The Psychoanalytic Study of the Child

VOLUME THIRTY-FIVE

The Psychoanalytic Study of the Child

VOLUME THIRTY-FIVE

New Haven
Yale University Press
1980

Designed by Sally Harris
and set in Baskerville type.
Printed in the United States of America by
Vail-Ballou Press, Inc., Binghamton, N.Y.

Library of Congress catalog card number: 45-11304
International standard book number: 0-300-02607-2

10   9   8   7   6   5   4   3   2   1

Contents

DREAMS AND SLEEP

CLINICAL CONTRIBUTIONS

APPLICATIONS OF PSYCHOANALYSIS

SPECIAL ARTICLE

In Memoriam
Dorothy Burlingham
1891–1979

Dorothy Burlingham's interest and influence were an abiding intellectual and personal presence in the history of *The Psychoanalytic Study of the Child*. Though she was never a formal member of the Editorial Board, her pioneering contributions and her imagination, curiosity, concern for children's well-being, and scientific standards in child psychoanalysis provided a generous, responsive resource for the Editors, which we now formally acknowledge. Our loss, personally and scientifically, is great. We shall miss her quiet steadfastness and her patient considerateness.

In more formally acknowledging her scientific contributions, we shall dedicate Volume 36 of *The Psychoanalytic Study of the Child* to her continuing influence and legacy.

In the present volume, with the collaboration of some of her closest friends and colleagues, we indicate our mourning in a more personal sense.

Quietly, always with modesty and grace, Dorothy Burlingham used psychoanalysis as a method and theory to make the world a better place for children, at the same time as she helped to build the theory and to advance the practice of child and adult psychoanalysis.

THE EDITORS

The following three tributes were read at memorial meetings held in London, November 22, 1979 and February 6, 1980. They are published simultaneously in the *Bulletin of the Hampstead Clinic*.

ANNA FREUD

Dorothy Burlingham would have been pleased as well as surprised about this meeting. During her lifetime, she was much too modest either to demand or to expect adequate recognition for her work.

Colleagues who have not known her well may be under the misapprehension that her interest in and work for psychoanalysis began here in England. In fact, this was not the case. Whatever she did here was preceded by a long active period in Vienna of which her activities here were no more than a continuation. There are not many people alive now, or present here, who can report on this, a fact which is my own justification for claiming to be one of the reporters today.

Dorothy Burlingham came to Vienna in 1925 and remained there until 1938, i.e., for 13 years which became decisive for her further life. She was at the time a young woman of 34, separated but not divorced from her husband, mother of four young children whom she protected from having to grow up in the shadow of the severe illness of their father. What she expected from psychoanalysis in Vienna was a new interest for herself as well as active help in the upbringing of her children.

She began her personal analysis with Theodor Reik and when he, after one or two years, moved from Vienna to Berlin, she changed over to my father. This latter treatment lasted a considerable time and, very gradually, developed into a training analysis which led to her entry into the newly opened Vienna Institute. As a candidate in good standing, she became in due time a member of the Vienna Psychoanalytic Society. It may be of interest at this point to reflect that none of this could have happened then if conditions of acceptance had been what they are now: her application would have been rejected out of hand on the basis of insufficient professional preparation or evidence of scientific involvement. If, with this fact in mind, you listen to the survey of her psychoanalytic achievements, you may well wonder whether our present selection proceedings are the best and how many people like her have been missed out on by us, or by the psychoanalytic institutes and societies since then. However, reflections like these belong in another context.

So far as child analysis was concerned, Dorothy Burlingham came to it the hard way. Any mother with children in analysis—and in her case there were four—has to meet the inconvenience of ferrying them to and from their treatment hour; to sit around in waiting rooms; to meet the difficulty of sharing responsibility; to tolerate their allegiance to a stranger; to have her own attitude and actions scrutinized, etc. She tolerated all these hardships admirably and, in later days, after changing roles and becoming a child analyst herself, she extracted from this period the ability never to criticize the mothers of her patients for complaining about or even breaking down under the inevitable strain. Several sensitive papers about child analysis and the mother, empathy between child and mother, etc., stem from this period.

Her involvement with child analysis did not preclude taking an active interest in the more general aspects of education. As American, and worse still, analyzed youngsters, her children did not fit into the conventional schools of Vienna without an amount of discomfort which threatened to interfere with their intellectual curiosity and pleasure in learning. The to her obvious remedy was to found a modern school of her own, a venture not easy to achieve at that period of time: there was, after all, no place, no house, and there were no teachers. However, none of these obstacles deterred her. A place was found in the pleasant garden of Eva Rosenfeld (who later became an analyst) in a suburb of Vienna; a small wooden schoolhouse was built; and the search for teachers produced two young men in their 20s, modern-minded, not yet settled in a career, and willing to join an exciting venture of this kind. The school counted altogether something like 15 children and proved a great success. There is no place to examine in detail what it did for the pupils. What needs mention, however, are the names of the two teachers who both acquired renown in the psychoanalytic world of later years: Erik Erikson and Peter Blos. It seems evident that this early contact with Dorothy Burlingham and her ideas did not remain without significance for their further careers.

From the more private concerns with her own life and that of her children, Dorothy Burlingham then took a decisive step into public work. This was the time when the City of Vienna, represented by two Inspectors of Schools, took an early interest in psychoanalysis. Dorothy Burlingham joined me in setting up the first psychoanalytic seminar for nursery school teachers in which the day-to-day problems of difficult children were discussed and their links with traumatic family events, internal conflicts, and developmental deviations were demonstrated to the teachers. This was also the time when Willie Hoffer had started his psychoanalytic course for pedagogues in which both of us could take an active part. One of the best members of first the nursery school seminar, later the course for pedagogues, entered analysis with Dorothy Burlingham.

It is also well worth noting that Dorothy Burlingham's interest in the blind can be traced back to these early days. Entirely on her own, she opened contact with the headmaster of a large Jewish residential home for blind children, observed their educational methods, and accepted her first blind child patient into analysis.

Apart from and alongside these excursions into applied psychoanalysis went the development of clinical child analysis itself. Dorothy Burlingham joined the first technical seminar in this respect, together with those few individuals now known as the first generation of child analysts: Jenny Waelder, Editha Sterba, Anny Katan, Marianne Kris, Berta Bornstein, and others. Siegfried Bernfeld and August Aichhorn came in where diagnostic and social issues, especially of older children and adolescents, were concerned. Since supervision for beginners had not yet come into existence at this period, it was this seminar where we reported cases to each other, corrected each other's mistakes, discussed technique, shared doubts and misgivings as well as pleasure and excitement about new discoveries.

On the side of the analysis of adults, Dorothy Burlingham joined a technical seminar formed by young members of the Vienna Society (Ernst and Marianne Kris, Edward and Grete Bibring, Robert Waelder, Heinz Hartmann, Richard Sterba, Wilhelm Reich, etc.) which served the same purpose.

Busy as this period sounds, there still was interest left over for a further venture, this time for an investigation into developmental issues. Discussions with nursery school teachers had supplied us with observational data concerning the ages from 2 to 5, child analytic treatments with analytic material concerning children under and over 5 years of age. What was not available to us, quite apart from infant observation in the first year of life, was detailed knowledge of the important developments between age 1 and 2. Since these toddlers are of prenursery school age and access to their families cannot be gained, our solution was to create a separate organization for a group of them, something between a crèche and a nursery school, which would provide the opportunities for their study. The American analyst Edith Jackson, together with Dorothy Burlingham, provided the financial means to rent an empty part of the newly built Montessori School and engage the necessary staff. Josefine Stross joined us as our pediatrician. We chose 20 toddlers from the poorest families of Vienna, their fathers beyond the dole and begging in the streets, their mothers at best doing some work as charwomen. Prerequisite for acceptance was a measure of independent movement, crawling in some cases, rather than walking. Home care was so poor that the children had to be washed, dressed in proper clothes, and medically examined each morning on arrival, after which they spent the day like older children, approaching toys, playing indoors and outdoors, eating, resting, etc. Their parents were delighted with their good care; the children thrived and, on their part, recompensed us by providing knowledge about a child's first steps out of the biological unity between infant and mother; about the increases in ego control of motility at this age; about the advances from primary to secondary process functioning and the age-appropriate backward and forward moves from one to the other; about the child's reactions to food intake and elimination; about the initial advances toward peer relationships and early community life.

In fact, what we learned from these children in the short year and a half before the incoming National Socialists closed the crèche gave Dorothy Burlingham and me the courage to embark on the even more difficult venture of the Hampstead War Nurseries. It was thus the so-called Jackson Nursery which formed the real bridge for Dorothy Burlingham between work in prewar Vienna and her later work beginning in wartime England.

HANSI KENNEDY

Dorothy Burlingham's early papers, published between 1932–39, are based on her psychoanalytic work with children and reflect her budding interest in the mother-child relationship, an interest which remained a dominant theme in her diverse later publications. Her approach to this topic differed profoundly from the abounding psychoanalytic studies exploring the earliest mother-child interactions and their impact on later pathology. She worked on the assumption that a specific bond existed between a mother and her child which affected the child's functioning, adaptation, and difficulties throughout his development. She attached great importance to what happened within this relationship, not only in the past but also in the child's current life, and for this reason she believed strongly that the long-term success or failure of psychoanalytic work with children also depended on the work the child analyst was able to do with the mother.

In several of her papers she referred to the strong unconscious "contact," "communication," "empathy" between mother and child, with its positive and negative implications for child psychoanalysis. She felt that the power of unconscious forces in the interplay between mother and child was, in some cases, so marked as to appear uncanny and must be taken into account as an unknown quantity that will bring uncertainties into the analysis (1935). In a later paper, "Present Trends in Handling the Mother-Child Relationship During the Therapeutic Process" (1951), which again examined the difficulties relating to the interplay between mother and child, especially as they confront the child psychoanalyst in his work, she pinpointed these phenomena more clearly. "It seems to me that even when one is trying to avoid giving the mother dynamic interpretations, the mother still receives them. When the analyst gives the child interpretations of a deeper kind, this material is bound to affect the mother. Even when the analyst does not explain these to the mother and does not connect these interpretations to the mother's conflicts, . . . the interpretations given to the child affect the mother as a kind of wild analysis. It is in answer to this secondhand analytic procedure that the mother reactivates her own childhood . . . and brings memories of her own childhood experiences" (p. 113f.).

In the excellent paper "Child Analysis and the Mother," which was written more than 45 years ago, has withstood time, and remains, I believe, the most comprehensive discussion of the advantages and disadvantages of including or excluding the mother from the analytic work with the child, Dorothy Burlingham came down firmly in favor of working with the mother as well. She based this not just on the need to get information about the young child's external life and environment but on the opportunity this affords the child analyst to pick up subtle connections between mother and child which would otherwise be lost and which will enhance a better understanding of the child. This she felt should amply compensate for the disturbances the mother creates in the child's treatment if one includes her in the analytic work. Dorothy Burlingham was, of course, fully aware of the problem of dealing with mothers who are severely disturbed in their own right. Whereas in the early 1930s it was thought that this difficulty could be overcome only by removing the child into foster care for the duration of his analytic treatment, it led in later years to Dorothy Burlingham's special wish to offer such cases simultaneous psychoanalytic treatment of mother and child in order to explore further the degree of interplay of their pathology.

These clinical issues were not the only aspect of the mother-child relationship that preoccupied her. Her interest extended far beyond this toward long-term developmental studies of mother-child couples in different settings (these will be referred to by the next speaker). I still want to say a few words about one special article (1951) in which Dorothy Burlingham approached the same topic from a historical perspective. Looking at some of the literature on education and pediatrics of the sixteenth and seventeenth centuries, she found that some of the present-day issues relating to feeding, illness, and the mother-child relationship were discussed then and that some leading doctors and educators advocated measures which we now consider psychologically sound. She referred to these as "Precursors of Some Psychoanalytic Ideas about Children" and pointed out that the controversy over the relative advantages of breast and bottle feeding during the last 50 or 60 years and the impact of early separation from the mother, considered to have been influenced by the discoveries of psychoanalysis, were preceded by similar controversies in the sixteenth and seventeenth centuries. Only then the controversy was not over breast and bottle feeding, but in respect to mothers who nursed their infants and those who handed over their babies to wetnurses. She found evidence in the literature that doctors and educators took up the fight against this prevailing practice and tried to influence mothers to feed their own babies. This provides fascinating reading because apart from warning mothers about the dangers that their baby might be "infected" with an illness or "suck in some bad characteristics with the milk," they also give psychological reasons. They point out the importance of breast feeding the infant for the sake of the mother-child relationship, that the nursing situation is a pleasure rather than a duty and has advantages for the mother as well as the child. This paper also contains most interesting quotations from the sixteenth- and seventeenth-century literature relating to additional advice on feeding infants: you should "not teach him to eat more nor oftener than nature requires. I do not think all people's appetites are alike; I would prevail . . . that the child be not awakened out of its sleep to be fed, as is commonly done." Evidently the idea of "feeding on demand" was not instigated by psychoanalytic teaching; but insightful observers, professionally engaged with young children, could come to similar conclusions. In this short paper Dorothy Burlingham also focused attention on precursors to "modern ideas" about the care of sick children. When inpatient treatment for sick children in England was first suggested, it was dismissed as an impossibility on the grounds that any thinking person could be easily convinced that to remove a sick child from his parents would break his heart immediately.

CLIFFORD YORKE

I came to know Dorothy Tiffany Burlingham comparatively late in her long and productive life. It was, for me, an uncommonly rewarding association in every respect, in the course of which I learned a great deal and in which acquaintance broadened unobtrusively into friendship. But, on this occasion, it is her scientific work of which I wish to speak, however briefly and inadequately.

She herself, in her diverse contributions to the literature, has pointed to a primary interest, a unifying theme, that both informs and is informed by the careful and detailed clinical observations in which the body of her work abounds: namely, the relationship between mother and child. Such an interest may sound unexceptional to those who do not know her work; but for her it was never a commonplace; and at no time did it embrace any attempt to reduce normality and pathology to mere reflections and elaborations of speculative constructs concerning early life. Indeed, her deep and abiding interest in this field sprang in large measure from her experience in the analysis of latency children where she was fascinated by her encounter with residua of what she called "rather obscure areas of contact between mother and child" and which she subsumed under the collective term of "empathy."

No doubt much of this enduring interest was stimulated by her early work in Vienna; by her early interest in progressive education; by her founding the first nursery for toddlers; and by the enormous intellectual and professional stimulation which she received there. Of none of this can I speak directly, but it seems that, at every step in her developing career, however involved in work with colleagues, she brought something of her own. When, for example, with Anna Freud, she founded the Hampstead War Nurseries, she was thenceforth remembered by her fellow workers for her sensitive and perceptive contributions to which she brought a psychoanalytic perspective that furthered observation and fostered inference without distorting it through preconception.

It was in the course of her work at the Hampstead Nurseries that her interest in twins received its particular impetus, although there were twins in her own family. Her ensuing work

concerned itself with some of the repercussions to be detected
when the child's first relationship is made with the peer rather
than with the mother. Her book on *Twins* (1952) is a classic; and
she pursued her subject in a memorable paper written in collaboration with Arthur Barron (1963).

She extended her interest in the interaction of mother and
child in an unusual and imaginative way: in the formulation
and implementation of her project for the simultaneous
analysis of mother and child. It is perhaps above all for her
work with blind children that she will be remembered; for the
devotion and dedication which she brought to the task and the
way in which she organized and welded together an active and
enthusiastic study group which led to a permanent change in
our understanding of the developmental problems of the blind
and the lessons which were to be drawn if deviant development
was to be modified. Here again her interest was deeply involved
in the difficulties faced by the blind child in building up an
effectively interactive tie to the mother when a vital element of
interplay between them—sight—was missing. This interest—
and that of the colleagues whom she inspired—did not of
course stop there: lessons about normality were drawn from the
pathology inseparable from blindness, and lessons about
pathology were drawn from normality. While publications
stemming from this work have permanently enriched the literature, the influence on workers in the field through extensive
teaching, through precept and example, has equally and decisively changed many prevailing attitudes and practices.

Lest it be thought that Dorothy Burlingham was unable to
step outside her chosen interest in the relationship between
mother and child, it should be added that her paper on the role
in the child's development of the preoedipal father (1973) is
itself a key contribution; and it should not be forgotten that it
was she who devised and founded the Hampstead Psychoanalytic Index. And, of course, her interest was everywhere, whether
in the meetings and activities of the Educational Unit or the
Group for the Study of Adult Psychosis. But no review of her
scientific and clinical interests can be even remotely inclusive, in
a brief tribute such as this.

It has been said of her—and more than a few times by those

who knew her well—that her clinical and observational capacities were second to none and formed a bedrock on which so much of what she had to say firmly rested. No doubt her close collaboration with Anna Freud was seminal; but wherever one looks—whether to her earliest writings or her most recent paper on the blind child in a sighted world (1979)—it is precisely this bedrock which is so forcefully in evidence. And here I would add one personal observation. If the qualities of a training analyst are to be judged by the qualities of her analysands, Dorothy Burlingham passed this test with flying colors. She leaves, in testimony, a body of distinguished psychoanalysts whose devotion to the science of the mind reflects her own.

Lastly, it is not possible to speak of Dorothy Burlingham without also stepping, however briefly, outside her scientific work. Of her generosity, of her concern for others, of her unswerving qualities of friendship and support, of her deep devotion to Anna Freud, and of her strength in the face of adversity, I make no more than a mention. But I would add this: true to the tradition of her family, she loved not only art, but beauty in all its forms. I do not know—and this is not the place to discuss—whether Beauty is Truth, and Truth Beauty. What I *do* know is that, in Dorothy Tiffany Burlingham, the love of both came together.

THE WRITINGS OF DOROTHY BURLINGHAM

1932   Kinderanalyse und Mutter. *Z. psychoanal. Päd.*, 6:269–289; Child Analysis and the Mother. *Psychoanal. Quart.*, 4:69–92, 1935; also in: *Psychoanalysis and the Occult*, ed. G. Devereux. New York: Int. Univ. Press, 1953, pp. 188–191; and as chap. 1 in: *Psychoanalytic Studies of the Sighted and the Blind* (1972)

Ein Kind beim Spiel. *Z. psychoanal. Päd.*, 6:245–248; also in: *Almanach der Psychoanal.*, 172–176, 1933; A Child at Play, chap. 2 in: *Psychoanalytic Studies of the Sighted and the Blind*

1934   Mitteilungsdrang und Geständniszwang. *Imago*, 20:129–143; also in: *Z. psychoanal. Päd.*, 9:127–137, 1935; The Urge to Tell and the Compulsion to Confess, chap. 3 in: *Psychoanalytic Studies of the Sighted and the Blind*

1935   Die Einfühlung des Kleinkindes in die Mutter. *Imago*, 21:429–444; Empathy between Infant and Mother. *J. Amer. Psychoanal. Assn.*, 15:764–780, 1967; and as chap. 4 in: *Psychoanalytic Studies of the Sighted and the Blind*

1937   Probleme des psychoanalytischen Erziehers. *Z. psychoanal. Päd.*, 11:91–97; Problems Confronting the Psychoanalytic Educator, chap. 5 in: *Psychoanalytic Studies of the Sighted and the Blind*

1938   Review of D. Seabury, *Adventures in Self-Discovery. Int. J. Psycho-Anal.*, 19:509

1939   Phantasie und Wirklichkeit in einer Kinderanalyse. *Int. Z. Psychoanal.*, 24:292–303; Fantasy and Reality in a Child's Analysis, chap. 6 in: *Psychoanalytic Studies of the Sighted and the Blind*

1940   Psychoanalytische Beobachtungen an blinden Kindern. *Int. Z. Psychoanal. & Imago*, 25:297–335; Psychic Problems of the Blind. *Amer. Imago*, 2:43–85, 1941; also: Psychoanalytic Observations of Blind Children, chap. 12 in: *Psychoanalytic Studies of the Sighted and the Blind*

Review of A. Adler, *Guiding Human Misfits. Psychoanal. Quart.*, 9:128–129

1942   (with Anna Freud) *Young Children in War-Time.* London: Allen & Unwin; also as chap. 12, Annual Report (January, 1942): Summary of First Year's Work, in: *Infants Without Families: Reports on the Hampstead Nurseries. The Writings of Anna Freud*, 3:142–211. New York: Int. Univ. Press, 1973. [This book also appeared, under various different titles, in several English and American editions and was translated into German, Spanish, and Japanese.]

(with Anna Freud) Tony. *New Era*, 23:126–128

(with Anna Freud) What Children Say about War and Death. *New Era,* 23:185–189

(with Anna Freud) Young Children in War-Time. *New Era,* 23:57–85

1943 (with Anna Freud) Tony and His Father. *New Era,* 24:21–23

(with Anna Freud) Regression As a Disturbing Factor in Child Development. *New Era,* 25:209–213

1944 (with Anna Freud) *Infants Without Families: The Case For and Against Residential Nurseries.* London: Allen & Unwin; also as Part II in: *Infants Without Families: Reports on the Hampstead Nurseries. The Writings of Anna Freud,* 3:543–664. [This book was also translated into Czech, Danish, Dutch, French, German, Italian, Japanese, Portuguese, Spanish, and Swedish.]

1945 The Fantasy of Having a Twin. *This Annual,* 1:205–210; also as chap. 1 in: *Twins* (1952)

1946 Children Without Families. *Health Educ. J.,* 4:33–39

Twins: Observation of Environmental Influences on Their Development. *This Annual,* 2:61–73; also as chap. 2 in: *Twins*

1949 The Relationship of Twins to Each Other. *This Annual,* 3/4: 57–72

Twins: As a Gang in Miniature. In: *Searchlights on Delinquency,* ed. K. R. Eissler. New York: Int. Univ. Press, pp. 284–287

1951 Present Trends in Handling the Mother-Child Relationship During the Therapeutic Process. *This Annual,* 6:31–37; also as chap. 8 in: *Psychoanalytic Studies of the Sighted and the Blind*

Precursors of Some Psychoanalytic Ideas about Children in the Sixteenth and Seventeenth Centuries. *This Annual,* 6:244–254; also as chap. 7 in: *Psychoanalytic Studies of the Sighted and the Blind*

1952 *Twins: A Study of Three Pairs of Identical Twins.* London: Imago Publ. Co.; New York: Int. Univ. Press

1953 Notes on Problems of Motor Restraint During Illness. In: *Drives, Affects, Behavior,* ed. R. M. Loewenstein. New York: Int. Univ. Press, pp. 169–175; also as chap. 9 in: *Psychoanalytic Studies of the Sighted and the Blind*

1955 (with Alice Goldberger & André Lussier) Simultaneous Analysis of Mother and Child. *This Annual,* 10:165–186; also as chap. 10 in: *Psychoanalytic Studies of the Sighted and the Blind*

1961 Some Notes on the Development of the Blind. *This Annual,* 16:121–145; also as chap. 13 in: *Psychoanalytic Studies of the Sighted and the Blind*

1963   (with Arthur T. Barron) A Study of Identical Twins: Their Analytic Material Compared with Existing Observation Data of Their Early Childhood. *This Annual,* 18:367–423; also as chap. 11 in: *Psychoanalytic Studies of the Sighted and the Blind*

1964   Hearing and Its Role in the Development of the Blind. *This Annual,* 19:95–112; also as chap. 14 in: *Psychoanalytic Studies of the Sighted and the Blind*

1965   Some Problems of Ego Development in Blind Children. *This Annual,* 20:194–208; also as chap. 15 in: *Psychoanalytic Studies of the Sighted and the Blind*

1967   Developmental Considerations in the Occupations of the Blind. *This Annual,* 22:187–198; also as chap. 16 in: *Psychoanalytic Studies of the Sighted and the Blind*

1968   Occupations and Toys for Blind Children. *Int. J. Psycho-Anal.,* 49:477–480

       (with Alice Goldberger) The Re-education of a Retarded Blind Child. *This Annual,* 23:369–385; also as chap. 17 in: *Psychoanalytic Studies of the Sighted and the Blind*

1969   Review of S. Fraiberg, *An Educational Program for Blind Infants. J. Spec. Educ.,* 3:141–142

       Kinderanalyse und Mutter. In: *Handbuch der Kinderpsychotherapie,* vol. 2, ed. G. Bierman. Munich: E. Reinhardt Verlag

1972   *Psychoanalytic Studies of the Sighted and the Blind.* New York: Int. Univ. Press

1973   The Preoedipal Infant-Father Relationship. *This Annual,* 28:23–47

       Preface to *Beyond the Best Interests of the Child,* by Joseph Goldstein, Anna Freud, and Albert J. Solnit. New York: Free Press

1975   Special Problems of Blind Infants: Blind Baby Profile. *This Annual,* 30:3–13; also as chap. 7 in: *Psychoanalytic Assessment: The Diagnostic Profile.* An Anthology of the Psychoanalytic Study of the Child. New Haven & London: Yale Univ. Press, 1977

1976   A Neglected Classic III: K. R. Eissler's "Mankind at Its Best." *J. Philadelphia Assn. Psychoanal.,* 3:78–79

1979   To Be Blind in a Sighted World. *This Annual,* 34:5–30

       Preface to *Before the Best Interests of the Child,* by Joseph Goldstein, Anna Freud, and Albert J. Solnit. New York: Free Press

THEORETICAL AND CLINICAL CONTRIBUTIONS TO PROBLEMS OF DEVELOPMENT

The Family and the Psychoanalytic Process in Children

E. JAMES ANTHONY, M.D.

> The answer to technical problems in psycho-analytic practice is never obvious.
>
> FREUD (1922)

PSYCHOANALYSTS ARE BY PERSUASION AND TRAINING ORIENTED toward the individual, whether adult or child. Their therapeutic vision is directed intrapsychically, although the technique they use to achieve inwardness has an important interactional component. In earlier days, they referred to themselves as "depth" psychologists, signifying their profound and almost exclusive concern with the realm of the unconscious; but as the ego and the self assumed greater prominence in theory, the extrapsychic world has been increasingly acknowledged (Anthony, 1980). One of these outer formations is the family, the milieu in which the child spends many years crucial to his development. Parts of this familial environment are gradually internalized into the conflictual spheres of the psyche, while other portions gain varying degrees of object representation. A further aspect of the family is incorporated into the conscious life of the child as he gradually comes to understand the complex elements that hold it

Ittleson Professor of Child Psychiatry at Washington University, St. Louis; training and supervising analyst (for adult and child analysis) at the St. Louis Psychoanalytic Institute; and currently President of the Association for Child Psychoanalysis.

3

together as a group and his own place within the system of relationships.

The answers to the technical problems in child psychoanalysis have never been obvious, and when one considers the catalog of psychic deficiencies, it is surprising how the child even came to be considered analyzable. The inability to free associate, the absence of insight, the nondevelopment of a sustained transference neurosis, the lack of voluntarism with regard to treatment participation, the immaturity of the psychic apparatus, and above all the ubiquitous actuality of the parents would seem to constitute insuperable obstacles to a truly psychoanalytic mode of therapy. "Any history of child analysis is more or less synonymous with the history of efforts to overcome and counteract these difficulties" (A. Freud, 1965, p. 29).

By various forms of substitution, child analysis has changed remarkably within a few decades, becoming "more analytic." Child analysts have ceased to be on the defensive, and they no longer talk of their treatment procedures as "wild analysis," applied analysis, analytically oriented psychotherapy or analytic play therapy. With the recognition of the transference developments in the child, the analytic view of the child altered dramatically, although the transference is not yet given quite the emphasis accorded it in adult work. We no longer feel it necessary to prepare every child for analysis; we are now inclining to the view that insight may grow with development and at times surprise us with its acuity; we systematically analyze defenses that seem to impede development; and we interpret in accordance with our better understanding of cognitive capacity at different age levels. It is child analysis that has thrown new light on the preoedipal phases, which are generally less accessible in the analysis of the adult. Our new technical confidence is allowing us to analyze more children prior to and following latency, and we are also analyzing children who would have been deemed unanalyzable years ago. Altogether, we have come a long way since Freud's early doubts about the psychoanalytic treatment of the child.

Quite early in the history of child analysis, technical problems with regard to families became obvious. This was because the analyst frequently treated children of friends and close associates within their own homes and with play equipment drawn from the child's own toys. The child could therefore see the analyst in his own familiar milieu and relate to him in a variety of family activities. This would give the analyst extraordinary insights but also many difficulties. He would know at firsthand how his patient was treated by his parents and siblings, but his own relationship with the family would undoubtedly reduce his capacity, essential in analysis, to view the outer environment mainly, if not completely, through the eyes of his patient. Moreover, the problems involving confidentiality would rapidly reach unanalyzable proportions since the child would naturally assume that his analyst discussed his case fully and openly with the parents. Although technically impracticable, this early period in the history of child analysis did provide a wonderful opportunity for the psychoanalytic study of the child *in his family* and the family's influence on the psychoanalytic process.

As mentioned earlier, the psychoanalytic "deficiencies" of childhood have compelled child analysts to become skillful substituters, and it was not long before they were drawing parents into the therapeutic ambience as supervised therapists, co-therapists, simultaneous patients, and systematic reporters. Some child analysts, with an experience of family therapy and diagnosis, have either diagnosed and treated the family prior to the analysis of the child or else followed up the child's analysis with a period of family therapy, presumably to resolve the individual transference more completely. Most orthodox child analysts would tend to find such procedure reprehensible.

This presentation has two aims to explore: the construction of a dynamic family model that could serve as a useful frame of reference for the child analyst during his treatment of the child; and second, the investigation of how much impingement the family makes on the psychoanalytic process. In order to carry out these aims effectively, it will be necessary to examine the ways in which psychoanalysis has looked at the family previously and currently.

Psychoanalysis and the Family

It would not be an exaggeration to state that the family has had a somewhat checkered career in psychoanalysis, and the same would be true of the group. Freud developed an interest in both, initiated some interesting and compelling theories for both, and then, for a while, abandoned the environment, returning to a more attenuated form of it when he created psychoanalytic ego psychology. Of all of Freud's work, these incompleted formulations are among the most provocative since they open doors to so many exciting new worlds that clinicians, other than psychoanalysts, have avidly explored.

Freud's family theory did not have the benefit of a continuous development since it was interrupted earlier by his self-analysis and later by the development of his metapsychology. His initial view of the family was shaped by his training in neuropathology, and subsequently by his work with Breuer when traumatic possibilities governed both their thinking. The family as an internal system was conceptualized later. Since his focus of interest lay elsewhere, not all of his ideas in this area have significance for a comprehensive psychoanalytic theory of the family, but all of them present elements that still need to be considered in dealing with either the psychology or psychopathology of family life. I will attempt to examine them sequentially.

1. Freud attached much importance to the transmission of a neuropathic tendency through the family, but did not consider the effects on the family as a whole of interaction between hereditarily disturbed members. In his own extended family group there was, for example, a cousin who was a hydrocephalic imbecile, a second cousin who became psychotic at the age of 19, a third whose psychosis developed in her 20s, and a fourth who died of epilepsy. "I have to admit to having a regular 'neuropathological taint,'" he said, and he included the fact that both his sister Rosa and he had "a pronounced tendency to neurasthenia." Subsequently, Freud was quite clear of the "complementary" interchanges between endowment and environment; "tainted" family members could seriously complicate both intrapsychic and interpersonal existence within the family (Jones, 1:4).

2. His interest then shifted from the family as a genetic transmission system to its environmental role in pathogenesis. "It follows from the nature of the facts which form the material of psycho-analysis that we are obliged to pay as much attention in

our case histories to the purely human and social circumstances of our patients as to the somatic data and the symptoms of the disorder. *Above all, our interest will be directed towards their family circumstances"* (1905, p. 18; my italics).

3. His first general theory of neurosis (which he never quite relinquished) was largely a familial one, although it appeared, on first statement, that the causal agents were extrafamilial. Later it became apparent that fathers were largely responsible for the "appalling" and "disgusting" pedophilic practices that occurred in his sample of 18 subjects. After much heartache and self-analytic soul searching, this seduction hypothesis underwent an internal transformation, paving the way for a revolutionary discovery (1896).

4. The problem of incest (whether external or internal) became a central concern that he explored anthropologically. In *Totem and Taboo* (1913), he set out three postulates that could have laid the foundation of systematic family theory and therapy from the psychoanalytic point of view: that there was a family psyche whose psychological processes corresponded fairly closely with those of the individual; that there was a continuity of emotional life in the family psyche from one generation to the next; and that the mysterious transmission of attitudes through the generations was the result of unconscious understanding that made the latent psychic life of one generation accessible to the succeeding one. This thesis presumed a collective psychological life of the family, a process of intergenerational transmission of emotional disturbances, and an unconscious understanding that assimilated conflicts and generated family pathology (Anthony, 1971). Why did Freud stop at this critical point? The focus on the individual was becoming paramount and to create a psychoanalytic theory and practice for the individual was certainly sufficient for a lifetime—even one as productive as Freud's.

5. In dealing with group psychology (1921), Freud also took a look at the family as a group, and the mechanisms that he found operating in the group could therefore be extrapolated to the milieu of the family. Morphologically, Freud would have described the family as a natural, permanent, heterogeneous, organized, and leadered group since these were the classifying

criteria that he proposed. By implication, the dynamics of the family group would include mechanisms of identification, feelings of mutual empathy, qualities of parental leadership, and a system of cohering elements that furthered relatedness—common interests and purpose, the sharing of the parents; and the projection of the individual narcissism onto the family as a whole and onto the parents in particular, so that both family and parents become something special. On the basis of an idea conjectured by Darwin, Freud described a primal family ruled over despotically by a powerful father whose sons became envious of his women and eventually aspired to overthrow him and devour him. Three separate psychologies were therefore in operation: the psychology of leadership involving the parents, the psychology of follower involving the child, and the psychology of the family as a group. In actual life, the child continues to transact daily with his family, while continuing to deal intrapsychically with various elements of it deriving from an earlier period.

6. In his general theory of the neuroses (1916–17), Freud took a closer look at the conscious and unconscious matrix that constituted the life of the family. At the center of what he called the "family complex" was the spontaneously occurring oedipus complex, circling around which was a transactional series that varied from family to family. The following elements made up this "family complex": the nuclear complex itself, aggravated by overly seductive or aggressive behavior on the part of the parents; sibling births that occasioned repeated narcissistic injuries and could be accompanied by intense feelings of jealousy, envy, and hostility more easily directed toward the sibling than toward the parents. Embitterments from these experiences could become a permanent part of the personality; the use of siblings for sexual and aggressive experimentation and the important role that they played in the discovery of sex differences that precipitated the castration complex; the use of siblings as "duplicates" of parental oedipal figures with the result that the girl in the family often turned to an older brother as a father substitute and to a younger sibling as the substitute for the baby the father failed to give her; "the extreme importance" (as Freud put it [p. 334]) of the birth order within the family in shaping the personality and psychological reactions into later life; and finally the

profound impact of the actual death of a sibling on personality development, particularly when this coincided with a period of heightened death wish. In elaborating this "family complex," Freud compounded the intrapsychic unfolding of the nuclear complex with the extrapsychic events occurring in the family such as parental attitudes and behavior, sibling birth and rivalry, the exigencies of ordinal position, and finally such traumas as death, illness, and abuse in the family.

7. The dynamic concept of two families, the manifest and the latent, was given expression in the "poetic fiction" as Freud (1909) referred to it, of the "family romance," in which the child's enormous overvaluation of the parents in the earliest years gives place, under the influence of rivalry and disappointment in real life, to a critical and disparaging attitude. As a consequence, he develops the illusion of having two families—an aristocratic and a humble one—both reflections of the child's own family as it appeared in successive periods of life. Like the oedipus complex, the family romance has deep roots both in the life of the individual and in myth and legend. The actual family with its faults and frustrations often stimulates the day-dream of the fantasied family that was so much better in every respect and met the child's every need in "royal fashion." In addition to the bread-and-butter family of everyday life, and the preconscious family from which the child was "adopted," there was also the unconscious family culminating in oedipal wishes and feelings which can by no means gain overt and satisfying expression in current family life. All three families contribute to the "family complex" and, at times, occasion "uncanny feelings" as they surface and submerge during analytic treatment. What holds the family together when there is so much fear and perse-cution rampant at the more primitive levels of functioning where killing and cannibalism form unthinkable ideas? Freud's answer was that the "indestructible strength of the family as a natural group formation rests upon the fact that this necessary presupposition of the father's equal love can have a real applica-tion in the family" (1921, p. 125). Favoritism spells disaster for the child in the family and may occupy a great deal of his time in analysis.

In the subject index of the *Standard Edition* of Freud's work

(1954) there is an extreme paucity of references to the family, to the family as a group, to the "family complex," or to the "family romance," as compared with references to "fathers," "mothers," and "parents"; and, to a large extent, this apparent bias has persisted in the psychoanalytic literature. The adult psychoanalyst does not appear to have much interest in the family since his patients are generally not dealing with the "family of origin" on a current basis. Flugel (1921) was the first and last psychoanalyst to describe the interpersonal structure of the family on the basis of the psychoanalytic theory of his time. In the center of his investigation was the oedipus complex as it functions unconsciously in the parents and sets the goal of development for each of the children. "Just as the oedipus complex is a psychic representation of the patriarchal family, so was Flugel's study inescapably based on the conditions prevailing within Western patriarchal cultures at the time, which conceptualized parenthood as mature and relatively unchanging" (Anthony and Benedek, 1970, p. xxi). In spite of these limitations, his contribution is significant. He emphasized that the development of the child requires corresponding readjustment in the parent's attitude and behavior at every stage; that the heterosexual development of parents is, to a considerable extent, related to the heterosexual development of the child; and that the hostile feelings of parents toward their children are often powerfully stimulated and reinforced by the unconscious process that identifies the child with the parents' own parents, so that there tends to be some similarity between the parent-child relationship of one generation and the parent-child relationship of the earlier generation. New parents, he observed, found themselves at times incompatible with their children, and this led to strong resentments as the "hostages to fortune" increasingly interfered with the parents' work and aspirations.

With respect to the family, one would expect to get more from child analysis and one does.

CHILD PSYCHOANALYSIS AND THE FAMILY

When the references to family in the literature of child psychoanalysis are closely examined, the striking fact is that they hardly deal at all with the family as an actual environment for the developing child and make no mention of any impact that daily living within a family might have on the course and process of psychoanalysis. The focus is mainly on the relationship of the parent (in almost all cases, the mother) to the child or to fantasies existing in the child prior to treatment. There are three interesting phenomena that have obtained notice: the family myth in which a particular child may be credited with a particular attribute that may compel the child to behave accordingly to meet the needs of the family; family fantasies, such as the ubiquitous family romance, the fantasy of being a twin, and the fantasy of a reversal of generations within the family; and, finally, family secrets which the child is sworn to maintain and which may ultimately disrupt the treatment. In Lustman's case (1962), a 4-year-old girl was regarded by her family as "absolutely fearless," and acted accordingly. In the analysis, it was clear that she had internalized the parental ego ideal mutually projected onto her to the extent that it had become an element of her ego and was relatively refractory to change. Her courage predictably made its appearance in the analytic situation.

One would have expected that the family romance also would have manifested itself during analytic treatment of children with the genesis of transference, but it was an adult analyst (Greenacre, 1966) who picked up elements of it in the over-idealization of the analyst. Such deifications are often related to a narcissistic countertransference disguised as therapeutic enthusiasm.

One of the problems confronting the child analyst is that while the parent-child relationship has been admitted into psychoanalysis, the family is still regarded as "environment" and kept out. To consider the family is tantamount to becoming an environmentalist, the modern equivalent of the "wild" analyst. Anna Freud (1965) has pointed out that the analyst of adults, because of his firm belief in psychic as opposed to external reality, is in no danger of becoming an environmentalist. The child analyst, however, is constantly aware of the powerful influence of the environment:

> In treatment, especially the very young reveal the extent to which they are dominated by the object world, i.e., how much

of their behavior and pathology is determined by environmental influences such as the parents' protective or rejecting, loving or indifferent, critical or admiring attitudes, as well as by the sexual harmony or disharmony in their married life. The child's symbolic play in the analytic session communicates not only his internal fantasies; simultaneously it is his manner of communicating *current family events,* such as nightly intercourse between the parents, their marital quarrels and upsets, their frustrating and anxiety-arousing actions, their abnormalities and pathological expressions. The child analyst who interprets exclusively in terms of the inner world is in danger of missing out on his patient's reporting activity concerning his—at the time equally important—environmental circumstances [p. 50f.; my italics].

Here we have echoes of Freud's statement 60 years earlier: "above all, our interest will be directed towards their family circumstances."

There is always a warning latent in extreme positions: if the adult analyst is too eager to discount the value of current happenings in reality, the child analyst must constantly bear in mind that the bad family environment generates pathology through interaction with dispositional characteristics and acquired and internalized libidinal and ego attitudes. Here Anna Freud (1965) helpfully counsels us, both adult and child analysts, to preserve the "balanced outlook" of Freud's theory of a complementary series of internal and external influences. We need to keep an eye open for "accidental environmental influences": "In the analysis of older children and the reconstructions from adult analysis we have found the forces embodied in the parents' personalities, their actions and ideals, *the family atmosphere,* the impact of the cultural setting as a whole" (p. 86; my italics). Fixed neurotic symptoms in the child will respond only to analysis, but outside this area, the personality of the child can also respond flexibly to the many influences exerted by the family during treatment. The child tends to externalize his conflicts in an interpersonal struggle with the analyst or in battles taking place at home. Such externalizations must not be confused with transference and should not be interpreted as such. With children, one is not so aware of what Rapaport (1960) referred to as "the private world of the individual," meaning by that the way in which a person experiences his environment, analytic or familial, in terms of his own likes and dislikes, which are products of his cumulative history. In child analysis, the internal family never becomes the exclusive focus of attention, with the external family subsiding into comparative nonexistence.

Erikson (1968) has been critical of the concepts of the limited "outer world" or "environment" that are often used "to designate an uncharted area which is said to be outside merely because it fails to be inside," that is, just a vague omnipresent "outerness" (p. 221). He is also critical of the "stubborn tendency" that persists in treating the mother-child unity as a biological entity more or less isolated from the actual environment. One cannot get away from a particular individual's particular family circumstances by the broad postulate of an "average expectable environment" or even an integrated series of average expectable environments. As one theorist has remarked, life would be simpler, theoretically and therapeutically (but clearly not practically) if one could dispense with the family altogether and perhaps even, in Erikson's words (1968), with "the indifferent or annoying fact of the existence of other people."

There is no doubt that the child's parents may either help or handicap the treatment; and since there are always resentments, manifest and latent, at the child analyst "taking over," unconscious sabotage from even well-disposed parents can always be expected. The more neurotic are the parents, generally speaking, the more difficult is the child's treatment. As Freud remarked way back in 1909, "The treatment of nervous disorders in children will always encounter one great difficulty: the parents' neuroses which will build a wall around the child's neurosis" (see Jones, 2:445). There is no doubt that the maternal neurosis does create a problem for the child analyst, and that many neurotic mothers frequently transmit their symptoms to their children, collude with the child in the maintenance of symptoms, and sometimes form *folie à deux* connections with them. Furthermore, many of these neurotic parents (and psychotic ones as well) do develop a strong need to keep a disturbed or infantilized child dependent on them (A. Freud, 1965).

The relationship between parent and child psychopathology

cannot therefore be a simple matter of "contagion" or "reaction": if such was the case, the analysis of the parent would inevitably cure the neurotic child, but, apart from transient situational stresses involving parent-child management, this simply does not occur. Neurosis is much more than a "reaction" and "contagion" is much less than an introjection. Both terms are therefore inadequate and insufficient explanations to account for the many interlinking complexities that contribute to the structural formation of a neurosis, even at its inception. A second fact is that once the interpersonal struggle between parent and child has become internalized within the child and made his own, it becomes much less amenable to direct interpersonal interventions. Speaking of the effect produced by the disturbed mother, Winnicott (1965) had this to say: "It must be remembered, however, that *the child's illness belongs to the child* ... the child may find some means of healthy growth in spite of environmental factors, or may be ill in spite of good care" (p. 74). This process of assimilating aspects of a disturbing environment into the internal psychic structure in a way analogous to the intake of food is still far from understood and needs more psychoanalytic inquiry (Anthony, 1980). For example, most infant observers have been aware that depressed mothers make for depressed babies. Anna Freud (1965) has suggested that such infants establish a rapport with the depressed mother, not by enthralling them with their developmental successes, "but by producing the mother's mood in themselves" (p. 87). The same cannot be said of the latency child who is provoked by the parental disorder but generally responds by a wide variety of defensive maneuvers in relation to the stimulus provided to his internal situation.

The impact of environment (and surely this would include the family) on the analyzability of the child has been considered by both Anna Freud (1965) and Winnicott (1954). Anna Freud has suggested a dichotomous classification of childhood disorders into conflicts that are external, related to the environment and relieved by its improvements, and conflicts that are internal and that need shorter or longer periods of analytic treatment. This has similarities to Winnicott's therapeutic nosology in which analytic treatment and environmental management are portioned out according to the predominance of internal or external factors. When the environment is good, as in the case of patients who develop difficulties in the course of an otherwise good-enough home life, analysis is indicated, but when there is a failure of environment, management needs to enter increasingly into the therapeutic work.

These considerations raise questions as to the necessity for treating the parent as an integral part of child analysis. "Although this is overtly a technical point," says Anna Freud (1965), "the issue at stake is a theoretical one, namely, the decision whether and from which point onward a child should cease to be considered as a *product of and dependent on his family* and should be given the status of a separate entity, a psychic structure in its own right" (p. 43). She also questions (1960) whether there is a need for parents to participate in treatment in order to make life easier for the changing child in analysis or for the changed analyzed child, declaring that she remained "a heretic" in some of these respects (p. 293), refusing to believe "that mothers need to change their personalities before they can change the handling of their children" (p. 298). Although mothers cannot alter the unconscious fantasies of their children, they can help to reinforce conscious, healthy progressions in development.

The cross-fertilization of unconscious fantasies in mother and child undergoing simultaneous analysis has been illustrated by Burlingham (1935) in the well-known case of the gold coin. During her analytic session, the mother spoke of a gold coin that had played a particular part in one of the scenes of her childhood. When she returned home, her 10-year-old son brought her a gold coin which he asked her to keep for him. She asked in astonishment where he had got it from, and he reminded her that he had been given it as a birthday present several months earlier. There seemed to be no reason whatsoever why the child remembered the coin precisely on this particular day when it came up in the mother's analysis. The child's analyst could throw no light on the matter and it looked as if the act had forced its way on that particular day into the child's life "like a foreign body." A few weeks later, the mother was writing down an account of the experience when in came the boy and asked for the gold coin back as he wanted to take it with him to show in his analytic session. Once again, the child analyst could find no reason for this wish. Freud (1933) was impressed by the account and felt that such observations helped to confirm the reality of thought transference. If this phenomenon does indeed prove to be a regular occurrence, there is no reason why it should not occur between other members of the family. One might therefore assume that the conscious and unconscious thoughts and fantasies of family members would continuously impinge on the psychoanalytic treatment of the child. Carefully observed, this might afford us significant information on the nature and direction of the child's transference and on the relative importance to him intrapsychically of the different members of the family at any given period.

The repercussions of parental psychopathology are many and varied: it may generate unconscious resistances in the child under analysis based on the unconscious fear that treatment will reveal negative, critical, and unloving wishes toward the parent; in the same context, it may play a crucial role in determining the child's analyzability since the resistances of both parent and child may summate to form insurmountable impediments; and it can create interpersonal difficulties that affect the family as a whole and drive it to scapegoat a particular child and make him the symptom-bearer and patient for the family. The situation is easier to handle analytically when the family suffers from the child's pathology rather than the other way around. Shifts in the dynamics of the family can then often sabotage the treatment and bring it to a standstill.

There is really no mysterious leap from parent to family in child analysis: the family simply represents the next horizon, but the level of intimacy involved is much the same. One has developed the habit of negotiating with the parents, but one could as well deal with the family and at least help to dissipate some of its paralyzing secrets.

The feeling is growing that if the child analyst is to do his best work with the child, he must maintain some psychoanalytic perspective on the family of the child. Smirnoff (1971) sums up this point of view in the following way: "One is tempted to envisage the problem under its two distinct aspects; that of the child on the one hand, and the parents on the other, with a view to establish a division of responsibilities. *In fact, the entire family is involved and the situation must be understood in terms of a family neurosis, with each member of the family participating, as it were, in the total clinical picture"* (p. 201; my italics). Here we have evident the interest of French child analysts (or at least some of them) in the so-called family neurosis, and the need to appreciate the family dynamics as part of the analytic treatment of the child. The family neurosis has not, however, been accepted so far by orthodox child analysts who tend to view it as an "unanalytic" term. Smirnoff himself is caught in the "division of responsibilities," since he does not talk about family pathology in the way that family pathologists do, but instead discusses parental pathology as it relates to child pathology. He castigates parents who are irritable, angry, and impatient; overwhelmed by their own aggressiveness; anxious, overprotective, indecisive, and devoid of authority; fearful of their children and helpless to deal with them; self-absorbed and narcissistic, preoccupied with achievement, obsessional, exacting, fussy and rigid to the extent of imprisoning their children in a strict code of rules and manners; immature, hypochondriacal, bullying and bullied—in fact, the entire gamut of character neuroses. As a result of living with parents like these, children may develop "reactive" disorders that rapidly become internalized even if the parental attitude is mitigated. Smirnoff merely emphasizes that parental pathology is not "a simple backcloth" against which the child's pathology runs its course. The child's pathology interacts constantly with the parental pathology to constitute a total family pathology, but the parts and the whole are interrelated in a way that is not yet clear to us as child analysts. According to Dare (1975), working with the Hampstead Diagnostic Profile, "the psychoanalytic understanding of the internal world of the child can be used in a detailed way to consider the interrelationship between the psychology of the child and that of his parents within the history of the development of the family as a group."

The advantages of analyzing the child in his own home, surrounded by his family, carried a lot of sense for the child analytic pioneer, Hug-Hellmuth in 1920.

> Just as the first meeting between the analyst and the young patient should take place in the latter's home, so should it be with the treatment itself. The analysis must go on indepen-

dently of the whims of the patient, who can very cleverly contrive to have a slight indisposition which prevents him coming, or arriving in time, or he may play truant in the analysis hour. . . . Of course, every child when at the height of a positive transference tries to transfer the analysis to the home of the analyst; but I have always gained the conviction that even when external circumstances demanded this change of place, such a change proved not to be lasting. However much the time and energy of the analyst is burdened by this demand, . . . and although an absolutely undisturbed and private talk in the patient's own house is difficult to obtain, nevertheless these evils seem to me trifling compared with the greater one of letting the child decide the external conditions of the analysis. Another consideration is that the parents, in spite of all their devotion, very soon feel that chaperoning of the child to and from the analyst's house becomes impossible and this difficulty is used as a reason for terminating the treatment—a situation well known to every child analyst [p. 291f.].

Since those days, the pendulum has swung in the opposite direction, with a relative encapsulation of the child analytic situation and the relative exclusion of parents from it, depending on the age of the child.

The Dynamic Family Model Pertinent to the Needs of the Child Analyst

Redl (1974) made reference to "the gang beneath the couch," signifying that whether we liked it or not, the child in analytic therapy brought in an imaginary peer group, an extension of the imaginary companions of the earlier child. The gang is often a fiction, a compensatory fantasy, or occasionally an actual group carefully selected to act out the fantasy.

In my own work as a child analyst, I have become equally aware of "the family under the couch"—the family that has long been the milieu of development, the arena of conflict since infancy, the safe environment for sexual and aggressive experimentation, and the home ground for the "family complex." Instead of talking in organismic terms of a "family neurosis" (the existence of which is very doubtful), I would prefer to speak of a neurosis relating to the family, that is, a neurotic reaction on the part of the child to his family. By this I mean, in the words of Rapaport (1966), an interplay between drive and environment, where environment would correspond to Freud's "family circumstances." Here again, we have something to learn from the work of Anna Freud (1965). While both adult and child analysis make it their primary aim to widen consciousness (without which ego control cannot be increased), the adult technique struggles with the undoing defenses against id derivatives rejected from consciousness at some time and then proceeds to the lifting of primary repressions. With the child, the ego must master reality on the one side as well as the amorphous emotional states existing within. When these vague impressions can be put into thoughts and words and logically understood during the work of analysis, new levels of development are reached, with enhancements of ego control, reality testing, and secondary process thinking. When the child gets better, it is generally because of a combination of treatment and maturation.

It is my belief, evolving with "increasing positiveness," that the differences between child and adult analysis can be further reduced without losing the inherent characteristics that make child analysis the analysis of a child and not of a pseudoadult. We should not try and stretch the child so that he fits the dimensions of the couch. The child analytic process is distinctly different from the adult analytic process and is experienced differently by the analyst. In place of introspections and periods of self-analysis, there are meaningful connections made, with the help of the analyst, between what is transpiring in the analytic situation, what is occurring currently at home, and what is recalled during the process of growing up. In some child analyses, current family situations seem to dominate the reported material and stir up curiosities and comparisons regarding the analyst's family. What often happens is an intermingling of oedipal family material associated with oedipal fantasies, current family material, family myths and secrets, and a family romance that first makes its appearance in the transference.

One needs to construct working family models belonging to the outside and reported by the patient as well as working models of the family as it is more permanently represented in the

patient's psyche. The usefulness of these working models increases with time as the external model becomes more accurately
and realistically reported and the internal model emerges in
transference as a wish-fulfillment structure that blends with the
romanticized re-creation of the analyst's family.

We can look at the external family in several different
developmental-transactional ways. Cognitively, within the
framework of Piaget, it is represented by a very heterogeneous
group of members at the sensorimotor, intuitive, representational, concrete, and abstract operational levels, with each
level implying a radically different mode of thinking and communicating. It is not surprising that the transactions, as reported, appear confused and that the members fail to get
through to one another. There is no doubt that a great deal of
incomprehensibility is taken for granted in family living. The
communications that do come across are often grossly distorted
because of semantic and syntactical deficiencies. The size of the
vocabulary itself sets limits to understanding for different members. To some extent, this inherent problem of understanding
and communicating is overcome by the fabrication of a basic
family language, which, like Esperanto, serves the purpose of
everyday life by the use of simple concrete expressions and
neologisms that have been manufactured for private family use.

On the psychosexual scale, children who are predominantly at
oral, anal, phallic, and genital levels may not be able to empathize
too easily with one another. A child who has put the anal phase
for the most part behind him is capable of behaving unsympa-
thetically to the child still in the throes of bowel and bladder
training. Older children may react with repugnance to the cop-
rophilic interests of toddlers or the gluttonous preoccupations of
the infant, while, at the same time, indirectly expressing both
envy and jealousy. Preoedipal children, struggling with problems of separation, may attempt to monopolize the mother,
while oedipal and latency children may become vehemently
rivalrous over the parent of the same or opposite sex. Somewhat
similar conflicts may make early adolescents sympathetically responsive to the needs of the toddlers. Nevertheless, during this
phase of reactivation, other adolescents may display an extreme
degree of intolerance for all the younger children in the family.

Many children pass through childhood trailing unresolved conflicts behind them, and these are the ones that resonate to all the developmental conflicts occurring within the family at any given time.

To a certain degree, being in a certain developmental phase offers the child some immunity from stimulations and provocations of other developmental phases and, for the same reason, he has some protection from traumas that are not phase-specific. In disturbed families, the children tend to react diffusely across overlapping phases, whereas in more healthy families, the children react in more circumscribed ways and remain compartmentalized within their respective stages of development.

On the psychosocial scale, while younger members may be struggling to assert their autonomy, sharpen their identities, carry out tasks, and work industriously at mastering basic skills, the older children may feel themselves isolated and different as they set out to emancipate themselves from family life.

With such incompatibilities built into the family situation, it is surprising how any family is able to achieve a sense of unity and harmony. The leadership given by the parents, the responsibilities that are taken by them, and the care that becomes available as needed are able to bridge both stage and generational gaps. Family life, as lived outside the analytic situation, is like an unending orchestral performance with instruments of different range and sound playing together, but not always harmoniously (Anthony, 1973).

The internal representation of the family reflects the developmental stage of the individual. It provides him with some indication of how members will react and interact, and the more experience he has of family life, the less surprises there are for him. At times he may try to manipulate the external family to correspond more closely to his internal construction and this may occasion angry and bewildering exchanges. Lebovici (1970) has attempted to formulate a psychoanalytic theory of the family, using the Oedipus schema to show how the pattern of interpersonal relationships is linked to the intrapsychic conflicts that are constantly reprojected onto the members of the family. He believes that the study of roles and modes of communication within the family can be incorporated into psychoanalytic theory, excluding its metapsychology. It seems to be his conviction that a knowledge of small group dynamics can enable the analyst to be more therapeutically helpful to his child patient.

I have to consider here whether my own strong interest in the external family as a unit may engender internal family responses during my psychoanalytic treatment of a child. Before I start analysis, I find myself curious about the family structure and the child's place in it; in my patient's neurotic reactions to his family as a whole as well as to its parts; and in the extent to which a "family complex" (with all its component fantasies, fictions, fabrications, and feelings) has been set up with the child competing with his siblings for the parents, substituting siblings for his parents, or acting as a surrogate parents toward his siblings. I am especially alerted to dissatisfactions with the parents, disappointments suffered at their hands, and family romances created to compensate for this. Predictably, I not infrequently find my patient elaborating a family romance during the transference in a series of fantasies that link his unconscious oedipal family with my hypothetical one that he reconstructs differently as we move along. His own real family at home falls into place somewhere along the spectrum.

The more that I become aware of the actual family as when I am treating the children of colleagues, the more I have come to realize how closely its style of presenting itself to the world, its patterns of interpersonal conflict, its repertoire of defense mechanisms, its mode of verbal and nonverbal communication, its manner of reconciliation following upheaval, and its overall sense of family feeling and family likeness become reflected in the child under analysis. I am reminded here of Winnicott's description (1971) of how the child sees himself in his mother's face, using her, as it were, as a mirror. It seems to be that the child experiences similar mirror responses from his family. "When a family is intact and is a going concern over a period of time, each child derives benefit from being able to see himself or herself in the attitude of the individual members or in the attitudes of the family as a whole . . . this would be one way of stating the contribution that a family can make to the personality growth and enrichment of each one of its individual members" (p. 138). I would paraphrase the last sentence to include the contribution that a family can make to the psychoanalytic treatment of one of its members.

Kramer (1968) has expressed the view that the child is less likely to be analyzable when there is a good deal of external conflict and family pathology, especially when the onset of the child's symptoms coincide with some gross disturbance in a family member or with some disaster such as divorce or death. In such cases, he advises work with the family as a whole until the child is freed enough to undertake analysis. If the child is hypercathected by the parent or the parent by the child, insistent instinctual discharges interfere with structural development, leaving the child "open" to the libidinal and aggressive impulses of the parents.

Conflicts between the parents are frequently projected into the parent-child relationship and keep both interpersonal and intrapsychic disturbances going. In such cases, a preliminary "separation" of the family neurosis from the child neurosis by family therapy is required, so that the mutual projections are interrupted and the child becomes capable of developing an analyzable transference. Kramer believes that simple mother guidance would not prove as effective.

My own procedure is different since my purpose is to learn in detail about the outside family in order to be in a position to reconstruct, along with the child, the internal family, both unconscious and representational. From the initial diagnostic interviews, I learn as much as I can about the family background, its structure, its historical experiences, and its characteristic functioning and malfunctioning. I have, on occasion, seen the family as a whole, but I generally obtain the family information from the parents. This working model of the real family in its everyday life is carried inside me during the analysis, undergoing modifications as my knowledge of it grows and changes. With the preschool child, the outside family is experienced through the "affective living through," as abreactions, reactions, and transactions are brought almost unchanged into the analytic situation. The domestic tantrum sets the mood for the session. The child is more likely to be tempestuously upset by minimal therapeutic frustrations and is unsure whether to hate the analyst or the family member responsible for the earlier storm.

Clarifying his feelings and placing them in the context of where
they belong are important parts of the work with the smaller
child.

In latency, the situation is different. Echoes from family life
are filtered indirectly through play and communication. A
9-year-old boy, Michael, was spending his session telling me
about all the things that he did at school and at home. I remarked
on his busyness and thought that it must surely stop him from
becoming bored. He quickly responded that he still often got
bored at home because the house seemed empty and there
seemed nothing to do. I commiserated with his situation, pointing out that it was hard to fill a space when one's father left the
house. It was like a hole with a lot of sad feelings inside it. His
eyes teared, but he reminded me that there were other kids at
schools whose parents had divorced and, though it hurt for a
while, they got over it. He had spoken to some of them and they
were just as happy as before. I wondered whether these other
kids were sure that their parents still loved them even though
they were separated. He said that he did not think that his parents cared about him because they were both trying to get married again. He asked whether I was divorced, and I thought that
he was wondering whether I had children and whether I also was
causing them to become sad and bored. He said that he did not
think that I would do that because I always listened to him and
talked to him. He bet my kids were happy and that I took them to
ball games and MacDonalds. I said that it was not easy to keep
everything fair in a family: sometimes one kid needed something
and sometimes another one; sometimes the mother needed
something and sometimes the father needed something; the
father might love his family but not be able to do something for
each one of them all the time; and then they would think that he
did not care. He shook his head, remarking that sometimes they
don't really care and it was no good pretending they do. His
father liked his sister and his mother liked his brother, but no
one seemed to like him. Then he looked at me and said that
perhaps he should be adopted—*if* he could find a happy family
that wanted him.

As the material becomes less defended, one receives kaleido-
scopic impressions of the family outside, but the main analytic

work involves the construction of an imaginary family, the family romance, in relation to the analyst's family, and the reconstruction of the early family with its system of memories and screen memories. In the case of Michael, most of the current feelings were bound up with the breaking up of the actual family. The trauma reactivated a "family complex," the oedipal feelings, the sibling jealousy, the sense of exclusion and loneliness. There was some tendency to idealize the past before his siblings had arrived and a strong tendency to idealize the family of the analyst.

With the working through of the oedipal conflict in the transference, the interpersonal relationships within the family often improve. The various families—the intrapsychic oedipal one, the idealized representational one, the actual interpersonal one, and the analyst's hypothetical one—may all appear in symbolic play with the family figures provided by the analyst. This imaginary miniature family, which may have quite an ongoing life in the course of the treatment, can be put to the service of libidinal and aggressive wishes, death wishes, family fantasies, family myths, and family secrets. It may reflect many of the current predicaments, such as marital difficulties, maternal depressions, paternal promiscuities, pregnancies and births, illnesses and accidents, and impending divorces. One does not really need an information service from the mother because the patient is generally an excellent "newsboy" and carries the family "headlines" with him. At all times, the "news" is doctored a little or editorialized a lot, but these processes are themselves significant in that this is how a child needs at a particular time to present his family to his analyst.

I have found that the more the real family is excluded from the analytic situation, the more frequently do the transitional and transference families make their appearance. As part of my total analytic task, I try to disentangle the various components of the "family complex" as it becomes reactivated in the transference; I accept the displacements of interpersonal feeling from the real family and try to appraise them realistically for the child; I encourage the formation of the imaginary family whose *dramatis personae* may help us to sort out the vicissitudes of family feeling; and I explore the disappointments, disillusionments, and wishes bound up with the family romance that often emerges in relation to the analyst's hypothetical family. Finally, I attempt to make the patient aware of his own neurotic reactions to the family and to the family circumstances.

AN UNUSUAL CASE FOR THE CHILD ANALYST

Theresa was a 9-year-old girl who was referred to me by her parents "for psychoanalysis" because she suffered, they said, from "hypnopompic hallucinations" and overwhelming fears of dying and death. She imagined herself in a coffin, shut in and all alone, unable to breathe and very frightened. She was the youngest of six Roman Catholic children whose father was principal in a high school. Four months before the referral, the parents had separated and then divorced (in defiance of their religious beliefs). The father had developed a state of depression and made a suicidal attempt. The mother's explanation for leaving her husband after 19 years of marriage and six children was simply that she had never loved him, found him "insufferably chauvinistic," and decided she wanted a life for herself. The situation then became critical for the family: the father left for Europe "to recuperate" from the injury meted out to him by his "psychotically irresponsible" wife, and she left for the Rockies "to meditate" on the options open to an emancipated woman. With both parents in flight, the oldest girl, Mary Sue, aged 17, was left to look after the home, care for the children, and continue, at the same time, at high school. There was an aunt, a career woman, who promised somewhat vaguely "to keep an eye on things." The parents had both agreed on only one thing, and this in itself was bizarre: they wanted Theresa "to be analyzed" by me and left explicit instructions and a letter, cosigned by the father and mother, instructing me "to go ahead."

I have to confess that I was a little taken aback when Mary Sue called me on the phone and said that Theresa was in a state of great panic, could not be reassured, had "weird feelings," and *please* could I analyze her as her parents had suggested. I realized that Mary Sue was in as much a state of panic as her little sister and that her maturity was not up to the maternity so unexpectedly thrust upon her. After much consideration of the situation, of the plight of the children and the strain on Mary Sue, I decided that I would do what the parents had requested: I would assess the girl for analysis and then analyze her if she needed to be analyzed. For the first and most probably the last time in my professional life as an analyst, I started a case without any contact with parents or parent substitutes. It was arranged for Mary Sue to drive Theresa to her sessions, do the family shopping, and then take her home. The extraordinary thing was that Theresa could hardly wait to get to my office, but when she got there, she did not seem to have anything to say to me. She made only five comments during this first session: "You sound foreign"; "Will you be staying in St. Louis?"; "I thought it was going to be quite different"; "nothing happened"; "I feel better!"

I said that I understood her to be telling me that she found me very different from her parents; strange in my appearance as compared with them, and this made her anxious and caused her to miss them even more. She came with the idea that I was going to make up for the loss and that this had not happened, and it felt as if nothing had happened. Yet, she had felt better because she knew that someone was interested in her and prepared to take care of her. When she had asked me about my remaining in St. Louis, she was clearly worried that I too might leave her; if I was planning to go away, how then could she trust me. I also pointed out that I might have disappointed her in another way. She had probably expected me to comfort her the way that her parents used to do, but this had not happened. Perhaps I could help her in other ways to deal with her unhappy feelings. She stared at me in a very troubled way, and I told her I would be seeing her every day from now on. In fact, I saw her six times a week for the first six weeks that the parents were away; during this time, her acute symptoms rapidly subsided and she began to reconstruct a picture of her family and family life that turned out to be both accurate and devastating. The rage against her parents was extreme, and she said that she wanted them to die wherever they were because they had no concern for their children. She dwelt upon the narcissism of both parents who cared only about themselves, upon the impulsivity of the father and the immaturity of the mother ("She looks like a teen-ager; she dresses in dirty jeans and has frizzed her hair"); upon the insecurity of all the children in the family with herself the worst in this respect; upon the fact that Mary Sue gave them all jobs to do but had no power to enforce the orders; upon her anger that her brothers expected, like their father, that the sisters would wait upon them ("They think that they are our husbands!"); that at night they had all decided to sleep in the same room and she would get into bed with Mary Sue. She wondered whether I would see her until the end of high school when she went off to college. She expected that I would attend her graduation and throw a party for her. She wondered what she would wear—not jeans like her mother. During this period there was a childish, unrealistic quality about much of her material and I mainly listened to her without too much interruption except to point out any change in feeling.

When I asked her why she was coming to see me, she said that it was her parents' wish, and when I again asked her why, she said, "to be analyzed." When I asked her what this meant to her, she said that she did not know, but Mary Sue had told her that I was supposed to help her with her fears and "weird feelings."

She began to tell me how things had been before the parents had separated. The father had always been like a school principal and she used to be afraid of him. She always felt that she was saying something wrong when they spoke together. He once told her that her grammar was poor, but that this did not matter too much for girls because he did not expect her to want to go to college. He said that her mother had been a good mother, even though she had no higher education. There was no reason, he insisted, for Theresa to feel bad about her inadequate diction because her strength lay in cooking and all her family enjoyed her cooking. If she specialized in cooking, she would become "a real woman" and men would be eager to marry her. On her eighth birthday, he presented her with four or five simple cookery books and told the family that she was on the way to becoming "a great chef." She told me that she did not feel any of these things that he said; they did not seem to apply to her; he seemed to be talking about someone else.

Toward the end of the third week, Theresa announced that she wanted to tell me something but that it would be wrong for her to do so. I told her that it was for her to decide what to tell me and that I was only there to help her to understand things that were in her. The next day, she decided that she would tell me because it did worry her. It appeared that the father had called a family council over a year previously and had told them all that their mother had gone on a spending spree against his wishes and against the best interests of the family. They had only a limited amount of money for a large number of people and she had taken it independently into her head to buy a large number of household articles that did nothing useful. He had sent these back to the stores and he wanted the children to realize that since they were a democratic family, he was going to ask their mother to hold out the back of her hand to him while he smacked it. If he had done something as stupid, he would expect the same treatment from her. Quite passively, the mother held out her hand and he administered a smack. Theresa burst into tears, and the rest of the children had been silent and mainly looking guilty.

Following the separation, the children and in particular Theresa missed their mother. Theresa developed strong fears of the dark and began to experience terrifying dreams. Her father took her into his bed and would hold her until she fell asleep.

She began to have a fantasy that her mother had found a "wonderful man who had a great deal of money and was always kind to everyone." (Actually, the mother was dating a man, but he was already married.) One day Theresa was sure that they would both drive up to the door, ask for the girls, and carry them off to a beautiful house which would then become her "real home." She would miss the boys, but they would be better off with Dad. She compared this imaginary home that was light and airy and colorful to the grim and dark and frightening atmosphere of her father's house. When the boys were older, they could come and live in "our house."

Transference feelings were rapidly generated, as one would expect when a child patient is separated from her parents. She became curious about my home life and wondered if it was as beautiful as her imaginary one. She had a feeling that my wife did not look after me all that well, as she observed from the food spots on my shirt. She also remarked that my shoes had not been cleaned for a long time. She thought that maybe, from time to time only, she would leave her mother and her "new father" and come over to my house and tidy up for me. If my wife did not like this arrangement, she could leave. She could then look after me and I could look after her.

In the fourth month, the parents returned and I decided after much consideration that I would not see them. I talked with them briefly and separately on the phone and both reported that Theresa was doing "wonderfully on analysis" and that they felt no wish to interfere or interrupt. They had enough problems to settle between them and with the other children. The mother then revealed that Theresa had spoken about the possibility of being adopted by me and that she had informed her, in a somewhat literal fashion, that this might not be feasible because I probably already had "a large number" of children of my own. She said that she had found another Guru in a different city and had decided to go and spend some time with him.

The intensity of the transference was quite exaggerated for a child of this age and this stage of treatment. Some mild neurotic manifestations began to appear. Theresa was once again fearful at night and wished that she could sleep with me. She knew that this would make her feel safer. She felt ashamed of the way she spoke because I "talked so nice." She felt a constant need to urinate whenever she came for her session. She said that she had "hot feelings" between her legs and wanted to go to the bathroom. She found that the imaginary family which she had introduced into the analysis was a precursor of an early family romance when she was much smaller and her parents had first begun to quarrel. Her hypothetical construction of this family had similarities with the other two families she had created, and she began to wonder whether it would be better to stay with my wife and have me leave the house or vice versa, just as she did not know whether she had done the right thing remaining with her father and the rest of the children rather than leaving with her mother. "You lose whatever you do."

The depressive core became manifest in association with a conflict of ambivalence. She began to mourn the loss of her mother more openly and to say that she did not make things any better for her. I was just a man like her father, and men did not know how to treat girls properly. She became bored during the sessions because I only knew of "man" things to do. She said that Mary Sue was getting fed up with coming every day and was mad with her. The resistance grew and was associated with doubts in my mind about my collusion with the deserting parents, my reinforcement of their lack of responsibility toward their children, and my own unconscious wish to provide better parenting for Theresa. Her waiflike lonesomeness was certainly appealing to anyone with even average parental urges.

During the sixth month of treatment, Theresa raised with me the question that her parents needed treatment to make them better parents because "all the kids were getting fed up and Mary Sue was being 'worn out'." The children had had a council meeting under the chairmanship of Mary Sue, who was becoming more irritable, more reluctant, and more rebellious. Theresa was commissioned to tell me all about the meeting so that I could do something about it. And in this she acted like a go-between for her siblings. After discussing it at some length, she herself decided that the "best thing" was for the children to meet with both parents and recommend to them to undertake treatment. She did not want any of the children to come to see me because I was her therapist and they should find therapists for themselves. Following the meeting with the parents, during which Theresa had been quite vocal, the mother and father decided that they would go to see a family therapist, but one with analytic experience. A little later Theresa informed me that Mary Sue had decided herself to see a social worker because Theresa had become so much better through talking. This social worker had a couple of sessions with the parents and I heard from her that Theresa had given me an extremely accurate account of the family background and history, of the psychopathology of the parents, of their leaving the home to the jurisdiction of Mary Sue, and of their almost total irresponsibility. She felt that the mother had undergone regression and was behaving at times like a chaotic adolescent. The father was rigid and authoritarian with very little capacity for sharing feelings. His suicidal attempt had been in the nature of a weapon for the purpose of bringing his wife to heel. She reported that Theresa was now doing well at school after the initial slump. In her opinion, the birth of Theresa started the parents on the road to disruption. She was the straw that broke the mother's maternal back, and the mother had undergone a significant postpartum depression. The parents had often left the children in the past without preparation, without substitution, and apparently without any concern, compassion, or remorse.

The social worker and I agreed that Theresa needed a more stable and less disturbing home environment if she were to continue in analysis, and she then moved in with her aunt and uncle. Her depression came more markedly to the forefront, together with her now openly expressed rage and resentment at those that she referred to as her "so-called parents." Her new "real family" provided an environment that was both facilitating and holding. I could now work with her internalized libidinal and ego attitudes without being overwhelmed daily by the detrimental external factors. Nevertheless, during that critical first year one could observe, in gross form, the interaction of family and analytic processes, the impingement of family pathology during the course of treatment, the formation of the "family complex," the reactivation of the family romance within the transference, the intensification of the transference to neurotic proportions because of abandonment by the parents; the interplay between the "unconscious" family, the representational family, the actual family, and the analyst's hypothetical family; the development of the family myth (that she was a great cook); and the revelation of the family "secret" (the ritual smack administered to mother by father). In the second year, when she was recapturing the sense of hopefulness, her mother, predictably, remarried and, without any consideration for Theresa's treatment, moved her and her siblings to South Africa where she intended to settle. The accelerated termination was not easy for either patient or analyst, and it was made less easy by its coincidence with the onset of puberty and the removal to a strange new world. In a single follow-up communication, I learned that she was "doing well." It is, of course, quite impossible to say how much of this could be attributed to the outcome of the therapeutic measures and how much to maturation and spontaneous developmental moves (A. Freud, 1965).

This particular experience, however, helps to confirm my view that the psychoanalytic situation provides us with a unique opportunity to study the family in depth. This does not mean to imply that we are ready for a psychoanalytic theory of the family as Flugel had hoped 60 years ago. However, along with the groundwork laid by Freud, the reconstructions derived from the analysis of adults, the direct observation of families by psychoanalytic observers, and the study of family phenomena as they emerge in the child analytic situation, we are gradually learning more about the psychoanalytic mechanisms at work in the family.

Today one is in a better position to understand individuation within the context of the family; one can, in analysis, rediscover the original family that the child carries within himself and the inner dialogue conducted with it; one can analyze the "family complex" and the fantasies that go with it; and one can watch the interplay between the developing family, the developing phases of parenthood, and the developmental stages of the child. In all these senses, we need to bring the family as a psychic phenomenon more fully and more frequently into our analytic work, to recognize the impact of the actual family on the analytic process, and to uncover the repressed unconscious elements relating to it. This should provide us with the necessary experience to construct a more substantive theory than we presently have.

BIBLIOGRAPHY

ANTHONY, E. J. (1971), The History of Group Psychotherapy. In: *Comprehensive Group Psychotherapy*, ed. H. Kaplan & B. Sadock. Baltimore: Williams & Wilkins, pp. 4–31.

———— (1973), A Working Model for Family Studies. In: *The Child in His Family*, ed. E. J. Anthony & C. Koupernik. New York: Wiley, 2:3–20.

———— (1980), Psychoanalysis and Environment. In: *The Course of Life: Psychoanalytic Contributions toward Personality Development*, ed. G. H. Pollock & S. I. Greenspan. Washington: National Institute of Mental Health (in press).

———— & BENEDEK, T., eds. (1970), *Parenthood: Its Psychology and Psychopathology*. Boston: Little, Brown.

BURLINGHAM D. (1935), Child Analysis and the Mother. *Psychoanal. Quart.*, 4:69–92.

DARE, C. (1975), A Classification of Interventions in Child and Conjoint Family Therapy. In: *Proceedings of IXth International Congress of Psychotherapy*. New York: Karger, pp. 428–437.

ERIKSON, E. H. (1968), *Identity: Youth and Crisis*. New York: Norton.

FLUGEL, J. C. (1921), *The Psychoanalytic Study of the Family*. London: Hogarth Press.

FREUD, A. (1960), The Child Guidance Clinic As a Center of Prophylaxis and Enlightenment. *W.*, 5:281–300.

—— (1965), Normality and Pathology in Childhood. *W.*, 6.

FREUD, S. (1896), The Aetiology of Hysteria. *S.E.*, 3:189–221.

—— (1905), Fragments of an Analysis of a Case of Hysteria. *S.E.*, 7:3–122.

—— (1909), Family Romances. *S.E.*, 9:235–241.

—— (1913), Totem and Taboo. *S.E.*, 13:1–161.

—— (1916–17), Introductory Lectures on Psycho-Analysis. *S.E.*, 15 & 16.

—— (1921), Group Psychology and the Analysis of the Ego. *S.E.*, 18:67–143.

—— (1922), *Sammlung kleiner Schriften zur Neurosenlehre*, IV Folge. Vienna: Heller.

—— (1933), New Introductory Lectures on Psycho-Analysis. *S.E.*, 22:3–182.

GREENACRE, P. (1966), Problems of Overidealization of the Analyst and of Analysis. *This Annual*, 21:193–212.

HUG-HELLMUTH, H. VON (1920), On the Technique of Child-Analysis. *Int. J. Psycho-Anal.*, 2:287–305, 1921.

JONES, E. (1953–57), *The Life and Work of Sigmund Freud*, 3 vols. New York: Basic Books.

KRAMER, C. H. (1968), *The Relationships Between Child and Family Psychopathology.* Chicago: Kramer Foundation.

LEBOVICI, S. (1970), The Psychoanalytic Theory of the Family. In: *The Child in His Family*, ed. E. J. Anthony & C. Koupernik. New York: Wiley, 1:1–18.

LUSTMAN, S. L. (1962), Defense, Symptom, and Character. *This Annual*, 17:216–244.

PIAGET, J. (1958), *The Growth of Logical Thinking from Childhood to Adolescence.* New York: Basic Books.

RAPAPORT, D. (1960), *The Structure of Psychoanalytic Theory* [*Psychol. Issues*, 6]. New York: Int. Univ. Press.

REDL, F. (1974), Group Psychological Implications for Individual Therapy with Adolescents: "The Gang Beneath the Couch." *Psychosoc. Proc.*, 3(2):5–20.

SMIRNOFF, V. (1971), *The Scope of Child Analysis.* New York: Int. Univ. Press.

WINNICOTT, D. W. (1954), Metapsychological and Clinical Aspects of Regression within the Psycho-Analytical Set-Up. In: *Collected Papers.* New York: Basic Books, 1958, pp. 278–294.

—— (1965), The Effect of Psychotic Parents on the Emotional Development of the Child. In: *The Family and Individual Development.* London: Tavistock, pp. 69–78.

—— (1971), *Playing and Reality.* Hammondsworth: Pelican Books, 1974.

A Historical Sketch of the Use and Disuse of Reconstruction

PHYLLIS GREENACRE, M.D.

IT SEEMS TO ME THAT AN INTEREST IN RECONSTRUCTION IS NAT-
ural—that it has a beginning in the child's curiosity about growth,
i.e., getting bigger. When a child discovers that his parents were
once children like himself, he is amazed and unbelieving. This is
then followed by curiosity about these child-parents and how
they got that way. These inquiries may later be absorbed and
covered over by elements of the family romance and the family
saga.

In recent years, reconstruction seems to have almost completely dropped out of psychoanalytic thinking and literature,
although it must persist in a limited anonymous way in some
analytic practice. It is not clear to me exactly when the term
reconstruction gained status in the psychoanalytic vocabulary, nor
when its usage began to fade out. Its deeper roots probably lay in
the disruption of the original theory of the traumatic basis of
neurosis, and in the fact that the cathartic method of treatment
had proved inadequate. It had become apparent then that in
some instances the supposed sexual trauma had not occurred in
fact, but was the imaginative product of the patient's childhood.
It was then clearly necessary to understand how such imagina-
tions had arisen and been subsequently forgotten, completely or
in part. Some kind of reconstruction was necessary. With the

Member, New York Psychoanalytic Institute, and Professor of Clinical
Psychiatry, Emeritus, Cornell University.
Introduction to Panel on Reconstruction, International Congress of
Psycho-Analysis, New York, 1979.

verification that in infancy there were stages of sexual sensitivity and some degree of responsiveness, it could be seen that fantasies might be generated with slight stimulation from without. They would then form according to the particular condition and phase of the young child's development at that time.

When an accepted theory has to be drastically modified, as the "trauma theory" was, a polarization of attitudes may occur with a special interest in and emphasis on the new and a relative disregard of the older ideas. Sometimes it is a matter of "throwing out the baby with the bath." Those who stressed the primary importance of fantasy saw the genetically determined state as the answer to the question of the beginning of the neurosis. Reconstruction could then come to rest in an attenuated form, with the realization in the patient that his neurotic difficulties sprang from and were determined by disturbances in some specific early phase(s). This gave a degree of naturalness to any sexual trauma, whether actual or fantasied. The feeling of relief was enhanced by the therapeutic relation to the analyst. This situation did not always deal adequately with the emotional nature of the actual, historically true part of an early traumatic impression, unless it was specifically repeated in the transference or otherwise acted out in some detail. Such patients might sometimes gain an equilibrium through a defensive intellectualization, but be vulnerable if new stress was experienced.

The alternating rhythm between the work of clinical test (or experiment) and theoretical formulations—which seems to go on in the evolution of sciences in general—was especially evident in the period after the First World War and extended into the early 1930s. At this time Freud had made a number of discoveries that went far beyond his earlier formulation of the realm of psychoanalysis. These were presented under the newly defined title of *metapsychology* as a comprehensive science of the mind. All mental processes would be described psychoanalytically with an account of the dynamic attributes, the topographical features, and the economic significance (see Freud, 1925, p. 58f.; Jones, 1957, p. 85). Of the 24 papers planned, 21 were ultimately published. This is an impressive list of studies which, with some additions and modifications, form the fundamental basis of psychoanalysis as we know it today.

World War II, the emigration of many Europeans to New York, and the establishment of New York as the center of training at a time when the formal training had only recently been organized here probably had some effect on what was emphasized as being of general and academic interest in psychoanalytic practice and training. There was a special and natural enthusiasm for the metapsychological papers, though only the early ones were at that time generally available. The importance of trauma as well as of the traumatic theory of neurosis was generally treated as a thing of the past, whose only importance was as part of analytic history. Reconstruction may have almost died of inanition.

It was something of a surprise to me to realize the significance of the fact that one of Freud's last papers which dealt with construction and reconstruction (1937) gave a clear and succinct statement of the value of assessing the role of trauma and the use of reconstruction as a psychoanalytic technique. It was clear that he had by no means abandoned the concept of reconstruction as of basic importance in analytic technique. Further, in "The Analogy," a postscript to *Moses and Monotheism* (1939), he wrote explicitly of the nature and importance of early trauma and the reason for the use of reconstruction.

For those who would decry the influence of actual trauma, and stress only the fantasies adherent to it, I would quote as follows:

> We give the name of *traumas* to those impressions, experienced early and later forgotten, to which we attach such great importance in the aetiology of the neuroses. We may leave on one side the question of whether the aetiology of the neuroses in general may be regarded as traumatic . . . [as] it is not possible in every case to discover a manifest trauma in the neurotic subject's early history . . . all we have before us is an unusual, abnormal reaction to experiences and demands which affect everyone, but are worked over and dealt with by other people in another manner which may be called normal. When we have nothing else at our disposal for explaining a neurosis but hereditary and constitutional dispositions, we are naturally tempted to say that it was not acquired but developed.
>
> But . . . two points must be stressed. Firstly, the genesis of a neurosis invariably goes back to very early impressions. [A

footnote here states: "This therefore makes it nonsensical to say that one is practising psycho-analysis if one excludes from examination and consideration precisely those early periods—as happens in some quarters."] Secondly, . . . there are cases which are distinguished as being 'traumatic' because their effects go back unmistakably to one or more powerful impressions in these early times . . . [and] have escaped being dealt with normally, so that one is inclined to judge that if they had not occurred the neurosis would not have come about either. . . . But the gap between the two groups [of cases] appears not to be unbridgeable.

[Freud then goes on to say that how these two sets of determinants combine depends upon quantitative factors: the two interact in a reciprocal way. The greater the constitutional factor, the more susceptible the individual is to trauma and vice versa.] In this way we reach the concept of a sliding 'complemental series' . . . in which two factors converge in fulfilling an aetiological requirement . . . as a rule both factors operate together and it is only at the two ends of the series that there can be any question of a simple motive being at work. . . . [Thus] we can disregard the distinction between the traumatic and non-traumatic aetiologies as irrelevant [p. 72f.].

Subsequently in the same article Freud summarizes under three headings the reasons for the use of reconstruction in psychoanalytic work:

(a) All of these traumas occur . . . up to about the fifth year. Impressions from the time at which a child is *beginning to talk*[1] [are] of particular interest; . . . the ages of two and four seem to be the most important; it cannot be determined with certainty how long after birth this period of receptivity begins. (b) The experiences in question are as a rule totally forgotten . . . and fall within the period of infantile amnesia, which is usually broken into a few mnemic residues, which are known as "screen memories'. (c) They relate to impressions of a sexual and aggressive nature, and no doubt also to early injuries to the ego (narcissistic mortifications) . . . young children make no

---

1. Many—perhaps most—children "begin to talk" toward the end of the first year. "Beginning to talk" is different from what was often said—that nothing can be analyzed that cannot be put into words.

sharp distinction between sexual and aggressive acts, as they do later. . . . The predominance of the sexual factor . . . calls for theoretical consideration . . . the facts of their being forgotten and their sexual-aggressive content are closely interconnected. The traumas are either experiences on the subject's own body or sense perceptions, mostly of something seen or heard—that is, experiences or impressions. The interconnection . . . is established by a theory, a product of the work of analysis which alone can bring about a knowledge of forgotten experiences, or, to put it *more vividly* but also more incorrectly, bring them back to memory [p. 74; my italics].

Freud certainly had not given up the belief in the efficacy of reconstruction.

His explicit statements regarding reconstruction were written in 1937–38, seemingly as part of his effort to leave comprehensive studies that would elucidate the theory and work of psychoanalysis. It seems ironically paradoxical that even at the time of his writing this, much of its content had already been considered defunct and only of interest as a part of the historical past of psychoanalysis. This conflict in points of view was probably due to multiple factors connected with the onset of World War II, and later with Freud's death, which also occurred in 1939. There were the practical delays in publication and in getting translations. But the greatest obstacle may have been the prolonged period of mourning for a lost leader and the increased clinging to those metapsychological perspectives which had been his last gift before the war had forced emigration. At the same time that there was an apparent expansion in the intellectual framework of analysis, there was a somewhat reactionary tightening in the teaching of technique. The precise interpretation began to take the place of reconstructive interest.

That the death of a great leader always brings forth complicated ambivalent reactions from those who have been devoted followers is well known. The ever-present crises of the war period certainly interfered with an adequate assimilation of the loss. It was only after the war was over and the training of psychoanalysts was in a period of temporary expansion that other derivatives of ambivalence began to break through: rivalries with the lost father-leader and competition with sibling colleagues. New theories began to emerge, giving different emphases in the basic psychoanalytic theses with corresponding modifications in treatment.

In the present decade psychoanalysis is experiencing various pressures, resulting from the social revolution of the 1960s, with its many paradoxical trends. There is an emphasis on the here-and-now with a demand for quick and dramatic cures—a strange mixture of a mechanistic approach to behavior and a faith in arcane and primitive remedies. Psychoanalytic and psychiatric terms are taken over with distorted meaning into the popular vocabulary. It is a bit surprising and perhaps heartening to me to find that *reconstruction* is a topic of interest at this particular time. To me, however, it seems to be the cornerstone of psychoanalytic practice, understanding, and research. I must add, too, that the functions and significance of screen memories still seem of marginal importance to many analysts. In my estimation, they form the fundamental skeleton of reconstructive methods.

BIBLIOGRAPHY

FREUD, S. (1915–17), Papers on Metapsychology. *S.E.*, 14:105–323.
——— (1925), An Autobiographical Study. *S.E.*, 20:3–74.
——— (1937), Constructions in Analysis. *S.E.*, 23:255–269.
——— (1939), Moses and Monotheism. *S.E.*, 23:3–137.
JONES, E. (1957), *The Life and Work of Sigmund Freud*, vol. 2. New York: Basic Books.

Cognition in Personality and the Treatment Process

A Psychoanalytic View

SEBASTIANO SANTOSTEFANO, Ph.D.

IN 1955, THE UNIVERSITY OF COLORADO CONVENED A SYMPOSIUM to discuss cognition because the sponsors believed, "For a long time psychology in America has slighted what may be considered to be its ultimate purpose, the scientific understanding of man's cognitive behavior" (Bruner et al., 1957, p. v). To compensate for this slight, leaders of the day were invited to discuss cognition. Several theoretical views were represented, including that of psychoanalysis by David Rapaport.

Following this symposium, research flourished under the label of "the new look in perception." What was it that was new? An attempt was being made to correlate cognition, needs, and personality. Among the leaders of this "new look" were psychoanalytically trained psychologists, notably George Klein, Philip Holzman, and Robert Holt. At about the same time, Piaget's writings were beginning to receive attention in this country, and researchers following Piaget also launched studies of cognition. In contrast to investigators wearing the "new look," Piagetian researchers were studying cognition as a domain separate from personality and needs.

Director of Child Psychology and Psychoeducation, Hall-Mercer Children's Center, McLean Hospital, and Associate Professor of Psychology, Harvard Medical School.
Presented as the Eighth Annual Beata Rank Memorial Lecture, the Boston Psychoanalytic Society and Institute, April 26, 1978.

Since the 1950s these two approaches to cognition have followed quite separate courses, in spite of the fact that they have shared a basic point of view: that cognition plays a pivotal role in adaptation. Investigators following the lead of George Klein have attempted to examine cognition as fibers weaving one fabric with those of personality. Piagetians have examined cognition as fibers which weave a fabric separate from that of personality. The issue I am noting here has important implications for my topic, and I shall return to it after completing the historical sketch.

As the "new look" elaborated its concepts and observations, Robert Holt (1964) published a communication some 10 years after the Colorado symposium, informing psychoanalysts that cognition was emerging as a powerful point of view and urging them to consider how this view could influence their clinical work and concepts.

Apparently Holt's suggestion was not followed by many. John Benjamin (1961) pointed out that the field of cognition was a stepchild in clinical practice. And Arieti (1970) expressed a similar opinion in commenting that cognition has been the "Cinderella" of psychiatry and psychoanalysis and that no other field of the psyche has been so consistently neglected by clinicians.

The neglect has not been total, however. Several psychoanalysts have addressed cognition and its significance for personality theory and practice. One particular feature of these statements has impressed me. In relating cognition and personality, these writers have turned, by and large, to Piaget's cognitive psychology rather than to the cognitive psychology that emerged from the "new look" research and psychoanalytic ego psychology. While a systematic review of this literature falls outside the scope of this paper, I would like to cite a few examples. Reminding child psychiatrists that in addition to understanding the dynamics of feelings one must also learn to understand the dynamics of thinking, Anthony (1956) reviewed and offered Piaget's concepts as serving this task. Peter Wolff (1960) provided psychoanalysts with a comprehensive comparison of Piaget's model and psychoanalysis. To explore cognitive aspects of object relations, Décarie (1965) studied children through Piaget's lens. And to construct a synthesis of cognitive and personality development, Melvin Lewis (1977) relied exclusively on Piaget's cognitive psychology.

These writings as well as others I have not mentioned illustrate that cognition is not being completely neglected by clinicians, and that there is clinical and theoretical value in understanding further the dynamics of thinking. At the same time these writings, in my opinion, also illustrate significant limitations which Piaget's concepts present for psychoanalysis. The goal of this paper is to illustrate how the psychology of cognition which has grown out of the "new" look research, and within ego psychology, is a viable alternative to Piaget's model and holds considerable promise for psychoanalytic theory and technique with both children and adults.

To pursue this goal I shall first review highlights of the synthesis of cognition and personality which Melvin Lewis offered psychoanalysis. I select his synthesis because it serves to illustrate both the advantages and limitations for psychoanalysis when one attempts to integrate cognition, as formulated by Piaget, with personality and the treatment process as formulated by psychoanalysis. His synthesis also serves as a comparison for the ego-psychological model of cognition, which, I propose, has more heuristic value for psychoanalysis.

To begin we should pause to remind ourselves of the meaning of the term *cognition* and recall Piaget's basic model. In the fields of psychology and psychiatry, cognition refers to any process by which an individual becomes aware of, obtains knowledge of, and uses information about an object, person, fantasy, thought, or feeling. Mental functions typically included are attending, perceiving, recognizing, conceiving, judging, reasoning, and remembering (English and English, 1958).

In Piaget's view of how humans obtain knowledge (Flavell, 1963), a person passes through three developmental periods. In the first, sensorimotor period (birth to 2 years), information is gathered primarily through physical contact. Cognition is entirely "practical" in that it involves perceptual-motor actions and responses to things rather than to symbols and representations of things. In the second period of concrete operations (2 to 11 years), information is increasingly engaged through the manipulation of symbols of objects rather than the objects themselves. In the third period of formal operations (11 to 15 years), a new and final reorganization of cognition takes place. Information is now gathered not only from the existing reality but in particular from the realm of possibilities, abstractions, and propositions.

Let us now review the synthesis constructed by Lewis (1977) which I will use as a point of comparison. Lewis uses Piaget's model to integrate language and cognition with personality. First he defines language as spoken words which are symbols for an individual's experiences. But how do words become symbols of one's experiences? He opts for the notion held by Piaget, and by many others including psychoanalytic workers, that since the child comes to know about objects through his actions on them, language emerges within this action process. Lewis next elaborates language by making a distinction between what he calls "symbolic verbal language," that is, spoken words, and "nonlinguistic representational thinking," that is, images and actions.

From this distinction, Lewis goes beyond Piaget because of two developmental observations made in the psychoanalytic situation. One concerns what he terms "symbolic dysmaturation." A child may have the capacity to represent in images and actions but not in spoken language, or the reverse. The other concerns the degree to which the symbols of spoken language are free from, or glued to, immediate events and perceptions. To deal with these issues Lewis turns to Piaget's stage of concrete operations and its unique process of conservation. In Piaget's model, conservation is the cognitive process by which concrete information and actions on that information are transformed into and conserved as images. As a result of conserving more and more information in the form of images, the child experiences images and language as autonomous from actions and immediate perceptions. The child becomes freer to think about his thinking and his representational world.

To complete his synthesis Lewis weaves one fiber of personality development closely to that of conservation. In resolving ambivalence and the dominance of oedipal strivings, Lewis proposes, the child is progressively conserving information in images and gaining distance from immediate events. As a result, the child becomes free to employ language as a tool to describe and conceptualize his perceptions and experiences, however contradictory and emotionally laden.

This synthesis brings several issues to the attention of psychoanalysis. First, Lewis asks us to be mindful that before the age of 7, a child has not yet achieved sufficient conservation provided by symbols to think about his own thinking and to talk about needs, conflicts, and feelings without experiencing them. Similarly, a child above the age of 9 could continue to conserve information inadequately, because of uneven development, and have difficulty taking appropriate distance from events and feelings.

In both instances delays in the development of cognitive conservation and language result in the child's experiencing anxiety states, since the child does not have the cognitive equipment to understand and resolve events and perceptions. It is here that Lewis makes a particularly important contribution. Psychoanalysis usually considers anxiety as it relates to intrapsychic conflict between, for example, wish and superego prohibitions. Lewis urges us to consider anxiety in additional ways—as related to the mismatch which could exist between a person's cognitive organization and the complexity of information the person is attempting to master. This consideration points to technique. For Lewis, therapeutic intervention should take place on a two-way street: the analytic process should promote not only emotional development but also growth in language and cognition, since the latter are tools by which information and perceptions are mastered.

Even with these contributions the synthesis proposed by Lewis, to my mind, does not address particular issues of importance to psychoanalysis, primarily because of limitations in Piaget's model. Piaget's model does not consider:

that individuals differ in the ways they gather information;

that cognitive functions temporarily regress and progress and become fixated;

that information is obtained both from external reality and from the world of fantasy;

that feelings are regulated while an individual is engaging information from the environment and from fantasies and memories;

that rather than marching from one cognitive stage to the next, individuals employ simultaneously several methods for gathering and expressing information.

To illustrate these limitations and to set the stage for an alternative model which I believe handles them, I shall at this point describe behaviors I observed in the analytic situation.

1. A 7-year-old boy is restlessly bristling with anxiety and anger. For a moment he fingers and kneeds pieces of a formboard game and then abruptly spills them on the floor, shouting to me, "Shut your shit mouth!" A few moments later he looks over small plastic soldiers and aligns them to wage war with my soldiers to determine which army will learn secrets from the other.

2. An 11-year-old girl, who is usually placid, stands in a tense position, arches her index finger as a hook, and touches her face over which freckles are distributed in abundance. Simultaneously she remarks, "My sister hates my freckles." Then her affect becomes industrious and eager, as she touches spots on a table top, while talking freely about school and a weekend trip her family took.

3. A 30-year-old man is associating to his dream of a child whose front teeth are missing. He seems quite anxious, and his stream of thinking is sporadic. He associates to one detail in his current reality, only to leap back to the manifest content of the dream; he ventures toward another reality detail, which is close to the first, only to leap back again to the dream image. Further, while associating, he sometimes grasps the edge of his trousers, near the knees, with the thumb and forefinger of each hand. After about 10 minutes of this style of cognitive activity he abruptly assigns a label to his dream, exclaiming, "It's a castration dream!" Upon verbalizing this label, the patients stops touching his trousers and his manifest anxiety and tension subside, as he now talks freely but about and within the narrow limits of the term castration.

With these vignettes I hope to illustrate that at all ages we can observe persons using multiple cognitive functions simultaneously, and in different ways, to acquire and use information; that these functions shift abruptly, regressively and progressively; and that affects also shift in concert. The 7-year-old boy verbalized the word "shit" (an instance of symbolic verbal language in Lewis's model), yet at the same time he physically manipulated pieces of a game with actions which seemed to represent the same issue (an instance of nonlingualistic representational thinking). Further, although in Piaget's model this boy was at the early levels of the concrete stage, he shifted from acting aggressively and directly toward the person of the analyst to acting more indirectly by conserving the analyst within the metaphor of an army war. The 11-year-old girl at one moment engaged information on her body (freckles) with a physical motion (hooked finger) and with words, while experiencing intense anxiety. At another moment she physically engaged spots on the table (symbols of freckles) while simultaneously surveying information in her reality of school and a family trip. I shall return to these examples, and that of the adult patient, after developing my thesis further.

Piaget notwithstanding, then, all of us have observed in the analytic situation that an 11-year-old child does not always function cognitively with the benefit of conservation and distance, nor does an adolescent or adult always operate cognitively in terms of possibilities and propositions. We have also observed children and adults who, at one moment, calmly examine and talk about a memory viewed from some distance, and who, at the next moment, are fused to a memory, reexperiencing it in fantasies and actions with affective storm.

My discussion to this point leads to several questions. How and why do persons differ in the way they gather and manage information? For example, some always need to touch information; some make physical contact with information only at certain times; some typically look only at narrow segments of information; while others typically direct their attention at many, broad, seemingly unrelated bits of information. How and why do individuals temporarily change their usual way of gathering information? And how and why does a person's emotional quality change as information is gathered and manipulated?

In synthesizing language, cognition, and personality, then, psychoanalysis needs a model which systematically takes into account the following issues: (1) individual differences, regression, progression, and fixation in cognitive functioning; (2) multiple cognitive functions which operate simultaneously at all stages; (3) cognitive functions which gather information from the external environment and from the environment of fantasies and memories; (4) cognitive functions which participate in balancing and regulating affects; and (5) language as one cognitive ego activity which is located developmentally among others. Moreover, each of these factors would need to be considered continuously in the analytic process as issues are repeated, as the unconscious is made conscious; as psychic conflict is resolved; and as thinking, emoting, and behaving are restructured.

The beginning of such a model is available if we integrate two concepts that have developed within psychoanalytic research. One concerns the concept of cognitive controls; and the other, the concept of action, fantasy, and language as developmentally ordered ego modes.

COGNITIVE CONTROLS

The concept of cognitive controls was formulated by George Klein (1949, 1951, 1954). In his clinical and research work Klein observed that individuals consistently use particular cognitive ego strategies or attitudes to approach, avoid, select, register, pace, compare, and cluster information, and that individuals differ in the use they make of one or another strategy. He also proposed that in managing information with these ego strategies, individuals balance information from the external environment and the environment of thoughts, fantasies, motives, and feelings. The model of a dynamic system of ego strategies which process information parallels, as can be seen, the psychoanalytic concept of mechanisms of defense. For Klein, then, individuals habitually use particular ego functions to remain in control of information, hence the term *cognitive controls.*

From Klein's seminal writings, the concept of cognitive controls has been developed and refined over the past 25 years and includes at this time a complex set of propositions and observations. Here I will survey only major aspects that rely upon my own work (Santostefano, 1978). While Klein and others studied cognitive controls primarily in normal adults, I have attempted to study cognitive control functioning in children at different stages of development, as well as in adults, and in both normal and psychopathological groups. I have also attempted to study directly the role cognitive controls play in adaptation and in the treatment process.

I shall define each cognitive control and the developmental course of cognitive controls observed in longitudinal studies of normal children from the ages of 4 years to adolescence. Following this, I shall consider observations of clinical groups.

WHAT ARE THE COGNITIVE CONTROLS WHICH CAN BE IDENTIFIED IN THE FUNCTIONING OF NORMAL CHILDREN AT DIFFERENT STAGES AND IN ADULTS?

When children and adults deal with information, how many distinctively different processes, or mechanisms, account for their cognitive activity? Of the several cognitive controls identified to date, five have withstood the test of numerous experiments. In the following, it should be noted that each cognitive control defines a developmental range of particular cognitive behaviors and that the controls are hierarchically related. The levels within each control, and from one control to the next developmentally higher one, represent stages of cognitive ego maturity, from cognitive behaviors that characterize the young child to behaviors that characterize the adolescent.

Body-ego tempo regulation. The first cognitive control concerns the manner in which an individual registers and manages information that comes from perceptions and images of the body, and the manner in which an individual regulates body motility. At one end of the continuum, the young child registers vague body percepts represented in global images. In addition, body motility is undifferentiated so that when asked to move fast or slowly, the child produces the same tempo. With an increase in age, perceptions and representations of the body gradually become more detailed and differentiated. Moreover, many body tempos are refined and regulated, each distinguished from the other.

Focal attention. This principle concerns the manner in which an individual scans and surveys a field of information. The young child typically scans information slowly and passively and gives attention only to narrow segments of the field of information before him. With an increase in age, the child directs attention more actively and sweeps attention across increasingly larger segments of a field of information.

Field articulation. Here the issue is the manner in which an individual deals with a field of information which contains elements that are both relevant and nonrelevant to the task at hand. The young child gives attention nearly equally to relevant and nonrelevant information. By adolescence, attention is actively withheld from nonrelevant information and selectively sustained for longer periods of time on what is relevant to the moment.

Leveling-sharpening. This cognitive control concerns the manner in which an individual manages information in memory images. The young child typically constructs global images of past information which are readily confused and fused with present perceptions so that subtle changes are not registered. As the child becomes older, sharper memory images are constructed and subtle similarities and differences between past and present information are noticed. This cognitive control relates most to the process of conservation defined by Piaget.

Equivalence range. This principle concerns the manner in which an individual categorizes information in terms of concepts. The young child relates or groups information in terms of a few categories that are narrow and concrete. With development, increasingly broader and more abstract categories are used. Language as a tool appears here in the model of cognitive controls. An individual may or may not construct a verbal label which guides the organization he imposes on information. However, the model holds that the highest developmental level involves labeling or verbalizing categories.

The key differences between this psychoanalytic model of cognition and that of Piaget should be apparent. From the viewpoint of cognitive controls, a child does not march first through a sensorimotor stage and then through a stage of conservation and so on. Rather, at all stages of development, a child and adult at some level: regulate body tempos and construct images of body percepts; scan fields of information; articulate relevant from nonrelevant; compare present perceptions with images that conserve past information; and conceptualize information. While one or another cognitive control mechanism might dominate at a particular stage of development, or at any given moment, all processes operate simultaneously to balance information from the environment, and from feelings and fantasies, and all processes are subject to progressive changes, regressions, and fixations.

WHAT IS THE PURPOSE OF COGNITIVE CONTROLS? WHAT ROLE DO THEY PLAY IN ADAPTATION?

In general, cognitive controls are conceptualized as maintaining a balance between feelings, drives, and fantasies, all registered as information by cognition, on the one hand, and the requirements and opportunities of information presented by the outer environment, on the other. This process is referred to as maintaining a cognitive-affective balance and is viewed as fostering adaptations, psychological development, and learning.

My developmental observations of normal children and adults suggest at present two distinct phases in the cognitive-affective balance maintained by cognitive controls within total personality development. During the first half of latency (5 to 9 years), cognitive controls quickly and steadily become more oriented toward information in the external environment. That is, the child's tempo regulation, scanning, selecting relevant information, constructing memory images, and categorizing increasingly work upon information in the external environment. In this position the cognitive-affective balance provided by cognitive controls enables the child to keep a distance from *internal* information (e.g., emotionally laden fantasies, representations of drives and wishes).

By focusing work on reality information during the first half of latency, cognitive controls facilitate the growth of other ego functions. These functions are critical if the child is to negotiate and resolve successfully the egocentric position of the oedipal phase before the age of 9 years. For example, the child should construct identifications with the standards of parents and teachers; construct defenses which manage the wish-dominated position of the oedipal phase; and develop capacities flexibly to accommodate to the demands, limits, and opportunities of the environment, especially school.

During the second half of latency (age 9 to adolescence), my developmental observations further suggest that cognitive controls shift to a position that is both outer- and inner-oriented.

With ego gains made during the first half of latency in constructing identifications, defense mechanisms, and control of the environment, the child in the second position of cognitive controls maintains a cognitive-affective balance by performing work upon information from both the external environment and the world of fantasies and feelings. When registering body percepts, regulating motility, scanning, segregating relevant from nonrelevant, comparing memory images with current perceptions, and categorizing information, the older child flexibly responds to the requirements and information of external reality, a response that is related to some intention or task as well as to the requirements and information of the internal world of fantasy and wish.

During the second half of latency, then, cognitive controls in normal development become highly flexible and mobile. From situation to situation controls can remain stable. They may also shift regressively (e.g., to more narrow scanning) or progressively (e.g., to broader scanning) as the environment and internal information demand. And cognitive controls shift back and forth between an inner and outer orientation. In flexibly responding to both worlds of information, the older child and adolescent broaden their source of information, continue learning, and achieve successful adaptations to changing environments.

A STUDY OF CHANGE IN AFFECTIVE-COGNITIVE BALANCE
LATENCY BOYS UNDERGOING SURGERY

My students and I attempted to study directly this shifting in the orientation of cognitive controls in the service of adaptation. In these initial studies our strategy has been to observe a person first in an environment which for him is average and expectable (e.g., his home), and then again in an environment that is atypical and stressful. In this way we hoped to optimize the opportunity of observing changes in cognitive-affective balance and of understanding their significance. In one study (Shapiro, 1972; see also Santostefano, 1978), psychologically normal boys 8 to 11 years old were observed in their homes, then again in a hospital just hours before they were to undergo surgery for hernia repairs, and then for a third time at home again, 30 days after leaving the hospital. One comparison group consisted of children observed at home and again in the dentist's office before they were to experience the repair of tooth decay for the first time. A second comparison group was observed in their homes (representing "usual" stress) at three comparable points in time. We measured the leveling-sharpening cognitive control as well as personality dimensions such as castration anxiety, fantasied aggression, fantasies representing body barriers and penetration, and behavioral signs of emotional upset.

In summarizing our results, I will note the differences which distinguished the surgical group. First, while in the hospital setting, all children in the group shifted their cognitive control functioning to more extensive and increased leveling. That is, relative to their cognitive functioning while in the home setting, the children insulated themselves from information in the external hospital environment. They formed global images of external information and did not notice subtle changes in this information. We also observed that the children who shifted most toward leveling external information produced at the same time more vivid, organized fantasies expressing aggression and fears of castration.

In brief, in response to a short-term change in the environment (surgical stress), these normal children shifted their cognitive-affective balance so that they insulated themselves from external stimulation while working on the internal information of castration and aggression associated with the stress. Last, we also observed that the children who shifted most flexibly toward an internal orientation received behavioral ratings from their mothers which suggested that they adjusted best after surgery.

I propose that this adaptive success was facilitated by the boys' capability to withdraw cognitively from external information, while attending to and working cognitively on personal interpretations of castration and aggression, rehearsing these in fantasy. As a result, unconscious, distorted interpretations and anxieties interfered less with postoperative adjustment.

To this point I have considered the normal course of the development of cognitive controls and the role they play in adaptation. I now turn to these same issues in psychopathological populations.

COGNITIVE CONTROLS IN PSYCHOPATHOLOGY

I have conducted a number of studies of children, adolescents, and adults who were hospitalized in psychiatric facilities because of severe mental disorders or who came to the outpatient clinic with severe learning disabilities and adjustment problems. Our observations to date suggest that the cognitive control orientation of these clinical groups appears to be opposite to that of normals. Before the age of 9 years, the cognitive work of children with emotional and learning disorders is much more occupied with information from fantasies, wishes, and impulses (inner-oriented). For example, when dealing with reality information, they scan more passively or at narrow segments, compared to normal counterparts. On the other hand, from 9 years through adolescence, we have observed that the cognitive controls of these children are either excessively outer-oriented or excessively inner-oriented. More importantly, their cognitive controls fail to shift flexibly, back and forth, from inside to outside information in keeping with opportunities, limits, and demands.

As a result, the efforts of these persons to adapt to and assimilate information usually are limited, whether the task involves learning in school, learning in a hospital milieu program, or learning in psychotherapy sessions.

ACTION, FANTASY AND LANGUAGE AS EGO MODES

As a complement to the concept of cognitive controls, I shall discuss briefly the concept of action, fantasy, and language as developmentally ordered ego modes, the second fiber required by the model I am proposing. I have previously attempted to illustrate how this psychoanalytic hypothesis could guide laboratory research as well as observation in the psychoanalytic situation (Santostefano, 1970, 1977a). Here I shall present only highlights of the concepts and research findings.

    1. Action, fantasy, and language are ego modalities which represent alternative means for expression.

2. A developmental principle defines the relations among these modes. Early in development the individual is fused to objects in his environment and responds immediately with actions. With differentiation of self from world, and with the growing capacity to delay and to represent objects in imagery, the individual postpones action and develops the capacity to employ fantasy. With further development, fantasy and action behaviors become subordinated by, and integrated within, the language system which dominates. However, the action and fantasy modes are not replaced by the language mode, but remain potentially active so that at each point in development they *codetermine* subsequent structures and expressions.

3. All three modalities are potentially available to the individual. Short-term changes in environmental conditions and expectations and/or shifts in the emotional-psychological state of the individual could result in temporary regression to a developmentally more primitive modality or to a developmentally more primitive level within a modality or to temporary progression.

We have explored various aspects of these hypotheses in formal studies. Psychological tests were designed to permit a wide range of action, fantasy, and language behaviors as responses. To study developmental changes within each mode the tests were administered to different age groups. Our results provide empirical support for the notion that early in development there is relatively little delaying of actions, and actions are executed directly on objects. With development, there is an increase in delay, and actions are executed more and more indirectly and at a greater distance between the person and the object. We observed the same progression toward an increase in delay, indirectness, and distance with development in fantasy and language behaviors.

In terms of relations among modes, we have observed that the action mode dominates to the age of 7 or 8, after which fantasy rapidly emerges as dominant. It is not until the age of 12 or 13 that language appears to become the preferred tool and effectively to regulate and connect with the processes of fantasy and action.

To study regression and progression in these ego modes, children were first classified as tending to express aggression either in the action mode (action-oriented) or in the fantasy mode (fantasy-oriented). Both types of children were then subjected individually either to an experimental laboratory condition that invited aggressive actions or a condition that invited aggressive fantasies. For example, in the former ("action") condition, a child broke wooden sticks, punched a Bobo doll; in the latter ("fantasy") condition, the child sat in a chair and viewed a film of a boxing match and pictures portraying violence. Psychological tests, measuring action aggression and fantasy aggression, were administered to each child before and again after the experimental condition. We found that following the "action" condition, each child regressed in one mode, and shifted progressively in the other, depending upon whether or not the "action" condition matched the child's current ego stage (i.e., action- or fantasy-oriented). For example, action-oriented boys who experienced the "action" condition showed a progressive shift in the action mode (i.e., an increase in delay and indirectness of action); at the same time they showed a regressive shift in the fantasy mode (i.e., less delay and more directness and primitivity in fantasy expressions). On the other hand, fantasy-oriented boys who experienced the "fantasy" condition regressed in the action mode while shifting progressively in the fantasy mode. I have discussed elsewhere (1977a) some of the implications of these research findings for psychoanalytic treatment especially of children.

INTEGRATING THE CONCEPT OF COGNITIVE CONTROLS AND THE CONCEPT OF ACTION, FANTASY, AND LANGUAGE AS EGO MODES

At the present time the synthesis I am using views cognitive controls as operating continuously within, and in the service of, the ego modality which dominates at the time. For example, if a child is functioning developmentally within the action phase, in addition to observing the form and content of actions, I also attempt to observe how body percepts are registered and body tempos regulated, how a field of information is scanned, how relevant information is distinguished from irrelevant, how past information is related to present perceptions, and how information is conceptualized. I make the same observations if the same child is functioning within the fantasy phase.

Several interlocking hypotheses are suggested by this model. The following hypotheses illustrate how the conceptual model could be elaborated.

1. Cognitive controls balance information from all sources and thereby mediate personality development as it moves through ego developmental phases of action, fantasy, and language.

2. The assimilation of new ego ideals is particularly important in the acquisition of new cognitive strategies and new action, fantasy, and language ego behaviors.

The following illustrates hypotheses that could serve the further systematization of analytic techniques with a cognitive-developmental model as a guide.

1. Unconscious conflicts and fixations should be progressively organized, repeated, resolved, restructured, and made conscious within the action, fantasy and language modes. The repetition of conflicts within each mode is served by cognitive controls.

2. Developmentally immature or fixated cognitive controls (for example, habitual narrow scanning; articulating all details as equally relevant) maintain a balance of information and emotions which fosters neurotic conflicts or fixations. Accordingly, these cognitive controls require formal analytic work and restructuring.

3. The form and content of an intervention by the analyst should be timed in terms of the patient's cognitive ego status and readiness for cognitive growth. That is, the analyst uses the patient's cognitive status to select activity, or fantasy, or language behaviors as well as to select the breadth of information the patient is asked to scan, the number of details articulated as relevant, the sharpness with which an image of past information is related to perceptions of present information, and the level of abstraction to label or conceptualize (i.e., interpret) a cluster of information.

To illustrate aspects of these hypotheses I now return to the clinical examples described at the start (p. 46). First I shall consider the 7-year-old boy. Once we resolved that we did not need to battle each other for secrets but could join each other in learning about them, the boy launched into a theme of play-acting, which persisted for more than a year. During this phase he enacted with macroactions the role of a king rat, assisted by a servant rat, who captured and punished rats whenever they sucked the tails of other rats into their anuses.

This phase then gave way to another in which the fantasy mode dominated. Now sitting on the floor, and using an area of about two square feet, the patient manipulated small plastic monster figures in elaborating fantasies which went far beyond the miniature actions involved. A scientist monster, assisted by a half-human monster, struggled to control, punish, and civilize dirty monsters who frequently escaped into a nearby village, who enjoyed wallowing in filth, and who engaged in many bad games, including putting their fingers in each other's anuses.

A year and a half later this mode gave way to a phase of storytelling. At that time fantasy was assisted in a major way by the language mode as a tool. The patient authored a mythical child character who was president of "The Ass Club" and the editor of a newspaper called the "Ass Times." The boy drew pictures for the newspaper, but mostly sat telling stories about the mythical character and the activities of his club. It was after this phase that the patient introduced discussions of objects and events in his reality, past and present, and of his own behaviors, all of which were concerned with his anal masturbation and play and the fantasies which accompanied them.

This necessarily brief case report is intended to emphasize several points that relate to the ego-cognitive model I have proposed: (1) the severe anal fixations which blocked this boy's development were originally repeated and worked through in phases dominated by body activity; then they were repeated and worked through in the fantasy mode; and then in the language mode. (2) Throughout this process, within each mode, the boy imposed increasing delay on actions; he widened the field of information he scanned; he articulated and distinguished increasingly more details as relevant; he compared with increasing clarity past images of information with present perceptions; and he conceptualized. (3) At the end of the four years I have summarized, words used by the boy such as "My ass has been the most important thing in my life" were connected both to deep, widespread roots at the developmentally lower level of a well-elaborated fantasy-representational mode and to the developmentally earlier level of action. With these cognitive roots which tied together and integrated the three modalities, the words patient and analyst exchanged did not float detached as intellectualizations but became steering posts which served the patient in gaining insights into his anal conflicts and fixations and subsequently into his wish for and fear of phallic pursuits.

The treatment process authored by the 11-year-old girl seemed to suggest similar developments. The first year of analysis of this girl, unlike that of the boy I just considered, was characterized by the language mode; that is, for the most part she talked about events and persons in her current reality and recent past. Gradually she regressed to the action and fantasy modes, repeating issues in each. She moved from touching spots on furniture, to scrubbing furniture, to scrubbing dolls, to play-acting in which she and I constructed and wore face masks, to puppet play of dolls who had no faces, to a fantasy world where no spots were allowed because they were bad. All of this happened before she gradually revealed how her father's frequent erotic yet hostile remarks about her "dirty freckle face" served to implicate her freckles as a major issue in her oedipal struggles.

The case of the 30-year-old patient illustrates still another point. During the first year of analysis, his habitual use of obsessional defense mechanisms (e.g., isolation, intellectualization) joined with intense selective repression became apparent. At the same time as I listened to the patient for the better part of a year, I was also struck by the observation that the style of his thinking was characterized in part by the habitual use of narrow scanning. When associating he tended to scan what appeared to me to be narrow fields of information, whether the field consisted of his thoughts about the present, memories of the past, or dreams. He would survey a few bits and pieces, each standing alone and unrelated to the others. Most importantly, when engaged in this cognitive process, he seemed to be at ease. With my prejudice for the model of cognitive controls, I speculated that this manner of scanning was a lifelong strategy which served a particular cognitive-affective balance that helped maintain his neurosis.

Before approaching the task of analyzing his defenses, I approached the task of analyzing this particular cognitive control (i.e., focal attention) with the assumption that the patient should first grow cognitively, scanning increasingly broader fields of information and balancing the accompanying affects. I speculated that when this growth took place, he could make gains in articulating relevant and irrelevant, comparing past and present, and conceptualizing, and he could then more successfully restructure his obsessional defenses.

As often as seemed appropriate, I engaged him in scanning more broadly, a step at a time, by bringing into his view and attention a detail from his previous material that was more distant, to some degree, than the percept on which he was fixed at the moment. I also brought this cognitive attitude of narrow scanning to his attention. As we worked on it repeatedly, he gradually perceived that he became anxious whenever he shifted his attention away from some narrow event, issue, or object and attempted to scan or associate more broadly. He gradually elaborated the perception that when he tried to scan more broadly, he felt as if he were walking through an unfamiliar place without a handrail to guide him. It was at this point in the analysis that he could make use of the awareness that he held onto the edge of his trousers whenever his attention seemed to leave some relatively narrow percept or issue. Following this work he showed a steady increase in the breadth of thoughts and experiences he scanned during his associating.

Only several years later did we learn one possible genetic source of his cognitive control of narrow focal attention. The patient had already authored the metaphor, over which he usually chuckled, that if he focused his attention on a relatively narrow detail, he felt secure, as he would holding the string attached to a balloon (his trousers). But if he let go of the string, the balloon floated away and he was anxious and confused about which way to look. As we explored this fantasy and metaphor, he uncovered a memory. At the age of 4, in a crowded amusement park, he had become separated from his father. The patient pictured himself standing there, crying, and clutching the string of a balloon in terror, not daring to look in any direction. While oedipal issues were certainly implicated in this experience and its representation, I believe it was only after his cognitive controls of focal attention and field articulation had matured that these issues could be included in his understanding of why he was afraid to scan his thoughts and feelings broadly and actively.

CONCLUDING REMARKS

I have attempted to illustrate the need for a model of cognition that includes multiple cognitive functions which are both flexible and stable and which interact with ego modes. Cognitive controls together with ego modes gather and balance information and affects throughout development. In the treatment process, these cognitive ego mechanisms serve to restructure developmental arrests and neurotic conflicts. The model I have suggested proposes cognition as the mediator in development and in the treatment process. In turn, the model points to several theoretical and technical issues that require further study. In closing I would like to mention several of these.

THE NEED FOR A FURTHER UNDERSTANDING OF ACTION AND NONVERBAL ASPECTS OF BEHAVIOR

This need is receiving growing attention by analysts as illustrated by the panel devoted to this topic (Lilleskov, 1977).

While the position of psychoanalysis is clear that a neurosis must be transformed from a compulsion to repeat in everyday life, and in the transference, to constructing memories and verbalizing, cognitive psychology suggests that we need to learn more about whether and when, and in what forms, behaviors that are usually viewed as acting in or acting out are part of a developmental thrust which requires that some issue be organized and expressed in the action mode before that issue re-emerges in fantasies, memories, and words. George Mahl (1977) has been one of the more active investigators of body movements in adult analysis. He suggests that some microactions of the patient while on the couch, such as curving the arms, anticipate and perhaps facilitate the recall and verbalization of some issue. From my work with children, I would suggest that we need to learn in which instances a body activity is more than anticipation and facilitation and becomes an organization of issues within the developmental mode of action, a behavioral organization which must be constructed to provide the foundations for restructuring the issue in fantasy and language.

This consideration relates in particular to technique in child analysis. We need to understand more about whether and when the child analyst should sit constantly like Whistler's mother or crawl around the floor joining the action mode of the child. In both adult and child analysis we need to learn more about whether and when an interpretation by the analyst of some action prematurely serves to block the process of constructing an action organization of behavior. If I had pointed out too soon to my adult patient that he was holding his trousers, would I have delayed or blocked the emergence of fantasies from this microaction? Is there more to learn about the timing when an organization of action should be connected with fantasies and these, in turn, with words and concepts?

THE ISSUE OF THE ROLE OF LANGUAGE IN THE TREATMENT PROCESS

Considerations of action and nonverbal aspects of behavior relate to the need for a better understanding of the role of language in development and the treatment process, especially in child analysis. From his synthesis employing Piaget, Lewis concluded that spoken language is the most useful therapeutic instrument in child therapy, "the royal treatment highway" and "the great mediator between cognitive and emotional development" (p. 659). The model I propose suggests that the royal treatment highway is made up of five or six lanes, with language occupying only one; that cognition mediates personality development; and that language is not especially effective in promoting cognitive change. There is some research which supports this contention. For example, when children who do not conserve information well were taught relevant words used by children who do, the cognitive process of conservation was not developed and restructured (Sinclair-de-Zwart, 1969).

THE NEED TO DEVELOP TREATMENT TECHNIQUES FOR PATIENTS
WITH COGNITIVE LAGS AND DEFECTS

If language does not effectively restructure cognition, what does? With growing analytic attention to patients who show wider and deeper cognitive ego disorders than the classically neurotic patient, there is the need to develop technical modifications for such patients. From the view of the model proposed here, these patients maintain an excessive inner or outer cognitive orientation and show fixated, immature, or deviant cognitive control functioning. Therapists are familiar with the child who spends two years playing checkers, refusing to venture from the information on the checkerboard. And both adult and child analysts are familiar with patients who rarely depart from the information of dream life and fantasy play, or who rarely turn their attention away from the infinite details contained in their current environments.

When a patient rigidly segregates information from inner and outer environments, or when a patient shows fixed cognitive defects, such as the tendency to scan only narrow segments of a field of information, do these cognitive control orientations limit the effectiveness of the treatment process? Does the process typical of psychoanalytic psychotherapy and psychoanalysis effectively restructure deficient cognitive controls? And if not, are there techniques uniquely suited to the task of restructuring cognition?

With patients who present moderate cognitive control deficits we can explore how the therapist can use the information the patient generates and organizes (i.e., a dream; a set of thoughts) as the material on which the patient is asked to perform particular *cognitive* actions designed to restructure the deficient cognitive control and to promote a more effective cognitive-affective balance and a cognitive orientation which flexibly shifts between inner and outer information.

Applying these formulations to patients who present severe cognitive deficits, I have observed that these deficits are not restructured within the process and experience provided by the usual treatment situation in psychoanalytic psychotherapy. With these patients the therapist sets particular cognitive tasks before the patient for work, either within psychotherapy, in a treatment program that supplements psychotherapy, or as a phase preparatory to psychotherapy. I have called these technical modifications "cognitive control therapy" to emphasize that the focus of the work is cognitive restructuring, and have reported the use of these techniques with borderline children (Santostefano and Berkowitz, 1976). The management of transference and resistance within a therapeutic focus that is cognitive as well as other theoretical and technical considerations of cognitive control therapy are described elsewhere (Santostefano, 1978).

THE NEED TO REVISE THE CONCEPT OF MOTIVATION AND ENERGY THEORY IN PSYCHOANALYSIS IN THE LIGHT OF COGNITIVE PSYCHOLOGY

Increasing attention has been given to this need by a number of writers (e.g., Rosenblatt and Thickstun, 1977), and I have expressed some of my views elsewhere (Santostefano, 1977b). Here I point only to a few implications for technique suggested by a theory of motivation that gives central attention to cognition.

For example, when the affect surrounding a simple percept or idea is very intense, global, and unorganized, should the unconscious fantasies and their affects be analyzed first, as some suggest, or the defenses against them, as others suggest? Or should the analyst first promote growth in cognitive functions, which would then effectively organize and balance affects and fantasies as they are analyzed? In the analysis of dreams, should we work first on the organization of the dream, or on the patient's repeated tendency to scan only narrow segments of the dream, or on the patient's tendency quickly to transform the dream into a verbal conceptual label, all before we analyze the libidinal content and defenses revealed in the dream?

These questions, and the issue of a cognitively based concept of motivation, point to the relations between cognitive controls and defenses and to the methods of "cognitive control analysis" and "defense analysis." Unlike defenses, cognitive controls have been proposed as placing no particular restrictions upon need-satisfying objects, since they also appear when "neutral" stimuli are involved, and as subjugating need to immediate reality requirements without affecting the aim of the need itself (Klein, 1970, p. 198). Furthermore, while cognitive controls have correlated to some degree with mechanisms of defense, they are not isomorphic with them; and cognitive controls are viewed as contributing to the structuring of defenses (e.g., Gardner and Moriarty, 1968).

Because cognitive controls serve in the structuring and maintenance of defenses, I am working with the hypothesis that the analysis of cognitive controls should precede the analysis of defenses. As a cognitive control is reformed (e.g., the narrow scanning of the patient discussed above), the restructuring of defenses (e.g., that same patient's isolation and selective repression) can then take place more effectively with the assistance of the cognitive scaffold constructed. Analytic work could move from cognitive controls to defenses to controls and back to defenses and so on in point-counterpoint fashion. At each step throughout this process, the gradual reformation and growth of cognitive controls is seen as serving the reformation of defenses.

In conclusion, I have tried to illustrate the conceptual and technical issues suggested by the psychoanalytic view of cognition which I have proposed. Whether we consider this model of cognition, or models proposed by others, I hope the field of psychoanalysis responds to the Colorado symposium of more than 25 years ago and returns cognition to its rightful position as a major lens through which psychological functioning is studied and treated.

BIBLIOGRAPHY

ANTHONY, E. J. (1956), The Significance of Jean Piaget for Child Psychiatry. *Brit. J. Med. Psychol.*, 29:20–34.
ARIETI, S. (1970), The Role of Cognition in the Development of Inner Reality. In: *Cognitive Studies*, ed. J. Hellmuth. New York: Brunner/Mazel, 1:91–110.
BENJAMIN, J. D. (1961), The Innate and Experiential in Development. In: *Lectures in Experimental Psychiatry*, ed. H. W. Brosin. Pittsburgh: Univ. Pittsburgh Press, pp. 19–42.
BRUNER, J. S., BRUNSWIK, E., FESTINGER, L., HEIDER, F., MUENZINGER, K. F., OSGOOD, C. E., & RAPAPORT, D. (1957), *Contemporary Approaches to Cognition.* Cambridge: Harvard Univ. Press.
DÉCARIE, T. G. (1965), *Intelligence and Affectivity in Early Childhood.* New York: Int. Univ. Press.
ENGLISH, H. B. & ENGLISH, C. A. (1958), *A Comprehensive Dictionary of Psychological and Psychoanalytical Terms.* New York: Longmans, Green.
FLAVELL, J. H. (1963), *The Developmental Psychology of Jean Piaget.* New York: Van Nostrand.

GARDNER, R. W. & MORIARTY, A. (1968), *Personality Development at Preadolescence.* Seattle: Univ. Washington Press.

GREENSPAN, S. I. (1975), *A Consideration of Some Learning Variables in the Context of Psychoanalytic Theory* [*Psychol. Issues*, 33]. New York: Int. Univ. Press.

HOLT, R. R. (1964), The Emergence of Cognitive Psychology. *J. Amer. Psychoanal. Assn.,* 12:650–665.

KLEIN, G. S. (1951), The Personal World Through Perception. In: *Perception,* ed. R. R. Blake & G. V. Ramsey. New York: Ronald Press, pp. 328–355.

—— (1954), Need and Regulation. In: *Nebraska Symposium on Motivation,* ed. M. R. Jones. Lincoln: Univ. Nebraska Press, pp. 224–274.

—— (1970), *Perception, Motives, and Personality.* New York: Knopf.

—— & SCHLESINGER, H. J. (1949), Where Is the Perceiver in Perceptual Theory? *J. Pers.,* 18:32–47.

LEWIS, M. (1977), Language, Cognitive Development, and Personality. *J. Amer. Acad. Child Psychiat.,* 16:646–661.

LILLESKOV, R. K. (1977), Report of Panel: Nonverbal Aspects of Child and Adult Psychoanalysis. *J. Amer. Psychoanal. Assn.,* 25:693–705.

MAHL, G. F. (1977), Body Movement, Ideation and Verbalization During Psychoanalysis. In: *Communicative Structures and Psychic Structures,* ed. N. Freedman & S. Grand. New York: Plenum Press, pp. 291–310.

ROSENBLATT, A. D. & THICKSTUN, J. T. (1977), Energy, Information, and Motivation. *J. Amer. Psychoanal. Assn.,* 25:537–558.

SANTOSTEFANO, S. (1970), Assessment of Motives in Children. *Psychol. Rep.,* 26:639–649.

—— (1977a), Action, Fantasy, and Language. In: *Communicative Structures and Psychic Structures,* ed. N. Freedman & S. Grand. New York: Plenum Press, pp. 331–354.

—— (1977b), New Views of Motivation and Cognition in Psychoanalytic Theory. *McLean Hosp. J.,* 2:49–64.

—— (1978), *A Biodevelopmental Approach to Clinical Child Psychology.* New York: Wiley.

—— & BERKOWITZ, S. (1976), Principles of Infant Development As a Guide in the Psychotherapeutic Treatment of Borderline and Psychotic Children. *McLean Hosp. J.,* 1:236–261.

SHAPIRO, I. F. (1972), *Cognitive Controls and Adaptation in Children.* Doct. diss., Boston College.

SINCLAIR-DE-ZWART, H. (1969), Developmental Psycholinguistics. In: *Studies in Cognitive Development,* ed. D. Elkind & J. Flavell. New York: Oxford Univ. Press, pp. 315–336.

WOLFF, P. H. (1960), *The Developmental Psychologies of Jean Piaget and Psychoanalysis* [*Psychol. Issues*, 5]. New York: Int. Univ. Press.

Consciousness of Self and Painful Self-Consciousness

BEULAH KRAMER AMSTERDAM, Ph.D. AND
MORTON LEVITT, Ph.D.

> I dote on myself, there is that lot of me and all so
> luscious,
> Each moment and whatever happens thrills me with
> joy.
> WALT WHITMAN, *Song of Myself*

> Hold it up sternly—see this it sends back
> (who is it? is it you?)
> Outside fair costume, within ashes and filth . . .
> Such from one look in this looking-glass ere you
> go hence,
> Such a result so soon—and from such a beginning!
> WALT WHITMAN, *A Hand-Mirror*

SINCE DARWIN (1872), THE NEGATIVE EMOTION OF SHAME HAS BEEN described as a consequence of a heightened awareness of self. There appears to be a prevailing belief, both in the lay and the psychological literature (Izard, 1978, p. 408), that self-consciousness invariably is a painful affect associated with being the center of attention. Even Genesis tells us that Adam and Eve became embarrassed and ashamedly self-conscious as a conse-

Dr. Amsterdam is Clinical Associate Professor of Psychology in the Department of Psychiatry, School of Medicine, University of California, Davis. Dr. Levitt was Acting Dean and Professor of Psychology in the Department of Psychiatry, School of Medicine, University of California, Davis. He died on January 13, 1980.

quence of eating from the Tree of Knowledge and becoming aware of their bodies.

In studying infants' responses to their mirror images, Amsterdam (1968) noted the presence of a variety of self-conscious behavior, including embarrassment, coyness, showing off, and clowning, starting at 14 months of age. In the first year of life, infants responded to their mirror images with unrestrained enthusiasm and delight. In the second year of life, children no longer respond to the mirror with naïve joy, but they withdraw and become wary of their images. Self-conscious behavior follows and continues through the period when children show objective recognition of the image starting at 18 months. Therefore, we are pressed to ask: What happens to the early narcissistic delight of the infant playing with his own body and its image? How does it turn into the painful self-conscious feeling most of us experience when we view our own image, or hear a recording of our own voice? The following questions are pivotal to this inquiry: (1) Is the feeling of self-conscious inevitably painful? (2) What is the process by which consciousness of self may become the painful affect of self-consciousness? (3) How is early genital development related to self-consciousness?

DEFINITIONS OF SELF-CONSCIOUSNESS

Since this is a relatively new area of infant study, we will define the key terms relating to the ontogenesis of self-knowledge during infancy. The word *self-conscious* has multiple meanings, including (1) an awareness or sense of oneself, (2) an awareness of oneself as distinct from others, (3) an awareness of being the focus of attention of others, and (4) the explicit state of awareness of being the focus of one's own attention. We will refer to the above meanings by using the term *self-awareness*. The words self-conscious or self-consciousness will be used to refer to the affective states of being shy, embarrassed, coy, "showing off," which usually are the result of being the focus of attention.

In our culture, the affective definitions of self-consciousness usually focus upon shame, shyness, and embarrassment. Izard (1977) treats self-consciousness as a subcategory of shame. However, this definition of self-consciousness appears to be peculiar to American and English culture and language, as Robert Solomon (1977) attempted to show:

> "Self-consciousness," which gives significance to our actions, meaning to our lives, and is the ultimate source of self-esteem, means something approximating "embarrassment" in American English. We think of a person as "being self-conscious" when he is ashamed of his flabby body caught out of sorts by a candid photographer or "put on the spot" by a question he is unable to answer. When that same term appears in European philosophy, however, it does not have that meaning at all. In France, "self-consciousness" is a matter of dignity, or at least vanity . . . in German *Selbstbewusstsein* means pride and self-importance, even with an uncritical touch of arrogance [p. 85].

Implied in this definition is an a priori awareness of self, as in the first definition.

It is important to remember that self-consciousness is not like consciousness of other things. Solomon notes: "In self-consciousness, the self is the subject, the consciousness and what consciousness is about" (p. 86). Thus, we are speaking, not of an entity, but of a process.

Since we will be exploring the origins of self-consciousness, we will attempt to define different developmental points in self-consciousness, as they appear in the first years of life. These include (1) *the early sense of self,* (2) *self-other differentiation,* (3) *affective self-consciousness,* and (4) *self-recognition.*

Most observers agree that the earliest sense of self is based in bodily kinesthetic and sensory feeling and appears to be present at birth (Lewis and Brooks, 1975). The sense of self as distinct from others appears to be present in some form during the first months of life, as seen in the ability of 3- and 4-month-old infants to differentiate between mother and female stranger, an ability they demonstrate by a variety of responses (Lewis and Brooks, 1978). By 8 months of age, the self-other distinction is obvious in stranger "anxiety" reactions.

Affective self-consciousness or the embarrassed, shy, or coy response has been shown in children starting at 14 months of age (Amsterdam, 1972) and in preschoolers between 2 and 5 years of age (Marvin and Mossler, 1976). Affective self-consciousness includes a spectrum of feelings ranging from shame and embarrassment to coy, vain, and prideful behavior.

Self-recognition is the child's ability to identify his image in a mirror. He can indicate this by the objective and nonverbal means of touching a mark previously placed on his face. This achievement occurs between 18 and 24 months of age and precedes the child's ability to identify his image by verbal means, such as using his name or saying "me." This visual self-recognition is accompanied by the self-conscious affective behavior of embarrassment or coyness (Amsterdam, 1968, 1972).

OBSERVATIONAL DATA

Mirrors have long been used as the obvious and primary object in experiments to elicit self-awareness, both with primates and humans (Gallup, 1970), but only recently have they been used to observe affective self-consciousness.

Mirrors have been extensively used in infant intelligence scales (Bayley, 1933; Cattell, 1940; Gesell and Amatruda, 1941); however, no clear criteria for self-recognition were devised. Arnold Gesell, after observing over 500 subjects, doubted that mirror self-recognition occurred in early childhood. In a study of twins and singletons, Dixon (1957) observed coy and other self-conscious behavior in the second year of life, but failed to establish a clear criterion for self-recognition. Working independently, Amsterdam (1968) and Gallup (1970) developed the technique of placing a red mark on the subject's face, and then observing the subject's use of the mirror to examine that mark. With the help of this technique, Gallup (1977) has established that chimpanzees are capable of self-recognition, while lower-order primates are not.

Observing 88 human subjects between the ages of 3 and 24 months, and following 2 subjects longitudinally, Amsterdam (1968) discerned a regular sequence of behaviors in response to the mirror. The results of this study pointed to three distinct phases in the child's reaction to his mirror image: (1) The first prolonged and repeated reactions of an infant to his image were those of a sociable "playmate"; the infant smiled at and vocalized to his image, expressing delight and enthusiasm and making playful approaches to the "other" child. This occurred in over 85 percent of the subjects from 6 to 12 months of age. (2) In the second year of life, the children no longer responded to the mirror with naïve joy; they became wary and withdrew from it, although some would intermittently smile or vocalize at the image. In this period, 90 percent of the subjects observed withdrew from the mirror. Self-admiring and embarrassed behavior suggesting self-consciousness first appeared at 14 months, and was seen in 75 percent of the subjects after 20 months. (3) Between 20 and 24 months of age, 65 percent of the subjects showed recognition of their images. Recognition inevitably appeared as one element in a complex pattern of behavior, which included the child's avoidance of looking in the mirror and embarrassed and other self-conscious affect.

While affective behaviors have been largely ignored by most investigators of mirror behavior (the exception being Schulman and Kaplowitz, 1977), Amsterdam's objective red-mark technique has been repeated in other studies. In observations of mirror behavior in 18 subjects at 6, 12, and 18 months of age, Dickie and Strader (1974) found that only 2 of their 18-month-old subjects manipulated a red dot placed below their eyes. This study essentially confirmed the results obtained by Amsterdam (1968). Schulman and Kaplowitz (1977), in a replication of Amsterdam's work but with the addition of distorted mirrors, supported her findings, and statistically justified their use as stages. Lewis and Brooks (1974) observed 24 infants at 16, 19, and 22 months, and found that none of the 16-month-olds, one third of the 19-month-olds, and all of the 22-month-old subjects touched a red spot on their noses. In another study, they observed "silly or coy" behavior in 18-, 21-, and 24-month-old subjects (Lewis and Brooks, 1975).

In 1977, Gallup pointed to the "striking discontinuity between several species of great apes and monkeys in the capacity for self-recognition . . . because the identity of the observer and the mirror image are one and the same, the ability to infer correctly the identity of the reflection would seem to be predicated on an already existent identity on the part of an organism making that inference. Without at least a rudimentary sense of identity, self-recognition would be impossible" (p. 283). These words might be equally applicable to infants' mirror-image responses before and after about 18 months.

While affective self-consciousness was elusive to define behaviorally and to observe and record with confidence when only the mirror was used, it could be measured and observed with high reliability when video tapes were added. In an initial video study, Amsterdam and Greenberg (1977) asked the question whether the child's self-conscious reaction is an instance of thinking that the image, taken as another child, is looking at him. While comparing 10-, 15-, and 20-month-old subjects, this study also provided the child with the opportunity to observe both his own image and that of another child; the results revealed that self-consciousness is more likely to occur when the older subjects look at their own simultaneous self-image rather than at that of another child or their own previously video-taped image.

The results of both studies are confounded by the possibility that the self-consciousness stemmed from awareness of being observed by a stranger (the observer) and the mother, of being the focus of the attention of the adults present. That seems entirely plausible because an adult also might feel embarrassed if placed before a mirror with others looking on. With observers present across all conditions, however, children did show the most self-consciousness with the self-simultaneous image.

This led to a second video-taped study of maternal and contextual determinants of self-consciousness. The infant's self-consciousness was greater under the direct admiring attention of a live stranger than when given no deliberate attention or exposed to his simultaneous video image. Thus, at this time it appears that being the focus of another's direct admiring attention is more likely to evoke self-conscious feeling than being the focus of one's own attention, at least when electronically mediated on closed-circuit TV.

Amsterdam's narrowly focused experimental findings are consistent with the observations made by Mahler et al. (1975) in a more normal nursery school setting. In the final stage of "hatching" to psychological birth, i.e., consciousness of self, which Mahler calls *rapprochement,* the toddler reaches the first level of identity—that of being a separate individual entity.

With the acquisition of upright, free locomotion and with the attainment of the stage in cognitive development regarded as the beginning of representational intelligence, the human being has emerged as a separate and autonomous person. During this time, the child begins to take possession of his own body and protect it against being handled as a passive object by his mother: for example, he struggles against being put in a reclining position. This subphase coincides with the self-conscious, embarrassed-type expression which Amsterdam first observed in 14-month-olds in response to the mirror image.

"Consolidation of individuality and the beginnings of emotional object constancy" comprise Mahler's final subphase, which starts at 20 months. "From the point of view of the separation-individuation process, the main task of the fourth subphase is twofold: (1) the achievement of a definite, in certain aspects lifelong, individuality, and (2) the attainment of a certain degree of object constancy" (p. 109). This is the period when the child shows recognition of his mirror image, by his touching the spot of rouge on his nose. This behavior necessitates the attainment of sufficient object constancy to associate his own face with the face in the mirror, and coordinate his visual-motor response so that he can look at the spot on the image's face and simultaneously touch his own.

Galenson (1978) investigated the emergence of genital awareness during the second year of life as part of the separation-individuation process. She observed 70 children, each for approximately one year, and found the following pattern: "Boys usually begin genital play at about 6 to 7 months of age, whereas girls begin at about 10 to 11 months. In boys, early genital play is continuous until the onset of masturbation at 15 to 16 months of age, whereas in girls a pattern of intermittent genital play is seen" (Galenson and Roiphe, 1974, p. 230).

Intentional reaching for the penis is correlated with the attainment of the upright posture and locomotion (Galenson, 1978). The intense interest in looking at and touching the genitals is an integral part of establishing a sense of self, separated and differentiated from others. After the initial pleasurable exploration of the genitalia, both boys and girls (by 18 months of age) became more covert in masturbatory behavior, revealing a range of affective self-conscious behavior, e.g., coyness, shame, shyness.

THEORETICAL EXPLANATIONS

At the beginning of the second year of life, there occur three key events which appear to be critical to the onset of painful self-conscious behavior: (1) the beginnings of representational thinking, which allows the bodily self to be taken as an object; (2) the infant's struggle to attain upright posture and locomotion; and (3) intentional reaching for and self-stimulation of the genitalia.

Piaget (1937) has shown that as the child develops a conception of the permanence of objects in the environment, he is then able to place himself as an object in the environment in relation to other objects, and thus to take himself and his own body as an object. Merleau-Ponty (1964) analyzed the self-conscious reaction to the mirror image in terms of the child's ability to take an attitude of self-observation toward himself and to turn away from the sense of self as experienced, to a new awareness of the self as a perceived object.

Merleau-Ponty postulates that embarrassment and self-consciousness occur when the child experiences himself most as an object of observation, whether the observer is himself or another; and when, in viewing himself or being viewed as an object, the child feels alienated from his experienced living self. The mirrored or perceived self thus becomes the ego ideal. The child must first understand that the visual image of his body which he sees over there in the mirror is not himself, since he is not in the mirror, but here, where he feels himself. Next, he must realize that while he is located here where he feels himself to be, he can be seen by another where he is, and also over there in the mirror.

This external perception of the self, as being in two places at one time, is also found in many dreams, in certain hypnotic states, and in near-death experiences. "Primitive" people are capable of believing that the same person is in several places at one time and that their mirror image is their soul (Frazer, 1957). This discrepancy can be resolved, according to Merleau-Ponty, only by passing to a higher level of spatiality that is no longer the intuitive space in which the images occupy their own space.

At 12 months of age, the specular image has become the subject of a game, in which the child first playfully and later desperately searches for the image. The child's understanding of the
specular image consists of his recognizing the visual appearance
in the mirror as his own. The recognition of his mirror image
necessitates his learning that a viewpoint can be taken on him;
the child becomes capable of being his own spectator, as it were,
and notices that he is visible to himself and others. "At the same
time that the image of oneself makes possible the knowledge of
oneself, it also makes possible a sort of alienation. I am no longer
what I felt myself, immediately, to be; I am that image of myself
that is offered by the mirror. Thereupon I leave the reality of my
lived me in order to refer myself constantly to the ideal, ficti-
tious, or imaginary me, of which the specular image is the first
outline" (Merleau-Ponty, 1964, p. 136).

This analysis elucidates the self-conscious behavior of infants
as they transcend their awareness of self-as-being to their new
viewpoint of the self as an object of observation. Thus, embarrassment and other self-conscious behavior are greatest when
the child experiences himself most as an object of observation,
whether the observer is himself or another.

Mirroring theories basically hold that the individual acquires a
conception of self from the reactions to his own behavior that are
reflected back from others. Mead (1934) maintained that consciousness of self comes about when the person becomes aware
of another's perspective; then he can view himself as a social
object. While Freud did not utilize mirroring in his developmental hypothesis, both Melanie Klein (1932) and Harry Stack Sullivan (1953) ascribe key importance to mirroring in the infant's
relationship with his mother as a major determinant of personality organization. Winnicott (1967) developed this viewpoint in
object relations theory terms.

UPRIGHT POSITION

While the attainment of upright posture is a critical task of infancy, its role in psychological development has been largely
ignored; almost no research has focused on this key event. Humans are the only species to attain consistent upright posture,
and perhaps the only species to inhibit self-conscious affective

behavior in a wide range of situations. Several theorists have speculated on the relationship between consciousness of self and upright posture.

Erwin Straus (1952) views gravity as a critical determinant of human development, knowledge, and civilization. He regards standing as the key to the individuation process:

> In getting up, man gains his standing in the world. . . . The child enjoys no less the triumph of his achievement. There is a forceful urge toward the goal of getting up and resisting, in a state of dangerous balance, the downward-pulling forces. There need not be any other premium, like satisfaction of hunger, attention, or applause. . . . He enjoys the freedom to stand on his own feet, and the freedom to walk [p. 536].

Erikson (1950) likewise sees the origin of self-consciousness in the upright posture:

> The development of the muscle system gives the child a much greater power over the environment in the ability to reach out and hold on, to throw and push away, to appropriate things and to keep them at a distance. . . . For as he gets ready to stand more firmly on his feet the infant delineates his world as "I" and "you," "me" and "mine" [p. 82].

Erikson further suggests that self-consciousness is shame, and is a result of the child's moving to the upright posture and becoming capable of greater autonomy. In practicing walking, the child not only becomes aware of his smallness, but, as a result of falling down and getting hurt, also begins to lose his sense of omnipotence. Erikson therefore recommends: "His environment must back him up in his wish to 'stand on his own feet' lest he be overcome by that sense of having exposed himself prematurely and foolishly which we call shame, or that secondary mistrust, that looking back which we call doubt" (p. 85). The onset of walking typically introduces the child's first prolonged conflicts with his parents and environment. The child's increasing mobility permits incursions on objects and running off, which are likely to trigger disapproval in parental figures. Likewise, the child's "holding on" or "letting go" in response to parental demands may also lead to shame, which may result from interactions with overly controlling parents.

Mahler et al. (1975) point out that during the acquisition of upright locomotion:

> Narcissism is at its peak! The child's first upright independent steps mark the onset of the practicing period par excellence, with a substantial widening of his world and of reality testing. Now begins a steadily increasing libidinal investment in practicing motor skills and in exploring the expanding environment, both human and inanimate. The chief characteristic of this practicing period is the child's great narcissistic investment in his own functions, his own body, as well as in the objects and objectives of his expanding "reality" [p. 71].

Heinz Kohut (1977) views prideful or self-assertive behavior in the relation to antigravity movements. He asks:

> Is it the "upright posture" . . . which, as the newest acquisition in the sequence of developmental steps, lends itself most aptly to become the symbolic act that expresses the feeling of triumphant pride? The flying dream and the fantasy of flying could then, of course, if this speculation has merit, be taken as the individual expression of the delight of the race—reexperienced by each new generation of toddlers—in fact that the head is now above the ground, that the perceiving eye, a central organ of the self, has moved upward, has overcome the pull of gravity [p. 113].

PAINFUL SELF-CONSCIOUSNESS

Galenson and Roiphe (1974) have suggested that genital behavior is universally and actively enjoyed by children at 6 to 7 months in boys, and at about 10 to 11 months in girls. During the second year of life, this activity becomes an intensely pleasurable and pronounced experience. We propose that painful self-consciousness develops as children are either quietly restrained and distracted, or more directly chastised and punished for exhibiting their bodies (nakedness) and for looking, touching, and playing with their genitalia. Thus, the child learns that pleasurable sensations which arise from within, in response to his own stimulation, are not only unacceptable to mother and other adults, but may well be taboo when they are present. This contrasts with excretory functions, which are observed and may

even be applauded by the same authorities when the child produces according to parental expectations and demands. The
child learns to inhibit genital sensation and exploration in the
presence of others at precisely the same time as he also experiences affective self-consciousness before the mirror. It is important to note that both these behaviors follow the onset of walking,
the pleasurable and unself-conscious exhibition of the naked
body, and the intentional touching of the genitalia.[1]

We therefore suggest that a major source of painful self-
consciousness is the negative reaction of a parent who looks
upon the infant anxiously when the child is engaged in genital
exploration or play. Consequently, the body is taken as a shameful object. In extreme cases, the child may become alienated
from his body, since pleasurable genital sensations forebode loss
of mother. Because genital behavior is universal in infants, and
most parents inhibit such behaviors in our culture, we find that
painful self-consciousness appears in the second year of life
and then spreads from sexual expression to other body-related
activity.

Kohut (1971) describes shame (along with rage) as disintegration products created by the break-up of the original close tie to
the maternal object. His work is particularly interesting in reference to issues regarding the mother's attitude toward the child's
exhibitionistic display. He attributes special importance to the
visual interaction between mother and infant: "The most significant relevant basic interactions between mother and child lie
usually in the visual area: The child's bodily display is responded
to by the gleam in the mother's eye" (p. 117).

Kohut emphasizes, as have many others, that even the most
felicitous union of mother and child is interrupted by the inevitable shortcomings of maternal care. Thus, the infant comes

---

1. Freud (1930) explicitly linked man's erect posture to the visibility of the
genitals and shame (p. 99f.). Our observations of normal children link up with
Freud's theories of shame, which he related to early experiences of being
observed, being naked, and exhibiting oneself, and which subsequently may
appear both in dreams and in pathological states, especially paranoia. The
connections between research and Freud's early writings (1896, 1950 [1892–
99]) deserve to be examined in the light of current findings.

sooner or later to recognize that his mother's love is limited. The child's dream of his own perfection (the first stage in narcissism) shifts to an appreciation of the perfection of his unified relationship with another—his mother—as his ego develops. Then the whole notion of joint perfection (with all its grandiose overtones) also becomes diminished; through the recognition of his mother's separateness, self-other is gradually differentiated into self and other.

The dissolution of the child's symbiotic unity with the mother represents a major developmental step that is not inevitably painful for the child. Both Sander (1962) and Mahler et al. (1975) have shown how some mother-infant pairs successfully negotiate the differentiation process, while others struggle over autonomy, control, and increasing independence. The thrust of the healthy infant's growth is toward differentiation, individuation, and increasing independence rather than toward remaining in a passive-dependent, symbiotic position.

Extending the work of Kohut, we propose that even the most felicitous union of mother and child is interrupted with the onset of explicit genital activity. During the early months of life, the infant derived comfort and pleasure in his interaction with mother and such autoerotic activities as thumb sucking, which are usually unopposed. With the onset of intentional genital stimulation, the child is aware of another source of pleasure arising in his own body, unrelated to maternal care. One of the first major narcissistic injuries in the mother-infant relationship may be the mother's disapproval and prohibition of genital play. The child's bodily display is no longer responded to by the gleam in mother's eye. Mothers in our society do not beam while their children play with themselves. The child's dream of his own perfection is thus destroyed, and that which has been pleasurable, his own bodily sensations, now produce shame.

Consciousness of self is a process that invariably involves affect. While shame, along with fear, anger, and disgust, play crucial roles in the development of the self-concept, we feel that too little attention and emphasis have been given to the positive emotions. The child's exploration of his own body and the bodies of others is typically accompanied by delight and curiosity. The mastering of gravity and the attainment of upright posture, which involve differentiating oneself from the ground, frequently are also accomplished with joy and excitement. Mahler et al. (1975) have observed that concomitantly with learning to walk, the toddler deliberately separates from his parents, and that *elation* is the dominant mood of this period.

The overemphasis on shame, fear, and guilt as the builders of self-consciousness is the inheritance of the Judaeo-Christian tradition that pervades our child-rearing techniques. This is expressed in Genesis where man falls from grace and the state of deindividualized bliss, and feels embarrassment at his nakedness after eating from the Tree of Knowledge; awareness of oneself, especially the sexual self, with a sense of individuation and differentness from others is accompanied by feelings of shame. The Judaeo-Christian tradition also stresses the inferiority of the body and bodily processes and the superiority and sublimeness of the spirit.

Furthermore, the Anglo-Saxon Calvinistic culture intensifies shame about the body and individuation. This is especially true in the semantic meaning of self-consciousness as shame in English, as compared to the French and German synonyms. Standing up in our Calvinistic culture requires us to be erect in a rigid manner (e.g., straight spine, shoulders back, chest out, stomach in), but also is carried over into the social and societal demand of being erect, uprighteous, and above it all. Not only are we expected to stand erect in a specific way, but we are also required to control our eyes, mouths, noses, hands, feet, and genitals in distinct ways. Could such a culture generate much besides shame, fear, and guilt from the earliest bodily sense of self? In addition, pride is one of the seven deadly sins, and we are taught not to show off, boast, or even brag about ourselves.

Painful self-consciousness is undoubtedly the clearer and sharper experience, more memorable than one's fleeting feelings of pride and pleasure in one's existence, accomplishments, and experience. Confessions of shame, guilt, and sin are encouraged, self-praise is not. We are compelled to take note of ourselves and our actions when we feel shame, thus being motivated toward improvement. Shame promotes change and activity. However, Coopersmith (.967) has shown that pride based on high positive self-esteem is an even more potent motivator.

Concurrent with intentional stimulation of the genitals is the attainment of locomotion with upright posture. While we agree with Erikson (1950) that walking contributes to feelings of autonomy and increased consciousness of self, we would not endorse the upright posture and walking as inevitable precipitants of shame. The act of learning to stand upright and walk, as a key factor in the development of personality, calls for serious investigation. Since upright posture enhances the child's awareness of the genitalia, shame would follow parental disapproval of deliberate sexual exhibitionism which takes place at this time.

The formulations of Merleau-Ponty (1964), that painful self-consciousness occurs when the child experiences himself most as an object of observation, whether the observer is himself or another, and, in viewing himself or being viewed as an object, feels alienated from his experienced living self, may be expanded to include infantile genitality. The genitalia provide the child with a unique opportunity for directly pleasuring himself. Perhaps for the first time the child treats part of his body as a distinct object, or takes an objective view of that which produces intensive subjective feelings. Thus, the child treats his body as an object and, similarly to his experience with a mirror, experiences the alienation between the subjectivity of immediate being and treating this same self as an object. These feelings of alienation will be enhanced by the prohibition of parents, which serves to make the genitalia into an unacceptable or ambivalently experienced object.

In summary, we have attempted to extend the current theoretical formulations regarding narcissism by looking at the data from recent infant research. While we are in no way downplaying the critical role of the mother-child relationship, and the gleam in the mother's eye for the development of healthy narcissism, we emphasize three additional factors that occur in the second year of life: the beginning of representational thinking, which makes it possible for the self to be experienced as an object among other objects; the onset of upright locomotion, which elevates the child to a position of increased grandiosity and vulnerability; and the start of intentional genital behavior. These three intersecting experiences combine in accentuating the self-other polarity, contributing to the separation-individuation process. The pleasurable sense of being, in which one is merged not only with the mother, but also with the universe, is lost, as one becomes an object of one's own observation, and the gleam in the mother's eye is transformed into an accepting, bewildered, or troubled look.

BIBLIOGRAPHY

AMSTERDAM, B. K. (1968), Mirror Behavior in Children Under Two Years of Age. Doctoral dissertation, Univ. North Carolina. Order No. 6901569; University Microfilms, Ann Arbor, MI. 48106.
────── (1972), Mirror Self-Image Reactions Before Age Two. *Develpm. Psychobiol.,* 5:297–305.
────── & GREENBERG, L. G. (1977), Self-Conscious Behavior of Infants. *Develpm. Psychobiol.,* 10:1–6.
BAYLEY, N. (1933), Mental Growth During the First Three Years. *Genet. Psychol. Monogr.,* 14:1–92.
CATTELL, P. (1940), *The Measurement of Intelligence of Infants and Young Children.* New York: Psychological Corporation.
COOPERSMITH, S. (1967), *The Antecedents of Self-Esteem.* San Francisco: Freeman.
DARWIN, C. (1872), *The Expression of the Emotions in Man and Animal.* New York: Philosophical Library, 1955.
DICKIE, J. R. & STRADER, W. H. (1974), Development of Mirror Image Responses in Infancy. *J. Psychol.,* 88:333–337.
DIXON, J. C. (1957), Development of Self-Recognition. *J. Genet. Psychol.,* 91:251–256.
ERIKSON, E. H. (1950), *Childhood and Society.* New York: Norton, 2nd ed., 1963.
FRAZER, J. G. (1957), *The Golden Bough.* London: Macmillan, abr. ed.
FREUD, S. (1896), Further remarks on the Neuro-psychoses of Defence. *S.E.,* 3:159–185.
────── (1930), Civilization and Its Discontents. *S.E.,* 21:59–145.
────── (1950) [1892–99]), Extracts from the Fliess Papers. *S.E.,* 1:175–397; see esp. Drafts H and K.
GALENSON, E. (1978), Preoedipal Development of Boys. Newport Beach: Galaxy, audiotape.
────── & ROIPHE, H. (1974), The Emergence of Genital Awareness During the Second Year of Life. In: *Sex Differences in Behavior,* ed. R. C. Friedman, R. M. Richart, & R. L. Vande Wide. New York: Wiley, pp. 223–232.
────── ────── (1977), Some Suggested Revisions Concerning Early Female Development. *J. Amer. Psychoanal. Assn. Suppl.,* 24:29–58.
GALLUP, G. G., JR. (1970), Chimpanzees: Self-Recognition. *Science,* 167:86–87.
────── (1977), Absence of Self-Recognition in a Monkey (*Macca fascicularis*) Following Prolonged Exposure to a Mirror. *Develpm. Psychobiol.,* 10:281–284.

GESELL, A. & AMATRUDA, C. S. (1941), *Developmental Diagnosis.* New York: Harper.

IZARD, C. E. (1977), *Human Emotions.* New York: Plenum Press.

—— (1978), On the Development of Emotions and Emotion-Cognition Relationships in Infancy. In: *The Development of Affect,* ed. M. Lewis & L. A. Rosenblum. New York: Plenum Press, pp. 389–413.

KLEIN, M. (1932), *The Psycho-Analysis of Children.* London: Hogarth Press.

KOHUT, H. (1971), *The Analysis of the Self.* New York: Int. Univ. Press.

—— (1977), *The Restoration of the Self.* New York: Int. Univ. Press.

LEWIS, M. & BROOKS, J. (1974), Self, Other and Fear. In: *The Origins of Fear,* ed. M. Lewis & L. A. Rosenblum. New York: Wiley, 2:195–227.

—— —— (1975), Mirror-Image Stimulation and Self-Recognition in Infancy. Read at Society for Research in Child Development, Denver.

—— —— (1978), Self-Knowledge and Emotional Development. In: *The Development of Affect,* ed. M. Lewis & L. A. Rosenblum. New York: Plenum Press, pp. 205–226.

MAHLER M. S., PINE, F., & BERGMAN, A. (1975), *The Psychological Birth of the Human Infant.* New York: Basic Books.

MARVIN, R. W. & MOSSLER, D. G. (1976), Anesthesiological Paradigm for Describing and Analyzing Complex Non-Verbal Expressions. *Representative Res. Soc. Psychol.,* 7:133–139.

MEAD, G. H. (1934), *Mind, Self and Society.* Chicago: Univ. Chicago Press.

MERLEAU-PONTY, M. (1964), *The Primacy of Perception.* Evanston, Ill.: Northwestern Univ. Press.

PIAGET, J. (1937), *The Construction of Reality in the Child.* New York: Basic Books, 1954.

SANDER, L. W. (1962), Issues in Early Mother-Child Interaction. *J. Amer. Acad. Child Psychiat.,* 1:141–166.

SCHULMAN, A. H. & KAPLOWITZ, C. (1977), Mirror-Image Response During the First Two Years of Life. *Develpm. Psychobiol.,* 10:133–142.

SOLOMON, R. C. (1977), *The Passions.* New York: Doubleday.

STRAUS, E. W. (1952), The Upright Posture. *Psychiat. Quart.,* 26:529–561.

SULLIVAN, H. S. (1953), *The Interpersonal Theory of Psychiatry.* New York: Norton.

WINNICOTT, D. W. (1967), Mirror-Role of Mother and Family in Child Development. In: *The Predicament of the Family,* ed. P. Lomas. London: Hogarth Press, pp. 26–33.

The Development of the Self

A Psychoanalytic Perspective

GERALD STECHLER, Ph.D. AND SAMUEL KAPLAN, M.D.

THE OBSERVATIONAL DATA THAT WE RELIED UPON TO HELP US TO conceptualize the development of the self were collected as part of the longitudinal study conducted by Eleanor Pavenstedt, Louis Sander, Gerald Stechler, and others, starting in 1954. A brief excursion into history will set the stage for our definition of what is "psychoanalytic" in our formulations. The antecedent and corollary studies of the Boston University project were conducted under the leadership of Beata Rank, Marian C. Putnam, and Samuel Kaplan at the James J. Putnam Children's Center. A series of informal well-baby conferences begun in 1949 led in 1961 to a more formal research endeavor, "Developmental Study Centered on Mutual Communication." We fully believed that we were then embarked on a truly psychoanalytic study of infant development.

In both projects, however, it became evident that the meta-psychological concepts subsumed under the rubric of the economic, structural, and dynamic points of view were not applicable to the data flowing from direct observation. Furthermore, there was no way of bridging the gap between metapsychology and the data emerging from such fields as neurophysiology, ethology, psychology, and genetic epistemology (Piaget, 1936).

Dr. Stechler is Professor of Psychiatry and Chairman, and Dr. Kaplan is Clinical Professor of Psychiatry and Co-Chairman, Department of Child Psychiatry and Child Development, Boston University School of Medicine.

Unfortunately, most psychoanalytic investigators elected to perpetuate the focus and the terminology provided by metapsychology. This tendency, coupled with two conceptual fallacies, is selected by Peterfreund (1978) as characteristic of a dominant trend in that sector of psychoanalytic developmental research which has become increasingly barren. The fallacies which Peterfreund discusses are:

> ... the adultomorphization of infancy, and the tendency to characterize early states of normal development in terms of hypotheses about later states of psychopathology. ...
>
> Early infancy is described as a state of 'fusion', 'narcissism', and 'omnipotence'. The terms 'autism' and 'symbiosis' ... are used to characterize normal infantile states. We hear of 'hallucinatory wish-fulfilments' and other 'hallucinatory' experiences, and of the existence of a 'stimulus barrier' in infancy. Finally, the infant is described as 'disoriented' and even as 'delusional', e.g. as having a delusion of 'common boundary between' self and mother [p. 427].

Since there is no evidence to support any of these concepts or terms, nor is there any conceivable way of searching out the needed empirical evidence, we suggest that conceptual clarity and veridicality require their elimination from the vocabulary of developmental research and hypotheses.

The relevance of metapsychological concepts for psychoanalytic theory in general has come under close critical scrutiny over the past two decades. In a paper delivered in 1964, Home anticipates some of the questions and criticisms that were subsequently elaborated by Apfelbaum (1965), Gill and Holzman (1976), Holt (1972), Klein (1966, 1970, 1976), Rubinstein (1965, 1967), and others. It is in this spirit of scholarly inquiry that we continue our search for a fruitful statement about early development consonant with *clinical* psychoanalytic concepts, in contrast to metapsychological ones (Klein, 1976; Rapaport, 1960).

Freud's clinical research established the genetic dimension in the understanding of behavior, and thus provided the basis for the study of the epigenetic character of development. Crucial to Freud's model of development was the notion of the transformation of early conflicts into later ones. It is our basic tenet, as we understand psychoanalytic developmental theory, that intrapsychic order and motivations arise from experienced discontinuity. The capacity to function in accordance with an internal self-regulating organization is a developmental acquisition originating in innumerable attempts to resolve experienced breaches of expectancy. That is the external facet of the experience. Internally it may be viewed as an experienced breach of integration. The growing child's manifest behavior, viewed from within this perspective, can thus be understood as reflecting efforts to deal with incompatible tendencies that result in crises of integration.

We will try to demonstrate how these inevitable crises foster the development of self-regulating functions, and how these self-regulating functions, in turn, evolve into organizing principles which previously we had been content to label "psychic structures." The beginnings of the child's internal environment flow from these experiences and eventually become the internalized rules of relationships—rules that influence the ways in which desires, themselves the product of inner urgings, and external events are responded to. We repeat: the structures which are available to the person to guide his actions originate in these ongoing efforts to resolve the inevitable breaches in integration. In this we follow Klein (1976): "psychological growth, in the sense of differentiated affective and motivational structures, has two main bases. First, there is the development of conflict-free motivations (involving basic pleasures derived from the actualization of potentials in appropriate circumstances); second, there is conflict" (p. 168). Motivational and affective structures emerge when the primary pleasure sources clash with other tendencies. These clashes are signaled by painful experiences of estrangement from self, internal dissonance, and incompatibility.

Since we have assigned such a cardinal position to the role of breaches of integration, we will elaborate and clarify the concept of conflict, especially as it leads to the conceptualization of the self as the center of psychoanalytic propositions. We first underscore the fact that breaches of integration are not always the by-products of conflict. The growing child may experience failures of integration as a result of environmental crises, developmental crises, deprivations of functions, etc. Furthermore, in conceptualizing conflict, we suggest a shift of emphasis from conflict between opposing systems, e.g., id, ego, superego, or opposing forces, e.g., aggressive versus libidinal drives, to a focus on the state of the person's self-integration. Klein (1976) refers to the more general class of breaches of integration as incompatibilities, reserving the term conflict for the more restricted class of intrapsychic clashes. As Klein (1976) views it, conflict is not simply any occasion on which the individual feels frustration. It is for him a clash of mutually exclusive aims which the person refuses to relinquish. In tracing the infantile roots of conflict, thus defined, we will be looking for instances in which an expressed wish or desire of the infant runs up, not just against a parental prohibition, but against a prohibition which has already become internalized to some extent, so that the tug is felt within the infant. Early on it may indeed be difficult to distinguish internally experienced conflict from the frustration of an externally blocked, pleasure-seeking act. However, as we present some direct observations, the distinction should become clearer.

The common origin of conflict and the self poses a complex problem. In a sense each must be present for the other to exist. Conflict arises when the unity of the self is disrupted by opposing internal polarities. This statement would put the self as existing prior to experienced conflict. On the other hand, we and others see the self as arising via a series of syntheses which are the active resolutions of experienced conflict. One resolution of this dilemma would have early structures, or organizing principles, arise from a range of experienced incompatibilities that occur prior to the existence of the more narrowly defined conflict. These early structures, in turn, could be the springboard from which conflict begins to be experienced.

Psychoanalysts have paid increasing attention to the delineation and explication of the meaning of the self. A review of this literature would take us too far afield, so we simply refer to works of Hartmann (1950), Jacobson (1964), Kohut (1971, 1977), Lichtenberg (1975), Mahler and Furer (1968), Sandler and Rosenblatt (1962), Schafer (1968), Spiegel (1959), Tolpin (1972), and Winnicott (1965).

In a continuity with ideas explicated by Klein (1976) and Erikson (1954), we will try to demonstrate the interaction between two aspects of the developing self: (1) an autonomous component, as a locus of action and eventually decision; (2) that aspect of the self which is a necessary part of a larger unit transcending one's autonomous actions. It is the integration of the "I" and the "we" components which spells out a complete entity, i.e., a self or person. "A sense of identity [or self] implies that one experiences an over-all sameness and continuity extending from the personal past (now internalized in introjects and identifications) into a tangible future; and from the community's past (now existing in traditions and institutions sustaining a communal sense of identity) into foreseeable or imaginable realities or work accomplishment and role satisfaction" (Erikson, 1954, p. 53).

As an alternative to the language of subject and object, we define the self as having aspects of *both* separateness and membership in a more inclusive entity. We would therefore expect to find a simultaneous unfolding of the "I" aspects of the self and the "we" aspects of the evolving entity or self-identity. Furthermore, we would expect to see behavioral evidence of fluctuations between the harmonization of, versus the clash between, "I" and "we" aspects of the developing self. In fact, such moments of disunity and discontinuity in respect to being a differentiated unit or part of a larger unit would be the occasion for integration and synthesis. The requirements for integration lead to the development of self-regulating capacities which constitute a large part of motivational development. Leaping ahead in the developmental process, we note that it is the autonomous tendencies which eventually manifest themselves in ambition and the search for separateness and independence. The affiliative tendencies may be expressed through family ties and societal bonds and lead to cooperation and interdependence. We do *not* see these trends as the outcome of separate streams of development and do not find the need to hypothesize a separate line of development for the narcissistic sector of the personality. Rather, our approach emphasizes their mutual and persistent interplay and reverberations. Our data offer us the opportunity to examine this proposition. To summarize, the sense of identity, or of self, is the outcome of the integration within and between these "we" and "I" aspects. With time, there results that integrated self-structure which contains a sense of continuity, coherence, and integrity.

Sander (1962) has proposed a developmental model of mutual adaptation and regulation between mother and infant and has more recently (1976) pointed the way toward the transformation from adaptation and regulation to the evolution of the self: "in becoming internalized, adapted strategies which first characterized regulatory relationships with the interpersonal surround will now function as features of self-regulation and eventually characterize personality idiosyncracy" (p. 312).

In 1979, Sander stressed the function of the inevitable discontinuities in mother-infant interaction as a key element in the evolution of self-regulating capacities and ultimately self-structure. When juxtaposed against a background of basic harmony, these "open spaces" provide the challenge and the opportunity for the infant system to develop the abilities for self-regulation.

We have found Schafer's (1968) original definition of self a useful point of reference in tracing the steps leading to a baby's development of a self. Schafer outlines three functions by which we define the self-structure: (1) the self-as-agent (e.g., as knower or doer); (2) the self-as-object ("I see myself torn in different directions"); and (3) the self-as-locus (i.e., location of the experience in the body). It is the persisting quality of continuity in these three aspects of self which eventually provides for a stable self-identity.

THE PRESELF—STAGE I

By the end of the first month, there exists a state of adapted coordination, in which there are open spaces, i.e., a span of time in which action is not dictated by the requirement for the restoration of regulation. These are the first occasions on which the infant can take the initiative, can actively explore stimuli of low intensity, and can organize expectancy schemas. This open space thus represents a discontinuity in the family system and permits the development of a semi-independent source of (self-) regulation. This regulatory process is seen as active and as implying the integration by the infant of elements of inner state and of outer experience. The voluminous research data which support the inference that the infant has an early capacity to organize his experience is viewed by us as reflecting the first stage in the development of the self. We call stage I the *preself*. We know that "the neonate can screen perceptual input with reference to information stored from daily experience and can classify according to both categories of animate and inanimate and to visual and auditory matches—and that the neonate rapidly learns to exert an active choice for a preferential stimulus" (Lichtenberg, 1979).[1] But this is not viewed by us as meeting the criteria we have established for a conceptualization of a self, although it is a vital step in the pathway leading to the emergence of a self.

We now turn to the observational data from the longitudinal study and the inferences we draw from these data on the basis of which we construct a model of the development of the self. As one of its principal objectives, this study included the investigation of the mother-child relationship, the first contextual unit, a term introduced by Evelyne Schwaber (1980). Frequent opportunities were provided for the observation of mother and child in a variety of situations over a 6-year period. The interactional data for each mother-child pair were divided into sequences of time segments. Evaluations were then made of the interactions which were prominent in each time segment. It is these evaluations that led to the conceptualization of a series of *issues* that were being negotiated between mother and child in each of these time segments. Sander (1962) writes: "Our observational material of the first 18 months of life seemed to fall into five large segments, each with a prominent feature which was encountered extensively in our data for that period" (p. 144). In essence, we can view the issue prominent in each segment as reflecting the primary *adaptational* task facing the mother-infant unit. Sander and his collaborators found striking contrasts in their sample of a "normal" population: "the range of adaptation achieved lies truly on a broad spectrum. The extent of adaptation ranged from the barest semblance of a behavioral synchrony between mother and child that was consistent with life to a varied and

1. We are indebted to Joseph Lichtenberg (1979) for his superb summary of recent research on the neonate.

harmonious interaction, specific in its accuracy of matching stimulus and response, infant need and maternal care" (p. 146f).

We have selected the observations made on Nancy D. and her parents. When the researchers placed mothers on a spectrum with reference to capacity for specific appropriateness of maternal responses to the baby's state, Mrs. D. achieved a high score. Indeed, Nancy's growth takes place in the context of reasonably accepting, nurturing, and empathic responses by both parents. From the earliest observations and thence forward, this mother is repeatedly described as responding to her baby in a very competent, gentle fashion. For example, at 3 weeks of age, the observer notes: "Mrs. D. picked the baby up, not letting her cry very long, and cradled her very comfortably and gently in her arms, looking down at her with a very warm, half humorous, accepting expression."

The proportion of empathic versus nonempathic interactions cannot be established from the brief excerpts presented below. Since our model focuses on conflict and disharmony in the formation of the self, there will be some selective emphasis on those elements. This selectivity could lead to a biased impression of excessive harshness. There were, to be sure, harsh moments, but that was not the overall atmosphere.

The family discussed here was one of the most stable, most integrated, and most supportive of the child's development in a group of 25 families studied in considerable detail. It is against the background of that supportive atmosphere that the following excerpts should be viewed.

This is not to deny that there were clear-cut problems that could be discerned in the interaction and in the child's development. Our experience in studying young families suggests that such problems are ubiquitous. The long-range implications of these early disturbances which fall in the normal range remain to be established.

In Nancy's family, the father was a very active participant in child rearing, and the parents adapted and responded supportively to each other's strengths and foibles. We are impressed with the evidence that attests to his importance in the evolving process of Nancy's internalization of environmental input. Nancy, like so many other infants, learned to relate to more than one person, right from the beginning. She showed a capacity to discriminate and to attach to both mother and father and evolved different modes of relating to each. We have to be aware that we are witnessing a series of dyadic relationships, and that she faced the task of perceiving two different primary objects, each of whom was offering different kinds of stimulation. As she responded with discriminative functioning with respect to each of her parents, i.e., as she reacted differently under these two different sets of conditions, she evolved an appropriately complicated structure.

We are impressed with the unity of the baby's organization during these early months, so that we see evidence for coordination and discoordination between parent and infant, but no evidence of conflict or dualism within the baby. There are plenty of moments when different need states are mutually incompatible, e.g., hunger and fatigue, but whichever one is ascendant will govern behavior. It is only with growth and development that differentiation takes place, and the baby's functioning then reflects a shift away from responses which flow from this initial position. To summarize, the infant starts with a number of physiological states which lack definiteness and are accompanied by varying degrees of fussiness and fretting. The initial unity or preself that coalesces out of these physiological states is facilitated by good nurturance and by reciprocal interactions. When sufficient comfort and coordination are provided in the interactions between infant and mother, the baby is able to experience distinctly separate and clear states. The primary consequence of successful, mutual adaptation is the baby's acquisition of a capacity for the regulation of her own states. This development corresponds to what Sander (1962) has subsumed under the headings of "period of initial adaptation" (0 to 2½ months) and "period of reciprocal exchange" (approximately 2½ to 5 months).

THE PREAWARENESS SELF—STAGE II

When Nancy was 4 months old, her mother reported: "We play a lot with her. Sometimes I prop her up on my knees and hold her there and we jounce her or we sing to her and she is as happy as a lark. In fact, we spend more time laughing at her than we do anything else. She's a very contented baby. When she wakes up from a nap, she starts 'babbling.' She's just happy in her room because she looks at different things."

We are calling attention to the manifest interrelatedness of the "we" and "I" aspects of Nancy's development. It is precisely in the context of a maximum of adaptive, pleasurable interaction between the baby and her surround that Nancy develops a distinct capacity for functioning happily by herself, i.e., autonomously. The "period of early directed activity of the infant—5–9 months" (Sander, 1962, p. 155) is ushered in early in Nancy's life. Increasingly, we witnessed Nancy's taking the initiative in establishing areas of reciprocity with both mother and father. In fact, her capacity for differentiated responses and initiatives with each of her parents was striking. For example, Mrs. D. reported: "My husband will put her over his head and she laughs. The rougher he plays with her, the better she likes it." Various observers reported on the way he played "rough" with her, but there was never any evidence that she experienced this play with distress. The research observers reported that Nancy, at 4½ months, was "much interested in objects, in people, in what is going on around her generally. She seems to be a reactive and outgoing baby, reacting sensitively to changes in her external situation."

As we approach the data which permit us to identify a more definitive phase in the evolution of the self, we emphasize that there is no single indicator that specifies a precise moment when we can say "now there is a self." Rather, the confluence of bits and pieces of data permits us to make the inference that there is now a self operating, in contrast to a preself. From the longitudinal perspective, the glimmer of such a self will become increasingly clear and organized, and will manifest sufficient regularity, consistency, and intentionality to validate the earlier inference. Thus, there is a transitional period as the baby emerges from the stage of preself, which we label *preawareness self*—stage II. This delineation of a self which does not yet carry any self-recognition or self-awareness has to be viewed, then, as a stage clearly bounded on the two sides. In this period, the behavioral data lead to our inference that Nancy is developing the capacity to take the initiative, to sort out options, and to determine a goal and a means of achieving it. In addition, self-regulation becomes smoother and can be sustained for longer periods of time. Over the course of the subsequent months, further developmental progress will permit us to infer that she has acquired the capacity to be aware of herself not only as the agent (the doer) but as the locus for contradictory wishes which necessitate resolution. Early glimmers of such self-awareness will be evident in the data from stage II.

During this stage, the infant's experience of the self is promoted and facilitated by her joy in repeating and practicing new skills and in her experiencing herself as an effective doer.

The data support the importance we assign to the increasingly frequent, sometimes strident, and always inevitable clashes between the infant and the surround as a factor which promotes this crucial developmental step. The record contains a number of incidents, beginning at about 6 months, in which mother and/or father felt impelled to prohibit, scold, or spank the baby. As previously stated, these events took place in an essentially harmonious atmosphere, replete with indicators of a superb level of adaptation between infant and parents. In this atmosphere, there also were innumerable incidents which reflected Nancy's growing capacity to imitate parental behaviors. In general, Nancy was described as progressing smoothly in her development, as being able to maintain her own direction of interest and to adapt readily to a variety of external cues. She was very responsive socially, but, at the same time, very selective as to which stimuli she responded to. She was able to block out or accommodate to a range of intrusions. There was not always an inevitable clash between "we" and "I" aspects of her functioning—in fact, she began actively to orchestrate and contribute to a harmonization of these interests.

The Clash: When Nancy was 8 months old, her mother reported that she was "grinding her teeth!" Mrs. D. was obviously distressed by Nancy's behavior and felt impelled to make her stop. Her initial, explicit, verbal prohibition, "Don't grind your teeth," merely elicited a happy grin from the baby. Within the next two weeks, Mrs. D. reported that Nancy had begun to bite her mother's shoulder, to which the mother objected strenuously with a firm "uh uh!" Nancy would then persist, elicit a more forceful prohibition, and eventually cease. On another occasion, the baby picked up a piece of candy. The mother said, sharply, "Nancy, uh uh!" The baby looked at her, leisurely put the candy down, and went on to some other activity. A bit later, she picked up the candy again, elicited a sharp "uh uh" from her mother, and immediately dropped the candy. These were the first occasions on which the baby responded to a verbal prohibition with compliant behavior.

The father was reported to have been more impatient and more vigorous. When Nancy refused to take a nap, he gave her a spanking. Her angry response resulted in a second slap, a command that she put her head down, and compliance.

At 9 months, Nancy had a number of favorite toys and was able to play contentedly in her crib. Simultaneously, she delighted in playing peek-a-boo with familiar persons. We are again impressed with the simultaneous and mutually facilitating autonomous and affiliative aspects of the developing self. One of her favorite toys was a doll. When the examiner handed this toy to her, "she gazed at the doll with an expression of great delight, smiling, then taking it and letting go of the crib railing, sitting down and cooing to the doll." There seemed to be developing a new affiliative unit, i.e., baby and doll. We might even infer the beginning of symbolization in which the doll represents a fragment of the interpersonal dyad—mother and child.

Her behavior had a specificity which is reflective of a highly differentiated quality. Thus she could differentiate between her father's "spanking" her with a smile on his face, and enter the game with smiles and sounds of delight, and a similar spanking accompanied by his frown. Furthermore, when she was presented with the frown, her state of upset was followed by active efforts to engage him and to get him to smile—at which point she relaxed and joined the game. We see here early evidence of her awareness of different affects and her active searching for ways to influence events so that she could end with a pleasurable affect.

Ordinarily we expect an individual to gravitate away from, to avoid that which is evocative of, a painful affect. Although Nancy responded to her father's frown with distress, with non-pleasure, she nevertheless persisted in maintaining contact with him until she could change *his* behavior and eventually produce a pleasurable situation for herself. By making this impact on her surround, she could succeed in creating a new environment. We infer that she had a complicated sophisticated schema of her father, which included the notion that he could be fun—again. Such persistence can be maintained only if, indeed, she is at least sometimes successful in such an engagement. Her experiences inform her that she can influence events—what she does can make a difference in her interpersonal world.

In summary, her playfulness, her initiatives, the beginnings of an acceptance of prohibitions, the beginnings of an active inhibition of her own behavior, as well as her active imitative behavior are viewed by us as indicators of a developing capacity for self-regulation. What we have just described reflects two functions of the self, i.e., initiatory and inhibitory behavior. Effectance pleasure is seen as the consequence of and also a motive for the sequence: the baby starts something (initiative), carries it through, and is pleased with her accomplishment. We, the observers, then infer that we are witnessing an intact being who is "running the show."

THE SELF—STAGE III

At 11 months, Nancy was walking. As with each previous developmental achievement, she was delighted with her new capacity and showed great joy. By that time, she was very tuned in to her mother's prohibitions. For example, her delight in hearing people talk on the telephone had created a problem, eventually solved by Mrs. D.'s encouraging her to babble into a toy telephone. The mother's earlier, repeated instruction "go talk on your telephone" produced the self-initiated response to the ringing of the phone—Nancy grabbed her own phone and put it to her ear. This high level of imitation is a further indication that there is a sentient being who knows what is going on and is able to mimic her parents. We also suggest the more far-reaching inference that this behavior is reflective of a process of identification, as defined by George Klein (1976). Nancy was put in the position of the passive sufferer who was forbidden the use of the telephone. With her mother's help, she shifted from this passive role, participated in the prohibition, and took the active position with the aid of the substitute phone. This process of active reversal goes beyond the mere suppression of behavior and reflects an expansion of the self by her internalization of the mother's prohibition.

The mother reported: "We were down to this friend's house and Nancy was going after the radio knobs and I kept smacking her hand. She still kept going back. I slapped her hand so many times that it got red. Finally she walked away and didn't go back to it. I said, 'Well, you're gonna learn one way or another not to touch things in other people's homes.' She understands now."

During one developmental test, Nancy began to throw the cubes down on the floor. "She got quite deliberate about it and with considerable vigor threw the cube down on the floor, looking after it as it hit the floor. Mother expressed annoyance, then started a series of prohibiting 'uh uhs,' calling out her name with increasing loudness. There was a response in that Nancy did restrain herself, then looked searchingly at mother, followed by an aborted attempt to throw the block. She was poised to drop the cube, again looked at mother, and finally let the cube just slip out of her hand.She was now much more tentative, did not actually throw the cube, and kept checking back for mother's reaction."

When Nancy was 1 year old, she showed a well-developed capacity for self-restraint in response to prohibition. On the occasion of a home visit to take video tapes, the following incident was reported:

> Nancy greeted us at the door rather stolidly. She then became intrigued by all the equipment. She looked from one thing to another, gazing at each object with great interest. As she would reach out for some of the cords, mother would say no, and then move things out of her way quite matter-of-factly. Nancy would turn her attention to something else. But sooner or later she would go back to her original interest. Mother continued telling her not to touch whenever she reached out for the equipment. Nancy sometimes would stop her activity and look up at her mother as though questioning. She very clearly restrained herself from full activity and from reaching out and touching the camera under the impact of her mother's forbidding words. She would start to reach out; then, as her mother

admonished her, she would somehow finish the movements so that it was not an abrupt cutoff of the activity, but she was very evidently holding herself back. At one point when both the mother and the cameraman left the room and I was sitting on a chair in the corner, the baby began to reach up and manipulate the knobs, which she hadn't been able to do before, with a very serious purposeful exploring. She seemed to be completely unaware of my presence, and it seemed to me that her expression had about it a quality of a great deal of satisfaction as, at last, she had an opportunity to really go at this camera the way she had been wanting to for some time. She continued this activity with great absorption for several minutes, but then as her eyes lifted for a moment and she caught sight of me, she became more tentative at manipulating and looked at me as though gauging my reaction. As I spoke to her and smiled, she suddenly broke forth into a most enchanting smile, as though sharing with me what fun this was. At this point her mother returned to the room and Nancy immediately discontinued her activity with the camera and moved toward something else very quickly.

We have described a baby who has a wish, carries out her own plan on her own initiative, and then meets up with the forbidding parent. She then reduces the impulsive quality of the response and checks the result with the parent to see what the change in her behavior produces in the parent's reaction. She continues to test out alternative behaviors and alternative responses. From this we infer that there is a being, a self, who is carrying out an act in response to a desire or initiative, and a being, the same self, who is monitoring this sequence of events. If a child is behaving and monitoring her own behavior in the context of an interpersonal relationship, is observing and recording how the other person reacts to what she is doing, and is then influenced by her perceptions so that she proceeds to integrate her own acts with the social cues, we conclude that there is self-awareness. This is stage III in the development of the self-schema.

Tracing out a series of steps may enhance our understanding of the process that contributes to this awareness of the self. We assume that the baby experiences a desire but is not yet aware of herself as the locus of the experience. She then engages in those behaviors that eventuate in a fulfillment of that desire. Depending upon the hedonic value of the consequences of her behavior, she goes back to the beginning, in the fashion of a feedback loop, and reexperiences this sequence, usually in a contextual network. In this manner, the infant begins to make connections, i.e., she develops perceptions of and feelings about the events which preceded the action and which led to what are now predictable consequences. In this fashion, she gradually becomes aware of her intentions as the first step along a path that will lead to certain desirable or undesirable consequences. This process can take place only if the baby has developed the capacity to hold an intention in a state of abeyance. It is the continuation of an unfulfilled intention over some time that is most relevant for a consolidation of the awareness of the self. A crucial element in the climate of organization which enhances the infant's capacity to retain interest in the face of a nonfulfillment of an intention (or wish) is the occurrence and recurrence of gratification within a reasonable period of time after the baby experiences the wish. Thus, we note that Nancy's parents combined a clearly expressed definiteness about limits and prohibitions with a reasonable degree of flexibility. In general, they displayed a very nice balance in responding to Nancy, permitting her wide latitude and freedom within a framework of clearly defined, consistent, yet not always inexorable limits. Nancy adapted to this surround, accepted restraints, and gradually developed the capacity to impose limits on herself. On any number of occasions, her behavior increasingly reflected a choice: when, in an empathic climate, she was presented with the necessity to choose between behavior that reflected the pursuit of the desire versus that which constituted an alliance with the parent, she chose the latter. It seems to us that this is akin to the process described by Kohut (1971, 1977) as transmuting internalization (or identification, as defined by Klein, 1976). The pleasure experienced by the child is derived from the identification with the parent, and the by-product is the mastery over the impulse.

These data permit us to describe Nancy as now having a self, defined as the doer and knower, and a self-as-object, i.e., as containing contradictory wishes which must somehow be resolved, and a self-as-locus, i.e., the experience is located in the person, within a contextual surround. To state it differently, we now infer the existence of a conflict in Nancy. We witness the struggle between the wish to express, to act upon the desire, versus the wish to please and remain on friendly terms with the parent. Nancy develops the capacity to resolve this conflict in the direction of an inhibition or modification of the desire; she takes a step in the direction of identifying with her parents and aligns herself as being in opposition to the wish. We especially emphasize those solutions which imply the capacity to compromise, to find new solutions. We see the polarities of wish and internalized prohibition with the ensuing constructive solution of the conflict. She now *creates* a previously *never existing behavior;* e.g., the slow release of the cube is a creative solution to the incompatibility. This synthesis leads to mastery; it incorporates elements of both sides of the polarity and finds a satisfactory solution.

We are suggesting, as has Sander, that there is a close interplay between *adaptation* and the gradual acquisition of the capacity to engage in increasingly complex *self-regulatory* processes. These capacities, usually referred to as structures, evolve from discontinuities and incompatibilities, and are then available to the child to *promote* the next level of adaptation. These structures are *created* by an adaptational requirement and are then available to contribute to the creation of *new solutions.*

We have used the familiar language of "structure" and "structure building," but are not comfortable with terminology which lends itself to the possible translation of a process into a solid entity. We would prefer to conceptualize the psychological consequences of internalization as the development of an increasingly complex set of organizing principles that facilitate self-regulation.

A brief illustration highlights the crucial importance of the contextual surround for development and permits us to make a few comments about empathy. Nancy was caught in what by then had become a familiar struggle as she responded to her wish to bang on a table. When she was confronted with a series of maternal prohibitions, she began to wander around without purpose, displaying an air of discontent, and was unable to find a solution. Mrs. D. elected not to respond to Nancy's manifest wish to be picked up. We saw how even a child like Nancy, with a well-developed capacity for taking the initiative, could temporarily be rendered relatively nonfunctional if the surround did not respond appropriately—she simply lost her sense of purpose, became progressively more uncomfortable, and eventually dissolved in tears. At that point, her mother did respond with "I know—you have your troubles, don't you," and came to her rescue.

The notion of the empathic response includes the supposition that the parent has the capacity to empathize with a wide range of conditions, including the "in-between" states. Inevitably, there are moments of mismatch, when the child feels ungratified and frustrated. The parent's tolerance for such in-between states, the confidence that the baby can exist ungratified and will emerge intact, provides the child with a validation of self across a whole range of states. This makes for a fuller, richer experience of self.

The data we have presented also permit us to infer that intertwined with the child's evolving sense of self is the development of a sense of "the other." We see the merging and the separation of self and parent as being on a continuum, so that there is simultaneity in the development of what will increasingly be a clear-cut awareness of "me" and a clear-cut awareness of "the other." This was beautifully illustrated in the mock-aggression play that went on between Nancy and her father. She entered completely into the spirit of the game, and presumably pleased him as well as herself, as she crawled away from his pseudoangry face, looking back at him with an inviting grin on her face! We assume that her highly developed discriminatory capacity was related to frequent experiences in which she was validated. The process of validation in an empathic context encompasses a number of steps: (1) the parents have to recognize the child's intention; (2) respond to it in a fairly consistent way; (3) communicate back to the child sufficiently clear, consistent signals so that the child knows what their reaction is; (4) permit the sequence to go far enough so the child (a) has a sense of intention, (b) carries the act to fruition, and (c) receives some kind of message about the consequences of her action.

We may assume that the patients referred to in the literature as suffering from severe pathology of the self have been reared in an atmosphere in which this development was arrested or seriously distorted. Severely disturbed parents do not permit and/or do not foster this development of a separateness—they invade and live inside the child. We would expect such persons to remain locked into self-object relationships and transferences, because they did not develop an adequate internal regulatory capacity. Indeed, as described by Kohut (1971) and elucidated by Schwaber (1980), such a person requires the external agent to help him maintain even a minimal sense of unity and integrity of the self.

We bring this account of Nancy's development of a sense of self-awareness to a close with a brief report of the following incident. When Nancy was 15 months old, the observers made a home visit. She led her father to the table, pointing to something she wanted him to give to her, and said, "Me!" We feel that this was an articulated, verbal expression of an awareness of the self that had been growing over a period of several months. Language represented a culmination of an extraordinary human development and ushered in a new level of functioning.

CONCLUSION

We have been involved in developmental research for many years. Why did we now elect to reexamine our data and begin the process of defining and spelling out the origins and development of the self? The seminal contributions of Klein (1966, 1976), Kohut (1971, 1978), and Sander (1962, 1976) point to the necessity for the elucidation of a psychoanalytic psychology of the self. They and others also argue cogently how counterproductive it is to maintain and elaborate upon metapsychology. Therefore we are still searching for a clinical model of the self and, insofar as we are interested in its ontogenetic development, we must look for it, at least in part, via developmental research.

The task is to enrich and elaborate the concepts offered by Kohut and others via detailed study of the process, both on the couch and in the nursery. In time, and without adultomorphizing or pathologizing early development, we hope to find the appropriate bridges across what is a continuous process of development of the self in its autonomous and affiliative aspects.

Basic questions abound and are a goad to further investigation. The relationship between affect and the patterns we have traced in the development of the self remains to be elucidated. Assumptions which have been made about the conceptualization and definition of awareness must be examined more closely. The further course of the development of self-organization during the typically conflict-laden second year needs to be explored. The preliminary model we have advanced is perhaps best seen as a tool with which to carry out the investigative tasks.

BIBLIOGRAPHY

APFELBAUM, B. (1965), Ego Psychology, Psychic Energy, and the Hazards of Quantitative Explanation in Psychoanalytic Theory. *Int. J. Psycho-Anal.*, 46:168–182.
—— (1966), On Ego Psychology. *Int. J. Psycho-Anal.*, 47:451–475.
ERIKSON, E. H. (1954), The Dream Specimen of Psychoanalysis. *J. Amer. Psychoanal. Assn.*, 2:5–56.
GILL, M. M. & HOLZMAN, P. S., eds. (1976), *Psychology versus Metapsychology* [*Psychol. Issues*, 36]. New York: Int. Univ. Press.
HARTMANN, H. (1950), Comments on the Psychoanalytic Theory of the Ego. In: *Essays on Ego Psychology.* New York: Int. Univ. Press, 1964, pp. 113–141.
HOLT, R. R. (1965), A Review of Some of Freud's Biological Assumptions and Their Influence on His Theories. In: *Psychoanalysis and Current Biological Thought*, ed. N. S. Greenfield & W. C. Lewis. Madison: Univ. Wisconsin Press, pp. 93–124.
—— (1972), Freud's Mechanistic and Humanistic Images of Man. In: *Psychoanalysis and Contemporary Science*, ed. R. R. Holt & E. Peterfreund. New York: Macmillan, 1:3–24.
HOME, H. J. (1966), The Concept of Mind. *Int. J. Psycho-Anal.*, 47:42–49.
JACOBSON, E. (1964), *The Self and the Object World.* New York: Int. Univ. Press.
KLEIN, G. S. (1966), Perspectives to Change in Psychoanalytic Theory. Read at the Conference of Psychoanalysts of the Southwest, Galveston, Texas.
—— (1970), *Perception, Motives, and Personality.* New York: Alfred A. Knopf, pp. 357–412.
—— (1976), *Psychoanalytic Theory.* New York: Int. Univ. Press.
KOHUT, H. (1971), *The Analysis of the Self.* New York: Int. Univ. Press.
—— (1977), *The Restoration of the Self.* New York: Int. Univ. Press.
—— & WOLF, E. S. (1978), The Disorders of the Self and Their Treatment. *Int. J. Psycho-Anal.*, 59:413–425.
LICHTENBERG, J. D. (1975), The Development of the Sense of Self. *J. Amer. Psychoanal. Assn.*, 23:453–484.
—— (1979), Implications for Psychoanalytic Theory of Research on the Neonate. Unpublished manuscript.

MAHLER, M. S. & FURER, M. (1968), *On Human Symbiosis and the Viscissitudes of Individuation.* New York: Int. Univ. Press.

PETERFREUND, E. (1978), Some Critical Comments on Psychoanalytic Conceptualizations of Infancy. *Int. J. Psycho-Anal.*, 59:427–441.

PIAGET, J. (1936), *The Origins of Intelligence in Children.* New York: Int. Univ. Press, 1952.

RAPAPORT, D. (1960), *The Structure of Psychoanalytic Theory* [*Psychol. Issues*, 6]. New York: Int. Univ. Press.

RUBINSTEIN, B. B. (1965), Psychoanalytic Theory and the Mind-Body Problem. In: *Psychoanalysis and Current Biological Thought*, ed. N. S. Greenfield & W. C. Lewis. Madison: Univ. Wisconsin Press, pp. 35–56.

———— (1967), Explanation and Mere Description. In: *Motives and Thought* [*Psychol. Issues*, 18/19:20–77], ed. H. H. Holt. New York: Int. Univ. Press.

SANDER, L. W. (1962), Issues in Early Mother-Child Interaction. *J. Amer. Acad. Child Psychiat.*, 1:141–166.

———— (1976), Epilogue. In: *Infant Psychiatry*, ed. E. N. Rexford, L. W. Sander, & T. Shapiro. New Haven & London: Yale Univ. Press, pp. 311–313.

———— (1979), Ellen Stechler Memorial Lecture at Boston University School of Medicine.

SANDLER, J. & ROSENBLATT, B. (1962), The Concept of the Representational World. *This Annual*, 17:128–145.

SCHAFER, R. (1968), *Aspects of Internalization.* New York: Int. Univ. Press.

SCHWABER, E. (1980), Self-Psychology and the Concept of Psychopathology. In: *Advances in Self-Psychology*, ed. A. Goldberg. New York: Int. Univ. Press (in press).

SPIEGEL, L. A. (1959), The Self, the Sense of Self, and Perception. *This Annual*, 14:81–109.

TOLPIN, M. (1972), On the Beginnings of a Cohesive Self. *This Annual*, 26:316–352.

WINNICOTT, D. W. (1965), Ego Distortion in Terms of True and False Self. In: *The Maturational Processes and the Facilitating Environment.* New York: Int. Univ. Press, pp. 140–152.

Some Potential Effects of Adoption on Self and Object Representations

PAUL M. BRINICH

THE ADOPTION OF A CHILD IS, IN HUMAN TERMS, ALWAYS A PAIN-
ful and potentially traumatic event. In our culture, adoption
occurs only when something has gone quite seriously wrong: one
or both parents have died, or are unable or unwilling to care for
the child they have conceived. From the side of the adoptive
parents, the decision to adopt a child often follows years of failure in their attempts to conceive a child of their own. Whether it
is based upon physiological anomalies or upon psychological
conflicts, this failure is something with which the adoptive parents must painfully come to terms.

The tragedies, inabilities, and failures of both the biological
and the adoptive parents are reflected in the adopted child and
his psychological development. For the "realities" of the adult
world mean little to the young child; the sudden death of loving
biological parents may be experienced as a malicious abandonment; his adoptive parents may tell him that he was "chosen," but
he may choose to believe he was stolen. No matter how often the
adopted child is told that his adoptive parents are now his "real"
parents, he can never completely ignore his first parents and the
fact that they gave him up.

Assistant Clinical Professor, Department of Psychiatry, Case Western Reserve School of Medicine, and Staff Child Psychologist, Cleveland Metropoli-
tan General Hospital. This paper developed out of work begun while the
author was in training at the Hampstead Child-Therapy Clinic, London. Dr.
Philip Spielman of Mt. Zion Hospital, San Francisco, contributed greatly to
clarifying the direction of this paper through his helpful criticism of an earlier
draft.

Every child uses a combination of personal experiences, cultural materials, and constitutional givens to create mental representations of himself and of the people and world around him (Sandler and Rosenblatt, 1962). These mental representations are organized into a "representational world" used by the child to predict the outcome of his interactions with people and with the world. Thus, the child's mental representations of himself and others influence his object relationships.

The adopted child must include two separate sets of parents within his representational world. He must also integrate into his representation of himself the fact that he was born to one set of parents but has been raised by another set of parents. This paper attempts to outline how some adopted children have organized their representational worlds and the ways in which their mental representations (of both themselves and their objects) have affected their object relationships.

That adoption poses special hazards for the child's development appears to be borne out by the fact that adopted children are referred for psychological treatment two to five times as frequently as their nonadopted peers in countries as widely dispersed as Great Britain, Israel, Poland, Sweden, and the United States (Bohman, 1971; Eiduson and Livermore, 1953; Humphrey and Ounsted, 1963; Kadushin, 1967; Lifshitz et al., 1975; McWhinnie, 1969; Reece and Levin, 1968; Schechter, 1960; Simon and Senturia, 1966; Sweeney et al., 1963; Toussieng, 1962; Work and Anderson, 1971; Ziatek, 1974). In addition, there appears to be a consistent trend in the symptomatology of the adopted children who are referred for treatment. In the great majority of studies the referral symptoms include behavior that is characterized as impulsive, provocative, aggressive, and antisocial (Comments, 1972; Eiduson and Livermore, 1953; Goodman and Magno-Nora, 1975; Jackson, 1968; Menlove, 1965; Nevrla, 1972; Offord et al., 1969; Schechter et al., 1964; Simon and Senturia, 1966). There is no unanimity on the association between adoption and psychopathological development, however, and many hypotheses have been suggested to explain the preponderance of behavioral problems and personality disorders reported in adopted children (Barnes, 1953; Clothier, 1943; Eiduson and Livermore, 1953; Reeves, 1971; Sants, 1964;

Schechter, 1960, 1967; Schechter et al., 1964; Simon and Senturia, 1966; Toussieng, 1962; Wieder, 1977a, 1978).

Before discussing the problems often associated with adoption, I would like to emphasize that this paper is not a criticism of adoption per se. I agree with those writers who believe that adoption is very often of great physical, social, and psychological value to all parties concerned (Bernard, 1974; Gardner, 1972; Kadushin, 1967; Skeels, 1972; Winick et al., 1975). Regardless of the difficulties often associated with it, adoption remains the optimal social solution to the problem of the unwanted child. Other social solutions, such as foster care or institutional care, are generally more pathogenic than adoption.

PROBLEMS POSED BY ADOPTION

Goldstein et al. (1973) have emphasized that affection, stimulation, and continuity of relationships are prerequisites for the normal psychological development of a child. Observations of early mother-infant interactions by researchers from both psychoanalytic (e.g., Brody et al., 1976; Escalona, 1968; Mahler et al., 1975; Spitz, 1965) and behavioral (Fogel, 1977; Kaye, 1977; Pawlby, 1977; Schaffer, 1977a; Schaffer et al., 1977; Stern et al., 1977) perspectives have demonstrated that mothers and infants very quickly establish reciprocal patterns of interaction. These patterns, which take place in an affectively charged atmosphere, provide a foundation for all future interactions and communications.

Of prime importance in these early interactions is the mother's ability to attribute meaning to her infant's actions. While some actions by infants are universal, genetically coded signals (e.g., crying to indicate discomfort), the subtleties of mother-infant interaction are very much a function of each particular mother-infant pair. A particular mother responds to a specific action by her infant *as if* it has a particular meaning. That particular infant learns, through reciprocal experience with his mother, the meaning *she* assigns to the specific action. The establishment of such *shared meaning*, embodied in a smoothly reciprocal relationship, is an essential part of the normal symbiosis described by Mahler and her co-workers (1975).

The achievement of a reciprocal relationship is problematic for every mother-infant pair. There are, however, some specific difficulties associated with adoption that make the achievement of reciprocity more problematic for the adoptive mother-child pair.

First, many adopted children experience one or more actual disruptions in their early experiences of reciprocity; this happens every time they are moved from one caretaker to another. Second, adoptions are rarely finalized during the first months of a child's life. Until the adoption is finalized the adoptive parents quite naturally feel that they and their child are "on probation." This situation is not conducive to the close intimacy characteristic of the symbiotic phase; it hampers the formation of a smoothly reciprocal relationship between child and parents.

The first difficulty associated with adoption is usually an external one contingent upon the legal procedures governing adoption in different states and countries. One very common element of these procedures is a probationary period between the time of placement and the time of final adoption. Goldstein et al. (1973) have argued cogently that an adoption decree should "be made final the moment a child is actually placed with the adopting family" (p. 36). Unfortunately, not all the difficulties in establishing a reciprocal relationship between adopted infant and adoptive parents are so external.

Reeves (1971) has pointed out that the adoptive mother "has 'got' a baby, but has not 'had a baby'" (p. 167). This fact has important implications for her mental representations of herself and her adopted child; and these in turn will be reflected in the relationships between the adoptive mother and her adopted child.

While the biological mother has a sense that the child is a *part* of her, the adoptive mother knows that the child was part of someone else. It is normal for the biological mother to cathect her child with a great deal of (originally) narcissistic libido; this is a problem for the adoptive mother, especially insofar as the adopted child emphasizes her own infertility. This problem in cathexis sometimes finds expression in the adoptive mother's inability to accept her adopted child's expressions of instinctuality (e.g., soiling, sexual curiosity, aggression directed toward the adoptive parents).

The adoptive mother may see such instinctual behavior as a reflection of the child's "bad blood." In such situations the adoptive mother's internal representation of her child may in fact consist of two disconnected parts, one acceptable and the other unacceptable. It is obvious that such a division in the adoptive mother's mental representations of her adopted child will be reflected in and influence his development.

The fact that 8 to 14 percent of adoptive parents later have biological children of their own (Bohman, 1971; F. G. Brown, 1959; Humphrey and Ounsted, 1964) suggests that a significant portion of these parents have some psychological conflicts about sexuality, reproduction, and parenthood (F. G. Brown, 1959). Whether the conflicts were based in oedipal or preoedipal phases of development, it is clear that these parents were unable to accept and to actualize one facet of themselves prior to adoption. It is very likely that this state of affairs would be mirrored in their self representations. Indeed, several authors have remarked that some adoptive parents appear to feel as if they had stolen their adoptive children, a feeling which is probably related to unresolved oedipal conflicts (Toussieng, 1962; Walsh and Lewis, 1969).

Such feelings can become a special problem when they intrude upon the resolution of the separation-individuation phase (Mahler et al., 1975) in the adopted child. Some adoptive parents fear that their children will leave them for someone else; as a result, these parents find it difficult to allow their children the normal experiences of separation which are characteristic of this phase.

Thus far I have concentrated on external, legal factors and psychological factors within the adoptive parents which are related to the self and object representations of both parents and adopted children. The adopted child's specific experiences, however, also shape his view of himself and the world. In a sense, the fact that he has been adopted can act as an irritant in the mental life of a child much as a grain of sand can irritate the membranes of an oyster.

The adopted child experiences knowledge about his adoption as a narcissistic injury (Schechter, 1960). For this and other reasons Wieder (1977a, 1978) recommends withholding information about adoption until the child has entered latency. Clothier

(1943) cites problems in the adopted child's ability to achieve a sense of "fundamental security" and identity. She suggests that "the adopted child may even create outrageous situations that will force his adopted parents to prove their love for him and their wish to love him for their own" (p. 229). Simon and Senturia (1966) suggest that the "presence of the two sets of parents makes it more difficult to fuse the intrapsychic 'good' and 'bad' parent images of infantile object relations into a workable, more realistic identification" (p. 864). Schechter (1973) includes this factor as one element in his psychoanalytic case study of an adopted child. The failure to fuse the intrapsychic good and bad parent images frequently exists in parallel with a failure on the part of the adoptive parents to fuse their "good" and "bad" representations of their adopted child.

The split in parental images creates problems at each developmental phase. It certainly makes the resolution of oedipal conflicts much more difficult. Moreover, insofar as the prohibition of incest plays a part in the resolution of the oedipal conflict, the adopted child has a special problem, for he is *not* related to his adoptive parents by blood. Since he usually does not know the identity of his blood relatives, he is thrust precisely into the position of Oedipus, who did not know the identity of his own parents until it was too late. The difficulty in locating himself in a genealogical context may be related to the sexual promiscuity which is often reported in the referral symptomatology of adopted children. This genealogical ignorance can give rise to particularly powerful family romance fantasies, which persist well into adolescence.

Adoption also presents problems in the establishment of a sense of identity during adolescence (Di Leo, 1973; Sants, 1964). Knowledge about and experiences with one's parents usually contribute greatly to the establishment of a firm sense of identity in the adolescent (even if this firm sense is nothing more than a repudiation of the adolescent's images of his parents). The adopted child, however, rarely has access to much information about his biological parents. Ernst Kris (1956), writing on the "personal myth," emphasizes the importance of autobiographical memories to the formation of a coherent ego identity in adolescence. Adopted children, however, have a double handicap: (1) they find it difficult to locate their own personal history within that of their family; and (2) they are likely to experience their curiosity about their origins and early life as conflictual and dangerous.

Finally, many adopted children experience themselves as *unwanted* despite their adoptive parents' best efforts to emphasize how much they want and love their adopted child. These feelings are certainly related to the fact that the adopted child usually has been rejected by his biological parents, which cannot be concealed from the child. This real rejection clearly makes itself felt in the child's self representations (Brinich, 1977; Daunton, 1974; Wieder, 1977a). It also poses special problems in therapy for this is a situation where external reality reinforces the results of internal conflicts.

CASE PRESENTATIONS

The clinical illustrations which follow are from three adopted children, two of whom also had significant physical handicaps.

CASE 1

Sophie was referred for psychoanalytic treatment at 9 years of age because of a long-standing provocative and hostile relationship with her adoptive mother and because of her growing obesity. Sophie had been adopted by the Fords after 10 infertile years of marriage. She had been given up at birth into the care of an adoption agency, which placed her with the Fords when she was 8 weeks old.

Sophie was a "wanted" child, but her mother found some of Sophie's behavior upsetting. Mrs. Ford felt it was very important to keep Sophie neat and clean, especially around the mouth, which she constantly wiped when Sophie drooled. Mrs. Ford found it difficult to accept this normal, "messy" behavior. She also found it difficult to accept Sophie's moves toward separation and independence when, at 15 months, she began to walk. When Sophie was 3 years old, Mrs. Ford began to threaten that she would send Sophie away to boarding school or to the hospital if she were naughty. It was at this time that Sophie was first told that she had been adopted.

This issue was pushed to the surface by the adoption, when Sophie was 2½, of a second daughter, Cheryl. Sophie became very demanding and insatiable; Mrs. Ford responded by providing many sweets, as a result of which Sophie's weight suddenly increased from the 55th to the 90th percentile.

When Sophie was nearly 5 her mother became pregnant for the first time; in the 2 years following the birth of her brother James, Sophie again gained a great deal of weight: at 7½ years her 81 pounds put her well over the 97th percentile in weight for her age.

By the time Sophie was 6½ both parents were full of complaints about her and spoke openly of her "bad heredity." It was clear that they found a great deal of Sophie's behavior unacceptable and were externalizing its cause onto the biological parents. Sophie responded in kind; she expressed a wish to be called Ellen, the name given her by her biological mother, whose name had been Sophie. The Fords not only had made this change but also had shared this information with Sophie. Thus, from the beginning, the Fords clearly (albeit unconsciously) had forged a link between Sophie and her biological mother, an identification that carried with it those aspects of human instinctual life which Mrs. Ford could not tolerate in her children.

Mrs. Ford certainly found Sophie a messy baby, one that she could not keep clean enough to satisfy her own internal prohibitions. From this point onward, the mother-child relationship was colored by Mrs. Ford's unconscious message that "anything messy cannot be mine." This early maladaptation between mother and daughter was only a shadow of what was to come later when, in the midst of the anal phase, Sophie was simultaneously confronted with both the knowledge of her own adoption and a baby sister. Cheryl proved to be remarkably different from Sophie, both in appearance and in temperament, and these differences seemed to have encouraged Mrs. Ford in her efforts to put all of the "bad" out onto Sophie.

By the time Sophie was 7, her parents complained of her "stealing," "lying," greed, and jealousy. "Stealing" was a particularly important element in the interplay between Sophie's unconscious and that of her mother. It is likely that another determinant in Mrs. Ford's decision to give Sophie the name of her biological mother, beyond the above-mentioned externalization, was Mrs. Ford's own guilt about having "stolen" a baby by adopting Sophie. When Sophie began to enact this fantasy in displacement, both parents remained unable to see what lay behind her behavior; instead, they insisted that Sophie be judged by the rules appropriate to adults.

This was the state of affairs at the beginning of Sophie's analysis. It did not take long for Sophie to show how her own representations of herself meshed with her parents' representations of Sophie.

Sophie had asked me prior to the beginning of the analysis proper whether she might have a "Teeny Tiny Tears" doll to use during her analytic sessions. It turned out that Teeny Tiny Tears was advertised and sold with the slogan, "Your very own baby" (something which Sophie probably knew from television advertisements). As Sophie's "very own baby," this doll, christened "Sarah," became the vehicle par excellence for her fantasies, particularly those related to her adoption.

For example, after the first weekend break in Sophie's analytic treatment, she ran to her locker. Sarah had "suffocated" on the weekend. Sophie talked of how Sarah was getting fat and showed the doll's knickers to me. My interpretation that it seemed that Sarah thought getting fat meant getting pregnant led Sophie to announce proudly, "I'm pregnant!" This acknowledgment of her sexual wish provoked in Sophie a corresponding fear that she would be rejected because of it. To prevent this, she turned passive into active and rejected me by writing a note saying, "Well, good-bye." When I wrote back, "Well, hello," Sophie took another step and began to denigrate me by writing, "You pig face." When I tried to link this denigration to a feeling Sophie had experienced herself, she said, "Shut your fucking mouth" and began to pick with her fingernails at a sore on her arm, turning it into a large, bloody, open wound.

The week continued with a confusion of instinctual material from several phases. Sophie greedily ate oranges during her sessions, then spat out the half-eaten mess at me. She brought in her pregenital impulses and sexual curiosity via the doll, regularly inspecting its bottom and accusing the doll of being dirty. At the same time, Sophie punished herself for these instinctual eruptions: she repeatedly reopened the sores on her arms.

Interspersed with the instinctual material were two fantasies involving Sarah. In one, Sophie described how I had killed Sarah in the night; her Dad was going to come and kill me in revenge. In the other, Sophie claimed that she was Sarah's mother: when Sarah was born, she was all bloody; Sophie had not liked Sarah then and had closed her eyes. It appears that this fantasy of being bloody expressed one of her answers to the question, "Why was I given away?" She was rejected because she was bloody and messy; her anal impulses made her unlovable and she was therefore sent away.

Sophie followed this with more picking at her arms; she used some cotton wool, which she had brought with her, to stop the bleeding. After this, she took some of the bloody cotton and put it underneath Sarah's nappy. When I suggested that she was really worried about menstrual periods and about babies growing inside, Sophie left to go to the toilet (and perhaps to check and see whether she was alright inside). When she returned, I told Sophie that it was time to stop for the week, but that she and I would meet again next week at the same times. Sophie was very pleased by this and said she would bring something special for Sarah on Monday because she had to spend the weekend alone.

Here we see how Sophie took the active, caring role in relation to Sarah; she empathized with Sarah's loneliness (which was her own) and tried to make things better for her. Thus Sophie did not just try to get rid of her feelings via projection; she also took active, reparative steps to deal with the pain involved.

The fact that Sophie brought so much material, and especially sexual material, so quickly and openly seemed unusual; where was the repression characteristic of latency? One function of the sexual material began to become clear during the third week of treatment, when I began to take up the coming long summer holiday which was just two weeks away. I had begun a sentence suggesting that Sarah often wondered and worried about . . . when Sophie broke in and excitedly said, "Sex!" I agreed that that was probably true, but I added that something else was more on Sarah's mind just now: that her Dad was going away for a long time during the holidays. Sophie dropped the doll onto the floor and I agreed that that was how she herself felt.

This was a good example of Sophie's defensive use of sexual material. Had I followed her decoy, she would probably have elaborated some complicated, exciting, sexual fantasy. But since I did not take the bait and instead tried to pick up her underlying anxiety, Sophie was then able to acknowledge how "dropped" she felt.

During her third week of treatment Sarah remained at the center of Sophie's material: Sophie demanded that she and I play cards together; Sarah was used for what was won and lost in the betting. This was an eloquent expression of how Sophie felt about herself—a child who was transferred from one parent to another according to chance, with no concern for the feelings of the child.

When I won a hand, Sarah cried: she did not want to go with me as my hands were "smelly"; I'd been playing with "dog shit," Sophie said. This externalization of Sophie's own unwanted anal impulses onto me was good evidence for Sophie having internalized her mother's concerns about cleanliness. It served a defensive purpose here; for in denigrating me, she denied her growing attachment to me, which made her feel terribly vulnerable as we approached the summer holidays.

Sophie returned from the next weekend break and immediately "heard" Sarah crying for her father in her locker. The mother (Sophie) took the baby and threw it at me, screaming in a paroxysm of rage, "She's not my baby, she's adopted; throw her in the river!" It is impossible to overemphasize the intensity of Sophie's outburst. I assumed that in this sequence Sophie had expressed her feelings about herself, a self representation rooted both in her perception of her adoptive mother's attitude toward her and in her fantasies regarding her biological mother's attitude toward her.

Sophie seemed to have frightened herself with this outburst and quickly regressed to a passive role: she lay on the bed and demanded that I feed her with Sarah's bottle. When I complied, she repeatedly spat up the "milk"; when she finally swallowed it, it turned out to be "poison." Sophie then began to bite the nipple and refused to let go. As this play developed, Sophie demanded that I force the nipple into her mouth. In this she seemed to condense (1) her oral greed; (2) her penis envy and her wish to castrate; and (3) her self-punitive tendencies, which I had previously linked with Sophie's guilt about the expression of instinctual impulses. When I refused to force the bottle into Sophie's mouth, she did it herself, reacting to this oral self-assault by spitting, messing, and throwing. I repeated what was to become a constant theme: Sophie needed to find out if I would put up with her dirty, spitting, angry, and sexy feelings.

The fear that she would be rejected led Sophie into the area of sibling rivalry. At the beginning of a session later in the same week of treatment Sophie threw her locker key at me as hard as she could. "His name is Robert!" she shouted. Robert was an adolescent boy whom I saw in the hour following Sophie's session. Her jealous anger poured out in cupfuls of water which she threw and spat at me. I finally stopped her when interpretation of her jealousy had no effect. Clearly, this outburst of messy anger was a kind of reliving of Sophie's experience of rejection when her sister Cheryl was adopted into the family; but the material which followed suggested that Sophie was even more concerned about her brother James's birth. For after I again interpreted Sophie's need to know that I *wouldn't* throw her away, even when she showed me *these* feelings, she quieted and acted out a birth. Sophie was the mother and Sarah was the baby. After the birth was complete, Sophie used the syringe from a play doctor kit to take a blood sample (quite literally) from herself; this was "to see if she [Sarah] is adopted."

James was, of course, the one Ford child who was *not* adopted. Sophie's enactment communicated her confusion about adoption and birth; it also contained the implication that the child would not be kept if she were found to have been adopted.

Sophie's anger and jealousy filled the final week of treatment before the summer holiday. She killed off her rivals, saying that she was going to "wash Sarah's head in boiling water," and that "a baby boy in the hospital had had an injection in his head and died." She was furious that I continued to see Robert and accused me of being "engaged" to him. She tried to undo her adoption and thereby her feelings of rejection by insisting that she had been adopted by Sophie Robertson (her biological mother); by implication Mrs. Ford then became her "real" mother. And she tried to hit me in the groin, to castrate me so that I would not go off with my "wife" during the holiday. Thus, Sophie's reactions to the holiday included elements from the oral, anal, and phallic-oedipal levels of libidinal development. In terms of her object relationships, other people were seen only as unwelcome intruders who cost her my love.

Despite her painful feelings of rejection and anger, Sophie was still able to respond positively to interpretations. For example, when she took the active role and ordered me to "make something" with the plasticine, I began making links for a chain and said that she and I needed *something* to keep us together over the long holiday. While she was initially taken aback by this, Sophie herself repeated and elaborated the chain the next day; then she wrapped the chain around one of her wrists and around one of mine, handcuffing us together.

Not surprisingly, Sophie was unable to allow herself this feeling of attachment for very long; it made her feel too vulnerable to rejection. When the time to end the session approached, she pulled the chain off and threw it at me, then tried to kick and bite me.

Sophie was, however, aware that her worries and her pain were internal and that she needed treatment. Before the end of the last preholiday session Sophie ordered me to "drink some medicine" which would make me "nervous"; the same medicine would make her "less nervous," she said. She added, "I'm nervous too much and I don't want to be."

At the end of this initial phase of treatment it was clear that Sophie saw herself as someone who would be rejected because of her instinctual impulses; she was dirty, sexual, and aggressive, and would be abandoned or killed because of these feelings. In this she was very reminiscent of Barnes's (1953) case, Carl, who feared that he would be abandoned because of his messy enuresis. In the card game Sophie portrayed herself as the victim of chance, a child whose own feelings and attachments were ignored as others made decisions about her placement.

Many of these feelings and aspects of Sophie's self and object representations can be understood from what is known about Sophie's parents and their attitudes toward their first adopted daughter. We must realize, however, that the dynamics of the interaction between Sophie and her parents are not different in kind from those that take place between biologically related children and parents. What seems to have happened here is that the parents' tendency to repudiate the clearly instinctual parts of human life (a tendency which may well have been involved in their infertility) meshed with the external fact that Sophie was someone else's child and led to the parents' repudiation of important aspects of Sophie. Sophie was not able to conform to her parents' expectations and responded to their rejection with provocative attacks and rejections of her own.

CASE 2

Arthur was referred for treatment at age 11 because his provocative, aggressive behavior repeatedly disrupted his school classes. Arthur had been given up for adoption at birth and was placed for adoption at 1 month of age. At 5 months, when he was discovered to be profoundly and congenitally deaf, his adoptive parents returned him to the adoption agency. He was readopted a month later by Mr. and Mrs. Sprout.

Mrs. Sprout was a teacher of the deaf, and the Sprouts had been actively seeking to adopt a deaf child; they had three children of their own, aged 10, 8, and 6, at the time they adopted Arthur. A very religiously motivated family, they consciously decided to devote a great deal of their energy to helping Arthur become as much like a hearing person as they possibly could. To this end they enrolled him in special schools which emphasized speech training and forbade sign language.

At home Mrs. Sprout took it upon herself to continue the teaching which Arthur received during the day. She made a special point of turning his face toward her whenever she was talking to him; if Arthur was not looking at her, she would grab his chin and turn it, disregarding his obvious resistance to these intrusions.

The Sprouts elected not to discuss with Arthur the fact that he had been adopted, even though they had three older children in the house. When I first saw them for a consultation, they still believed that Arthur did not know he was adopted. At the same time they described to me how Arthur often put a "For Sale" sign on the door of his bedroom when he was upset.

The Sprouts did not repudiate Arthur's instinctual behavior, as the Fords did with Sophie. Actually, the Sprouts sometimes seemed to take a great deal of pleasure in relating the trouble which Arthur gave to his teachers. They presented Arthur's behavior problems as normal childhood responses to unreasonable demands by his teachers, in spite of the fact that the problems were so severe that Arthur was repeatedly sent home from school because of them.

Arthur's linguistic communication skills were very poor when he began treatment. Despite eight years of intensive educational efforts and average nonverbal intelligence scores, Arthur could not speak intelligibly or in sentences and could not write more than one- or two-word "sentences." He relied almost entirely on his facility in mimicry for communication, and his parents discouraged his use of sign language.

It was not until six months after the beginning of twice weekly treatment that the issue of enrolling Arthur in a program which would allow both speech and sign language came up. This idea met the fierce opposition of Mrs. Sprout, who believed that sign language would isolate Arthur from his hearing peers. Some intensive work with Mrs. Sprout, aimed at clarifying her motives in this very logically defended choice, led to the revelation by Mrs. Sprout that she was quite certain that she herself was unable to learn sign language. Moreover, she felt that if Arthur were allowed to learn sign language, he would then want to communicate only with people who knew sign language and she would be abandoned. Her refusal to entertain the option of sign language was based upon a fear she would lose her son.

From Arthur's material it emerged that he felt in danger of being rejected because he was deaf. He repeatedly brought a portable "citizen's band" 2-way radio (which had been given him by his parents) to his sessions and attempted to communicate with other people by using this. Unsuccessful, he again and again removed the back and tried to fix the insides of the radio so that he could hear. When I interpreted his wish for a set of ears that worked properly, Arthur looked away, putting himself "out of touch." He then began confronting me with choices: did I like this game or that game, this person or that person? I interpreted this as Arthur's wish to know if I liked him or someone else, adding that many children, and especially adopted children, had such worries. Arthur then closed his eyes and said that they "hurt."

Thus it appeared that Arthur's feelings about being deaf and being adopted were interwoven. His self representation seemed to include elements of a defective, unwanted boy who was in danger of being rejected. This image, when coupled with his inability to meet his parents' fantasies (of creating a "normal" child out of a profoundly deaf child), left Arthur with the need to test again and again whether or not he would be rejected.

When I linked Arthur's testing behavior to his anxieties about adoption and rejection, he drew signs which read "For Sale" and "Sold." Arthur then told me that his adoptive parents had paid 200 dollars for him when he was a baby. While it never became clear whether Arthur thought this was a small or a large investment, it was clear that he had constructed a fantasy that he had been sold to his adoptive parents. The connection we had made between Arthur's testing behavior and his "For Sale" feelings was a fruitful one, for Arthur expanded upon it by making "father," "mother," and "baby" hats. Arthur was dissatisfied with his first "baby" hat and wanted to discard it in favor of a new "baby" hat. I interpreted this to Arthur as an expression of his worry that he might not be good enough for his parents.

When I discussed some of this material with Arthur's adoptive parents (in Arthur's presence), his mother spontaneously brought up the fact that she and her husband actually were Arthur's third set of parents; his second set of parents had gotten rid of Arthur when they found that he was deaf. Mrs. Sprout added that she and her husband had never tried to explain this to Arthur because they were sure it would be too confusing for him. This discussion was followed by a marked improvement in Arthur's ability to limit his provocative behavior.

CASE 3

Anna was given up for adoption at birth and prior to the diagnosis of rubella syndrome pathology. While her vision turned out to be relatively intact, she was profoundly deaf and in need of heart repair surgery. During the preoperative diagnostic work at 2 months of age, a technical error led to the destruction of a major portion of the blood supply to her right arm, which had to be amputated just below the elbow. After spending an extended period of time in the hospital, Anna was eventually placed in a foster home, where she stayed until she was 3 ½ years old. At that time she was reported to have "autistic features"; her hearing loss had not yet been documented.

Anna was adopted by a single woman, Ms. Roberts, who had approached the adoption agency seeking a "handicapped female." Ms. Roberts, a nurse in a pediatric oncology unit, had herself been adopted as a child. Her memories of childhood were very painful as she recalled abuse by her adoptive parents; she was eventually hospitalized for 2 years, suffering from what she termed "anorexia nervosa" at the age of 11.

It was clear that Ms. Roberts had chosen a child who reminded her of her own childhood. It was equally clear that Ms. Roberts had managed to surmount tremendous odds in her own life and had dealt with her own experiences of deprivation by becoming a provider, as a nurse, for many other children. Ms. Roberts was quite aware of this as the result of many years of therapy.

Despite this insight, Ms. Roberts had not been able to avoid developing a very conflictual relationship with Anna. When Ms. Roberts brought Anna for an initial consultation, she reported that she and Anna, who was then 6 years old, were constantly angry with each other. Ms. Roberts felt that Anna often took pleasure in defeating her mother's attempts to help her, especially in the area of communication.

In treatment Anna quickly made it clear that her prosthesis, which ended in a grasping hook which she could manipulate very skillfully, was an important issue in her self image. She leaned against me with the prosthesis, touched me with it, came to one session without it, and finally played the part of a monster coming to attack me with it. Clearly, Anna sometimes felt that she was dangerous and frightening as well as defective.

Ms. Roberts, like Mrs. Sprout, chose to educate her deaf child without using sign language. She hoped to give Anna a "normal" childhood which would allow her to be fully integrated with nonhandicapped children in school and in other social situations. These wishes were not pathological in themselves; but insofar as they did not recognize Anna's very real limitations, they proved the source of great stress for both mother and daughter. At times Ms. Roberts demanded speech quality far beyond Anna's ability; at other times Ms. Roberts "gave up" and dropped all demands for communication with Anna. For her part, Anna learned to manipulate her mother via the quality of her speech, which was sometimes much worse than what Anna was capable of.

Ms. Roberts brought treatment to a sudden and early end when she decided that she would invest her limited resources in additional speech therapy for Anna, rather than in continued psychotherapy. Nonetheless, it had already become clear that Anna's self representation included an element which might be labeled the "defective monster who is rejected." It was also clear that Anna's adoptive mother had a similar self representation and that she was attempting to heal some aspect of herself by providing for Anna. Finally it was clear that Anna was engaged in a great deal of testing of her adoptive mother's commitment to her as she flirted with her mother's boyfriend in an openly sexual way.

DISCUSSION

The fact that a child is adopted does not by itself produce psychopathology. Nor are the psychological conflicts outlined in this paper and illustrated in the three cases different in kind from the psychological conflicts seen in children living with their biological parents. Nonetheless, there are some issues which appear to be particularly important in the psychoanalytic treatment of adopted children.

ISSUES IN ANALYTIC TREATMENT

The treatment of adopted children usually cannot be divorced from the treatment of the adoptive parents. This is because adoption is almost always linked in the parents with powerful affects and conflicts related to the issues of infertility, illegitimacy, and parenthood. Beyond these, the adoptive parents need to be able to deal with the instinctual sides of human life and with the ambivalence of their children without resorting to externalization and projection. They must also have resolved their oedipal conflicts sufficiently to permit them to take someone else's child as their own. In adoptive parents who have not resolved their oedipal conflicts, the adoption of a child can mobilize so much guilt that they are forced into the actualization of "rescue" fantasies. (This actualization is effective only if the act of rescuing and its consequent approbation somehow undo the act of stealing and its consequent guilt.)

Unresolved conflicts in adoptive parents can mesh with normal developmental conflicts in the adopted child to produce an extremely pathological result. Eiduson and Livermore (1953) clearly described a vicious circle in which the normal instinctuality of an adopted child produces anxiety in adoptive parents who have severely repressed their own instinctual lives.

The parental anxiety leads to attempts to repress the child's expression of his instinctual urges. If such attempts are not successful, the parents reject that (instinctual) part of the child and attribute it to the biological parents. The child, perceiving that he has been rejected because of his instinctual urges, must repudiate either a part of himself or the parental demands. If he does the latter, it is often by provocative behavior aimed precisely at the areas of instinctuality which have been repressed by his parents. Thus the cycle begins again, but usually is reenacted at an increasingly higher pitch. The cycle eventually leads to overt rejection of the child by the parents and of the parents by the child.

The adopted child has a particular difficulty in the resolution of ambivalence toward his parents. In describing their group of adopted children seen in treatment, Eiduson and Livermore (1953) concluded, "None of these children had 'accepted' the fact of adoption in the sense of facing [the fact] that these adoptive parents, with their good and their bad sides, *are* his parents, the ones with whom he is going to have to work out his own inner feelings of both love and hate" (p. 800).

In a similar fashion the adoptive parents have a particular problem in the resolution of their ambivalence toward the adopted child. While the child is loved, he is also representative of the parental failure to conceive. Furthermore, the child's obscure genealogy offers an excellent opportunity for the externalization of instinctual behavior; the child then becomes two different children to the adoptive parents: "our" good child and "their" bad child. These two parental representations of the child certainly are perceived by the child; indeed, it is likely that the child will incorporate them into his or her own self representation.

It is by now obvious that the treatment of an adoptive child will necessarily include analysis of transference manifestations deriving from both the adoptive parent and the (unknown) biological parents. The fact that the adopted child has little or no information about his biological parents does not prevent the child from constructing elaborate fantasies about these parents in order to make sense of his adoption.

Adopted children can be compared to children who have experienced real losses or traumas which reinforce their neurotic conflicts. All the psychoanalytic investigation and assistance in the world cannot undo the fact that the adopted child has been rejected or abandoned. This is one reason why adopted children present a particularly difficult therapeutic challenge.

Given the factual basis of his rejection by his biological parents, it is perhaps not surprising that the adopted child repeatedly tests the commitment of his adoptive parents. This testing is often extremely destructive, for the child's anxiety about rejection does not disappear after he has tested his adoptive parents. The child increases his demands for acceptance by engaging in behavior which becomes more and more unacceptable to his parents. Unfortunately such children often end up provoking precisely the outcome which they feared. It is important to help the adoptive child to recognize the self-destructive potential of this pattern and to limit it to the treatment.

Another issue which is particularly important in the treatment of adopted children is a wish to be adopted by the therapist. This wish sometimes appears in the treatment of nonadopted children and can at times be related to the family romance fantasies often seen in latency-age children. In adopted children, however, this wish has a special intensity; the child has, after all, been transferred from one set of parents to another in the past. More important, however, is the fact that his wish may conceal a fantasy that the therapist is, in fact, one of the adopted child's biological parents who has returned to reclaim his child.

The fantasy that the therapist is a biological parent come to reclaim the adopted child as his own expresses what is very likely the core problem for many adopted children—the creation of a self representation as a "wanted" child. This wish, which is certainly a healthy one on the part of the child, puts the therapist in a delicate dilemma. He must help the child to come to terms with a real loss without repeating the loss. He must help the child give up the fantasy that his biological parents have returned to claim him, while nurturing the child's sense of self-esteem and preserving his relationship with his adoptive parents. Here the family romances of adopted children may shed some important light.

Family romance may, however, be a misnomer. For while a biological child may make use of a fantasy of rich and powerful parents from whom he was stolen or adopted and thus maintain in fantasy some remnant of the relationship he once had with his parents in the days before he realized the limitations of their resources and power (Freud, 1909), the adopted child is faced with a more sobering reality. In the case of Sophie, her initial fantasies about her "other" parents included a murderous mother and an ineffectual father. Sophie's fantasies thus resembled those of the adopted children reported by Wieder (1977b) who felt that they had been "gotten rid of" by their biological parents. This observation is also supported by Glenn (1974) who noted that the adopted child may feel that his adoptive parents "consider him a possession rather than a person" (p. 415). It was only relatively late in Sophie's treatment that her self representation was modified to include some feelings of being wanted and valuable, that Sophie hesitantly began to speculate that her biological parents might have been richer and more generous than her adoptive parents. This observation suggests that an important contributor to the family romance in "normal" children may be their ability to recall a time when they experienced themselves as the unambivalently cathected "special" children of special and omnipotent parents. Such an experience would contribute greatly to the creation of a self representation in which the child sees himself as valuable and "wanted."

Adoption is an area in which preventive efforts have special importance. While acknowledging the limitations of our ability to predict who will be good adoptive parents (Goldstein et al., 1973), we can recognize that the parents of adoptive children are in need of some special support. The experience of F. G. Brown (1959) in group meetings with adoptive parents is one example of an effort to help parents deal with the affect-laden topics of infertility and illegitimacy. It is important to realize that such interventions are needed at several points during the development of the adopted child. An assessment of unresolved conflicts in the adoptive parents will provide some clues as to those stages in the development of the child at which the parent might be in need of outside help. In addition, adoption per se can complicate normal developmental phenomena such as oedipal conflicts, the family romance in latency, and the adolescent search for a coherent, independent identity.

Multiple placements, delay in placements, and delay in the legal ratification of adoptions all contribute to the association of adoptions with psychopathology. Goldstein et al. (1973) have written at length on this topic, as have Chestang and Heymann (1973) and Franklin and Massarik (1969). It is important to recognize that repeated interruptions and delays in the process of the adoption make it difficult for the child to develop a representation of himself as a wanted child. Such delays have an effect on the child even when they occur at a very early age, for they affect the adoptive parents' representations of both themselves and their adopted child.

Preventive intervention thus includes changes in the policies and procedures regarding adoption. It also includes changes in the laws surrounding adoption and the attitudes expressed in those laws. The statutes governing adoptions in California, while encouraging speedy resolution of decisions regarding the custody of a child, still assume that the "rights" of the biological parents of a child are paramount; they make no mention of the importance of psychological ties the child may have established with other parenting figures except in the case of a decision whether or not to remove a child already out of the custody of his biological parents from his foster parents (California Welfare and Institutions Code, 1977, Section 366.5). The laws do not recognize that their object—the adopted child—is actively creating representations of himself and of others based upon the experiences to which he is subjected under the law.

NEWLY EMERGING ISSUES

There has been strong endorsement in recent years of a change in philosophy in the administration of adoptions which allows for the adoption of "hard-to-place" children such as older children, children with disabilities, multiracial children, and children adopted by parents of a different race than their own (Chestang and Heymann, 1973; Franklin and Massarik, 1969; Young, 1971). The specific issue of transracial adoptions has been raised by the American Academy of Pediatrics, Committee on Adoption and Dependent Care (1973), W. T. Brown (1973), Fanshel (1972), Hagen and Hall (1973), Robertson (1974), and Spence (1975). All of these developments contain the implicit assumption that parents can successfully adopt and parent a child who has sustained important losses and who is quite obviously "different" from his adoptive parents. While I do not disagree with this assumption in principle, I believe that such adoptions will be particularly vulnerable to disturbances in the establishment of mutually satisfactory object relationships between the adopted children and their adoptive parents. This is because each of these groups—older children, multiracial children, and children adopted across racial lines—will experience special problems that will be reflected in their self and object representations, which in turn will influence their object relationships.

CULTURAL RELATIVISM: A CAUTIONARY NOTE

In closing I would like to stress the cultural relativism of the ideas presented in this paper. There is a vast range of cultural attitudes toward adoption. Among the Marquesans, for example, adoption occurred at the request of the adoptive parents and independently of the wishes of the biological parents; a family could requisition a child from another family even before the child was born, and refusal to accede to such a request was grounds for a serious blood feud (Linton, 1936). The Hopi developed a system of adoption which existed in parallel with blood ties, so that everyone within a tribe was related to everyone else by either blood or adoption (Thompson and Joseph, 1944). In Manus, adoption became a way of strengthening the economic status of the family; yet the relationship of the adopted person was always somewhat tenuous as, in times of crisis, the adoption might be repudiated in favor of blood ties (Mead, 1956). Among the Gusii in Kenya, there is a proverb which, roughly translated, says, "It is better to adopt an orphan cow than to adopt an orphan child." In that culture there is a belief that an adopted child will, sooner or later, abandon his adoptive parents and return to the household of the man who paid the bridewealth for his mother; a child who does not do this is considered deviant (LeVine, 1979). Even within Western European cultures there have been historical periods when great numbers of children were placed outside of their home for months or even years, to be fed by wetnurses or to be apprenticed into a trade (Aries, 1960). These examples, however brief, clearly demonstrate that the view of adoption presented in this paper is a very limited one.

BIBLIOGRAPHY

AMERICAN ACADEMY OF PEDIATRICS, COMMITTEE ON ADOPTION AND DEPENDENT CARE (1973), Transracial Adoption. *Pediatrics*, 51:145–148.
ARIES, P. (1960), *Centuries of Childhood.* Harmondsworth, Middlesex: Penguin.
BARNES, M. J. (1953), The Working-Through Process in Dealing with Anxiety around Adoption. *Amer. J. Orthopsychiat.*, 23:605–620.
BERNARD, V. W. (1974), Adoption. In: *American Handbook of Psychiatry*, ed. S. Arieti. New York: Basic Books, 2nd ed., pp. 513–534.
BLUM, L. H. (1959), Sterility and the Magic Power of the Maternal Figure. *J. Nerv. Ment. Dis.*, 128:401–408.
BOHMAN, M. (1971), A Comparative Study of Adopted Children, Foster Children and Children in Their Biological Environment Born after Undesired Pregnancies. *Acta Paediat. Scand. Suppl.*, 221:1–38.
BRINICH, P. M. (1977), "A Baby Has Been Stolen." Unpublished paper presented at the Hampstead Child-Therapy Clinic, London.

BRODY, S., AXELRAD, S., & MOROH, M. (1976), Early Phases in the Development of Object Relations. *Int. Rev. Psycho-Anal.,* 3:1–31.

BROWN, F. G. (1959), Services to Adoptive Parents after Legal Adoption. *Child Welf.,* 38:16–22.

BROWN, W. T. (1973), Racial Devaluation among Transracially Adopted Black Children (Doct. Diss., Ohio State Univ.). *Diss. Abstr. Int.* (Univ. Microfilms No. 74-10921).

CALIFORNIA WELFARE AND INSTITUTIONS CODE, Volume 1, (1977), North Highlands, Calif.: Department of General Services.

CHESTANG, L. & HEYMANN, I. (1973), Reducing the Length of Foster Care. *Soc. Wk,* 18:88–92.

CLOTHIER, F. (1943), The Psychology of the Adopted Child. *Ment. Hyg.,* 27:222–230.

COMMENTS (1972), Adoption. *Med. J. Austral.,* 2:1098–1099.

DAUNTON, E. (1974), The Opening Phase of Treatment in an Adopted Child with a Symptom of Encopresis. Read at meeting of the Association for Child Psychoanalysis, Ann Arbor, Mich.

DI LEO, J. H. (1973), The Special Needs of the Adopted Child. *Med. Insight,* 5:38–40.

EIDUSON, B. N. & LIVERMORE, J. B. (1953), Complications in Therapy with Adopted Children. *Amer. J. Orthopsychiat.,* 23:795–802.

ESCALONA, S. K. (1968), *The Roots of Individuality.* Chicago: Aldine.

FANSHEL, D. (1972), *Far from the Reservation.* Metuchen, N.J.: Scarecrow Press.

FOGEL, A. (1977), Temporal Organization in Mother-Infant Face-to-Face Interaction. In: Schaffer (1977b), pp. 119–151.

FRANKLIN, D. & MASSARIK, F. (1969), The Adoption of Children with Medical Conditions: Parts I-III. *Child Welf.,* 48:459–467; 533–539; 595–601.

FREUD, A. (1973), Infants Without Families. *W.,* 3.

FREUD, S. (1909), Family Romances. *S.E.,* 9:235–241.

GARDNER, L. I. (1972), Deprivation Dwarfism. *Sci. American,* 227:76–82.

GLENN, J. (1974), The Adoption Theme in Edward Albee's *Tiny Alice* and *The American Dream. This Annual,* 29:413–429.

GOLDSTEIN, J., FREUD, A., & SOLNIT, A. J. (1973), *Beyond the Best Interests of the Child.* New York: Free Press.

GOODMAN, J. D. & MAGNO-NORA, R. (1975), Adoption and Its Influence During Adolescence. *J. Med. Soc. N.J.,* 72:922–928.

HAGEN, C. & HALL, M. (1973), Transracial Adoption. *Clin. Soc. Wk J.,* 1:53–57.

HUMPHREY, M. & OUNSTED, C. (1963), Adoptive Families Referred for Psychiatric Advice: Part I. *Brit. J. Psychiat.,* 109:599–608.

——— (1964), Adoptive Families Referred for Psychiatric Advice: Part II. *Brit. J. Psychiat.,* 110:549–555.

JACKSON, L. (1968), Unsuccessful Adoptions. *Brit. J. Med. Psychol.,* 41:389–398.

KADUSHIN, A. (1967), A Follow-Up Study of Children Adopted When Older. *Amer. J. Orthopsychiat.,* 37:530–539.

KAYE, K. (1977), Toward the Origin of Dialogue. In: Schaffer (1977b), pp. 89–117.

KRIS, E. (1956), The Personal Myth. *J. Amer. Psychoanal. Assn.*, 4:653–681.

KRUGMAN, D. C. (1968), A New Home for Liz. *J. Amer. Acad. Child Psychiat.*, 7:398–420.

LEVINE, R. A. (1979), Personal communication.

LIFSHITZ, M., BAUM, R., BALGUR, I., & COHEN, C. (1975), The Impact of the Social Milieu upon the Nature of Adoptees' Emotional Difficulties. *J. Marriage & Fam.*, 37:221–228.

LINTON, R. (1936), *The Study of Man.* New York: Appleton-Century.

McWHINNIE, A. M. (1969), The Adopted Child in Adolescence. In: *Adolescence*, ed. G. Caplan & S. Lebovici. New York: Basic Books, pp. 133–142.

MAHLER, M. S., PINE, F., & BERGMAN, A. (1975), *The Psychological Birth of the Human Infant.* New York: Basic Books.

MEAD, M. (1956), *New Lives for Old.* New York: William Morrow.

MENLOVE, F. L. (1965), Aggressive Symptoms in Emotionally Disturbed Adopted Children. *Child Develpm.*, 36:519–532.

NEVRLA, V. (1972), [The Problem of the Adoptive Child.] *Psychol. Patopsychol. Dietata* (Bratislava), 7:79–82.

OFFORD, D. R., APONTE, J. F., & CROSS, L. A. (1969), Presenting Symptomatology of Adopted Children. *Arch. Gen. Psychiat.*, 20:110–116.

PAWLBY, S. J. (1977), Imitative Interaction. In: Schaffer (1977b), pp. 203–224.

REECE, S. A. & LEVIN, B. (1968), Psychiatric Disturbances in Adopted Children. *Soc. Wk*, 13:101–111.

REEVES, A. C. (1971), Children with Surrogate Parents. *Brit. J. Med. Psychol.*, 44:155–171.

ROBERTSON, D. C. (1974), Parental Socialization Patterns in Interracial Adoption (Doct. Diss., Univ. California, Los Angeles). *Diss. Abstr. Int.* (Univ. Microfilms No. 75-1998).

SANDLER, J. & ROSENBLATT, B. (1962). The Concept of the Representational World. *This Annual*, 17:128–145.

SANTS, H. J. (1964), Genealogical Bewilderment in Children with Substitute Parents. *Brit. J. Med. Psychol.*, 37:133–141.

SCHAFFER, H. R. (1977a), Early Interactive Development. In: Schaffer (1977b), pp. 3–16.

—— ed. (1977b), *Studies in Mother-Infant Interaction.* New York: Academic Press.

—— COLLIS, G. M., & PARSONS, G. (1977), Vocal Interchange and Visual Regard in Verbal and Pre-Verbal Children. In: Schaffer (1977b), pp. 291–324.

SCHECHTER, M. D. (1960), Observations on Adopted Children. *Arch. Gen. Psychiat.*, 3:21–32.

—— (1967), Psychoanalytic Theory As It Relates to Adoption. *J. Amer. Psychoanal. Assn.*, 15:695–708.

—— (1973), A Case Study of an Adopted Child. *Int. J. Child Psychother.*, 2:202–223.

—— CARLSON, P. V., SIMMONS, J. Q., & WORK, H. H. (1964), Emotional Problems in the Adoptee. *Arch. Gen. Psychiat.*, 10:109–118.

SIMON, N. M. & SENTURIA, A. G. (1966), Adoption and Psychiatric Illness. *Amer. J. Psychiat.*, 122:858–868.

SKEELS, H. M. (1972), Effects of Adoption on Children from Institutions. In: *Childhood Psychopathology*, ed. S. I. Harrison & J. F. McDermott. New York: Int. Univ. Press, pp. 757–760.

SPENCE, S. (1975), Some Considerations of the Adoption of Vietnamese Children. *Int. Soc. Wk*, 18:10-20.

SPITZ, R. A. (1965), *The First Year of Life*. New York: Int. Univ. Press.

STERN, D. N., BEEBE, B., JAFFE, J., & BENNETT, S. L. (1977), The Infant's Stimulus World during Social Interaction. In: Schaffer (1977b), pp. 177–202.

SWEENEY, D. M., GASBARRO, D. T., & GLUCK, M. R. (1963), A Descriptive Study of Adopted Children Seen in a Child Guidance Center. *Child Welf.*, 42:345–349.

THOMPSON, L. & JOSEPH, A. (1944), *The Hopi Way*. Chicago: Univ. Chicago Press.

TOUSSIENG, P. W. (1962), Thoughts Regarding the Etiology of Psychological Difficulties in Adopted Children. *Child Welf.*, 41:59-65, 71.

WALSH, E. D. & LEWIS, F. S. (1969), A Study of Adoptive Mothers in a Child Guidance Clinic. *Soc. Casewk*, 50:587-594.

WIEDER, H. (1977a), On Being Told of Adoption. *Psychoanal. Quart.*, 46:1-22.

——— (1977b), The Family Romance Fantasies of Adopted Children. *Psychoanal. Quart.*, 46:185-200.

——— (1978), On When and Whether to Disclose about Adoption. *J. Amer. Psychoanal. Assn.*, 26:793-811.

WINICK, M., MEYER, K. K., & HARRIS, R. C. (1975), Malnutrition and Environmental Enrichment by Early Adoption. *Science*, 190:1173-1175.

WORK, H. H. & ANDERSON, H. (1971), Studies in Adoption. *Amer. J. Psychiat.*, 127:948-950.

YOUNG, R. E. (1971), From Matching to Making in Adoption (D.S.W. Diss., Univ. Pennsylvania). *Diss. Abstr. Int.* (Univ. Microfilms No. 72-28819).

ZIATEK, K. (1974), [Psychological Problems of Adoption.] *Psychol. Wychowawcza* (Warsaw), 17:63-76.

Siblings of Twins

BETH A. BERNSTEIN

THERE IS AN EXTENSIVE LITERATURE WHICH FOCUSES ON THE FATE-ful significance of being a twin. However, the effects on a nontwin sibling of having siblings who are twins have not been examined.

Steff Bornstein (1935) reported the analysis of a 3-year-old boy whose twin siblings were born when he was 2½. He was brought to treatment because of anal symptoms and preoccupation with bowel movements. In the very first session, it was clear that he held back his stool, "not for the sake of autoerotic satisfaction, but out of anxiety" (p. 191). The analysis disclosed that he equated his stool with his little twin brothers and that his retention of stool was an attempt to prevent the birth of any more twin brothers. He was intensely rivalrous with the twins, had death wishes against his mother for bearing the twins, severe castration anxiety, and oral aggression manifested especially in a wish to eat the twins which he projected in a story onto a "bad boy." Bornstein did not stress that the siblings were twins.

Burlingham (1952) noted, "The fuss and excitement over the twins not only by the mother but by everybody who comes into contact with them can only increase the jealousy" of the older nontwin sibling (p. 9).

Lidz et al. (1962) studied identical schizophrenic twins and mentioned parenthetically, "We have, in this presentation, neglected the older brother of the twins. His situation was difficult and unenviable—rejected by his mother who wished to use him as she did the father as a pawn in preparing the way for her twin kings. He . . . had serious emotional problems" (p. 87). Lidz et al.

Member, Association for Child Psychoanalysis.

nevertheless demonstrated that the birth of the twins caused a disturbance in the entire family.

Joseph (1975) reported that the development of one of his patients was significantly influenced by the fact that she had older twin siblings. She complained that she was the only one who was alone; her parents had each other as a pair and the twins were a pair. "She felt a desperate need to unite with someone, so that she, too, could be part of a pair like the others" (p. 27).

I have analyzed several patients who were siblings of younger twins. The cases I shall present demonstrate that these siblings incessantly searched for a twin. As a result of the attempt to master their rivalry, they identified with the twins, but the attitude toward the twins was so ambivalent that the attempts were doomed to fail. These single siblings of twins had particular difficulty in separating, marked penis envy, oedipal rivalry, ambivalence toward love objects, depression, guilt, unusually strong reaction formations, competitiveness, and homosexual feelings and fears. All of these are, of course, universal phenomena, but in these siblings of twins, they were intensified. Many patients with no twin relatives have had the fantasy of having a twin, a constant companion, an alter ego, a mirror of the self. The actual experience of having twin siblings is, for the most part, painful and fateful for the nature of future object choices.

CASE PRESENTATIONS

CASE 1

Laurie L. was a slender, 4-year-old girl with long, dark hair, a lively expression, and sparkling, dark eyes. She was timid, shy, tense, withdrawn, fearful, and unable to leave the house unless one of her younger twin sisters accompanied her. Her parents feared that Laurie's phobia would spread and that she would be unable to start nursery school. Mrs. L. reported, "Laurie just loves her twin sisters and won't go anywhere without them." It mattered little which one of the twins; at that time, Laurie showed no preferences.

The parents also complained that Laurie bullied everyone in the house, that she was a terrible sleeper, was high-strung and willful. They agreed that when "Laurie is home, the house is in an uproar; she has always been a special person, not your run-of-the-mill child." On the one hand, everything had to be controlled for her; for example, she would ask anxiously, "How do I cross the street? Is Anne coming with me? Does she have to wear her boots? Is Joan staying home with Vera [the housekeeper]?" On the other hand, Laurie intimidated everyone and wanted to control everything.

Laurie was seen in five-times weekly analysis, which lasted five years. She came to her first appointments escorted by her mother; she clung to Mrs. L.'s hand, begging for "one more kiss," whispering secrets, grasping her mother's skirt in panic, demanding a hug or a final, and yet another kiss. Several weeks later, after this behavior had lost its frenetic quality, I remarked that I had once known a little girl who demanded kisses and hugs from her mother because she was afraid that her mother would be angry if she realized that her daughter was happy to stay and talk with me alone. Laurie answered simply, "It's the same with me."

By the seventh week of treatment, Laurie told me, "I have no problems, well, just one. When Mommy goes out. It doesn't bother me at all when the twins go out. In fact," at this point Laurie looked at me hesitantly, and then continued, "is it bad if I wish they would die? But I'll die first because I'm older. Mommy will die even sooner." All of this was said with no affect.

By the third month of analysis, the mother could remain in the car or go on a shopping trip during Laurie's analytic hour. From the beginning of treatment, Laurie was an obstreperous, demanding child who hurled toys around my office, crumbled cookies, methodically destroyed everything in the dollhouse, jabbed at everything until she had broken it. Yet, surprisingly, when it was essential to set limits on her wildness in my office, she responded with contentment. She ground crayons together in such a way that she would streak a yellow crayon across the paper and a red line would appear, or she would draw with a black crayon and a green line would appear. She crowed, "When I do this, one color doesn't have to be alone all the time." Asked what it made her think of, she answered, "That is the hardest part—to be alone. If I had a twin like Anne and Joan, I'd never have to be alone." After a silence she told me she would never play Farmer in the Dell with her friends because "I might end up as the cheese and I'd have to stand alone and everyone would walk around and sing Hi-O, the dairy-o, the cheese stands alone." Tears came to her eyes at the thought.

Laurie constantly complained that she was the only one in the house who had to sleep alone. Then one day she said, "I'm not really the only one. Vera sleeps alone, too. No, the hardest part for me is to be alone."

I had carefully prepared Laurie for a long weekend interruption. When, at the end of the session on Thursday, I reminded her that I would not see her again until Monday, she suddenly complained of dizziness, looked frightened, and collapsed onto her hands and knees. I had to dress her like an infant and, unable to stand on her feet, she wobbled her way to the door on her hands and knees. At the door she stood up, started down the stairs sedately, and, halfway down, she turned and asked, "Will you write to me while you're away? Two times or three?" Laurie's way of showing me how helpless it made her feel to face even a brief separation was so transparent that it needed no interpretation. In one way or another, it was repeated every time there was a separation from me, even for one session, if I initiated it. Her histrionic manner was both characteristic and frequently charming and expressive.

Laurie demonstrated her intense possessiveness, separation anxiety, and sibling rivalry in her fantasies, dreams, and behavior in the transference. For example, she would lock the door as she left the office in order to prevent my next patient from entering. One day Randy, the child whom I saw after Laurie, arrived early, waiting quietly outside. To express her disapproval, Laurie walked over sternly and locked the door. On another occasion, while Randy waited outside, Laurie held the clock, watching as the last few seconds of her session ticked away. Forlornly, she left complaining, "My dumb mother isn't even there yet. She never is there when she knows I'm waiting."

One day Laurie brought me a "book" she had made. It was a sheet of paper with a picture of the sun shining at the top left corner; the moon was in the right top corner. Between the two, a flower grew out of the grass on a tall stalk on which a large phallic-looking object sprouted. By this time her preference for Anne had emerged and she told me, "Anne is the sun and that stupid Joan is the moon. I'm the flower in the middle." She considered the drawing silently for a moment and then said, "I wish it could be just me and Anne. Then we'd be twins." Asked what the flower reminded her of, she replied impatiently, "It's me—because I'm not like other girls. I'm special."

Mrs. L. told me of Laurie's endless preoccupation with the sleeping arrangements for herself and the twins. One night Laurie would demand that Anne sleep with her, leaving Joan to sleep alone; the next night Laurie would decide that both twins were to sleep in her room and she would sleep alone in their somewhat larger room. Everyone in the family agreed to these demands, but Laurie slept no better elsewhere than she did in her own room. She complained to her mother, "The twins keep me awake because I have to watch them and listen to what they say to each other all night." Asked if she would like to share a room with one of the twins, Laurie replied angrily, "I would hate, hate, hate to share a room with either one of them." A more acceptable alternative occurred to Laurie a moment later: "I might like to share a room with Mommy and then if I had a bad dream, Mommy would be right there."

Laurie repeatedly called Vera to ask, "Are Anne and Joan home yet? Are they crying? Are they smiling? Are they eating already? Don't let them go into my room!"

Laurie repeatedly used the numbers two and three in a context which represented traces of her preoccupation with the twins and her wish to duplicate and triplicate objects, as we both came to understand. This was particularly apparent in her use of stuffed animals (Burlingham, 1952). She frequently lugged to my office large shopping bags crammed with all her treasures: animals always in doubles and later in triplicates. These stuffed animals unmistakably represented her identification with the twins, her longing to be a twin, and to possess and dominate the twins. She not only gave the animals twin names, e.g., Brown-Brown, but openly referred to them as twins. Laurie had never played with dolls, but she hung lovingly over her animal companions. The animals had such reality for Laurie that she once suggested, in all seriousness, that we teach Brown-Brown to eat with a knife and fork. Gradually the twin animals became triplets, still another indication of Laurie's wish to enter the twin relationship by any means. She had inevitably failed in her efforts to separate the twins in reality; now, with the animals, Laurie joined Joan and Anne as the dominant triplet. Asked who the third animal might be, Laurie replied breezily, "They're all twins."

Laurie also acted out the fantasy of being a twin by selecting two of her many girlfriends to form a threesome. She would then set one child against the other; the three children never got along harmoniously. She often wanted to give me a list of her many girlfriends. This long list served many purposes: (1) doubling and tripling; (2) denial of her feelings of aloneness; (3) defense against claustrophobia. She made certain that she was never close for long to any friend because of her fear of excessive intimacy, which was already becoming a character trait. She was also afraid of closed spaces, for example, playing hide-and-seek. In the transference, abusive references to me were opposed to wishes to be with me or be part of me forever.

Laurie played games with my hand puppets, especially with the alligator and the mouse. She wanted me to hold the mouse puppet while she held the alligator puppet. Anxiously Laurie remarked, "The alligator could hold hands with the mouse, but the mouse will bite me." When I asked why the mouse would want to bite Laurie or the Alligator, she said, "Because sometimes I get so angry at the twins that I'd like to bite them. And sometimes I do bite them—but just a small nibble." A day or so later, she became uneasy when a dog barked. She listened for a second bark which never came, and finally said, "G-R-O-W-L." I asked, "What does that sound mean?" "It means shut up or I'll bite you." Her language was often biting. The oral aggressiveness, seen sooner or later in most children, was unusually marked in Laurie, as were the defenses against it.

When Laurie's parents left for a vacation, her grandfather brought her to my office. She came tramping up the stairs, laboriously carrying bags of her stuffed animals, the inanimate victims of her fury. They had been mutilated; arms and legs dangled by a thread, eyes had been ripped out. "Will you help me fix them?" Asked why she wanted them repaired, tears came to her eyes and she said, "Sometimes I feel so bad for what I did to them and then I can't fall asleep." During the entire time that the parents were away, she was unusually placid and contented as we sat together and sewed.

One day, Laurie wanted to play ring-around-the-rosie with the puppets in a circle, holding hands. She began to sing "Eastside, Westside, all around the town, boys and girls together." She interrupted her song to comment "Yuck!" and then continued, "me and maybe a roar." I asked, "Why yuck?" "Boys are so noisy and wild and they think they're great just because they're boys." Her mishearing of the words "Mamie O'Rourke" from the song helped me to understand her intense penis envy and oedipal rage.

When the parents returned from their vacation, Mrs. L. told me that Laurie had had a bad dream, but refused to talk about it. When Laurie came for her session later that day, I told her about her mother's call and asked if she could tell me about the dream. "No, but I'll draw it for you." She proceeded to draw and told me it was the meat section of the supermarket; she pictured herself walking past the meat which reached out to grab her with red, bloody hands. Coming so soon after her mother's absence and her guilt over her destruction of the animal twins, her wish to be as close to me as the twins were to each other, and her feelings of helplessness to right these many wrongs, this dream represented her wish to devour the objects (mother and twin sisters), to be devoured by the mother, with resultant anxiety about these wishes and fear of punishment for them. This was confirmed when she told me that the meat wanted to grab her and eat her up. She added fearfully, "Sometimes I wish I could just grab the twins and bite them. Hard!" I asked, "Is it possible that you are afraid the meat wants to eat you up because you would like to eat your sisters up and make them disappear?" She looked at me steadily for a moment or two and started to gnaw at her knuckles.

Another manifestation of Laurie's wish to have me as the twin emerged when she drew something on a sheet of paper, covered it with her arm, and demanded that I guess what she had drawn. She gave me hints. "C-c-." When I still failed to understand, she gave me a further hint. "Ca-ca-ca-." I guessed "cat" and when that proved to be right, she snapped, "It took you long enough."

I asked, "Is it possible that you are sad that Joan and Anne know what the other one is thinking and it takes me longer to guess what you are thinking? Would you like me to be as close to you as Anne is to Joan?" She looked perplexed. "Aren't we that close?"

The twins wanted Laurie's favor on any terms, as did her friends. She frequently chose one twin and excluded the other, separating them as she did with any child who had an intimate relationship with another child. In this way, Laurie provided herself with the missing twin, separated them, entered the twinship, retaliated for her own aloneness, and made the twins know what it felt like to be an outsider. She became the phallic member of a threesome, as in her drawing of the sun, moon, and phallic flower; in her wish to devour the penis of a boy she played with; and in her persistent obsession with three and its multiples, as in the stuffed animals. In learning these devices for finding twin substitutes, Laurie had been able to give up to some extent her dependence on her mother and on the twins. This was partly because in the treatment she had found an acceptable twin in her bond to me and also destroyed the twins by finding in me a mother with no twin rivals.

The transference was ambivalent and maternal. After the first year of treatment, Laurie would come up to me at the end of the hour and hold her face up to be kissed. After this happened a few times, I asked if it was possible that she wanted me to kiss her good-bye. "I do not! I do not!" At that time she drew a picture of what looked like two large breasts and told me triumphantly, "It's Y-O-U. It's a boat." The transference image of me as a mother, feeder, and the vessel containing the two breast babies emerged here in her conflictual wishes to be inside the object, outside and self-sufficient, and yet to be fused with the object. This perception of me was omnipresent, and its elements were either openly stated or could be clearly derived from her behavior. It was a recapitulation of the behavior observed in the early days of treatment when Laurie clung to her mother. Her asperity was a characterological defense against clinging, tender feelings.

The mother continued to complain that Laurie was unable to fall asleep at night. Laurie insisted, "I have to stay awake at night to listen to the twins whispering together in their room. I try my hardest to listen to what they're saying to each other, but I never can make out the words." "What do you think they talk about, Laurie?" "I don't know, but I hate it, I just hate it that they talk and won't tell me what they're saying." There is no doubt that this was a displacement and an attempt to deny the rage at mother and father for their special relationship, but it was immeasurably intensified by the existence of the twins, by the impenetrable mystery of their intimacy, and by her helplessness to overcome her feelings of being excluded.[1]

Later in the analysis, as Laurie continued to talk about listening at night to the twins' whispering and laughing, or of hearing Vera go to the bathroom, or of Mommy and Daddy talking in their room, I asked, "What do you think Mommy and Daddy talk about together?" "I don't know." Laurie was quiet for a few minutes and then asked, "How do babies grow in the Mommy's belly?" This material illustrates again that Laurie's intense preoccupation with the whispering of the twins had two sources: her feelings of being excluded from the twinship; and her unconscious use of these obsessional thoughts to disguise her curiosity about the sexual activities of her parents. I said I would have a pregnant mother doll the next day, but Laurie arrived carrying a large Bugs Bunny; in one paw the rabbit had a plastic carrot which he held to his mouth. In this way, before I could show Laurie something she really did not want to know, she was showing me. She picked up the "pregnant" doll and said contemputously, "That's not a fat tummy. That's clay." She angrily removed the clay "tummy" and threw it in the wastebasket. Then she removed the tiny baby doll which I had tucked into the clay "tummy" and, holding the baby to the mother doll's mouth, she said softly, "Here's your baby." Laurie was telling me and the doll that she wanted to be the only baby her mother needed. The intensification of her sibling rivalry led to increased oral sadism in fantasies, dreams, symptoms, actions, and character traits.

Circumstances forced a premature termination of the analysis. Laurie understood her parents' wish to discontinue treatment. Faced with the inevitability of separation from me,

1. In conferences with groups of Mothers of Twins Inc. when I described this behavior pattern, all the mothers burst into laughter and then vied in reporting their own similar experiences.

the good mother and long-sought-for twin, Laurie had nothing to say. She spent the last session shuffling through the pile of records looking for her favorite song. She listened to it over and over again until the hour was up, moodily repeating the words of a girl who made up her mind never to get married. As Laurie left the office, she told me, "I'm never going to leave home either. Anne and Joan will and then we won't have to be bothered with the twins anymore."

Three years after the discontinuation of the analysis, I saw Mrs. L. in a follow-up session. She reported that Laurie had gone on an overnight camping trip and had tucked into the bottom corner of her sleeping bag a new, and favorite, stuffed toy, Casper the Ghost. Laurie, then almost 12 years old, had been afraid to spend the night without her twin companion, but she knew her friends would ridicule her if they discovered this childlike need for a stuffed toy. She never got the twin she had sought, but she still wanted a "twin"—for comforting. She chose a ghost figure, which points to the repression of painful infantile affects evoked by the birth of the twins. Such feelings are present in all children, but the reactions are unusually intense and persistent when the child has to deal with twin rivals who consume the mother's attention to an inordinate degree; the twins, in addition, have an almost supernatural, exclusive closeness. This makes the nontwin sibling feel lonely and incomplete. The existence of the twins enables the single sibling to justify unacceptable feelings, but the reality is insurmountable.

A few months later Laurie came for a visit. She told me that Anne was unquestionably her favorite twin, but she would like best to have a sister born a month after her own birthday. She questioned me closely and seriously as to how this could have been worked out. "Say I'm born December, 1975 and Anne is born January, 1976. We'd be in the same class. I'd be older, but we'd be almost the same age."

Laurie was carrying a book which she assured me she had read again and again. It was called *Betsy, Stacy, and Tib* and was about three girls aged 11 "who are best friends."

While Laurie was free of symptoms, successful in school, a leader in her social life, and easy to get along with at home, she still struggled with the problem posed by her being the sibling of twins. She still hoped to solve her dilemma by becoming one of triplets, by separating the twins, and by appropriating the preferred twin.

Naomi was 23 years old when she began her analysis. She was unable to form a stable relationship with a man, usually seeking men whom she recognized to be either sadistic or passive. She lived through long, lonely periods, interrupted by stormy and intense friendships which caused her so much suffering that she inevitably broke them off. She mourned that her effectiveness in her work was diminished because of her frequent depressions and she brooded with a sense of doom which intensified and diminished in the course of the analysis.

Naomi had twin brothers who were 4 years younger than she. She recalled a fantasy in which she was tied to a wall and two men nursed from her breasts. This fantasy related to seeing her mother nurse her twin brothers. As they grew up, her mother relied more and more on Naomi to help take care of them. Naomi felt that this had deprived her of her childhood, but she also felt that she could do a better job than her mother. She took it upon herself to discipline the twins, which she did by beating them severely with her father's belt.

Naomi's relationships with men began masochistically but invariably terminated with a destructive rage toward her partner. These aborted relationships derived from childhood fantasies of castrating her father and the twins—the twins, because they had intruded on her relationship with her parents; and the father, because, by siring the twins, he not only had betrayed her but had also made it impossible for her to contend successfully with two rivals who had arrived simultaneously on the scene and who "seemed to have it all."

She had a strong, unconscious feeling of envy because her mother had produced twins, an act which she could not hope to follow. This was a determinant in her inability to work productively in her profession. She equated her creative work with "baby" and, remembering the awe and adulation that the arrival of the twins had aroused, she felt helpless. Her feelings of penis envy were further intensified as a result of fantasies in which baby and penis were equated and because in reality her father had been enormously proud of his twin sons.

She could not please her father by producing twins, nor could she satisfy him by becoming a boy. She remembered vividly the night her mother's water broke. Naomi had been left alone and she referred to it as "a night of psychic terror." This was a screen for the fear and loneliness she had experienced when the twins were born and for her feelings of rage which subsequently emerged in her relations with men.

During the termination phase of the analysis, Naomi became involved in a project that required knowledge of her own field and the application of psychoanalytic insights. She suggested that the analyst assist her. In this wish she expressed not only her oedipal desire to have a child by the powerful analyst but also her yearning for a twin effort, involving two disciplines. In this way, she would represent the twins. Since it was her idea, her "baby," it demonstrated her triumph over the father, the mother, and the twins.

CASE 3

Mrs. Rose R. was a 39-year-old married woman, the mother of a teen-aged boy and a 2 ½-year-old girl. She was an orally aggressive woman, overweight, garrulous, and suffering from depression.

When Rose was 5 years old, the birth of twins, a boy and a girl, brought about many changes in her behavior. Her free associations about this period of her life showed that she viewed that time as depressing and frustrating. In later years she always suffered from feelings of being excluded, except for those few blissful occasions when she visited a spinster great-aunt in a small town in New England where she was adored and occupied the center of the stage.

Before the birth of the twins, she had been told of their imminent arrival and that she could share in raising them and helping her mother like a big girl and that the coming event would make her an extremely fortunate child. How fortunate she felt herself to be can be inferred from her reference to them as "Eskimos" because her mother's large abdomen looked to her like an igloo;

even then she anticipated that she would be frozen out, as indeed she subsequently was. She was hostile toward these strangers even before their arrival. After the twins were born, her mother had a postpartum depression, a situation that would be devastating for a young child even if she did not have twins to contend with. The euphemism was that mother was recovering from the birth of the twins in a bedroom from which Rose was barred because she "might bother her." A housekeeper and nurse cared for the mother; a second nurse cared for the twins. Mother and father made a pair, the two nurses were a pair, the twins were a pair, and Rose had to shift for herself. In addition, her father retreated into alcoholism at this time and was unable to function in his profession.

In treatment, Mrs. R. often complained of feeling lost, physically cold, and abandoned. Her face betrayed the hope of affection mingled with a fear of rejection. At other times she was petulant and reproachful. Her associations led to a comparison of her current state of mind and how she had felt when the twins were born. She felt she was not a good patient, that I did not care for her as her previous analyst had, that she was not truly associating freely as she imagined my other patients were; she felt helpless. She was getting nothing done at home; the day should have 48 hours; there should be two of her; she felt she was only half a person.

Mrs. R. had been under psychiatric care intermittently, but for long periods, since her late teens when she feared that in a state of unconsciousness she would stab her mother and father and that she would cut off her brother's penis; she visualized with horror the bloody stump. She could not be reassured by her parents and demanded psychiatric help. She was an intelligent and talented woman. Before seeing me, she had been in treatment for three years, but her relationship to her younger twin brother and sister had never been explored.

After the birth of the twins, she had been bitten severely by a dog toward whom she felt absolutely no resentment. The dog had only done to her what she fantasied doing to the twins. "I hated them so much, and all I could think of doing to them was to bite them."

As the twins grew up, they engaged in much sexual play.

When Rose tried to intrude herself into these games, she was made to feel like a clumsy, awkward oaf, which was how she still saw herself at the time she began her analysis with me.

The patient had known her husband and dated and necked with him since her early teens; he had been like a big brother to her and with him she felt she finally had her "twin." At the time of her analysis she had come to consider him a clown, a failure; he told "gag" stories. Often she timidly expressed the idea that she might be a lesbian. She was, in fact, more interested in women than in men. "I would have made a much better son than my brother."

Her first child was a boy with whom she immediately established a pathologically intimate relationship. She and he formed a "twinlike pair" from which her husband was locked out, as she had been following the birth of the twins. Mother and son were constant companions, shared loving secrets, and cut themselves off from other contacts. The father, in desperation, found comfort in devoting himself to his business. Mrs. R. felt, with reason, that she had ruined her son who would never be able to develop independently. She castrated him psychologically, as she had castrated her brother in fantasy when she was a teen-ager. She made him into the weak fool she had considered her brother to be. The twin sister had appeared to be the best endowed of the three children, but later in life this sister became somewhat of a derelict. The patient herself had competed in a predominantly male field and felt she had made more of a success of her life than either of the twins. When a tree fell over in a high wind, she mourned, "I feel amputated with the tree gone." She expressed her feeling that her son had been her substitute for a phallus; now she felt she was being punished by the "amputation," which she once wished to carry out on her twin brother.

During her second pregnancy, Mrs. R. again felt that now she would find a twin. "I felt at last I would have a girl, a lifelong companion, just like another part of me. A twin!"

She came to a session wearing shoes of identical style and noticed only while lying on the couch that they were different colors. She remarked ruefully, "Even my shoes are like the twins." All of this material expressed her wish to double herself, to be both boy and girl, and her unhappy awareness that she could never be more than half of what she wanted. The solution lay in her unconscious wish to be a twin, to get rid of the twins, and to prove to her parents that she could be everything they needed.

Early in the analysis she reported two dreams. In one, she was in school and was told her IQ was 113, which meant she was a genius. She rushed home to tell her parents, but no one wanted to listen. There were other people around, too, but she could not get any attention. This dream struck her as obnoxious because she felt she possessed an obviously superior intelligence. The affect in the dream was sad and nostalgic, but it reassured her that she was superior to the twins. It revealed her wish to be better than both of the twins put together, along with her need for self-punishment.

One of her associations to this dream was a homosexual fantasy about the analyst, which represented her wish for union with the superior twin, her sister, to be twin to the mother-analyst so as to make the twins unnecessary, and to retain her mother as she had been before the postpartum depression.

She had a "half-dream" which indicated her identification with the twins as well as her conviction that she was only half a person. In the hypnagogic state of the "half-dream" she felt that the analyst was caressing her breast as she masturbated herself. This fantasy also expressed her wish for the analyst-mother's love and to have in herself male and female identities and genitalia. The sense of incompleteness and the bisexual identification, apparent in this "half-dream," are often seen in siblings of twins. The patient spoke apprehensively of numerous homosexual fantasies which had both excited and humiliated her. Her nipples and clitoris were strong erogenous zones, but she rarely experienced vaginal sensation during intercourse. She occasionally masturbated in the manner of the "half-dream" and spoke at that time of being "androgynous." When I asked if, in this way, she could take the place of both brother and sister twin, she flushed, was silent, and later quietly replied, "Yes." These contrasting affects also appeared in the transference.

During the termination phase, Mrs. R. remarked, "I feel that my other half is gone now that my son is in college. I feel like nothing. I was at a dinner party and met a Jewish woman who wanted to be friendly to me; but I was afraid to get involved with her. I feel a whole half of me is missing and that you are hostile to me. I need someone to show me [to myself]." She explained that she needed to find, in the transference, a woman, a mirror of herself, who was complete. She felt her mother had never needed anybody else.

She reported experiences of "like E.S.P." This was particularly true in her relationships with her hairdresser, her internist, and her children's pediatrician. With all of these men, and with others, she felt there was an unspoken bond, like that between her twin siblings; toward all these men she felt a sexual longing which she believed was reciprocated, although it was never lived out.

This borderline patient experienced the birth of twin siblings as a lifelong abandonment, with enormous intensification of sibling rivalry and with repeated overt death wishes against both parents who had made the twins. She also expressed open death wishes toward the twins for "being," envy of the mother who had born them, rage at the father for siring them, a restitutive desire to enter the twinship, to separate the twins, to become herself a twin, to have a twin. The fact that her twin siblings were differently sexed greatly increased her bisexual problems. In her marriage and in her role as mother as well as in her bisexual identifications, she attempted to repair the damage which she felt had been done to her. In the transference all of these conflicts emerged and were worked through.

DISCUSSION

All children react to the birth of a sibling with various degrees of envy, jealousy, and hostility. Most case histories are replete with the impact that the birth of a younger child has on the older one and the variety of ways this trauma is subsequently coped with. When two babies arrive at the same time, however, all the child's reactions are intensified.

To begin with, the child feels displaced, ousted from the love of the mother, who in reality has to give more care and time to two new babies. Moreover, for many mothers having produced twins is a narcissistic gratification that will induce them to spend much time in awe and adulation of the twins.

In this climate, the single child will begin to feel abandoned, helpless, and enraged. His savage feelings toward the twins and the mother give rise to overwhelming death wishes and inadequate defenses against them.

In the cases I described, there was increased oral aggression— wishes to bite and to devour the unwanted intruders—but there were also equally strong wishes to join them, to become part of a pair, to separate them, and gang up with one to exclude the other. The preoccupation with the twins formed a lifelong pattern that carried over into other relationships. The nontwin siblings sought the twins in friendships, love relationships, work partnerships, and their own children, and in relation to the analyst who, the patients hoped, would be the twin or provide a twin. The object relationships of these patients showed evidence of a frequently unconscious, but fierce, desire to be a twin and to seek out people who would serve as twin surrogates.

The impossibility of fulfilling this aim in reality led to disillusionment, increased ambivalence, and the need to repeat this pattern over and over again, with the result that they experienced repeated failures in their object relationships.

In part, these failures were also due to faulty identifications. These are crucially important in human development and get their greatest impetus from the oedipal situation. Under ordinary circumstances identification is preceded by imitation and introjection of the mother in order to achieve the lost oneness of the symbiotic phase (Maenchen, 1968). Claustrophobia, as observed in Laurie and in Mrs. R., should be understood as a defense against the wish to be a twin within the mother's body: introjected, united, and blameless.

The attempts to fuse with mother were interspersed with periods of negativism which were phase-specific and seemed to represent a prolonged struggle to establish an individual identity. All of these processes were disturbed, partially aborted, and the identifications occurred precociously in the siblings of twins because of the fear of loss of the mother, which may be transferred onto the twins. As a result, what I saw was more in the nature of overpossessiveness than mature identification (Glenn, 1966). These patients all had a heightened dread of loneliness—due either to intense separation anxiety or to the fear of loss of the love object—a fear that was omnipresent. Without the object's presence, they never felt complete.

The siblings of twins whom I have studied did not seem able to achieve a clear feeling of self; such autonomy as they attained was quickly abandoned under stress. Arlow (1960) described the twins he studied as feeling envious of their siblings for being complete and for having a clear identity. In contrast, the siblings I studied were intensely envious of the twins. "They have it all; they're never alone; they don't need anyone else." They continued to search for some form of twinship in order to experience a sense of autonomous self.

This was especially true in the case of Mrs. R., who always felt she was only half a person, who attempted to complete herself by establishing a twinship first with her husband and then with her children. The fact that she was the sibling of differently sexed twins also led to an exacerbation of bisexual problems since she identified with each, alternately and simultaneously, and therefore could not experience a sense of sexual identity.

In the case of Naomi, who had twin brothers, there was no doubt that her penis envy had been enormously intensified. In her adult relations with men she repeated the sadomasochistic pattern she had had as a child with her twins of whom she took "better care" than her mother but whom she also disciplined mercilessly. Yet, she continued to feel lonely and incomplete.

One wonders, in this context, how Laurie, who had twin sisters, will solve the problem of establishing her sexual identity. At present, her manner, appearance, and interests are distinctly feminine and she is popular with both boys and girls. While in many respects her analysis helped her to develop normally, she has retained her wish for a twinship, a wish that characterized all the cases I have presented.

None of the problems these patients had is unique to siblings of twins. All these characteristics are present in ordinary sibling rivalry, but the birth of two rivals exacerbates all the child's feelings. As Jeanne Lampl-de Groot (1979) pointed out, the chronically ill or disabled child manifests similarly intense reactions of exclusion, helplessness, and rage. The aspect that differentiates the single sibling of twins is the intense wish to separate the twins, to destroy the twins, and to become a twin. The intensification of the ordinary sibling rivalry together with the urgent desire to replace the twins and become a twin oneself constitutes, I believe, a syndrome that is characteristic of single siblings of younger twins. While all my cases happened to be female, I have no reason to believe that this particular syndrome would be substantially different in males.

Nevertheless, it would be worthwhile to investigate the specific problems faced by boys who are siblings of twins, as well as a variety of other factors which I have not discussed in this paper. Among these are: whether the presence of other nontwin siblings, younger or older, makes a difference; the age difference between the single child and the twin; the effects of having older twins; the question of who appeared on the scene first; the sexual differences; the effects of the twins on other members of the family. These questions should be further researched.

SUMMARY

Twinship has a fateful effect not only on the twins themselves but on all the other members of the family, especially the siblings. The cases presented in this paper demonstrate that the nontwin sibling reacts to the arrival of twins with intensified sibling rivalry and a pervasive sense of being excluded from the rest of the family of couples—mother and father, the twins. In the attempt to compensate for these feelings of incompleteness and loneliness the siblings of twins unconsciously but unsuccessfully and interminably seek a twin surrogate. Thus, the reality of being a sibling of twins is very different from the fantasy of having a twin.

BIBLIOGRAPHY

ARLOW, J. A. (1960), Fantasy Systems in Twins. *Psychoanal. Quart.*, 29:175–199.
BORNSTEIN, S. (1935), A Child Analysis. *Psychoanal. Quart.*, 4:190–225.
BURLINGHAM, D. (1945), The Fantasy of Having a Twin. *This Annual*, 1:205–210.
——— (1952), *Twins*. New York: Int. Univ. Press.
DEUTSCH, H. (1929), The Genesis of Agoraphobia. *Int. J. Psycho-Anal.*, 10:51–69.
GLENN, J. (1966), Opposite-Sex Twins. *J. Amer. Psychoanal. Assn.*, 14:736–759.

Joseph, E. D. (1975), Psychoanalysis—Science and Research. *J. Amer. Psychoanal. Assn.*, 23:3–31.

Lampl-de Groot, J. (1979), Personal communication.

Lidz, T., Schafer, S., Fleck, S., Cornelison, A., & Terry, D. (1962), Ego Differentiation and Schizophrenic Symptom Formation in Identical Twins. *J. Amer. Psychoanal. Assn.*, 10:74–90.

Maenchen, A. (1968), Object Cathexis in a Borderline Twin. *This Annual*, 23:438–456.

Asceticism in Adolescence and Anorexia Nervosa

S. LOUIS MOGUL, M.D.

THE INCIDENCE OF ANOREXIA NERVOSA IS INCREASING (CRISP ET al., 1976) and there is a corresponding increase in the number of articles and books about it. Hilde Bruch (1973) and Mara Selvini Palazzoli (1978) have written the most comprehensive clinical accounts, giving much attention to the familial and early developmental origins of the condition. This paper focuses on one particular aspect—the relationship between adolescent development and anorexia nervosa, and the ways in which asceticism links them. While I do not view adolescent conflicts as the basic cause of anorexia nervosa, I propose that each throws light on the other and that a better understanding of the mental life of anorectics and of adolescents can be gained by examining the relationship between them. This understanding is a matter of considerable practical importance in the treatment of anorexia because there is wide agreement that correction of the weight problem alone, which can often be accomplished with behavioral therapies, may leave the psychic experience of the patient largely unchanged. That is, even with body weight shifted into the normal range, preoccupation with struggles over food and weight, to the exclusion of other interests, may continue. To the outsider, the problem seems solved, but, as one artistic and intellectually interested patient said after a good recovery, "The worst thing about being anorectic was the enormous waste of

Assistant Clinical Professor of Psychiatry, Harvard Medical School at Massachusetts Mental Health Center, Boston, Massachusetts, and a member of the faculty of the Boston Psychoanalytic Institute.

time and energy in always thinking of food." Thus, there is no avoiding the difficult task of effective psychotherapy if one is to provide meaningful help for the psychological suffering of anorectics.

A goal of this paper is to demonstrate that viewing anorexia in the light of adolescent developmental issues, especially those on the continuum from self-discipline through self-denial to asceticism, adds to those psychotherapeutic tools that Bruch and others have provided by their elucidation of the role of early developmental aberrations. Attention to the more contemporary adolescent issues involves the search for what is potentially adaptive in this most seriously maladaptive disease. This search presents difficulties in resolving contradictions, stemming in part from the many mysteries that anorexia poses, and from the considerable variation in development, dynamics, and function in anorectics, despite the remarkable uniformity of the descriptive picture. Some cases are in fact so unremittingly destructive of what humans generally value that one's credulity is strained when one attempts to find the psychological sense of this syndrome.

Anorexia nervosa is a disease largely of middle-class adolescent girls. (Over 90 percent of the cases are in females, and the percentage is even higher if one includes only the typical cases. Therefore the feminine pronoun will be used in referring to anorectics in this paper.) In an established case anorexia nervosa is described by the following characteristics:

1. Thinness is pursued relentlessly, in many instances without limit, by means of food restriction, exercise, and variably by induced vomiting, purging, and diuresis.

2. Cognitive functioning (or reality testing) is impaired: there is a distortion of the body image and of the true nature of body signals indicating tiredness, hunger, or satiety. Moreover, there is a staunch denial of illness and even the claim of well-being—a denial, not just to others, but also resulting in the patient herself not being consciously aware of the condition in herself, although she can spot even subtle signs of it in others.

3. Alertness, restlessness, and lively activity are pursued often to the point of fierce regimens of exercise that belie the emaciated state of the body.

4. Amenorrhea is a regular finding and often is a very early sign before significant weight loss sets in.

5. There is preoccupation with food and weight to the exclusion of other interests and relationships, especially as the condition progresses. Life offers less and less pleasure.

6. Families of anorectics are tightly knit and very involved with each other. Broken homes are the exception.

My interest in the relationship between anorexia and adolescent development stems from the frequent observation of teenage patients with a variety of eating, weight, and menstrual problems that are connected with typical adolescent conflicts. These problems may take the manifest form of the girl refusing to be seen eating in public or by a boyfriend, or a variety of overeating and undereating conditions, including fragments and intimations of the anorectic syndrome. The symptoms are often reversible and are not experienced as a serious impairment, though in some instances they progress to full-blown anorexia nervosa. The frequency of these manifestations in this age group, especially in such subcultures as ballet students (Druss and Silverman, 1979), raises the question of their possible adaptive role.

A starting point in considering this relationship is the striking fact that anorexia nervosa almost always has its onset in the adolescent years. There are a few cases which start in preadolescence, and some where the first definitive appearance of the condition is in early adult life. In my experience, most of the cases in the latter group have clear antecedents in adolescence and are always triggered by major developmental milestones such as marriage and, especially, pregnancy. The way in which pregnancy can serve to precipitate the open outbreak of the anorectic syndrome, and yet can be, along with mothering a child, a ground upon which the anorectic works toward freeing herself from earlier symbiotic attachments, is worthy of a separate study.

Normal adolescent development involves the moving away from childhood attachments to, and dependencies on, the real parents and the internalized parent images to new objects with the opportunity for appropriate emotional and sexual experience. It also involves the establishment of the maturing person as a relatively independent being with an autonomous sense of self and identity.

The adolescent calls on a variety of inner resources to aid in this difficult task. To counter the upsurge of drive energy, the girl, one hopes, has an ego and superego strong enough to protect her against the danger of being overwhelmed and adaptive enough to allow exploration and mastery of new potentialities. In this effort, the ego makes use of defenses established or consolidated in latency, and, according to Anna Freud (1936), also can call on two defensive attitudes characteristic of adolescence, namely, intellectualization and asceticism, the latter of which is crucial for my consideration. Anna Freud describes the defense of asceticism as follows:

> ... adolescents are not so much concerned with the gratification or frustration of specific instinctual wishes as with instinctual gratification or frustration as such. Young people who pass through the kind of ascetic phase which I have in mind seem to fear the quantity rather than the quality of their instincts. They mistrust enjoyment in general and so their safest policy appears to be simply to counter more urgent desires with more stringent prohibitions. Every time the instinct says, "I will," the ego retorts, "Thou shalt not," much after the manner of strict parents in the early training of little children. This adolescent mistrust of instinct has a dangerous tendency to spread; it may begin with instinctual wishes proper and extend to the most ordinary physical needs. We have all met young people who severely renounced any impulses which savored of sexuality and who avoided the society of those of their own age, declined to join in any entertainment, and, in true puritanical fashion, refused to have anything to do with the theater, music or dancing. We can understand that there is a connection between the foregoing of pretty and attractive clothes and the prohibition of sexuality. But we begin to be disquieted when the renunciation is extended to things which are harmless and necessary, as, for instance, when a young person denies himself the most ordinary protection against cold, mortifies the flesh in every possible way, and exposes his health to unnecessary risks, when he not only gives up particular kinds of oral enjoyment but "on principle" reduces his daily food to a minimum, when, from having enjoyed long nights of sound sleep, he forces himself to get up early, when he is reluctant to

laugh or smile, or when, in extreme cases, he defers defecation and urination as long as possible, on the grounds that one ought not immediately to give way to all one's physical needs [p. 154f.].

This valuable protective mechanism, ascetism, readily becomes converted, or, more accurately, perverted, into maladaptive states by what Anna Freud calls the "dangerous tendency to spread."

The situation is even more complicated when one considers the important role of asceticism not just in defense against drives, but also in establishing the sense of strength and freedom from dependence on parents that allows for the exploration of the wider world, an endeavor which is so central a part of adolescent development.

The discovery that one does not have to have three meals a day prepared by one's mother, but that one can skip a meal to have something more desired than food, or even survive for days on small amounts of simple, portable food has a liberating, even exhilarating impact on teen-agers. Similarly, the experience that one can withstand the discomfort or pain of severe exertion allows the freedom for long hikes, mountain climbing, and other feats of skill, strength, and endurance that in fact expand one's world and also add enormously to the inner sense of strength and autonomy.

These are such ordinary matters that their designation as asceticism may seem unwarranted. Yet, much more extreme examples are quite common; I have encountered numerous instances of even grotesque forays into asceticism, especially among adolescent boys, which clearly were adaptive and growth-promoting. For instance, a 15-year-old boy struggling to gain some freedom from quite protective parents had been refused permission to go camping in the middle of winter in the White Mountains of New Hampshire with friends. He proudly reported to me that, instead, he had slept in his own backyard in an arctic tent and sleeping bag when the temperature was $-10°$ F. He needed to know for himself that he could survive this experience, and his relationship with his parents became considerably less combative after this event.

What distinguishes adaptive asceticism from pathological

states is not so much its extent, or even the subjective experience of gratification from it, but the degree to which the asceticism becomes an end in itself. In this connection I refer once more to *The Ego and the Mechanisms of Defense:*

> ... in the repudiation of instinct characteristic of adolescence no loophole is left for substitutive gratification: the mechanism seems to be a different one. Instead of compromise formations (corresponding to neurotic symptoms) ... we find almost invariably a swing-over from asceticism to instinctual excess, the adolescent suddenly indulging in everything which he had previously held to be prohibited and disregarding any sort of external restrictions. On account of their antisocial character these adolescent excesses are in themselves unwelcome manifestations; nevertheless, from the analytical standpoint they represent transitory spontaneous recovery from the condition of asceticism. Where no such recovery takes place and the ego in some inexplicable way is strong enough to carry through its repudiation of instinct without any deviation, the result is a paralysis of the subject's vital activities—a kind of a catatonic condition, which can no longer be regarded as a normal phenomenon of puberty but must be recognized as a psychotic affection [p. 156].

It seems to me that the clinical condition which best illustrates Anna Freud's point is not catatonia, but anorexia nervosa, especially in view of the frequent swing-over from bulimia to anorexia and vice versa.

What happens when the potential anorectic youngster approaches the developmental tasks of adolescence? In many ways their responses are similar to those of other adolescents, but the reliance on asceticism as the answer to all of their conflicts over these tasks becomes more and more extreme. Asceticism can be considered from three viewpoints: (1) as a defense against drives; (2) as a defense against the sense of powerlessness; and (3) as the expression of a wish for aesthetic and moral transcendence.

1. Initially there is considerable struggle between drives and wishes and the puritanical repudiation of them. "Anorexia," meaning lack of appetite, is a misnomer. In most instances there is a strong urge to eat, which, may, as the condition progresses,

be displaced onto mental preoccupation with food and acts of feeding or even stuffing others. True sustained loss of appetite is mainly a late finding and may be a physiological result of inordinate starvation. Severe anorexia ends with a remarkable suppression of the libidinal side of instinctual life, but with a flowering of aggression as expressed against the self and the body and against others in the form of puritanical moralizing. In essence, the anorectic's use of asceticism as a defense against libidinal drives is not qualitatively so different from that of other adolescents, but it is taken to an extreme and then reinforced from other directions, to which I now turn.

2. Hilde Bruch (1973) refers to a pervasive sense of powerlessness as the fundamental developmental defect in anorectics and the key to understanding this condition. There is, also, the sense of not owning oneself, of not even knowing clearly one's own body indicators of needs and wishes; in short, there is not a secure sense of identity as separate from the mother.

I have been struck with how often the onset of anorexia follows what appears to be a major growth accomplishment that should enhance the sense of greater freedom and independence, such as a first major departure from home for school, camp, or a long trip, finding a boyfriend, or, as in one instance, the announcement of an important academic award and scholarship. These youngsters do not respond by being encouraged to go ahead, but rather, as if terrified of their progress toward independence, beat a hasty retreat back to feelings of helpless impotence. From this perspective, asceticism provides the way to an exhilarating sense of power, not to accomplish practical growth objectives, but as a subjective experience divorced from the external world. The anorectic makes a strong assertion of self-determination which is limited mainly to food refusal and has the effect of returning the adolescent to a profoundly regressed interaction with and dependence on the parents. The anorectic's use of asceticism as a defense against the sense of powerlessness involves qualitative differences from that of other adolescents. Here the asceticism takes on a life of its own and lends itself readily to distortion in which what is called "strength" serves weakness and what is called "independence" serves helpless dependence.

3. Another aspect of adolescence that is pertinent to the focus of this essay is the tendency, not just to be somebody distinct from the parents, but to be somebody special. Many adolescents mobilize and sustain great amounts of energy for social, athletic, and artistic attainments that are the expression of lofty ambitions and ideals. These often require disciplined self-denial and strenuous, painful exertion, at times of heroic proportions. Here the emphasis is not on asceticism but on the quest for heroic, transcedent, or artistic ideals in terms of both external achievement and inner subjective experience.

This striving can be expressed in many forms. For example, high school athletic teams are routinely expected to spend much time in training and exercise in the pursuit of small approximations toward excellence. This tendency is even more pronounced in such individual endeavors as the serious pursuit of figure skating, music, and ballet. These activities have in common with anorexia the self-disciplined mastery of the body and great absorption in the quest for artistic excellence that provide the feeling of being exalted above ordinary life.

Anorectics generally have a sense of being concerned with the "higher things" in life and have a disdain for the worldliness of those around them. They become "hunger artists" more interested in satisfying their own standards than in expecting applause, but they are often hurt when their difficult achievement is little appreciated and even seen as "sick" by others. The subjective sense of moral purity and of being in quest of an aesthetic ideal is fiercely maintained by the anorectic, despite results which are hideously ugly to others.

In addition to this quest for heroic and lofty ideals as a part of anorexia, I have found it highly characteristic of the personality of people who become or who have been anorectic to be very ambitious and hardworking in the service of attaining real athletic, artistic, and intellectual accomplishments and recognition. Several of my patients have focused on the impact that the pressure for excelling from people around them has had on their anorectic experience. Bruch (1975) believes that the recent increase in the expectations for performance from women has contributed to the increased incidence of anorexia. There is much that is puzzling here, but it fits with the picture of anorexia as involving conflicts over intense striving and the response to feeling great pressure to excell.

Thus far I have painted a discouraging picture of anorectics reaching out for normal adolescent attitudes such as struggling against instincts and the sense of impotence, vigorous self-discipline, and lofty idealism, which misfires by virtue of being taken to absurd extremes, resulting not in growth but disaster. The anorectic also is concerned with asserting her autonomy and the reality of her separate self, but in most instances she is so ill prepared for this separateness, and her heart is so ambivalently in it, that she ends up, via widespread regression, distressingly reduced to childlike dependence.

How does one find a therapeutic opening in this often relentless downward spiral? Everyone agrees it is very difficult. Bruch (1973) wisely recommends avoiding interpretations, which, however accurate, are experienced as intrusions into the mind, like forced feeding, and waiting for authentic feelings to surface so that the patient gains a sense of her right to exist. In my experience, the approach derived from viewing the anorectic's positive investment in the adolescent aspiration of a strong and separate self provides some opening for more active intervention.

In view of the difficulty of devising therapeutically effective tools for working with anorectics, I have found it useful to travel far afield in my search for a better understanding of these patients; I shall cite instances from East and West which have added to my empathic appreciation. Some perspectives from Indian theology and mythology provide a kind of validation for the peculiar route to "power and salvation" that the anorectic pursues. I take the following material from Heinrich Zimmer's *The Art of Indian Asia* (1955).

The oldest Indian religion, Jainism, had a standard of extreme asceticism for its monks, representing "a condition of absolute detachment from the world, from the social order, and from the common values of earthly life. For the Jaina gospel of release from the bondage of life and rebirth was unremitting in its disciplines of renunciation: through a sustained process of ascetic cleansing, the monk's career was to culminate, ideally, in self-starvation" (p. 15). This is a rather oversimplified view of the extreme anorectic position in which asceticism is espoused without conflict or complication.

Among the Buddhist legends is one relating the experience of "the ascetic Gautama" in which the Buddha describes his ascetic experience to his monks in the following manner:

> 'What if I should take food only in small quantities, only as much as my hollow palm would hold?' My body became extremely thin. . . . When I thought to touch the skin of my stomach, I would actually take hold of my spine, and when I thought to touch my spine, I would actually take hold of the skin of my stomach—so closely did the skin of my stomach cling to my spine, from the little food. . . . Yet through this severe mortification I am not attaining superhuman, truly noble knowledge and insight. Perhaps there is another way to enlightenment.
>
> Then I remembered a time when I was . . . a youth, at home. I was . . . without sensual desires, without evil ideas. . . . Then there arose in me the consciousness that this was the way to enlightenment. . . . And then I thought, 'It is not easy to gain that happy state while my body is emaciated' [p. 348f.].

The ascetic Gautama seriously considered, but eventually rejected, extreme asceticism as the way to enlightenment, in favor of spiritual purity without the somatic and material preoccupations that go with starvation. There is a valuable lesson here, sadly ignored by anorectics, that extreme mortification of the body empirically leads, not to psychological freedom from its needs, but to mental enslavement to them (see fig. 1).

There are a number of Hindu legends in which the central feature is the enormous power of asceticism. In one of these, the asceticism has a heroic and in a way worldly, creative aspect. The demon Tāraka, like others before and following him in the Hindu view of history, had acquired the power, by severe penances, to force Brahmā, the all-pervading spirit of the universe, to grant him his wish of invulnerability. The wish was granted with one limitation—that Tāraka could choose the one being from whom his invulnerability was exempt—and he chose an infant seven days old, thinking, "What infant of seven days could kill me?" Thereafter he set forth to conquer the universe, driving the gods from their thrones and realms; and because of his virtual invul-

Figure 1. *The Fasting Buddha* (2nd–3rd century A.D.; Gandhara)

Despite the extremity of emaciation, the serene spirituality shines through without a trace of anguish—an ideal the anorectic seeks but fails to obtain.

Original in Central Museum, Lahore, Pakistan Reproduced from Zimmer, *The Art of Indian Asia,* vol. 2, plate 65, copyright 1955, 1960, by permission of Princeton University Press nerability, none could withstand him. Filled with despair, the gods took themselves in impotent wrath to Brahmā, begging his assistance and advice, but he replied:

> "The being to kill Tāraka does not yet exist; for what infant possesses strength enough to kill this demon? What parents, moreover, should be potent enough to generate such an infant-hero? None but the Great Goddess could bear the child; no male but the Great God, Śiva Mahādeva, has, through his timeless austerities, stored up the boundless energies needed to beget such a being." . . . The goddess . . . Umā, the daughter of King Himālaya, out of compassion for the gods and the universe . . . longed to become Śiva's wife. . . . And her problem, again, was that of arousing the god from his profound yogic trance; for Śiva, steeped in a continuous contemplation of the pure void of his own being, is the archetypal yogī, who cares nothing for the world. Śiva cannot be tempted by sensual pleasure, nor by the prospect of a blissful married career. It was in vain, therefore, that the gods tried to stimulate his passion when the goddess came to adolescence.
>
> . . . the gods sent the god of love to pierce Śiva's side with his shafts of desire, but the great deity merely opened the eye in the middle of his forehead—his third eye—and a flame burst from it with the force of a lightning flash, burning the beautiful body of the sweet god of love to cinders. . . . Umā, the lovely maid, wept. . . . And so, though her mother forbade her absolutely and her father consented only reluctantly, she resolved to gain Śiva's favor through a regimen of prolonged ascetic exercises severe enough to match his own.
>
> Departing into the mountains, quite alone, without attendants to protect her against wild beasts and other dangers, the beautiful young goddess-princess took an extremely rigorous vow and began her work. First she lived on fruits. . . . [She spent the hot season in the merciless rays of the sun and when the cold came, she entered the ice-cold water of the Ganges and stood there neck deep in meditation.] She reduced her diet and subsisted on water. She reduced it again and ate only the leaves and twigs that the wind tore from the trees. And finally, she gave up even this and lived on nothing . . . and when thirty-six thousand years had passed, she felt that the god might draw near to her and fulfill her selfless wish [p. 118f].

And, of course, he did. It occurred to me as I read this story that t corresponded to an anorectic girl's vision of the mystic way out of the sense of powerlessness (see figs. 2 and 3).

Western asceticism may at times be concerned with spiritual power, but, from fasting to self-flagellation, it is centrally concerned with moral power, the expiation of sin; consistent with this, submissiveness and meekness are great virtues. The Hindu ideal and myth depict asceticism as the means to magical power which may then be used for good or evil, but the issue of punishment or expiation does not occur. The Indian myth provides images which correspond more to the asceticism of anorectics than does Western religion with its emphasis on morality. However ascetic, the anorectic is not meek and brooks no opposition to the pursuit of her anorexia, as though the salvation of the world depended on it. The Hindu myth provides an idealized image that helps visualize the anorectic's psychology in pursuing power through fasting. This does not imply that one can uncover explicit fantasies of this kind. Anorectics are notorious for not revealing their fantasies. Rather, the behavior and utterances of anorectics can be put together to compose a mosaic corresponding to this myth.

Turning from Eastern to Western imagery, I found a remarkable story by Kafka, "A Hunger Artist" (1922), which seems to come from inside an anorectic's mind, especially in the crucially important area of narcissism, including its triumphs and despairs. The story is not at all clinical and I have no idea whether Kafka knew of anorexia or an anorectic person. He was clearly concerned with the issue of finding the right food or fasting and gave this an important place in other stories, especially "The Metamorphosis" and "Investigations of a Dog." "That he had ascetic tendencies is demonstrated by his vegetarianism, his abhorrence of uncleanliness, and the ice-cold baths he took in winter in spite of his frail condition" (Politzer, 1962, p. 283). Kafka's hunger artist, like an anorectic, conveys intense pride in self-starvation as a kind of art form, hypersensitivity to the least imputation of dishonor, yet ultimately sad hopelessness and a sense of the utter futility of his existence, and even of his death. According to Bruch (1973), "in the beginning of this century, when there was much interest in oddities of behavior and endurance, hunger artists, locked in cages, would exhibit themselves

Figure 2. *Kali (or Umā) praying to Siva* (12th–13th century, bronze;
Southern India)

Does the austere elegance—one hesitates to say "beauty" to a Western audience
—of this bronze, thin, but powerful, and even sensually attractive, convey the
consciously held, but actually unattainable ideal of the anorectic of whom one
could say, "The spirit is willing, but the flesh is weak"?

Courtesy of Nelson Gallery-Atkins Museum, Kansas City, Missouri (Nelson Fund)

Figure 3. *Devi as Umā* (15th century, bronze; Southern India)
Umā or Kali, in her more usual, well-nourished, and voluptuous state.
Courtesy of Museum of Fine Arts, Boston, Mass. (Marianne Brimmer Fund)

and show to an awed public that they cheerfully and artistically endured hunger, fading away before their eyes. This professional fasting has gone out of style" (p. 13).

The hunger artist, like the anorectic, obtains enormous satisfaction from the strength of self-denial expressed in fasting. In a characteristic way, one 16-year-old anorectic expressed pride in her weight loss, in contrast to the contempt she had for her mother, who had been dieting almost constantly for 20 years without losing her chubbiness. After a 20-pound weight loss heralding anorexia, a 14-year-old girl triumphantly reported, "They never thought I could do it." She had a real feeling of being a champion, like one of the characters in the Kazantzakis essays (1963), who declared, "In hunger I am king." This capacity to starve oneself is so rigidly limiting, unnatural, and ultimately self-destructive that the initial triumph is regularly followed by the feeling of being unappreciated and hopelessly trapped as the hunger artist or the anorectics pursue their cruel goal.

I now turn to clinical material to illustrate my view that the way to an alliance with the anorectic's narcissism is through her wish for transcendent strength and goodness.

A 16-year-old, quite emaciated girl presented the typical problem of being in great need of treatment but was extremely reluctant to acknowledge any difficulty. Like a child who felt her play was being taken too seriously, she insisted that there was nothing wrong with her: her family was ideally happy, very close, and loving; she was eating less to lose weight because she found fat people to be ugly and disgusting. She firmly maintained that she was just trying to make herself attractively slim, though she had long since gone beyond that point and was grotesquely thin. Besides, she surely could not be faulted for avoiding unhealthy foods such as meat, because of cholesterol; fish, because of chemical poisons; vegetables and fruits, because of sprays and artificial fertilizers and coloring; carbohydrates were nothing but calories; and everyone knew that sugar was very unhealthy. Whatever it was, she had the rationalization immediately at hand.

I saw few openings to engage her in treatment. I therefore perked up when she began to talk with great interest and expectation about an upcoming Jewish holiday, Yom Kippur, the day of atonement by fasting. As she was enthusiastically relating how meaningful this holiday was for her, I suggested that by analogy the fasting of Yom Kippur might provide another view of her own fasting. She gave me a contemptuous look, as though what I was saying made no sense. When I tried to explain, she was even more offended.

When I listened more carefully, however, and allowed her to clarify what interested her in this religious holiday, it became clear that it was not the moral issue of atonement for sin through fasting, but was the lofty spirituality of the day in which the materialism of everyday life had no part. When I acknowledged this aspect of her, she could respond to me more as ally than enemy. Similarly, when I responded to her wish to strengthen herself in vigorous exercise, rather than to the self-punitive and masochistic element, she felt helpfully supported.

It is noteworthy that depression with its concomitant psychology of crime and punishment is often a part of the experience of the anorectic, but is usually not accessible to therapeutic work in the acute anorectic phase. During the phase of weight loss there is an exhilarating sense of spiritual power, very much like that of the Hindu ascetic. Depression is more prominent either when the patient experiences the bankruptcy of this ideal, like Kafka's hunger artist, or when she is pressed into gaining weight by whatever means, including even her own partial insight gained in therapy. At this point, the more classic dynamic of depression, the sense of evil to be paid for with punishment, has more meaning for the patient, and she may even feel valued for her strong moral sense.

Early in treatment, this patient, like many other anorectics, was quite unready to find any narcissistic enhancement from my considering her conflict a struggle against sin; in fact, quite the opposite was true. On the other hand, she felt very much enhanced when I showed interest in her wish to be a strong person with lofty ideals, to be clearly distinguished from the "petty, materialistic" people around her.

I would like to close with a rather unusual clinical experience which connects anorexia nervosa to adolescent development in a positive way. A young woman who had had some psychotherapy for depression during her high school years experienced considerable turmoil in deciding which college to attend. She had been very pleased to be accepted at an excellent college some distance from her home, but felt the strong, not always explicitly stated, pressure from her family to attend another excellent college nearby. With considerable unresolved conflict, she finally decided on the out-of-state school to further her feeling of independence.

In her first week at college, and immediately after a friend had been sexually assaulted, she was quickly caught up in what Anna Freud called the "swing-over" from instinctual excess to asceticism. There were eating and drinking bouts with vomiting, followed by days of fasting. Uncharacteristic for this person, hedonism went out of control. It involved much time with boyfriends, little time studying, and excess spending, leading to large debts. She had a painful confrontation with her father during the Christmas vacation, resulting in a sense of mortification over her weakness and an intense anger over feeling owned by her family rather than being considered a person in her own right. She then felt the necessity to assert self-control in her life to establish a sense of autonomy.

In her second term at college, she imposed a rigorous regimen of diet and abstinence, and worked hard at her courses and to earn money to repay her debt. She accomplished all of this, but when she came to see me at the end of the term, she was a full-blown anorectic. She had lost over 30 pounds, was amenorrheic, and had lost interest in drinking, boys, and having fun in general. In fact, she had lost interest in life except for her academic accomplishment and carrying out the regimen she had set for herself.

She felt enormously proud of what she had done without denying the suffering she had experienced. She further insisted that she could get over the anorexia, which she did not call by its name, by spending the summer working away from home and also away from the pressures of school. I felt anything but reassured by this plan, but since I was given no choice about her going (the patient insisted on her need to take care of herself on her own), I arranged for medical supervision of her nutritional state and telephone and letter contact with me. When I saw her at the end of the summer, she was no longer anorectic but proceeding on the long and difficult task of defining and establishing her life.

In contrast to most anorectics, this woman's anorexia involved to some extent a consciously determined struggle against the real excesses of out-of-control hedonism, which presented a real danger to her. She was able to locate the source of the danger within herself. Although she was frightened of being controlled by her parents, she felt separate enough to contend against this control, actively, and avoided the extreme of regressive dependence. She spoke retrospectively of anorexia as having been the means to some very specific ends, namely, separating herself from dependent closeness and defining herself as an autonomous being who had to make her own life.

The clinical findings in this case were rather typical and severe enough to be worrisome; the course was unusual, though not unique. Cases like this one, seen in conjunction with numerous instances of clear but fragmentary, fleeting manifestations of anorexia in teen-agers, indicate the adaptive roots of anorexia nervosa which are obscured and lost as the condition takes on a destructive life of its own.

Discussion

The progress from childhood to psychological adulthood is long, complicated, and variable. Despite regressions, the overall thrust is clearly forward toward the assertion and attainment of meaningful independence and involves variable degrees and kinds of rebellion. Painful states, Weltschmerz, and even depression are expected parts of adolescent experience, but so are the embracing of life on new levels and interest in changing so as to be able to take advantage of the pleasurable and creative opportunities of the real, adult world.

Self-discipline, frequently extending to ascetic discomfort and self-denial, is a vital adaptive resource which the adolescent needs, not only to defend against the danger of drive excess, but also in establishing the capacity to survive independently and in mastering the requirements and skills for life, especially the creative life.

The youngsters who develop anorexia in adolescence often have progressed through childhood without manifesting gross distortions in their functioning. This is not to dispute the early developmental disorders on which Bruch and Palazzoli focus. Indeed, the often extreme, even symbiotic, closeness of mother and child is apparent in the compliant, good behavior of these girls. The adaptive requirements of childhood do not greatly challenge this limited separation which is so acceptable, even necessary, within these families. Adolescent development, by its very nature, not only challenges this arrangement, but threatens to disrupt the rigid mother-child bond.

Anorectics, as teen-agers, caught up in the strong pull of adolescent development and conscious of some wish for independence, make many movements to grow and expand their lives with successful academic, athletic, social, and even beginning heterosexual activities. The observation that the onset of anorexia nervosa follows closely a striking step in the development of disengagement is consistent with the hypothesis that this very success, as it threatens the closeness of mother and child, frightens the youngster into a regressive retreat. This same struggle between the strong drive for separateness and independence and the reluctance to loosen family ties is at the heart of adolescent developmental conflicts. It is precisely at this point in development that healthy adolescents vigorously assert themselves, their rebelliousness being the more extreme, the stronger the tie that needs to be loosened. Anorexia frequently appears when one would expect to find adolescent assertion of independence and rebelliousness. The anorectic, unable to tolerate progress toward genuine independence, musters the assertion of stubborn negativism, most especially by not eating, as an expression of her control of her own life and to some extent of the lives around her.

The adolescent phenomena of self-denial and asceticism lend themselves most naturally to this undertaking and become the guiding principle in the mental life of anorectics. This mechanism subserves whatever there is of self-control and independence, however misguided, that the anorectic can achieve. The reliance on asceticism makes the anorectic triumphant over the libido in general. In severe cases the libidinal basis of adolescent development seems to have been removed, and in extreme cases interest in life itself is extinguished.

As in serious depression, regression is extreme and sustained in anorexia, and it is difficult to find even a trace of libidinal pleasure in a severe case other than a joyless masochism. Most importantly, the self-respect of the anorectic is based almost exclusively on this pernicious, extreme self-denial and asceticism. Thus, rather than being a means to achieve difficult, demanding, but adaptive ends, as in healthy adolescents, the asceticism becomes identified with the anorectic's vital narcissism and is pursued for its own sake, as though without it there would be nothing.

SUMMARY

In focusing on the place of asceticism in the mental life of anorectics, this paper has sought a link between normal adolescent development and anorexia nervosa. Better understanding of the adaptive roots of this disease can be obtained from viewing the spiritually motivated asceticism of anorectics, as exaggeration, at times to grotesque extremes, of the creative self-discipline of healthy adolescents; this view, in turn, offers additional avenues for psychotherapy.

BIBLIOGRAPHY

BRUCH, H. (1973), *Eating Disorders.* New York: Basic Books.
———— (1975), Personal communication at Boston Psychoanalytic Society discussion.
CRISP, A. H., PALMER, R. L., & KALUCY, R. S. (1976), How Common Is Anorexia Nervosa? *Brit. J. Psychiat.,* 128:549–554.
DRUSS, R. & SILVERMAN, J. (1979), The Body Image and Perfectionism of Ballerinas. *Gen. Hosp. Psychiat.,* 1:115–121.
FREUD, A. (1936), The Ego and the Mechanisms of Defense. *W.,* 2.
KAFKA, F. (1922), A Hunger Artist. In: *The Penal Colony.* New York: Schoken Books, 1948, pp. 243–256.
KAZANTZAKIS, N. (1963), *Spain.* New York: Simon & Schuster.
PALAZZOLI, M. S. (1978), *Self-Starvation.* New York: Jason Aronson.
POLITZER, H. (1962), *Franz Kafka, Parable and Paradox.* Ithaca, N.Y.: Cornell Univ. Press.
ZIMMER, H. (1955), *The Art of Indian Asia: Its Mythology and Transformations,* 2 vols., ed. J. Campbell. Bollingen Series XXXIX. Princeton, N.J.: Princeton Univ. Press.

DREAMS AND SLEEP

Children's Dreams Reconsidered

STEVEN LURIA ABLON, M.D. AND
JOHN E. MACK, M.D.

> And dreams in their development have breath,
> And tears, and tortures, and a touch of joy;
> They leave a weight upon our waking thoughts,
> They take a weight from off our waking toils,
> They do divide our being; they become
> A portion of ourselves as of our time,
> And look like heralds of eternity:
> They pass like spirits of the past,—they speak
> Like Sibyls of the futures; they have power—
> The tyranny of pleasure and of pain.
>
> LORD BYRON, *The Dream*

DREAMS HAVE BEEN INTRIGUING TO MAN THROUGHOUT HISTORY. Man has been fascinated by the way dreams capture powerful feelings and experiences. Children's dreams are of particular psychological interest. They express concisely and vividly what matters most to the developing child. They reflect, sometimes in a profound way, children's developmental struggles as well as their creativity, capacities, and emotional problems. Children's dreams reveal and communicate powerful affective experiences. Often, early dreams are remembered into adulthood with clarity, deep feeling, and a sense of lasting personal significance.

The purpose of this article is to review what has been written

Dr. Ablon is Assistant Professor of Psychiatry at The Cambridge Hospital, Harvard Medical School; Director of Child Psychiatry Training, Cambridge-Somerville Mental Health and Retardation Center, Cambridge, Massachusetts. Dr. Mack is Professor of Psychiatry at The Cambridge Hospital, Harvard Medical School; senior staff member, Cambridge-Somerville Mental Health and Retardation Center, Cambridge, Mass.

179

about children's dreams and, more importantly, to raise questions for further exploration and research in this area. A great deal more has been written about adults' than about children's dreams. Much of what is known about adults' dreams may also be applicable to the dreams of children. For this reason we have drawn on observations and studies involving adults where they seemed relevant to the understanding of children's dreams. It is essential that any study of children's dreams be undertaken in the context of child development. In the past 25 years new and sophisticated techniques have evolved to study sleep physiology and the neonatal and infant period. At the same time, there have been many advances in understanding the psychology of child development. These advances have taken place in the establishment of developmental lines, and in the areas of separation-individuation, mother-infant bonding, temperament, cognition, affect, and the concept of the self, to mention only a few. These developments provide a basis for reexamining some fundamental questions about children's dreams.

THE NATURE OF CHILDREN'S DREAMS

An important initial question is: what is a child's dream? The *Oxford English Dictionary* defines a dream as the "train of thoughts, images or fancies passing through the mind during sleep." Such a definition does not require that the dreamer remember his dreams for it to be said that he has dreamed. This is consistent with the observation that children often describe a dream at night but have no memory of it in the morning. It is also supported by the observation of Ernest Hartmann (1973), a major contributor to our understanding of the physiology of sleep and dreaming, that "the functional roles of sleep and dreaming sleep are fulfilled whether or not any dreams are actually recalled" (p. 131). The *psychological* purpose or value for a child of consciously experiencing, thinking about, or telling a remembered dream to another person is, of course, a different matter. In addition, during sleep children have words or body movements that seem to indicate that they are dreaming and sometimes even suggest the content of the dream. A related problem is the nature of the state of consciousness of the dreamer and the relationship of the dream to reality. This dilemma was nicely expressed over 2,000 years ago by the Chinese philosopher Chuang Tsu:

> Once upon a time, I, Chuang Tsu, dreamed I was a butterfly flying happily here and there, enjoying life without knowing who I was. Suddenly I woke up and I was indeed Chuang Tsu. Did Chuang Tsu dream he was a butterfly or did the butterfly dream he was Chuang Tsu? [p. 48].

Children, for whom dreams have an intense vividness and special power, are often perplexed by such questions.

Consideration of the definition of a child's dream leads inevitably to the question: how early do children have dreams? This problem has intrigued many clinicians and researchers. It is now well known that there is a high proportion of REM sleep in earliest EEG recordings of premature infants. However, before the child develops language, only behaviors and sleep polygram patterns can be used to suggest dreams. Hug-Hellmuth (1919) and Fraiberg (1959) believe that infants and children dream in the first year of life. Their inferences are based on movements, smiles, and cries occurring during sleep. Erickson (1941) describes his observations of an 8-month-old girl. When her father was away, her activity and laughter during sleep resembled her customary activity playing with him before her 6 P.M. feeding. Erickson felt it was questionable to say that an 8-month-old could have "a dream of definite psychic content and affective components" (p. 383). He wondered whether a child of 8 months who missed her play with her father and experienced affective deprivation could resort to a dream in order to provide a substitute satisfaction. In the light of observations in sleep physiology, early infant-parent bonding (Klaus and Kennel, 1976), and affects in infancy (Izard and Tomkins, 1966), Erickson's interpretations now seem less questionable.

During the second year of life it becomes easier to identify the occurrence of dreams in children. This progress is closely related to language development. Children who are fluent early and have a relatively large vocabulary are most able to communicate their experience through dreams. Mack (1965) describes a

13-month-old boy who cried "boom boom" during an apparent nightmare (p. 409). He suggests that the child saw a frightening vacuum cleaner in the nightmare, because the boy had shown similar behavior when the vacuum cleaner was running during the daytime and would point at it with the same words. Isaacs (1932) relates how a boy of 14 months woke with a fear that "a white rabbit was going to bite me." She attributes the dream to the "child's own angry biting impulses at the breast" (p. 96). Levy (1945), describing children's dreams following operations, places some as early as age 12 months. Fraiberg (1950) writes about a 15-month-old boy who screams in his sleep, "Let me down. Let me down" (p. 286). This follows a visit to the doctor in which he was restrained for a throat culture. Niederland (1957) reports a boy's nightmares at age 17 and 20 months, which the child could not yet describe in words. At age 2½ this boy was able to verbalize the content of his dreams.

Two of the earliest reported dreams of children come from Freud's own family (1900). These examples are memorable for their charm and liveliness. Freud reports that his youngest daughter, at age 19 months, cried out in her sleep, "Anna Fweud, stwawbewwies, wild stwawbewwies, omblet, pudden!" At age 22 months of age, Freud's nephew woke with news that seemed to have originated from his dream, "Hermann eaten all the chewwies" (p. 130f.). Grotjahn (1938), Piaget (1945), and numerous other observers have confirmed that, varying with the child's mastery of language, children begin giving verbal accounts of dreams around age 2.

Many observers have asked when a child learns to distinguish dreams from actual events of the night. From Freud's description (1900) of the dreams of Anna at age 19 months and Hermann at age 20 months, it seems likely that these dreams were experienced by the children as actual events. Piaget (1929) describes three stages in the child's understanding of dreams. During the first stage (age 5 to 6), the child experiences the dream as coming from outside; it remains external. The memory of the dream is confused with other memories, such as of recent events in the child's life. During the second stage (age 7 to 8), the child may locate the source of the dream in his own head, thought, or voice; nevertheless the dream seems external to the child, in front of the child, or in the room. Finally, at about age 9 or 10, the child experiences the dream as taking place internally in the head or eyes and also as being thoughts occurring internally. A child's ability to distinguish dreams from real events is a gradually learned process, which seems to depend on a number of variables. These include the rate of cognitive development, development of language skills, the child's intelligence and imagination, and the help provided by adults during the night or in the morning in teaching the child the difference between dreams and reality. With this in mind, our observations and those of others such as Piaget (1929) and Greenacre (1964) suggest that under normal circumstances a recognition of the difference between dreams and actual events of the night begins to take place in the fourth year of life.

In describing a child's dream, we should try to distinguish what is the dream itself from elaboration, secondary revision, unconscious ordering, and storytelling. Each of us has seen children, who, having told us a dream, then proceed to elaborate it into an imaginative story. In addition to the fertile material the dream provides for story making, which children of course enjoy, the story may give order and cohesion to an emotional experience, i.e., the dream itself, which may seem threatening, perplexing, or disorganizing.

Foulkes et al. (1969) studied childhood dreaming during REM sleep by waking children and asking them about their dreams. In this situation the report followed dreaming with only a very short time interval. Nevertheless, the authors state that the descriptions the children offered did not necessarily report the actual content of their dreams. This was particularly true in children of preschool age. Foulkes et al. attribute this phenomenon to limitations in the child's vocabulary and in the concepts available for communication, and possibly even to confabulation. DeMartino (1955), in his review of the literature on children's dreams, also emphasizes that children have a limited descriptive vocabulary and tend to fill in the gaps in dreams indiscriminately. He adds that children may fail to report material in dreams that is contrary to their own experience. In addition, as Becker (1978) points out, when children describe dreams from the night before, especially in the prelatency age group, fantasies, dreams, and events of the day are combined in a variety of ways.

DEVELOPMENTAL ISSUES AS SEEN IN THE DREAM

Children's dreams reflect the mutual interaction of drive and ego development. They depict the most pressing concerns and tasks for children at different phases of development. At the same time dreams highlight the development of ego functions such as verbalization, language development, competence in handling affect, and cognition.

Although language is essential for describing dreams, the core perceptual and affective experience of dreaming may precede the development of language. The earliest dream experience may not yet be verbally structured. Dreaming may be part of the experiences which children build into language, especially because dreams may have such intense affective power. Parents' interest in their children's dreams encourage children to put their dreams into words. The importance of communicating dreams in language is eloquently stated by Monchaux (1978):

> ... there are some special features of dream telling which offer
> great advantages to the ego in its task of recognizing, *en route* to
> reconciling, the two sides which are intrinsic to any argument
> in the unconscious ... Nowhere do we see this more clearly
> than in the use of symbols in the dream text, and ... in the very
> use of dream telling as a medium for communication between
> internal object, self and other; in the expression of the conflict
> between acknowledged and disclaimed intention; and finally
> in the detection, not only of what the person wants in his life,
> but also, and perhaps pre-eminently, if we pay sufficient atten-
> tion to it, of the capacities of a given person's organizing func-
> tion at a given time [p. 452f.].

Monchaux reminds us not only that dreams help structure internal and external experience, but also how communicating dreams helps the dreamer master these experiences. Although Monchaux emphasizes the importance of dream telling for adults, it is certainly equally important in children, for whom communicating dreams is related to the crucial role of verbalization in ego development. Hirschberg (1966) makes a similar point about the ego development required to describe dreams. He explores how when a young child draws dreams, the process of looking and seeing can help him define and delineate the limits of reality. Dreams are of great interest and value for the way they reflect conscious and unconscious conflicts, wishes, powerful affects, reality, and the child's efforts to organize and cope with these important dimensions of his life. The dream thus reflects the ego's activities, can itself place demands on the ego, and can thereby stimulate the development of organizing psychic structure.

For children, dreams are expressive of fears and other intense feelings, fantasies, events of daily life, perceptions of important people, in short, what matters most deeply to the child. Foulkes et al. (1969) argue, from laboratory studies, that children's dreams are realistically related to their waking life and that dreams are more bizarre and unpleasant when children are struggling with some "dysfunction in waking personality" (p. 641). Normal children's dreams, according to Foulkes, describe ordinary play and recreational activities. This is consistent with the importance of these activities for children. When additional data are made available, however, the unconscious and symbolic aspects of these dream reports may be seen to relate to deeper conflicts and development issues. Observers have shown that many important dimensions of a child's life may influence the manifest content of dreams, including elements of his culture, family life, and the peculiarities of parental personality (Foulkes et al., 1969; Green, 1971; Markowitz et al., 1963, 1967). As we have described (Ablon and Mack, 1979), developmental stresses such as toilet training or oedipal conflicts as well as separation, birth of siblings, deaths, marked alterations in a parent's emotional state, changes in home or school situation, illnesses, operations, injuries, frightening events of the day, and similar stresses or traumas will naturally find their way into the manifest content of the child's dream.

Dreams are powerfully connected to the affectively significant elements of human life. If the meaning of a dream is explored in relation to its latent content, the central life dilemmas of the individual may be found to be economically expressed. This is particularly true in the case of children, whose major conflicts often have a quite specific focus and content. The focus and content are structured by the context of the child's developmental level and cognitive capacities. In the dream the child gives symbolic or metaphoric expression to specific developmental struggles. We will illustrate these points with an example.

Martin, an intelligent 8-year-old boy, went with his father to stay with friends of his parents for the weekend. Martin's father and mother were divorced and lived in separate cities. Martin lived with his mother but spent some weekends and vacation periods with his father. His father brought with them for the weekend visit a young woman friend, Karen, with whom he had been living and traveling. Martin and Karen appeared to get along well. Karen and Martin's father shared a room for the weekend. Martin had his own room close by.

In the morning Martin told Karen a little about a dream he had had during the night. She encouraged him to tell it to one of us (J. M.) the next day, which he did:

"My hermit crab. It was really big and was climbing into another shell. He was climbing out of his shell and climbing into another shell. " When asked further about the dream, Martin said that the hermit crab was very big, about a foot long, and that it was in a tank where there were two other shells and two other hermit crabs. The crab had become "too big for the shell he was already in" and so he climbed into the larger shell, which was the right size for him. Martin added, "He was happy there was another shell that he could get to because if he was much bigger he would be stuck in there." He soon would be growing out of the new shell as well, and there was a still *larger* shell waiting for him that was too big and would not fit in the tank. "We would have to take another shell out, or put a few shells out, to put that one in and we didn't think he was ready for that." The dream, Martin said, was a good one because the crab "found a new home."

In further conversation Martin said that he did in fact have various pets, including a tank with hermit crabs of the land-based type. He liked to look after these crabs and was careful to supply them with shells of various sizes so they would find new homes when they grew out of their old shells. Also, he said, he liked snakes, especially water snakes, but had none of these pets.

How a dream such as Martin's is to be interpreted will depend upon the context in which it is dreamed, the child's associations to it, the circumstances of its being told, and the amount of additional information available that can shed light upon its meaning or deepen our understanding. If Martin's manifest dream is examined without regard to the context, it would appear to contain little more than a quite realistic reflection of his interest in his pets and their activities. A hermit crab in a tank climbs out of its shell and into another shell. This is quite ordinary and seemingly nonsymbolic, much as many dreams in a sleep laboratory seem to be when reported without additional information (see pp. 185 and 199). Further meanings and significance become apparent when additional details of the dream and associations to it are obtained.

When Martin was asked about his dream, he added that the creatures were not the size of hermit crabs but a foot across, nearer the size of a small child than a hermit crab. The dream seemed to reflect the boy's interest in growing and growing up and the pleasures and concerns connected with it. There even was a still larger shell outside the tank (not mentioned in the initial telling of the dream)—possibly a reference to his anticipatory thoughts about the time when he would be grown up and leave home altogether. In the context of his parents' divorce it was not unwarranted to infer that Martin was dealing with the question of which home he belonged in, and with anxieties about losing his home. Martin apparently also was dealing with his curiosity and worry about his father's leaving their house and finding a new one with Karen; or leaving Martin's mother and finding a new woman.

Martin's situation of traveling with his father and his father's lover and sleeping in a room next to them was conducive to the activation of sexual interests and anxieties. Moreover the conversation at the dinner table the evening before had focused on the activities and relationships of adults with each other and of parents to children. Martin's dream and his comments in relation to it seemed to reflect genital interests and concerns as well as wishes and fears about growing big or growing up. In the dream, hermit crabs, in reality but an inch or so in size, expanded to a foot in length; a crab might get stuck in the shell if he grew too large. The receptive shell might represent a vagina or womb, suggesting an interest in pregnancy and birth processes. The hermit crab grown large and out of his shell conveyed a sense of the child's vulnerability. But we would need more evidence to know if these speculations are valid.

We can say, however, that Martin's dream reflected in displaced and condensed form the developmental issues with which he had to deal as well as the conflicts activated by his specific situation. As a bright 8-year-old he could draw upon rapidly expanding cognitive abilities and scientific interests in constructing his dream. The dream itself told a story and provided a creative and quite economical solution to a number of Martin's problems. Yet, it would be an unjustified teleological inference to conclude that such mastery or problem solving is the dream's purpose in a consciously directed sense. We believe it would be more accurate to think of dreaming, as in this example, as a versatile and symbolically rich dimension of mental life through which the child can give creative and highly condensed metaphoric expression to the central dilemmas of his current existence.

The importance of affect in motivation and personality has been developed in the work of Tomkins (1962, 1963) and Izard and Tomkins (1966). Freud (1900) also emphasized the importance of affect in dreams. However, Tomkins's work, which classifies fundamental affects in descriptive terms based on facial expressions in young children, opens new pathways. Classifying affects makes possible research aimed at understanding the motivational aspects of affect. Izard and Tomkins (1966) describe:

> . . . a model of the human being, stressing the importance of relatively independent but interacting personality subsystems. The homeostatic system, the drive system, and the affect system are the three motivational systems. The homeostatic system under normal circumstances is the silent, 'automatic' regulator of vital functions. The drive system is concerned with physiological and safety needs. The affect system is the primary motivational system, the principal provider of blueprints for cognition and action. Drives, though necessary for biological survival, are relegated to a place of little importance in the behavior we consider uniquely human: constructive interpersonal relating, complex cognitive processes, creative activity.

These kinds of human behavior can be understood and predicted only when we conceive affect as the dynamic, motivating, cue-producing experience [p. 123].

Observation of a child's affects and ways of dealing with them can lead to valuable insights into the mechanisms of drive regulation and the development of ego functions. Dreams, because of their affective intensity, are especially fertile sources of data from this point of view. Serog (1964) also emphasizes the importance of affect in children's dreams: "Prelogical thinking has, instead of logical coherence, the unity of feeling, instead of logical truth, the self-evidence of immediate impressions" (p. 52). In dreams, in addition to prelogical thinking, a further emotional impact is contributed by the preponderance of visual images. Perhaps this is related to the fact that visual perception precedes language development. Visual images represent thoughts, experiences, and feelings in a concise, trenchant way, whereas language spreads its meaning over a series of words. Other direct sensory perceptions in dreams, such as taste or smell, also have intense emotional impact. However, sensations of taste and smell are less common than visual images in dreams, as are auditory perceptions or written words. These sensory modes seem to require more imaginative work from the dreamer than do visual images.

Another reason why a child's dream is so affectively powerful is that most often he experiences himself as at center stage of an intense drama. Dreams are thus narcissistically focused; i.e., they concern what the child is experiencing within himself and not the realities or problems of the outside world. Hartmann (1973) notes another aspect of this "self-centeredness" in the observation that "usually missing in dreams are emotions which depend on feedback from the environment—for instance, the feeling of anger which changes gradually to sympathy depending on a turn that a conversation may be taking" (p. 137). Castle (1971) emphasizes, in language derived from Piaget, these aspects of dreams in his observation: dream thinking is mostly assimilated, i.e., is focused on internal experience. "It is assimilative because of the circumstances under which it is carried out, namely, during sleep, when of necessity the focus of thought is on the self rather than the outer world" (p. 103). In terms of the importance of images in dreams, Castle states, "Dreaming is image thinking... it permits among other things a high degree of specificity, immediacy and personal relevance" (p. 104). Piaget (1945) underscores the primacy of assimilation and the affective point of view in children's dreams:

> In the child this primacy of assimilation constantly occurs, as we saw in considering play, both as regards intelligence and feelings. But in the adult, even when his intelligence is normally adapted, there is at least one kind of situation in which this primacy continues from the affective point of view, quite apart from the pathological states in which there is general regression. This is in dreams, during which affective life goes on, but without the possibility of accommodation to reality [p. 209].

Dreams and fantasy share many characteristics. Both involve symbolic expression of thoughts, images, emotions, memories, and unconscious impulses. Primary process thinking is usually less disguised or transformed in dreams than in fantasy. Dreams, fantasy, myth, poetry, and art reflect related creative and symbolic processes. Visual imagery, symbolism, prelogical thought, strong emotions, and immediacy are common characteristics of these diverse human activities.

Awareness of the importance of powerful emotions in dreams of adults and the usefulness of understanding dreams goes back to ancient times. In the epic of *Gilgamesh* immensely moving dreams are related and interpreted. In *The Republic* Plato wrote about dreams:

> [Desires]... wake while we sleep, when the reasonable and humane part of us is asleep and its control relaxed, and our fierce bestial nature, full of food and drink, rouses itself and has its fling and tries to secure its own kind of satisfaction. As you know, there's nothing too bad for it and it's completely lost to all sense and shame. It doesn't shrink from attempting intercourse (as it supposes) with a mother or anyone else, man, beast or god, or from murder or eating forbidden food. There is, in fact, no folly nor shamelessness it will not commit [p. 392].

Freud (1933) described clearly the common aspects of dreams, legends, and myths.

In the manifest content of dreams we very often find pictures and situations recalling familiar themes in fairy tales, legends and myths. The interpretation of such dreams thus throws a light on the original interests which created these themes, though we must at the same time not forget, of course, the change in meaning by which this material has been affected in the course of time. Our work of interpretation uncovers, so to say, the raw material, which must often enough be described as sexual in the widest sense, but has found the most varied application in later adaptations [p. 25].

THE LANGUAGE OF CHILDREN'S DREAMS

Attempts to understand the language of children's dreams relate directly to the characteristics of prelogical thinking which they as well as myths and other creative and artistic endeavors possess. Freud (1900) made his famous and revolutionary observation that the language of dreams involves the language of the unconscious and that the *"interpretation of dreams is the royal road to a knowledge of the unconscious activities of the mind"* (p. 608). In 1915, Freud described the unconscious and primary process as characterized by displacement, condensation, mobility of cathexis, exemption from mutual contradiction, timelessness, and replacement of external by psychical reality. Fisher (1957) used the tachistoscope to expose subjects to pictures and then studied the manifest content of subsequent dreams. Partly based on this work, Fisher suggested a broader definition of primary process. Included in this definition would be transformations and distortions such as fragmentation, spatial rotation, and symbolic transformation (see Arlow, 1958). The language of dreams is structured by the characteristics of primary process thinking. The language of dreams utilizes another group of operations involved in transforming the latent into the manifest content of dreams. These are defensive operations, including repression, reaction formation, reversals, omissions, sublimations, projections, secondary revision, which were defined by Freud and expanded and elaborated by Anna Freud (1936) in relation to children.

Modern dream theorists have focused on the information-processing and problem-solving aspects of the language of dreams. In contrast to Freud's emphasis on wish fulfillment, drive discharge, disguise, and censorship, the adaptive aspects of dreams have been emphasized by French and Fromm (1964), Greenberg and Pearlman (1975, 1978), and Jones (1970). From this perspective, the manifest content of dreams, rather than being seen largely as a vehicle for important latent thoughts, reflects a person's attempts to cope with emotionally important material of that day or the days just preceding the dream. In this sense, the language of dreams can be compared to a computerlike retrieval system that processes experiences, feelings, knowledge of the present and past in an attempt to find possible solutions or new viewpoints. Such efforts can involve attempts to find solutions to emotional conflicts as well as intellectual and scientific problems.

Sternlicht (1966) has made interesting observations on the dreams of adolescent and adult retardates. He reports that although their dreams were relatively simple, with a minimum of dream symbolism, one can still detect the basic aspects of wish fulfillment and problem solving even in this group. Foulkes and his associates (1969) studied preschool children and normal and emotionally disturbed adolescents in a sleep research laboratory. The children were woken during REM periods and asked to tell their dreams. The investigators concluded that in the absence of

> ... disturbances introduced by personality pathology, the child's dream is characterized by generally realistic, life-related content in which impulse and affect are noticeably absent. The dream of the young adolescent is more impulse-laden, but this correlates well with the shifting dynamic interrelation of ego and impulse that accompanies the onset of adolescence [p. 641].

In this study, children reported dreams that in the usual course of their lives they would, most likely, not recall and certainly not report. Perhaps the few dreams remembered—the few seconds or minutes recalled out of the several hours of REM sleep—express the deeply felt or emotionally urgent matters that break through the barriers which guard the sleeper against the intrusion of most dreaming into consciousness. It is possible that the long hours of dreaming that are usually forgotten may have, as one of their functions, information processing and problem solving.

In the study of dreams, a systematic way of scoring and coding them and an orderly set of rules for analyzing them would be very helpful. Foulkes (1978) presents a model of dreaming and a method of dream analysis which he calls a Scoring System for Latent Structure. Utilizing this system, he illustrates how underlying structures of dreams can be elucidated, and (with a mathematical analysis and digraph theory), mechanisms of dream formation can be identified. Foulkes also raises a number of fascinating research possibilities that could be investigated. An important unanswered question is how easily learned such a system would be for others, as well as how congenial or useful other dream researchers would find it. In any case, Foulkes underscores the importance of the use of language in understanding dreams. This is a varied and fertile area much in need of investigation and elaboration.

For the French school of psychoanalysis led by Jacques Lacan the unconscious is best approached as a special language with its own rules of logic and structure. Lacan (1978), writing about dreams says, "What concerns us is the tissue that envelops these messages, the network in which, on occasion, something is caught" (p. 45). This tissue involves the structure of language. The central idea in Lacan's approach is expressed in his statement: "The unconscious is structured like a language" (p. 20). Using the examples of Chuang Tsu and the Wolf-Man, Lacan (1978) suggests some of the possibilities of looking at dreams from a linguistic, philosophical, and poetic perspective:

> ... When he is the butterfly, the idea does not occur to him to wonder whether, when he is Choang-tsu awake, he is not the butterfly that he is dreaming of being. This is because, when dreaming of being the butterfly, he will no doubt have to bear witness later that he represented himself as a butterfly. But this does not mean that he is captivated by the butterfly—he is a captive butterfly, but captured by nothing, for, in the dream, he is a butterfly for nobody. It is when he is awake that he is Choang-tsu for others, and is caught in their butterfly net.
>
> This is why the butterfly may—if the subject is not Choang-tsu, but the Wolf Man—inspire in him the phobic terror of recognizing that the beating of little wings is not so very far from the beating of causation, of the primal stripe marking his being for the first time with the grid of desire [p. 76].

What Lacan offers is a certain complexity and an unexpected perspective which are consistent with his description of dreams, parapraxes, and wit as having a sense of "impediment," "discovery," and "surprise" (p. 25).

Lacan (1968) suggests that a child's dreams may be the first primal linguistic expression of the unconscious, its first text.

> Remind yourself that the dream has the structure of a sentence or, rather, to stick to the letter of the work, of a rebus; that is to say, it has the structure of a form of writing, of which the child's dream represents the primordial ideography and which, in the adult, reproduces the simultaneously phonetic and symbolic use of signifying elements, which can also be found both in the hieroglyphs of ancient Egypt and in the characters still in use in China (p. 30).

In a Lacanian framework, the images of Martin's dream—the big hermit crabs, the shells, the tank—would, for example, be seen as linguistic elements. They would be understood as metaphoric or metonymic signifiers linked in an overlapping and interrelating chain of meanings to the things signified (vagina, boy-grown-to-man, home) and the latent dream thoughts (rivalrous wishes, desire to possess, longing to be bigger, wish for a safe womb or home) (see Leavy, 1978). It is not clear in "reading the text" how Lacan would deal with the powerful drives which inspire the symbolic transformations of the dream, or with the resistances that children put in the way of too direct revelations of the intense wishes and feelings that are embodied in the dream's latent content.

The impact of Lacan, and other structuralists such as Claude Levi-Strauss and Jean Piaget, has been considerable in the French-speaking intellectual and psychoanalytic communities, but their work does not yet seem well understood or integrated elsewhere. The same may be said of the work of Noam Chomsky and other linguists whose contribution to understanding the language of dreams has been limited, perhaps in part because of the inaccessibility and difficulty of their work for psychoanalysts.

THE FUNCTION OF CHILDREN'S DREAMS

Many of the questions previously discussed are important in exploring the function of children's dreams. Interestingly, with all the criticism and modification of Freud's theories about dreams, his view of "dreams as *the guardian of sleep*" and his sense that "In the case of children's dreams there should be no difficulty in accepting this statement" (1901, p. 678) have been generally accepted. Child analysts seem to agree with the observation that dreams protect the sleeper from awakening. Looking at the question from the perspective of studies in sleep laboratories, Foulkes et al. (1969) take a similar view. "Under conditions of systematic presentation of external stimuli during sleep there is still further evidence of the adaptive ego functioning. As the examples of incorporation . . . indicate, the disturbing stimulus is most often displaced or externalized in the REM-sleep dream" (p. 641). Discussions in the literature which emphasize censorship and the disguise of infantile wishes and conflicts in dreams, and those which stress adaptive work of the ego or problem solving, do not contradict each other. Rather, they approach the theory of dream formation and function from different perspectives.

In his book *Dreaming and Memory*, Palombo (1978) combines in an interesting and fruitful way the traditional psychoanalytic view of dreams and the newer information-processing models. He describes "an autonomous mechanism of nonconscious, adaptive ego functioning called 'the memory cycle'" and writes,

> The memory cycle is a sequence of processes through which new experiential information is introduced into adaptively suitable locations in the permanent memory structure. The most striking hypothesis of the memory cycle model is that the critical step in the sequence—the step which matches representations of new experiences with the representations of closely related experiences of the past—takes place during dreaming [p. 13].

Palombo also discusses the therapeutic effects of psychoanalytic dream interpretation:

> Dream interpretation appears to have a special efficacy in the building of those intrapsychic structures which restore and renew the incomplete self and object representations acquired during the patient's childhood. This effect results from a synergistic collaboration between the analyst's interpretive activity and the adaptive functioning of dreaming in the memory cycle. It is distinct from, but complementary to, the role played

by dreams in providing new data from that part of the patient's memory structure which is ordinarily inaccessible to consciousness [p. 14].

Palombo describes the development of a "new dream" during the analytic work with dreams:

The intrapsychic counterpart of the analyst's dream interpretation is a new dream which incorporates the originally reported dream together with the new information supplied by the interpretation. This new dream, which I have called "The Correction Dream," results in the introduction of information contained in the interpretation into the precise location in the permanent memory structure which contributed its contents to the originally reported dream [p. 14].

These points are illustrated with detailed psychoanalytic clinical material.

Hartmann (1973) has interpreted the characteristics of dream thought in the light of possible functions of the brain during sleep. He suggests, "primary process in dreaming—primitive connections, large discharges of energy, opposites occurring together—can all be seen as characteristics of a 'reconnecting' process in which daytime residues are reconnected to large, old, and thus 'primitive' pathways or brain storage systems" A vivid dream element, Hartmann postulates, "may indicate a nodal point representing interconnections between multiple brain pathways which somehow achieve enough prominence to be noticed by dreaming consciousness" (p. 133).

The repetitive or recurrent nature of children's dreams, especially frightening ones or nightmares following traumatic or disturbing experiences suggests a process of mastery or integration by the ego. In particular such experiences as injuries, operations, or prolonged separations during the day are often revived in dreams (Jessner et al., 1952; Levy, 1945). As we have described in a previous paper (Ablon and Mack, 1979), this is consistent with children's attempts at mastery through repetition. Freud (1920) too spoke of this when he described dreams in traumatic neuroses as attempts to restore control over catastrophic experiences. "These dreams are endeavouring to master the stimulus retrospectively, by developing the anxiety whose omission was the cause of the traumatic neurosis" (p. 32). In addition, as Mack (1965, 1970) points out, in a child's nightmares and dreams, not only recent, but unresolved traumatic experiences from earlier periods of development may be revived and expressed. In considering the phenomenon of recurrent frightening dreams, one must be cautious in the use of concepts such as "working through of traumatic experiences" or "mastery," which imply purposive activity on the part of the sleeping ego. This caution is warranted because recurrent nightmares may also reflect the failure of the dream's guardian function, or the inability of the "dreaming ego" to contain and even master the disturbing day residue or memory trace within a "normal" dream structure. Fisher et al. (1970) differentiate—correctly, we think—between the REM anxiety dream, which "appears to have a mechanism for tempering and modulating anxiety," and the stage-4 nightmare or night terror, which "represents a massive failure of the ego to control" anxiety.

The effect of the dream itself upon the waking ego of the child is an insufficiently studied subject. In 1957 Harry Leavitt stated, "Much more could be learned about the function of dreams if we were to focus more attention on the effect that dreams have on the wakening ego" (p. 212).

Winnicott (1945) clarifies how dreams may help a child integrate the difference between being asleep and awake: "I think there is not necessarily an integration between a child asleep and a child awake. This integration comes in the course of time. Once dreams are remembered and even conveyed somehow to a third person, the dissociation is broken down a little, but some people never clearly remember their dreams, and children depend very much on adults for getting to know their dreams" (p. 151). Grolnick (1978), in "Dreams and Dreaming as Transitional Phenomena," explores an important aspect of dreams where further observation and study is clearly indicated. He considers the possibility that the symbols in dreams can serve as a bridge for the child between past and present, between fantasy and reality. Furthermore, for a small child, traumatic dreams and traumatic life events may be experienced in a similar way and are stresses that provide an opportunity for mastery and growth. The mood or dramatic content of a child's or adult's vivid dream

may linger throughout the day. The child is unlikely to tell anyone about it, because many adults are not interested, do not take
the dream seriously, or offer responses which strike the child as
silly. Rochlin also points out that we know very little about the
effect of the latent or manifest content of dreams upon the daytime experience (see Mack, 1969). This is clearly an unexplored
and intriguing area for further study.

THE SIGNIFICANCE OF A CHILD'S SPECIFIC DREAM

Freud (1900) felt that children's dreams demonstrate especially
clearly the wish-fulfillment character of dreams. "The dreams
of young children," he wrote, "are frequently pure wish-
fulfilments and are in that case quite uninteresting compared
with the dreams of adults" (p. 127). The word "frequently" was
added in 1911 with the comment, "Experience has shown that
distorted dreams, which stand in need of interpretation, are
already found in children of four or five." As examples of wish-
fulfillment dreams, Freud describes his daughter Anna's dream
at age 19 months of strawberries and his nephew Hermann's
dream at age 22 months of cherries. Again, in a footnote added
in 1911, Freud further modified his position that children's
dreams are simple expressions of wish fulfillment. "The fact
should be mentioned that children soon begin to have more
complicated and less transparent dreams. . . . [There is a] wealth
of unexpected material that may occur in the dreams of children
of four or five" (p. 131). Niederland (1957), in his observations
of dreams of young children, corroborates Freud's view of the
importance of wish fulfillment, but adds that there is a "wealth of
manifest and latent dream material, of symbolism, of immediate
and remote sources used by the dream work" (p. 202) in a small
child's dream. Niederland also emphasizes that "the obscurities
in a young child's mental productions can be largely clarified by a
full knowledge of the various circumstances, family setting, external and internal influences operating in the child's life, and
their proper evaluation" (p. 202). Anna Freud (1965) in her own
observations of children's dreams also highlights the central importance of wish fulfillment: "With children, better still, there
are simple fulfillment dreams which reveal the underlying

wishes" (p. 14f.). Anna Freud (1935, 1965) emphasizes how a specific child's dream also reflects the child's repertoire of defense mechanisms. She points to how the dream's meaning can provide a survey and inventory of the functioning of the child's ego apparatus at a given time.

In their studies of normal children's dreams, Foulkes et al. (1967, 1969, 1978) found little evidence of wish fulfillment or of unresolved infantile conflict. They see children's dreams almost entirely from the side of the ego:

> ... the content of the child's dream often seems directly related to the predominant foci of his social adjustment during wakefulness. Moreover, the treatment of these situations in his dream life does not generally appear to be markedly disguised, nor are there extensive intrusions of socially unacceptable impulses, frightening fantasies, etc., or of bizarre symbolism which might mask such content. This is not to say that disguise is by any means totally lacking in the present sample of children's dreams, only that many of the dreams seem comprehensible from the simpler and more direct perspectives of a dream theory . . . which stresses the close ties between nocturnal fantasy and contemporary social adjustment and the forward-looking exploration of one's own roles and of his relations to others rather than regressive content, autistically expressed [1967, p. 466].

This viewpoint seems determined to a large extent by the laboratory setting where the children are encouraged to report dreams to satisfy the experimenter. The child's associations, play, and life history are not emphasized as ways of understanding the dreams. In a clinical setting, in which the child is encouraged to share worries and troubles, conflict is much more likely to be reflected and appreciated in dreams. This is true even in nonclinical settings where a strong interest in the meaning of dreams is present.

Specific dreams may provide a clear reflection of the level of a child's cognitive development and his cognitive style. Aaron Beck (1971) points to this when he notes,

> According to the cognitive model of dreams, certain cognitive patterns structure the content of the waking fantasies and

other waking ideational experiences as well as the content of the dreams. These cognitive patterns are specific to the individual. . . . When the individual is asleep and external input is withdrawn, the cognitive pattern exerts a maximum influence on the content of the dream [p. 7].

Piaget's theories initiated a vast amount of work in the field of cognitive development in children, but children's dreams have not been used sufficiently as a lens through which cognitive development can be explored in statu nascendi.

Nightmares are another area that offers opportunities to study the child's ego functioning in relation to dreaming. Nightmares have become an important subsection of the subject of dreams. In his studies of nightmares, Mack (1965, 1970) emphasizes the "desperate creativity" that functions simultaneously as defense and tension discharge. A nightmare can reflect mastery and a developmental advance, or indicate areas of vulnerability that lead to the child's being overwhelmed, with resultant impairment of ego functioning or more lasting symptom formation.

There has been increasing acceptance of the notion that severe night terrors of children, or pavor nocturnus, can be distinguished from the ordinary nightmare. The former, the less common stage-4 nightmare (Fisher et al., 1970), is a phenomenon of S- or non-REM sleep, while the more familiar nightmare occurs during D- or REM sleep (Fisher et al., 1970; Gastaut and Broughton, 1965; Hartmann, 1967, Mack, 1970). Hartmann and Russ (1979) have offered the interesting hypothesis that there may be some relationship between frequent D-nightmares in adults and vulnerability to schizophrenia. This possibility was suggested by the psychopathology discovered in the examination of 20 adult subjects (mean age 22) who reported at least one nightmare per week; 19 of the 20 subjects in this pilot study "had suffered from nightmares for as long as they could remember, which usually meant since age 4–6" (p. 11). It would be most interesting to follow a group of children suffering from nightmares into adulthood to determine whether the occurrence of unusually frequent nightmares in childhood may be a predictor of later emotional difficulty or psychopathology.

There has been little or no research as to how the occurrence of or susceptibility to frequent nightmares applies to the concept of the self, the development of a cohesive self, and impairments or vulnerability in the development of the self. Hartmann's (1973, p. 137) statement, "some sort of continuous feeling of the self is not present in dreams," might be taken as a hypothesis for systematic exploration. As dreams led the way for Freud in his studies of mental processes, children's dreams, and particularly nightmares, could be an important source of information in clarifying and further conceptualizing the development of the psychic structures and content which comprise a cohesive self.

DIFFERENCES BETWEEN CHILDREN'S AND ADULTS' DREAMS

It is important to clarify some of the differences between the dreams of children and adults. From the perspective of sleep physiology, premature infants have the largest amount of REM sleep. REM sleep makes up approximately 80 percent of the total sleep in premature infants. By the second half of the first year, REM sleep comprises about 30 percent of total sleep. In normal young adults, 20 to 25 percent of sleep is REM sleep. In addition, not until the end of the first year of life are sustained periods of stage-4 sleep present, which is non-REM sleep and the deepest level of sleep. If children are woken during stage-4 sleep, characteristically single vivid images are reported, in contrast to the elaborate dreams recalled during REM sleep. Stage-4 sleep is the period of the sleep cycle during which arousal may be associated with night terrors (or pavor nocturnus), somnambulism, and enuresis. Stage-4 sleep comprises 20 to 25 percent of sleep in children from age 1 year to young adulthood, approximately 10 percent in young adults, and is minimal to absent in people over 65 years of age.

Children's dreams are also distinguished from those of young adults by being more obviously related to the current issues in the child's life and structured in accord with the level of his cognitive and other ego developmental capacities. The child's developing capabilities in the areas of language and cognition are the very loom upon which the dreams are woven. At different ages children's dreams focus upon those aspects of their daily lives which are of greatest contemporary importance. Children's dreams, especially anxiety dreams, may show how these current issues are linked with earlier developmental conflicts and stresses. Some experimental confirmation of this often-noted clinical phenomenon has been provided by Witkin (1969) who studied the anxiety dreams of children following the viewing of stressful films. He notes that such dreams in their content "go back to events in the dreamer's early childhood" and that "sometimes the subject's very earliest memory is implicated" (p. 315).

There is a rich literature concerned with the content analysis of dreams, including children's dreams (see Despert, 1949; Hall and Van de Castle, 1966; Van de Castle, 1970). For example, the dreams of children in the third and fourth year of life are found, not unexpectedly, to contain images of parents, playmates, and domestic animals. More specifically, Van de Castle (1970) examined 450 dreams of children ages 4 to 16. He found that the percentage of animal dreams was much higher in the 4-year-olds than in the older children; in fact, there was a linear decrease with age. Statistical research of this nature could be of value for psychoanalysis in generating hypotheses or encouraging further work that could explore the meaning of such findings. During the oedipal period, along with pleasant dreams of everyday life, aggressive and sexual issues and anxiety about masturbation are clearly evident. Dreams at this age often involve fighting and punishment, and images of kings, queens, witches, snakes, wolves, fire and water. Ames (1964) and Green (1971) have provided nice descriptions of the changing common themes in children's dreams up to age 16. Common themes in the latency-age period are related to the prominence of the child's conscience and the child's investment in school and peers. Common subjects are authority figures such as teachers and police, friends, games, and recreational activities. In adolescence, the increased capacity for abstraction and intellectual activity is reflected in the imagery and complexity of the dreams. The upsurge of aggressive and sexual feelings in adolescence also leads to the expression, sometimes in a less well-organized structure than was present in latency, of impulse-laden interests and conflicts.

Comparing children's and adult's dreams, Freud (1901) wrote:

> But in the case of adults, anyone with some experience in analysing their dreams will find to his surprise that even those dreams which have an appearance of being transparently clear are seldom as simple as those of children, and that behind the obvious wish-fulfilment some other meaning may lie concealed [p. 646].

As we saw earlier, Freud eventually modified this view, acknowledging the increasing complexity and sophistication in children's dreams as they reach the preschool age. From the perspective of child analysis, Anna Freud (1927) offered this observation:

> When it comes to dream interpretation, . . . we can apply unchanged to children what we have learned from our work with adults. During analysis the child dreams neither less nor more than the adult; and the transparency or obscurity of the dream content is, as in the case of adults, a reflection of the strength of the resistance. Children's dreams are certainly easier to interpret, though in analysis they are not always so simple as the examples given in *The Interpretation of Dreams*. We find in them all those distortions of wish fulfillment that correspond to the complicated neurotic organization of the child patient [p. 24].

THE THERAPEUTIC USE OF CHILDREN'S DREAMS

Rexford has stressed that there are divergent opinions as to the extent to which children's dreams are accessible to the analyst (see Blom, 1960). At one time Anna Freud (1927) wrote enthusiastically about the value of dream interpretation in child analysis:

> But there is nothing easier to make the child grasp than dream interpretation.
>
> At the first account of a dream, I say, "No dream can make itself out of nothing; it must have fetched every bit from somewhere"—and then I set off with the child in search of its origins. The child amuses himself with the pursuit of the individual dream elements as with a jigsaw puzzle, and with great

satisfaction follows up the separate images or words of the dream into real life situations.

Perhaps this comes about because the child still is nearer to dreams than the adult; it may again be merely because he feels no surprise to find a meaning in dreams, not having heard the view that they have no meaning. In any case he is proud of a successful dream interpretation. Incidentally, I have often found that even unintelligent children, who in all other respects were quite unsuited for analysis, did not fail in dream interpretation. I have conducted two such analyses for an extended period almost exclusively by using dreams.

But even where the child's associations to a dream fail to appear, an interpretation is nevertheless often possible. It is so much easier to know the child's situation, the daily happenings and significant people in his life. Often one may venture to insert missing ideas into the interpretation from one's own knowledge of the situation [p. 25].

This confidence in the therapeutic value of working with children's dreams was later qualified:

Free association, the mainstay of analytic technique, had to be counted out as a method; young children are neither willing nor able to embark on it. This fact affects dream interpretation, the second main approach to the unconscious. Children tell their dreams freely; but without the use of free association, the interpretation of the manifest dream content is less fruitful and convincing [1945, p. 6].

The question of whether there are satisfactory substitutes for free association in work with young children has been the subject of rather heated debate. The view that play technique can provide similar access to the unconscious has been advanced by Melanie Klein (1932) and supported by many others. Anna Freud's position on this is clear:

Play with toys, drawings, painting, staging fantasy games, acting in the transference have been introduced and accepted in place of free association and, *faute de mieux*, child analysts have tried to convince themselves that they are valid substitutes for it. In truth they are nothing of the kind. It is one disadvantage that some of these modes of behavior produce mainly symbolic material and that this introduces into child analysis the element of doubt, uncertainty, arbitrariness which are inseparable from symbolic interpretation in general [1965, p. 29f.].

We would suggest that the potential arbitrariness of an interpretation can be balanced by the child's subsequent play and verbal response, which may or may not provide confirmation that the analyst is following a fruitful avenue.

The use of dreams in the analysis of children has been discussed at a number of panels. For example, at one (see Rangell, 1956), Editha Sterba maintained that in child analysis and therapy children's dreams play a surprisingly insignificant role. She noted, for example, that in Anna Freud's book on the psychoanalytic treatment of children only two dreams are reported. Although there was some disagreement about Sterba's observation and reports in the literature would not bear out her opinion (see, e.g., Bornstein, 1946, 1953), most participants seemed to concur and no compelling explanation for this observation was advanced.

In contrast to the views expressed by Sterba and others (see Rangell, 1956), Erna Furman (1962) discussed a severely disturbed boy in whose analysis dreams played an important role. She emphasized, "When his ego becomes strong enough to give up, in reality, a pathological behavior pattern which serves defensive purposes, the underlying conflict appears in intense dream activity" (p. 269). She also observed that when reality became less threatening and her patient felt in a better position to cope with it, "his ego allows certain of its own normal functions to appear first in dreams at a time when it still wards them off in waking life" (p. 269).

Marjorie Harley (1962) observed that her latency-age patients reported dreams only infrequently. Yet, when dreams are reported, they are useful for purposes other than direct interpretation:

> . . . either the child's explanation of the occasion for the dream, or the dream's manifest content, [has] offered a springboard to discussion of everyday events and feelings; or, usually unknown to the child, the dream has helped to clarify or to confirm preceding and subsequent material; or the latter have cast light on the implication of the latent dream thoughts,

often too unconscious to permit interpretation; or the dream has stimulated new and valuable play productions or daydreams [p. 272].

These comments are consistent with our experience, and that of others such as Lippman (1945), of the usefulness of dreams for expanding and clarifying material even when the dream is not interpreted or the child is not in as intensive a form of treatment as analysis. Harley (1962) observed that:

> ... those children who have made the most use of dream interpretation have been those under considerable inner pressure, with a corresponding weakness or weakening of the defensive barriers against their excessive excitations. It is for such children that the reported dream has seemed to me not only frequently to serve as a "safety valve" ... for the discharge of instinctual strivings, but also to provide a means of achieving some distance from which they may view their unconscious, as well as some focus for their often intense and diffuse anxiety [p. 272f.].

Harley also wonders why in recent clinical reports analysts and children use dream interpretation less in their analytic work. She suggests as a possible explanation that "the earlier methods of child analysis may have come closer, at times, to a seduction of the child's instinctual side and thus may well have led to a generally higher level of tension within the analytic situation" (p. 288).

Several panel participants (see Blom, 1956; Abbate, 1964) as well as Becker (1978) relate the role of dreams in analysis to the child's developmental stages. In the preschool age, dreams merge with fantasies and events of the day. Children in this age group share dreams as they would other natural and obvious events, but sharing dreams and working with dreams in analysis are different matters. Selma Fraiberg describes an analytic case in which dream analysis did not play a prominent role until age 6. Before that age the child did not recognize associations in his play and behavior as being related to the dreams he reported. Fraiberg reports that she had not observed any children under age 5 who could play the "what pops into mind" game (see Abbate, 1964).

During latency the child's emphasis on mastery of preoedipal and oedipal impulses, on reality, learning, and solidifying defenses results in dreams becoming less available, the child often being reluctant to explore them. However, bright children in the latency period with strong obsessive-compulsive defensive patterns may readily take to reporting and analyzing dreams as an enjoyable intellectual challenge. In early adolescence, when the ego is already struggling with the upsurge of aggressive and sexual impulses, dreams are rarely brought into therapy or analysis unless the dreams themselves are a symptom for which the child is seeking help.

That dreams are useful in child analysis, psychoanalytic psychotherapy, and even during a diagnostic evaluation seems now to be generally agreed. As has been previously noted, even the relating of dreams outside of the therapeutic context can be valuable for the development of ego skills such as the use of language, imagination, communication, reality testing, and memory. The question then arises how dream reporting by children in therapy and analysis can be facilitated. Anna Freud and Selma Fraiberg give examples in simple language of how children can be taught that "no dream can make itself out of nothing" (Anna Freud, 1927, p. 25) and how to play that "what pops into your mind game" (Fraiberg, 1965, p. 399). In addition, the analyst's interest, comfort, and enjoyment of dreams often are communicated to the child and encourage the child to talk about dreams. The vicissitudes of the transference, such as wishes to please the analyst or to withhold and frustrate him, are important factors determining whether a child will share dreams. The nature of the child's conflicts, ego structure, and developmental situation naturally affect his ability to relate dreams. Nevertheless, if the analyst has a basically positive relationship with the child and a firm therapeutic alliance, asking the child to talk about dreams performs an important educational function. It teaches the child one of the best ways to learn about the unconscious. Direct questions about dreams early in the treatment rarely have an adverse effect, or produce a negative response, except when the child opposes the treatment, or has paranoid or narcissistic problems that cause him to experience such questions as unwelcome or painful intrusions. In such cases, direct questions about whether a child has any dreams to tell should probably be avoided. Adults are often sophisticated enough to know about the importance of dreams, and after a period of treatment and analysis of resistance will usually report dreams spontaneously. This cannot be expected of children so that the responsibility for inquiring about dreams generally rests with the analyst.

In order to gain additional perspectives on the therapeutic value of children's dreams, we would like to report material from the analysis of a 5-year-old boy and compare the use made of the dream material with how Freud (1909) dealt with the dreams of Little Hans.

Jeff entered analysis at age 5 because of moderately severe stuttering. He was inattentive at school because of his preoccupation with aggressive fantasies that were elaborations of superhero television programs. He had very few friends because of his overbearing, controlling behavior and occasional outbursts in which he hit and cursed other children. In his early years, Jeff's parents had traveled a great deal. As a result he was precipitously toilet trained at 2½ during an assignment overseas. During these trips, Jeff's mother was often depressed and would threaten, punish, and withdraw from him when he was demanding or aggressive. At age 3½ the family settled in one location, but Jeff's father still traveled often and was away for long periods of time. He was a bombastic man, given to angry, frightening outbursts. Jeff copied and admired his father, while fearing his mother's repressive, punitive responses to his anger and disobedience. When Jeff was 4, his sister was born.

In the first months of analysis Jeff developed a very positive relationship with the analyst. This seemed to be based on his longing for his father, his sense that he was safe with his analyst, and that his analyst took a consistent interest in him. He developed the beginning of a therapeutic alliance, verbalizing his feeling that the analyst would help him to understand his anger so that he would not be so frightened of it. During his treatment hour Jeff was very enthusiastic, bright, and engaging. He was extremely polite, and there was little evidence of anger outside of his preoccupation with playing superhero games in which there were many miraculous adventures and victories with much shooting and bombing. In his play his interest in feces and smearing became prominent. This was connected with his ideas about fecal babies and fecal penises. It also became clear that he struggled with a great deal of castration anxiety in relation to his absent, frightening father and his controlling, but now very attentive, mother. The castration anxiety was so marked that he consistently retreated from phallic concerns to anal preoccupations.

After 6 months of analysis Jeff's stuttering had almost entirely disappeared and he was less bossy and aggressive with other children. His analyst had explained to him about dreams, and they talked about how much could be learned from dreams about his feelings and worries, and how to play "what pops into mind" as a way of learning about dreams. Jeff was intrigued with this and brought occasional dreams to analysis. These dreams were very brief and difficult to separate from his fantasies, what he saw on television, and what occurred to him as he told the dream and embellished it. Jeff had no interest in associating verbally to his dreams. When asked about this, he stated clearly that he did not want to talk about it anymore—he wanted to play. In the sixth month of analysis Jeff began an hour by telling about a popular science fiction movie he had seen with his father during the weekend. Then Jeff played a game he called rescue, in which an injured man is rescued by the police and an ambulance is called. At that point Jeff looked at the analyst and was reluctant to say what he was thinking. He said he was thinking that his analyst's voice had changed. Then he played a game in which there was an attack from evil spacemen, but Superman fought them, ultimately defeating them by throwing a bathtub at them and, as a second thought, a stove. The analyst suggested that perhaps Jeff was saying he would not tell the analyst anything if he got angry at him. Jeff agreed and then played darts, remarking that he had not gotten the bull's-eye. He moved up very close so he did get a bull's-eye. At this point Jeff said that he wanted to tell the analyst about "something scary at night—these men were digging a grave, they were half finished and they went for supper. The dead person rose up, went to the millionaire's house, broke in and killed him." Jeff said he was scared after the dream and thought he would not be able to sleep, but he did. Jeff said he had the dream twice. This seemed to occur to him at the time he was telling the dream.

Jeff would not play the "what pops into your mind game." He

wanted to describe a very scary movie his father had seen and told him about. Jeff said in the movie people are changed into monsters by radiation, and all come alive at dawn. He added that it was bad for dead people to come out of the grave. Jeff then asked the analyst whether he was growing a beard. He said his father had a beard. The analyst understood the dream as an expression of Jeff's competitive conflicts with his father, and his fear of his frightening father who watched scary movies. The fear seemed connected to retaliation for Jeff's wish to break in and kill his father and have the millionaire's house and his mother, whom he loved so much, all to himself. The millionaire seemed to represent both Jeff's father and his analyst, whom Jeff saw in a big house. For Jeff, who was in the grip of murderous transference feelings, his analyst, with his imagined different voice and beard, seemed to have taken on the characteristics of Jeff's father. At the same time the dream expressed the work Jeff and his analyst were doing—digging up feelings and memories and, symbolically, in the violent play killing his father. That the two men go to supper seemed to express a maternal, nurturing side of Jeff's relationship with the analyst and a longing for such closeness with his father.

The analyst chose at this point, because of the early stage of the treatment, and in order to respect the defensive functions of the ego, only gradually to interpret repressed material. In this way an effort was made not to raise the level of anxiety in the analytic situation to such an extent that it would impede the progress of the analytic work. The analyst chose, therefore, to say to Jeff that he thought the dream had to do with angry feelings that many boys have; Jeff might be angry at his father and be afraid that if his father knew about Jeff's anger, he would be angry at Jeff too. This seemed acceptable to Jeff, and the hour continued with his playing at fighting enemies from outer space. One of the men was shot dead, but was taken to a house where he became "all right" again. Then a dart board was used to close off the house and protect it from other attacks from outer space. At this point, Jeff ate a candy and earnestly told the analyst that as soon as he got home he would brush his teeth. He said that you always have to brush your teeth after sweets or you'll get cavities.

A comparison of how Jeff's dream might be worked with today

with how Freud interpreted Little Hans's dreams about 70 years ago presents some interesting problems. The situations in many ways are not, of course, comparable, especially since Little Hans's treatment was carried out by his own father under Freud's direction. In the analysis of Little Hans, three dreams are reported. In the work with these dreams a number of similarities are immediately apparent. For instance, the importance of the dream in the context of the child's daily life is clearly appreciated. Little Hans's dream of forfeits is referred to subsequently in the treatment, as was Jeff's dream of coming out of the grave. In addition, Hans's dream at age 4¾, "When I was asleep I thought you were gone and I had no Mummy to coax with" (p. 23), is not interpreted, but rather used as a way of understanding the child's conflicts which were only gradually brought into consciousness as the material developed and deepened. This is similar to how Jeff's dream was used. While Freud tended to focus primarily upon the repressed mental content revealed by the dreams, like the game of forfeits or losing his mother, today we would approach such material through the analysis of ego defenses. As in Jeff's case, we would make the child more of an ally or partner in the effort to understand the dream's significance. This effort would include emphasis on teaching about dreams and how to associate to them, and play would be perceived as a useful kind of associative activity. In addition, today there would be more emphasis on the dimensions of transference and on the revelation in dreams of levels of ego development, defensive capability, and cognitive style. In recent work with dreams greater attention also tends to be paid to preoedipal issues and to problems of aggression, which dreams often make transparent. Nevertheless, in the first report of a child analysis, Little Hans's father, with Freud's guidance, takes a remarkably thorough interest in Little Hans's dreams. Hans's father and Freud examine the dreams in relation to Hans's daily life, elucidate the defensive operations involved in the dreams, and formulate how these dreams reflect the child's wishes and conflicts. How much was done with Little Hans's dreams accentuates in many ways how little child analysts have subsequently developed and expanded the subject of analytic work with children's dreams.

SUMMARY AND CONCLUSION

The dream is one of our most fertile sources of knowledge about the inner world of childhood and the child's unconscious mental life. The dream, in its manifest content and latent meanings, is powerfully connected with the deeper emotional currents of the child's inner life, and is a vehicle through which he seeks to assimilate and integrate his ongoing experience. Certain dreams of childhood remain compelling for the adult and may provide a kind of signpost or landmark for the early memories which it both reveals and conceals. The dream provides a window into various processes of development. Anxiety dreams or night-mares in particular provide a rich source of data about the con-temporary struggles of children and their link to earlier fears and conflicts. Through the child's dream we can study affective and cognitive development and learn about the growth of men-tal organization. The developing structures of language and their link to powerful drives and compelling emotional experi-ences can be approached through the exploration of the child's dream. The impetus to creativity is best seen in the tendency of children to elaborate their dreams into stories and dramas— proclivities which can be facilitated when the child is encouraged to communicate his dream experience to others. In his novel *When the Tree Sings* (1979), Stratis Haviaras tells of a small boy who was trapped for several hours underground in a tomb. He relived the terrifying experience in repetitive dreams. In her advice to him his grandmother shows a deep understanding of the importance of dreams in childhood for keeping alive the memories of troubling experience and even permitting its ulti-mate integration through creative activity:

> She also said that I should try not to forget the details of my accident and what I was afraid of while I waited to be rescued. Nor should I forget the thoughts that were connected with it, or the dreams I'd had since then. "Because if you do forget them, a good part of you would be trapped in that tomb forever," she said. I started writing down everything on a sheet of paper, but I couldn't remember very much, and I soon realized that I was making up most of the dreams and stories,

so I decided to stop writing and start using my shadow puppets instead [p. 124].

Anna Freud and other child analysts have written of the potential usefulness of dream analysis in the treatment of children. Nevertheless, despite their richness as a source of knowledge about childhood, children's dreams have been little investigated by psychoanalysts, and there are relatively few reports of their use in the evaluation, psychotherapy, or psychoanalytic treatment of children. The reasons for this are unclear to us. Perhaps the emphasis in recent decades upon personality structure, object relations, parent-child attachment and separation, narcissism and the development of the self have led us away from the study of unconscious mental life as revealed in dreams in its deepest and truest sense. All of these subjects can also be well explored through the medium of the child's dream.

The discoveries beginning in the 1950s of the neurobiology of sleep and dreaming have perhaps put psychoanalysts on the defensive about the seemingly pedestrian activity of talking with children and their parents about dreams. But the findings of these studies, especially the discovery that infants and small children spend an especially high percentage of their sleeping hours in the D-state or REM sleep, should only encourage our interest in children's dreams. In fact, these findings suggest that dreaming is associated with central nervous system activities and functions which are of particular importance during the period in which the brain is undergoing its most rapid growth and change. Thus we may say in conclusion that if this review has any overriding purpose, it is to encourage a return to the study of dreams, especially the dreams of children. For it has been confirmed again and again that there is no shortcut to the discovery of the unconscious and that dreams are its royal road.

BIBLIOGRAPHY

Abbate, G. M. (1964), Report of Panel: Child Analysis at Different Developmental Stages. *J. Amer. Psychoanal. Assn.*, 12:135–150.
Ablon, S. L. & Mack, J. E. (1979), Sleep Disorders in Children. In: *Basic Handbook of Child Psychiatry*, ed. J. D. Noshpitz. New York: Basic Books, 2:643–660.

AMES, L. B. (1964), Sleep and Dreams In Childhood. In: *Problems of Sleep and Dream in Children*, ed. E. Harms. New York: Macmillan, pp. 6–29.

ARLOW, J. A. (1958), Report of Panel: The Psychoanalytic Theory of Thinking. *J. Amer. Psychoanal. Assn.*, 6:143–153.

BECK, A. T. (1971), Cognitive Patterns in Dreams and Daydreams. In: *Dream Dynamics [Science and Psychoanalysis, 19]*, ed. J. H. Masserman. New York: Grune & Stratton, pp. 2–7.

BECKER, T. E. (1978), Dream Analysis in Child Analysis. In: *Child Analysis and Therapy*, ed. J. Glenn. New York: Jason Aronson, pp. 355–374.

BLOM, G. E. (1960), Report of Panel: The Role of the Dream in Child Analysis. *J. Amer. Psychoanal. Assn.*, 8:517–525.

BORNSTEIN, B. (1946), Hysterical Twilight States in an Eight-Year-Old Child. *This Annual*, 2:229–240.

——— (1953), Fragments of an Analysis of an Obsessional Child. *This Annual*, 8:313–332.

BYRON, G. G. (1854), *The Works of Lord Byron Including The Suppressed Poems and Also A Sketch of His Life by J. W. Lake*. Philadelphia: Lippincott, Grambot Co., pp. 516–517.

CASTLE, W. (1971), Contributions of Piaget to a Theory of Dreaming. In: *Dream Dynamics [Science and Psychoanalysis, 19]*, ed. J. H. Masserman. New York: Grune & Stratton, pp. 98–116.

CHUANG TSU, *Inner Chapters*, tr. Gin-Fu Feng & J. English. New York: Random House, 1974.

DEMARTINO, F. (1955), A Review of the Literature on Children's Dreams. *Psychiat. Quart. Suppl.*, 29:90–101.

DESPERT, J. L. (1949), Dreams in Children of Preschool Age. *This Annual*, 3/4:141–180.

The Epic of Gilgamesh, tr. N. K. Sandars. New York: Penguin Books, 1960.

ERICKSON, M. H. (1941), On the Possible Occurrence of a Dream in an Eight-Month-Old Infant. *Psychoanal. Quart.*, 10:382–384.

FISHER, C. (1957), The Study of the Preliminary Stages of the Construction of Dreams and Images. *J. Amer. Psychoanal. Assn.*, 5:5–60.

——— BYRNE, J., EDWARDS, A., & KAHN, E. (1970), A Psychophysiological Study of Nightmares. *J. Amer. Psychoanal. Assn.*, 18:747–782.

FOULKES, D. P. (1978), *A Grammar of Dreams*. New York: Basic Books.

——— LARSON, D. L., SWANSON, E. M., & RARDIN, M. (1969), Two Studies of Childhood Dreaming. *Amer. J. Orthopsychiat.*, 39:627–643.

——— PIVIK, T., STEADMAN, H. S., SPEAR, P. S., & SYMONDS, J. D. (1967), Dreams of the Male Child. *J. Abnorm. Psychol.*, 72:457–467.

FRAIBERG, S. (1950), Sleep Disturbances of Early Childhood. *This Annual*, 5:285–309.

——— (1959), *The Magic Years*. New York: Charles Scribner's Sons, p. 79.

——— (1965), A Comparison of the Analytic Method in Two Stages of a Child Analysis. *J. Amer. Acad. Child Psychiat.*, 4:387–400.

FRENCH, T. & FROMM, E. (1964), *Dream Interpretation*. New York: Basic Books.

FREUD, A. (1927), Four Lectures on Child Analysis. *W.*, 1:3–69.

_____ (1936), The Ego and the Mechanisms of Defense. *W.*, 2.

———— (1945), Indications for Child Analysis. *W.*, 4:3–38.

———— (1965), Normality and Pathology in Childhood. *W.*, 6.

FREUD, S. (1900), The Interpretation of Dreams. *S.E.*, 4 & 5.

———— (1901), On Dreams. *S.E.*, 5:629–686.

———— (1909), Analysis of a Phobia in a Five-Year-Old Boy. *S.E.*, 10:3–149.

———— (1915), The Unconscious. *S.E.*, 14:159–215.

———— (1920), Beyond the Pleasure Principle. *S.E.*, 18:3–64.

———— (1933), New Introductory Lectures on Psycho-Analysis. *S.E.*, 22:3–182.

FURMAN, E. (1962), Some Features of the Dream Function of a Severely Disturbed Young Child. *J. Amer. Psychoanal. Assn.*, 10:258–270.

GASTAUT, H. & BROUGHTON, R. (1965), A Clinical and Polygraphic Study of Episodic Phenomena During Sleep. In: *Recent Advances in Biological Psychiatry*, ed. J. Wortis. New York: Plenum Press, 7:197–221.

GREEN, M. R. (1971), Clinical Significance of Children's Dreams. In: *Dream Dynamics* [*Science and Psychoanalysis*, 19], ed. J. H. Masserman. New York: Grune & Stratton, pp. 72–97.

GREENACRE, P. (1964), A Study on the Nature of Inspiration. *J. Amer. Psychoanal. Assn.*, 12:6–31.

GREENBERG, R. & PEARLMAN, C. (1975), A Psychoanalytic-Dream Continuum. *Int. Rev. Psycho-Anal.*, 2:441–448.

———— & PEARLMAN, C. (1978), If Freud Only Knew. *Int. Rev. Psycho-Anal.*, 5:71–75.

GROLNICK, A. (1978), Dreams and Dreaming as Transitional Phenomena. In: *Between Reality and Fantasy*, ed. S. A. Grolnick, L. Barkin, & W. Muensterberger. New York: Jason Aronson, pp. 213–231.

GROTJAHN, M. (1938), Dream Observations in a Two-Year-Four-Month-Old Baby. *Psychoanal. Quart.*, 7:507–513.

HALL, C. S. & VAN DE CASTLE, R. L. (1966), *The Content Analysis of Dreams*. New York: Appleton-Century-Crofts.

HARLEY, M. (1962), The Role of the Dream in the Analysis of a Latency Child. *J. Amer. Psychoanal. Assn.*, 10:271–288.

HARTMANN, E. L. (1967), *The New Biology of Dreaming*. Springfield, Ill.: Charles C Thomas.

———— (1973), *The Functions of Sleep*. New Haven & London: Yale Univ. Press.

_____ & RUSS, D. (1979), Frequent Nightmares and the Vulnerability to Schizophrenia. *Psychopharm. Bull.*, 15:10–12.

HAVIARAS, S. (1979), *When the Tree Sings*. New York: Simon & Schuster.

HIRSCHBERG, J. C. (1966), Dreaming, Drawing and the Dream Screen in the Psychoanalysis of a 2½-Year-Old Boy. *Amer. J. Psychiat.*, 122:37–45.

HUG-HELLMUTH, H. VON (1919), *A Study of the Mental Life of the Child*, tr. I. T. Putnam & M. Stevens. Washington: Nervous and Mental Diseases Publishing Co.

ISAACS, S. (1932), *The Nursery Years*. New York: Vanguard Press.

IZARD, C. E. & TOMKINS, S. S. (1966), Anxiety as a Negative Affect. In: *Anxiety and Behavior*, ed. C. D. Spielberger. New York & London: Academic Press, pp. 81–125.

JESSNER, L., BLOM, G. E., & WALDFOGEL, S. (1952), Emotional Implications of Tonsillectomy and Adenoidectomy on Children. *This Annual*, 7:126–169.
JONES, R. M. (1970), *The New Psychology of Dreaming*. New York: Grune & Stratton.
KLAUS, M. H. & KENNEL, J. H. (1976), *Maternal-Infant Bonding*. St. Louis: C. V. Mosby.
KLEIN, M. (1932), *The Psycho-Analysis of Children*. New York: Grove Press, 1960.
LACAN, J. (1968), *The Language of the Self*, ed. & tr. A. Wilden. Baltimore: Johns Hopkins Univ. Press.
——— (1978), *The Four Fundamental Concepts of Psychoanalysis*. New York: Norton.
LEAVITT, H. C. (1957), Teleological Contributions of Dreams to the Waking Ego. *Psychoanal. Rev.*, 44:212–219.
LEAVY, S. A. (1978), The Significance of Jacques Lacan. In: *Psychoanalysis and Language*, ed. J. Smith. New Haven & London: Yale Univ. Press, pp. 271–292.
LEVY, D. (1945), Psychic Trauma of Operations in Children. *Amer. J. Dis. Child.*, 59:7–25.
LIPPMAN, H. S. (1945), The Use of Dreams in Psychiatric Work. *This Annual*, 1:233–245.
MACK, J. E. (1965), Nightmares, Conflicts, and Ego Development in Childhood. *Int. J. Psycho-Anal.*, 46:403–428.
——— (1969), Report of Panel: Dreams and Psychosis. *J. Amer. Psychoanal. Assn.*, 17:206–221.
——— (1970), *Nightmares and Human Conflict*. Boston: Little, Brown.
MARKOWITZ, I., BOKERT, E., SLESER, I., & TAYLOR, G. (1967), A Cybernetic Model of Dreaming. *Psychiat. Quart. Suppl.*, 14:57–68.
——— MARK, J. C., & SEIDERMAN, S. (1963), An Investigation of Parental Recognition of Children's Dreams. In: *Violence and War* [*Science and Psychoanalysis*, 6], ed. J. H. Masserman. New York: Grune & Stratton, pp. 135–151.
MONCHAUX, C. DE (1978), Dreaming and the Organizing Function of the Ego. *Int. J. Psycho-Anal.*, 59:443–453.
NIEDERLAND, W. G. (1957), The Earliest Dreams of a Young Child. *This Annual*, 12:190–208.
The Oxford English Dictionary (1969). London: Oxford Univ. Press, p. 655.
PALOMBO, S. R. (1978), *Dreaming and Memory*. New York: Basic Books.
PIAGET, J. (1929), *The Child's Conception of the World*. New York: Harcourt Brace, pp. 88–122.
——— (1945), *Play, Dreams and Imitation in Childhood*. New York: Norton, 1951.
PLATO, *The Republic*. New York: Penguin Books, 1974.
RANGELL, L. (1956), Report of Panel: The Dream in the Practice of Psychoanalysis. *J. Amer. Psychoanal. Assn.*, 4:122–137.
SEROG, M. (1964), The Dream, Its Phenomenology, Its Theory and Its Interpretation. In: *Problems of Sleep and Dream in Children*, ed. E. Harms. New York: Macmillan, pp. 47–59.

STERNLICHT, M. (1966), Dreaming in Adolescent and Adult Institutionalized Mental Retardates. *Psychiat. Quart. Suppl.*, 40:97–99.

TOMKINS, S. S. (1962), *Affect, Imagery, Consciousness* vol. 1: *Positive Affects*. New York: Springer.

——— (1963), *Affect, Imagery, Consciousness*, vol. 2: *Negative Affects*. New York: Springer.

VAN DE CASTLE, R. L. (1969), Problems in Applying Methodology of Content Analysis. In: *Dream Psychology and the New Biology of Dreaming*, ed. M. Kramer. Springfield, Ill.: Charles C Thomas, pp. 185–197.

WINNICOTT, D. W. (1945), Primitive Emotional Development. In: *Through Paediatrics to Psycho-Analysis*. New York: Basic Books. pp. 145–156.

WITKIN, H. A. (1969), Influencing Dream Content. In: *Dream Psychology and the New Biology of Dreaming*, ed. M. Kramer. Springfield: Charles C Thomas, pp. 285–343.

Sleep Disturbance and Father Hunger in 18- to 28-Month-Old Boys

The Erlkönig Syndrome

JAMES M. HERZOG, M.D.

Erlkönig

Who is riding so late through dark and wind?
It is the father with his child.
He has the boy snug in his arms
He holds him safely; he keeps him warm.

'My son, why are you scared and hiding your face?'
'Father—can't you see the Erlking, the Erlking
with crown and robe?'
'My son, it is a wisp of cloud.'

'You, darling child, come, go with me!
I will play lovely games with you.
There are heaps of bright flowers on the shore,
my mother has lots of golden clothes.'

Director, Infant Follow-Up Clinic; Director, Clinic for the Development of Young Children and Parents; Staff Psychiatrist, Children's Hospital Medical Center, Boston; Assistant Professor of Psychiatry, Harvard Medical School.

'Father, father, can't you hear what the Erlking
whispers and promises me?'
'Hush, don't fret, my son, it is the wind
rustling in the dry leaves.'

'Pretty boy, will you come with me?
My daughters shall look after you nicely,
every night they will dance the round
and will rock and dance and sing you to sleep.'

'Oh, father, oh father, can't you see the Erlking's
daughters over there at that dismal place?'
'My son, my son, I can see it plain;
it is the old willows that gleam all grey.'

'I love you, your beautiful shape excites me,
and if you won't come willingly, I will use force.'
'Father, father, now he's taking hold of me!
He has hurt me, the Erlking has!'

The father is terrified, he rides fast,
he holds the groaning child in his arms
it is all he can do to reach the farm;
in his arms the child was dead.

GOETHE (1786)

THROUGHOUT THE LIFE CYCLE, DISRUPTIONS OF PHYSICAL FUNC-
tion accompany psychological distress and disorder. As psychiatrists and psychoanalysts, we are accustomed to encountering
problems in feeding, sleeping, elimination, and sexual function
as components of the natural history of a multiplicity of disorders. In infancy and early childhood, such physiological dysfunction is particularly striking because it is often the primary
indication of disequilibrium, either in the caretaker-child matrix
or within the developing psyche of the child (Richmond and
Lipton, 1958).

This paper will describe a particular kind of psychosomatic
disturbance, a sleep disorder occurring in a group of little boys as
the apparent concomitant of similar life experience, the recent
loss of their father through divorce or separation. An attempt

will be made to understand the mechanisms which underlie the specificity of the response to a developmentally heightened need which is being frustrated. Thus, this paper is not so much a contribution to the nosology of the dyssomnias as an inquiry into the consequences of a specific developmental deprivation.

REVIEW OF THE LITERATURE

In contradistinction to early infancy and to later childhood, sleep disturbance in the period from 15 to 30 months of age is almost universal (Gesell and Ilg, 1943). This appears to be equally so for male and female children. According to Anna Freud (1965),

> However carefully an infant's sleeping habits and arrangements have been handled in the first year of life, difficulties with sleep, or with the ease of falling asleep, intervene almost without exception in the second year . . . falling asleep is no longer a purely physical affair as the almost automatic response to a body need in an undifferentiated individual, in whom ego and id, self and the object world are not yet separated off from each other. With the strengthening of the child's object ties and of his involvement in the happenings of the external world, withdrawal of libido and of ego interests to the self becomes a prerequisite for sleep. This is not always accomplished without difficulty, and the anxiety aroused by the process makes the toddler cling all the more tenaciously to wakefulness. These symptomatic manifestations of the state [of wakefulness] . . . again disappear spontaneously when the child's object relationships become more secure and less ambivalent, and when his ego becomes stabilized sufficiently to permit regression to the undifferentiated, narcissistic state necessary for sleep [p. 157f.].

The most dramatic and distressing sleep disturbances of this period probably are the nightmares and the night terrors. Hippocrates attributed these frightening experiences to cerebral hyperperfusion (Chadwick and Mann, 1950). In 1500, the Belgian physician Roelans described the phenomenology of these occurrences and listed them as one of 52 diseases afflicting children. The first English pediatrician, Thomas Phaer, also discussed nightmares in his *Boke of Chyldren* published in 1545. In more recent times, Jones (1931), Fisher et al. (1970, 1973, 1974), and Mack (1965, 1970) have written on this subject.

Some authors draw a technical distinction between nightmares and night terrors (Kanner, 1957; Keith, 1975). The former are seen as severe anxiety dreams occurring in REM sleep; the latter, as one of the arousal disorders occurring in stage-4 non-REM sleep. Clinically, particularly in young children, it is often difficult to distinguish between night terrors and nightmares. The child awakens, usually early in the course of the night, and is terrified and inconsolable. He is often difficult to reach or make contact with. There are signs of autonomic overactivity, and the child's affect suggests that the terror that accompanied awakening has not yet abated. Incidence figures for this experience, principally reported for older children, are approximately 1 to 3 percent (Kales et al., 1968).[1]

Several analysts have focused on the meaning of these terrifying nocturnal occurrences of childhood. Freud (1895) regarded night terrors as a form of anxiety neurosis with hysterical features; Helene Deutsch (1932), as the most intense form of that infantile anxiety which lets us see the difficulties which even a child has to contend with in his psychological development. Abraham (1913) and Waelder Hall (1930) saw the symptoms as being related to oedipal conflicts; whereas Niederland (1957), Fraiberg (1950), and Sperling (1955), who described pavor nocturnus or night terrors in 2- and 3-year-olds, emphasized pregenital conflicts with marked oral and anal-sadistic components. Despert's study (1949) of 190 dreams of preschoolers tends to corroborate the latter findings. Klein (1932) found oedipal concerns in preoedipal garb in her analyses of children with night terrors. Levy (1945) reported that nightmares and night terrors were the characteristic form of disturbance in 1- and 2-year-olds following surgery. Nagera (1966) comments "that sleep, at first merely vulnerable in infancy, assumes the specific coloring of each successive libidinal phase and can gradually become a major area of neurotic conflict" (p. 423).

---

1. Comprehensive reviews of sleep disturbances in children of this age have appeared in both the pediatric and psychoanalytic literature (Fraiberg, 1950; Friend, 1956; Guilleminault and Anders, 1976; Sperling, 1955).

THE CLINICAL MATERIAL

During a six-month period, at two clinical settings in Boston, I saw 12 little boys between the ages of 18 and 28 months whose chief complaint was a syndrome resembling night terrors. In each of the cases, the disorder had had its onset during the preceding three weeks. The little boy would awaken early in the course of the night after falling asleep with greater or lesser difficulty. He would seem terrified, disoriented, and call for help. Often, he would sob, "Daddy, Daddy." The mother would attempt to comfort her child and feel that her ministrations were to no avail. Initial inquiry revealed a strikingly consistent family constellation. In each of the cases, the parents had separated or were divorced in the preceding four months. In 8 of the 12 cases, the father's departure had resulted in a change of sleeping arrangements. In 4 of these 8 cases, mother and son were sharing the same bed; in the other 4, they were merely sharing the same bedroom. Other identifying data, associated findings, and potential precipitants differed in these 12 cases. Developmental histories, ordinal position in the sibship, nature of the previous mother-child and father-child relationship, and antecedent sleep history all possessed a decidedly idiographic character. The nomothetic observation, however, was the onset of a night-terrorlike sleep disturbance within four months of the father's departure from the home.

Children progress rapidly along a variety of developmental lines. At 28 months, the child usually is at a place that differs significantly from where he was at 18. To exemplify these developmental differences and yet demonstrate the consistent refrains, I shall present 3 cases.

CASE 1

Gary was 18 months when his mother brought him to the clinic. She explained that he awakened every night for the past week, screaming as if something were after him. Gary and his mother were sharing a bed since the departure of his father one month earlier. The mother therefore observed each episode in its entirety. "Gary wakes suddenly," she reported, "he seems to jump off the bed. He screams uncontrollably, sometimes for 20 minutes to an hour. There is a look of fear in his eyes. He cannot be reached."

The pregnancy and early developmental history of this little boy were entirely within normal limits. He was the first child of a 23-year-old mother and a 25-year-old father. The three months preceding the father's departure had been most tumultuous and had involved considerable affective display in the household. When Gary's father would shout at his mother, the little boy would cover his ears or begin to cry. There had been no contact between Gary and his father in the intervening month. As Gary's mother was finishing her description, she suddenly looked quite angry and said, "Oh, I forgot to mention that when Gary wakes up and starts screaming, he calls for his Daddy. I don't know whether that should make me angry or make me sad."

Gary was a tall, blond, attractive boy who separated easily from his mother and ran smilingly into the playroom. He immediately got into my lap. Staying in constant physical contact with me, he began to play with some clay. He rolled it into long loglike pieces and then broke them into smaller parts. He laughed, seemingly with pleasure. I introduced a puppet into the play who picked up one of the pieces. The puppet could be taken for an adult male—a Daddy perhaps. Gary looked very frightened and said, "Daddy hurt Daddy hurt." I thought that Gary was indicating that the Daddy was hurt and I said, "What is the matter?" There was no response. Then I asked, "Who can help?" To this Gary brightened and said, "Daddy help Gary—please." He hugged me hard at this point. At a later time, a little boy puppet was sleeping in the same bed with his Mommy. Suddenly, he jumped up. I got out a pencil, called it a dream-machine, and put it on the little boy puppet's head. "What's happening?" I said, "Let's see if we can see what's happening to him." Gary peered through the pencil dream-machine and then looked very frightened. "Scare," he said. "Scare me—Daddy hurt quick get Daddy— Daddy help Gary." I had the Mommy puppet get up and try to comfort the little boy puppet. "No, no," shrieked Gary, looking very afraid, "Daddy hurt, get Daddy." I then introduced the adult man puppet. Gary put him next to the little boy. Then he had the man put the little boy in a separate bed and return to his wife's bed. "All better now," Gary said happily.

In real life, Gary's sleep disturbance lasted for about one month. His father did not come back and make it all better. He and I met twice a week during this period, at the end of which Gary's affection for me began to wane. The play seemed very similar in our eight meetings. Our work was interrupted when Gary's mother decided to move back to the city from where she came. She wrote me a note saying that she would look for a new Daddy for her son and for herself.

CASE 2

Ira was 28 months old when his mother, a physician, brought him to the clinic. He was the youngest of three children. Four months earlier, his father, also a physician, had announced that he was in love with a female colleague and moved out of the home. Both parents were "working on the situation" in couples treatment and Ira saw his father on weekends.

Ira's previous development had been unremarkable. Because both parents worked, he was cared for by a devoted housekeeper from the time he was 3 months old until the present. His two older brothers, almost 5 and 7, were functioning quite well. The mother attributed the continuing smooth functioning of the family to the steadying influence of the housekeeper, who accompanied them to the clinic. The chief complaint was that Ira had been awakening for the past two weeks every night screaming and tearful. He had his own room and would come darting out as though he were being chased. Neither the mother nor the housekeeper could comfort him at these times, and the situation was deteriorating rapidly. Ira had begun to refuse to go to bed; the previous three nights he had not fallen asleep until well after midnight.

On the weekend following his first symptomatic week, Ira had been with his father. He had awakened screaming as usual. His father had come to him, held the screaming child, and said, "It's a dream, Ira. Do not be afraid." The little boy had sobbed, "Daddy, Daddy," and clung to his father with all his might. "They're after me, please don't let them hurt me," he cried. The following week, in his mother's home, the night terrors continued. "Daddy said it's a dream," the little boy would say before going to sleep, as if to give himself courage. When he awoke in the night, he would scream for his father and could not be comforted by his mother. The housekeeper informed me that she had spoken to the boy's father and told him that he needed to come home, if not for his wife's sake then for his son's.

Ira was a very tired-looking boy with big sad eyes. He, too, separated from his mother and caretaker with great ease, taking my hand and saying, "You will help me. Are you a Daddy?" We began to play and, before long, I produced my dream-machine. Ira said, "This little boy is having a bad dream. I have them too. He is dreaming big bird. He eats the boy's head. The boy is scared." "What can we do to help the boy?" I asked. "Get the Daddy," Ira cried. He was literally in tears. "Why the Daddy? How can he help?" I asked. "He is *like* the boy. He can because he knows the boy. He is not a Mommy," Ira cried.

Ira's development was significantly more advanced than Gary's in a number of ways. He was able to recognize the notion of a dream entity. The dream was conceptualized as an external process (Piaget, 1945) but not yet as one created by the dreamer himself. As Kohlberg (1968) has shown, such realization usually does not occur until the age of 6 or 7 years.

Ira's father did come back and the boy's night terrors abated. I continued to see Ira in psychotherapy. He was greatly concerned about a number of big birds with blatantly aggressive proclivities and continued to employ phobic displacement as his principal defensive maneuver. He was not, however, blatantly symptomatic.

CASE 3

When Marvin's parents separated, he too developed a syndrome resembling night terrors. He would awaken screaming each night. He said that he was being pursued by a dog which would bark and then bite him. In happier times, Marvin and his father had played a "doggie" game. The father would get down on all fours, begin barking ferociously, and then chase the little boy. The child would flee amidst squeals and howls of what was thought to be mock terror. Sometimes, the roles were reversed and Marvin would attack, bark, and bite.

Marvin's mother did not seek assistance when her son's sleep was initially disturbed. She concluded to her satisfaction that Marvin's symptoms were a response to her husband's departure. When three weeks later, however, Marvin who was then 22 months old developed a daytime phobia of dogs, his mother decided that professional assistance was indicated. Marvin became afraid of Baba, his word for dog, and would shake with terror whenever dog or Baba was mentioned. He refused to attend his nursery school and grew ever more frightened and restricted. His previous history was more complicated than that of any of the other boys: he had a chronic medical illness, and his mother had a psychiatric illness.

Initially, Marvin was wary of me, as was his mother; but by the second interview both had become very attached and Marvin began to refer to me as Bubu, a name which to my ears was very similar to Baba. At this time, the little boy's language was quite impaired and he said very little. Whereas he previously had been able to leave his mother easily, both he and she now considered this an impossibility, to a degree which far exceeded any such phenomena observable in normal rapprochement. Marvin presented a full-scale phobia. His entire day revolved around the avoidance of Baba. Initially, the play was comparably monothematic. Baba was a merciless creature who attacked, and attacked, and attacked. Over time (a 10-month period), a modification occurred: Baba could be controlled by Bubu. Bubu originally and for a long time stood for me, but ultimately became a part of Boy-Boy. Marvin said that Boy-Boy needed to have Bubu control Baba in order not to be afraid of Baba. Bubu could become part of Boy-Boy because they were *alike*—not the same, but alike. Eventually, we learned that Baba was a part of Boy-Boy too. At the end of the treatment, Marvin, then 4 years old, said that Boy-Boy should now be called Bart. Bart was big and well and he contained Boy-Boy (sometimes now called bye-bye), Baba (sometimes called angry or mad), and Bubu (frequently called you-you).

DISCUSSION

The three cases presented varied in the degree to which the symptomatology was elaborated. Moreover, the children, whose

ages ranged from 18 to 28 months, were at different developmental levels. Nevertheless, common themes and mechanisms
could be discerned. Each was struggling with something scary
which at least initially proclaimed itself during sleep, and each
boy perceived his father's presence or return as a vital element in
controlling or combatting that fear. We know from the work of
Galenson and Roiphe (1976), Kleeman (1965, 1966, 1976), Maccoby (1966), Money and Ehrhardt (1972), Roiphe and Galenson
(1973), and Stoller (1968, 1976) that children have some perceptions of their genital equipment very early; that at some time
between 14 and 18 months of age, sexual differences are appreciated, and early castration anxiety makes its apperance. At
that time, core gender identity also appears to become fixed.
Abelin (1977) has posited that the little boy is biologically programmed by androgenization of the fetal brain to turn away
from the mother and toward the father at this very time. This
turning helps to dissolve his primary femininity. He suggests
that the boy's concept of self originates from a triangulation of
mother, father, and self. Narcissistic development is endangered
and core gender identity impaired if the male child lacks a male
parent at this critical juncture. He regards the need of little girls
for a male parent as less crucial at 18 months, but as mandatory
during the oedipal period. The little girl is not programmed to
turn away from the mother. Her identity is forged from generational triangulation rather than on the basis of gender differences.

The little boys whom I have observed and treated appear to
manifest yet another specific need for their fathers. They appear
to be overwhelmingly concerned with oral and anal-sadistic issues. Their aggressivity feels to them as though it is out of control, and their cognitive status does not permit rational assessment of the true state of affairs. The loss of the father seems to
them to be their own doing (Piaget, 1936) and simultaneously
deprives them of the wherewithall to control aggressive drives.
Particularly interesting is the recurrent reference to same and
different. The father's sameness (nonmotherness) is appreciated and needed. Earlier, during the practicing subphase
of separation-individuation, the little boy's greater aggressivity
(Maccoby and Jacklin, 1974) serves him in good stead. His "love

affair with the world" (Greenacre, 1957) allows him to explore and grow and move away from the mother. During rapprochement (Mahler et al., 1972, 1975), however, the boy's return to his mother seems to be vulnerable to impairment if she is cool because she is depressed or angry, as in the postdivorce state, overly eager, as in the sharing of one bed, or if he lacks a male model to show him how to manage his libidinal and aggressive impulses. The sequelae of these vicissitudes of rapprochement still need to be delineated (Mahler and Kaplan, 1977).

All 12 of my cases involved the loss, either partial or complete, of the father at exactly this critical juncture. Analysis of the dream and the play material supports the notion that the absence of the father at this time imposes a particular strain on the evolving psychic structure of the boy, a strain that demands discharge and restitution. Under the regressive and progressive sway of sleep a phobic transformation emerges in which the child's own aggressive impulses are seen as hostilely and mercilessly attacking the self in the guise of monsters, big birds, and so forth. This gives rise to the remembered content and affective coloration of the night terror or nightmare. The mother is unable to interrupt this process and may even fuel it by moving closer to her son, either physically or emotionally, possibly by increasing the confusion between libidinal and aggressive impulses. The father, however, or a male father substitute can stem this panic and break through the night terror symptom by reappearing and protecting the little boy.

While I have stressed the importance of the loss of the father for the 12 boys I observed, it may be more specifically the aggression mobilized by the loss. Solnit (1972) described a sleep disturbance in a 16-month-old girl after her very much loved father lost his temper with her. Subsequently she related a dream of a big black bird that would hurt her if she lay down to sleep. It became clear that "she felt overwhelmed by her father's aggressive outburst and by her own angry response and aggressive feelings toward her beloved father" (p. 447). The common element in this girl's dream and those of the boys I observed appears to be a fear of being unable to ward off the consequences of heightened aggression during the state of sleep. In the case of the boys, this aggression seems to be compounded by having witnessed the hostile exchanges between the parents prior to their divorce, the mother's continuing overt anger at her husband, and the child's own hostility over having been abandoned by his father.

The phobic structure of the nightmare content suggests that progressive forces are mobilized under the special ego circumstances which emerge during sleep. Ordinarily, one does not observe true phobias at this age, although exceptions to this statement have been reported (Renik et al., 1978). Ritvo (1974) states that children are capable of dreams which go beyond simple wish fulfillment and involve dreamwork. In children and perhaps also in adults, the dream may be not only the purveyor of archaic material from the distant coulisses of the mind but also the harbinger of new psychic structures. Phobic organization (Lewis, 1971) usually does not make its appearance until after the third year. In both the dreams and play of these little boys, however, it can be clearly observed. Only in Marvin was there a progression to a full-scale phobic disturbance, and he had more to contend with than simply the loss of his father.

A boy needs his father for the formation of the sense of self, the completion of separation-individuation, the consolidation of core gender identity, and the beginning modulation of libidinal and especially aggressive drives. I call the affective state which exists when these needs are not being met *father hunger*.

It appears to me that in the cases which I have described, the affective pressure of this father hunger reaches a point at which it cannot be simply ignored or endured. The ego is pushed to precocious creativity—the production of a phobic symptom. As I look at the night and day productions of Ira, Gary, Marvin, and the 9 other cases, I see this precocious creativity at work. The night terror is the creative work, but it is also a torment—the exact equivalent of the felt need and deprivation which produce it. The ultimate cost of this ego precocity to the developing personality remains to be seen.

The long-term implications of the absence of the father also are unclear (Herzog and Sudia, 1973). Nor do we know how necessary it is that every child have two parents, one of each sex. It seems important, however, to delineate symptoms, reactions, and behaviors which are associated more or less firmly with the absence of one of the parents at a critical developmental juncture, as they are recognized, particularly at a time when almost 50 percent of our children will spend some of their developing years in a single-parent family.

I have subtitled this paper the Erlkönig syndrome, after Goethe's poem immortalized in song by Schubert. The poem tells of a little boy pursued by a monster, the Erlkönig or elf king. The exact Danish etymology of the word suggests old woman or menacing woman as the root.

The little boy begs his father for help—to be saved from the Erlkönig. The father cannot perceive the threat and therefore cannot comply. In the end, the boy lies dead in his father's arms, a victim of Erlkönig—or, in terms of this paper's theme, a victim of his own aggression.

BIBLIOGRAPHY

ABELIN, E. (1977), The Role of the Father in Core Gender Identity and in Psychosexual Differentiation. Read at annual meeting of the American Psychoanalytic Assn., Quebec.

ABRAHAM, K. (1913), Mental After-Effects Produced in a Nine-Year-Old Child by the Observation of Sexual Intercourse Between Its Parents. In: *Selected Papers on Psycho-Analysis.* London: Hogarth Press, 1927, pp. 164–168.

CHADWICK, J. & MANN, W. N., eds. (1950), *The Medical Works of Hippocrates.* Oxford: Blackwell Scientific Publ., p. 191.

DESPERT, J. L. (1949), Dreams in Children of Preschool Age. *This Annual,* 3/4:141–180.

DEUTSCH, H. (1932), *Psycho-Analysis of the Neuroses.* London: Hogarth Press, 1951.

FISHER, C., BYRNE, J., EDWARDS, A., & KAHN, E. (1970), A Psychophysiological Study of Nightmares. *J. Amer. Psychoanal. Assn.,* 18:747–782.

—— KAHN, E., EDWARDS, A., & DAVIS, D. M. (1973), A Psychophysiological Study of Nightmares: I. *J. Nerv. Ment. Dis.,* 157:78–98.

—————————— & FINE, J. (1974), A Psychophysiological Study of Nightmares and Night Terrors: III. *J. Nerv. Ment. Dis.,* 158:174–188.

FRAIBERG, S. (1950), On the Sleep Disturbances of Early Childhood. *This Annual,* 5:285–309.

FRIEND, M. R. (1956), Report of Panel: On Sleep Disturbances in Children. *J. Amer. Psychoanal. Assn.,* 4:514–525.

FREUD, A. (1965), Normality and Pathology in Childhood. *W.,* 6.

FREUD, S. (1895), On the Grounds for Detaching a Particular Syndrome from Neurasthenia under the Description 'Anxiety Neurosis.' *S.E.,* 3:87–117.

232   *James M. Herzog*

GALENSON, E. & ROIPHE, H. (1976), Some Suggested Revisions Concerning Early Female Development. *J. Amer. Psychoanal. Assn. Suppl.*, 24:29–58.

GESELL, A. & ILG, F. L. (1943), *Infant and Child in the Culture of Today.* New York: Harper.

GOETHE, J. W. (1786), Erlkönig. In: *The Penguin Book of German Verse.* Baltimore: Penguin Books, 1966, pp. 214–215.

GREENACRE, P. (1957), The Childhood of the Artist. In: *Emotional Growth.* New York: Int. Univ. Press, 1971, pp. 479–504.

GUILLEMINAULT, C. & ANDERS, T. (1976). Sleep Disorders in Children. *Adv. Pediat.*, 22:151–174.

HERZOG, E. & SUDIA, C. (1973), Children in Fatherless Families. In: *Review of Child Development Research,* ed. M. Caldwell. Chicago: Univ. Chicago Press, pp. 73–79.

JONES, E. (1931), *On the Nightmare.* London: Hogarth Press.

KALES, J., JACOBSON, A., & KALES, A. (1968), Sleep Disorders in Children. In: *Progress in Clinical Psychology,* ed. L. Ast & B. F. Riess. New York: Grune & Stratton, 8:63–75.

KANNER, L. (1957), *Child Psychiatry,* 3rd. ed. Springfield, Ill.: Charles C Thomas. pp. 499–500.

KEITH, P. R. (1975), Night Terrors. *J. Amer. Acad. Child Psychiat.*, 14:477–489.

KLEEMAN, J. (1965), A Boy Discovers His Penis. *This Annual*, 20:239–266.

——— (1966), Genital Self-Discovery During a Boy's Second Year. *This Annual*, 21:21:338–392.

——— (1976), Freud's Views on Early Female Sexuality in the Light of Direct Child Observation. *J. Amer. Psychoanal. Assn. Suppl.*, 24:3–28.

KLEIN, M. (1932), *The Psycho-Analysis of Children.* London: Hogarth Press.

KOHLBERG, L. (1968), Early Education. *Child Develpm.*, 39:1013–1062.

LEVY, D. M. (1945), Psychic Trauma of Operations in Children. *Amer. J. Dis. Child.*, 69:7–25.

LEWIS, M. (1971), *Clinical Aspects of Child Development.* Philadelphia: Lea & Febiger.

MACCOBY, E. (1966), *The Development of Sex Differences.* Stanford: Stanford Univ. Press.

——— & JACKLIN, C. (1974), *The Psychology of Sex Differences.* Stanford: Stanford Univ. Press.

MACK, J. E. (1965), Nightmares, Conflict, and Ego Development in Childhood. *Int. J. Psycho-Anal.*, 46:403–428.

——— (1970), *Nightmares and Human Conflict.* Boston: Little, Brown.

MAHLER, M. S. (1972), Rapprochement Subphase of the Separation-Individuation Process. *Psychoanal. Quart.*, 41:487–506.

——— & KAPLAN, L. (1977), Developmental Aspects in the Assessment of Narcissistic and So-Called Borderline Personalities. In: *Borderline Personality Disorders,* ed. P. Hartocollis. New York: Int. Univ. Press, pp. 76–86.

——— PINE, F., & BERGMAN, A. (1975), *The Psychological Birth of the Human Infant.* New York: Basic Books.

MONEY, J. & EHRHARDT, A. (1972), *Man and Woman, Boy and Girl.* Baltimore: Johns Hopkins Univ. Press.

NAGERA, H. (1966), Sleep and Its Disturbances Approached Developmentally. *This Annual,* 21:393–447.

NIEDERLAND, W. G. (1957), The Earliest Dreams of a Young Child. *This Annual,* 12:190–208.

PHAER, T. (1545), *The Boke of Chyldren.* Edinburg: L. S. Livingstone, 1955, p. 28.

PIAGET, J. (1936), *Origins of Intelligence in Children.* New York: Int. Univ. Press, 1952.

———(1945), *Play, Dreams and Imitation in Childhood.* New York: Norton, 1951.

RENIK, O., SPIELMAN, P., & AFTERMAN, J. (1978), Bamboo Phobia in an Eighteen-Month-Old Boy. *J. Amer. Psychoanal. Assn. Suppl.,* 26:255–282.

RICHMOND, J. B. & LIPTON, E. L. (1958), Observations on the Psychological Development of Infants. In: *Emotional Problems of Childhood,* ed. S. Liebman. Philadelphia: Lippincott, pp. 17–33.

RITVO, S. (1974), Current Status of the Concept of the Infantile Neurosis. *This Annual,* 29:159–182.

ROELANS, C. (1500), On Diseases of Infants. In: *Pediatrics of the Past,* ed. J. Ruhrah. New York: Harper & Row, 1925, p. 99.

ROIPHE, H. & GALENSON, E. (1973), Object Loss and Early Sexual Development. *Psychoanal. Quart.,* 42:73–90.

SOLNIT, A. J. (1972), Aggression. *J. Amer. Psychoanal. Assn.,* 20:435–450.

SPERLING, M. (1955), Etiology and Treatment of Sleep Disturbances in Children. *Psychoanal. Quart.,* 24:358–368.

STOLLER, R. J. (1968), *Sex and Gender.* New York: Science House.

———(1976), Primary Femininity. *J. Amer. Psychoanal. Assn. Suppl.,* 24:59–78.

WAELDER HALL, J. (1930), The Analysis of a Case of Night Terror. *This Annual,* 2:189–227, 1946.

CLINICAL
CONTRIBUTIONS

Constructive and Reconstructive Activities in the Analysis of a Depressed Child

DONALD J. COHEN, M.D.

ANDREW WAS THE SECOND CHILD OF A PSYCHIATRICALLY ILL mother and a subdued father with a strong family history of depression. His infancy was lived under the shadow of marital crisis and maternal depression and hospitalization. His parents separated when he was 6 years old. Before age 7, he was failing in school and was persistently sad. He spoke little, lay on the floor sucking his thumb, ate with his hands, and, at times, crawled and barked like a dog. Psychoanalysis during three years, from ages 7 to 10 years, allowed him to understand his sadness and anger and the meaning of some of his symptoms. A newly discovered artistic creativity flowered, served its therapeutic purposes, and faded. Andrew was able to move forward in his development but remained sober and quiet.

During the course of Andrew's analysis, his experience of recurrent loss was reconstructed, mainly through the use of his nonverbal modes of communication (Solnit and M. Kris, 1967). In this discussion, I will describe these reconstructive activities

Professor of Pediatrics, Psychiatry, and Psychology, the Child Study Center and Yale University School of Medicine, New Haven, Connecticut.

I am indebted to Drs. A. J. Solnit, S. Ritvo, S. Leavy, S. van Amerongen, and H. W. Loewald, and P. Cohen.

The work was supported, in part, by National Institute of Health grant RR00125 and National Institute of Mental Health grant MH30929.

and review aspects of the theory and practice of child psychoanalysis and the analytic theory of affective development.

CASE PRESENTATION

BACKGROUND

Andrew's parents were born and grew up in England, where Andrew was born following his parents' first extended stay in the United States. On both sides, Andrew was decended from several generations of solid, somber, hardworking people. His great grandfather and grandfather were strict and harsh. Aunts and uncles were depressed, and some required active treatment. One uncle suffered mild organic impairment following measles encephalitis; relatives who were not themselves depressed tended to marry spouses who were. Andrew's father was a serious man, devoted to his family and to the clients in his legal practice. Several years of psychoanalysis before Andrew's birth, undertaken because of marital and professional unhappiness, helped clarify his professional plans but did not raise his low spirits; another try at analysis, after his divorce, and concurrent with Andrew's analysis, ended before completion.

Andrew's mother's psychiatric history was dramatic and tragic. A beautiful woman, she had the capacity for engaging and exciting friends and for bringing out the concern of others. While still in England, she spent many thousands of dollars on impulsive shopping. Long periods of bitter unhappiness and dissatisfaction with marriage and life in general preceded Andrew's birth and intensified over the next years. The move to the United States failed to alleviate her feelings of emptiness and despair. During episodes of acute depression she made suicidal gestures. Occasionally she appeared to suffer from hallucinations. She would take to bed, sometimes with Andrew near her and sometimes with little concern for where he was; she suddenly would rush from the house and drive away in her small red car, accompanied by her pet dog and wild, drug-using friends. Hospitalization was required for evaluation of vague somatic complaints which she suggested were the result of a dreaded disease, such as cancer, but which were manifestations of her emotional tension.

The family moved to the United States when Andrew was 3 years old. His parents separated when he was 6; three months later, Andrew and his 6-year-older sister were taken by their mother to live in the new house built by her second husband. Her psychiatric problems did not abate; when seven months later, this second marriage ended, she returned to her homeland and the children returned to their father, who cared for them with the help of a devoted South American housekeeper. During the next two years, Andrew's mother had considerable psychiatric trouble and was hospitalized following a very serious suicide attempt. Her contacts with Andrew were sudden, rare visits, lasting a few days at most, and frequent threats of visits, raising hopes and worries for Andrew and his family for months on end.

The mother who left but did not die was the central motif of Andrew's analysis. He yearned for reconciliation with his mother and knew that it could not occur. Vaguely, he felt he had wronged her, and he did not allow himself to recognize that he had been deprived and shunted aside. He felt guilty and avoided consciously experiencing his rage. Instead, he felt alone and empty.

DEVELOPMENTAL HISTORY

Andrew's gestation and delivery were normal, as were the first months of his life. By the second half of the first year, he was placed in child daycare in order to allow his mother more freedom; she often left him unattended at home. At age 1 year, he had a serious case of measles with a high fever; two weeks later his mother developed measles encephalitis, and her recovery was followed by a brief period of improvement in her psychiatric status. At age 2, Andrew had a positive tuberculin test, with normal chest x rays, and received one year of chemotherapy. His motor and general social landmarks were broadly normal. By age 3, his nursery school teachers felt he was not doing well in emotional development and social communication. By 4, nursery school teachers were concerned because he seemed "depressed" and both unable to keep up with agemates and uninterested in them. His quietness worried his teachers and all other adults who cared about and for him. His entry into kindergarten was marked not by explicit fearfulness, but rather by the stoicism that characterized his whole life: he was a boy who simply accepted what happened to him. After six weeks of kindergarten, his teacher notified the family that he was neither doing schoolwork nor playing with other children.

By age 6, Andrew began to spend increasing time huddled with his pillow on the floor. His father could find no way to provide any real pleasure for him. Andrew avoided new experiences and foods, barely spoke, and never about his feelings, and suggested nothing that could move him out of his shell. At times he played with a neighborhood friend, but he did not allow his father or sister into his private world.

THE ANALYSIS

First Phase

Andrew's father brought him for therapy, agreed that analysis was indicated, and remained supportive throughout the treatment, conducted four times weekly over three years. Discussions with Andrew's father occurred on the telephone weekly, at first, and then far less often. Face-to-face meetings occurred monthly, and then gradually every three to six months. Discussions could be brief and intermittent because Andrew's father had a clear, empathic understanding of Andrew's feelings and the effects of past and current events; he also appreciated the nature of psychoanalytic treatment. There was no communication with Andrew's mother at any time.

In light of his history, it may be surprising to learn that Andrew was an engaging, albeit very reserved, youngster during his first evaluation visits. Freckled and rather full-faced, he reflected the handsome good looks of his parents. During the first hours, preceding the decision for analysis, Andrew played with small figures, re-creating airplane trips, crash landings, and wars with cowboys, Indians, ambushes, and heroes on white horses. This introduction offered a promise for play that was not fulfilled. With the decision for analysis came a long, severe drought. Analysis started with days and weeks of virtual silence and simple responses to questions and prods.

Andrew became interested in making coffee and eating crackers or cookies, a ritual that was perhaps reinforced by the cold and dark early mornings when we met. Sitting with his coffee-warmed milk, he spoke little about daily events and, far less, about the events of his past life. In this way, analysis started by our being cast, by Andrew, as a quiet parent and a quieter child at breakfast. He was always hungry.

First Projects

Talk, in child analysis, is generally only one of several modes of communication. The child presents himself through action and gesture, through games and play and routines; he draws, writes, and lounges about. He pulls the analyst into movement and activities, or blocks and pushes him out (Bornstein, 1945; A. Freud, 1965). If all psychoanalysis, with people of every age, shares qualities with the creation of a dialogical play, the players of child analysis create and act out the stage instructions as well as the speeches. At the end, the actors must recognize the unique ontological status of the analytic drama—its transitional status between the world of true lovers, friends, teachers, students, parents and children, and the world of memories and wishes (Loewald, 1960, 1979a). The actors in the children's theater know that they have been closer than those in adult analysis to building and rearranging palpable stage props and scenery; they have served together, as coach and apprentice, in a hardworking road show.

From warmed-milk, second breakfasts, Andrew became involved in projects. At first, these led nowhere or only short distrances. Pages of neat and dull designs were colored with crayons; books of handmade mazes were too easily navigated or were put aside. One day, this desultory activity was altered by a creative move started by Andrew's finding a Polaroid camera in the cabinet. Andrew's muted curiosity led to his taking photographs of the office and of us. Soon, he began the historical documentation of the construction of a building which was occurring immediately outside the windows of the office. The meanings of a house being built—as a symbol of mother's return and of the search for inner strength and reunion as well as a reminder of the breakup of the family—were only later and

slowly understood and interpreted. Yet, around this activity
hours took shape and the analysis took on a sense of direction:
hours started with warmed milk with a cookie and moved to
careful observation, discussion, and photographing the emerging structure. From first clearing of the land and groundbreak-
ing through digging of the foundation and each successive stage
of physical growth, the picture album became an archive of
something taking shape and of continuity over analytic hours
and months. Interspersed with pictures of the building outside
were photographs of Andrew, his photographs of me, and short
notes about the date and what was seen through the window.

Andrew began to play with wooden stirrers one morning. The
stirrers were made into a life raft on the open sea, and then the
life raft became a wall of a pioneer's cabin. The pioneer home on
the prairie—later named the Strong Family Home—was the first
of a series of constructions, each becoming more solid and larger
and each taking its place in a frontier village. Andrew used
scraps of wood and ambitiously sawed wood to create the shacks
of Indians, the houses of settlers, and finally, a several-storied
fort surrounded by a wall behind which children and women
could flee, if necessary. But they had no need to hide, since in
Andrew's frontier, the Indians and cowboys too readily resigned
themselves to bland friendship rather than risk authentic dispute and achieve true rapprochement (Mahler et al., 1975).

During the second year of analysis, a foray into building
store-bought models represented a defensive withdrawal. Andrew felt secure with the structure provided by following instructions. Yet, little pleasure or emotional movement accompanied the completion of the tidy models. That Andrew had no
trouble at all in fine motor coordination was clearly revealed by
his dexterity in assembling the smallest parts of an explorer's
boat. When my fumbling led to the loss of several pieces, Andrew
said that we might wait until "later" before we tried completing
it. This, our only unfinished model, became a continuing personal joke, a metaphor, at the end of analysis, for the never-
ending process in which we were engaged.

The Scroll

There was a long period during the second year of analysis
when Andrew's silent brooding was vigorously interpreted: he

did not show his feelings because he feared he would be flooded with sadness and anger that he could not control; he feared that I would not understand how frightened and lonely he was, just as others did not seem to care; and he felt bad because of his anger at his mother, for leaving, and his father, for not keeping the family together. Why bother to show feelings? Why would anyone care? Whom can you trust, anyhow? If he wasn't so bad, why would he have been treated so badly? While Andrew maintained a quiet, "I don't know" distance, I used whatever was presented, and could reasonably be inferred, to attempt to form a bond of communication and understanding by attitude and word.

The cumulative force of this psychoanalytic inquiry and concern eventually penetrated the guarded walls of inhibition. Until this period, Andrew could not draw and was unwilling to sketch or paint with me. To justify this he told me of his lack of ideas and talent while describing school art projects. One day during this period of interpretation of his defensive withdrawal, Andrew took a crayon from the box lying on our work table and tentatively drew an oval, which became a raindrop and then a bolt of lightning. Above the lightning a rain cloud took shape, and from the clouds rain fell to the ground. The raindrops landed on a surburban highway with cars coming from a toll booth. This became a full, vibrant drawing—Andrew's first. I commented on his pleasure in the act of expression.

The "good" psychoanalytic hour has a shape: initial false starts are followed by a memory, dream, or thought which, because of the state of transference, leads to a shared experience of buried feelings or events (E. Kris, 1956a). Something new in the analytic process reinvests something old with energy, and the preconscious becomes conscious. Andrew's teardrop, drawn with me, ignited a spark of life. This liveliness appeared to have survived from some distant, past relationship, perhaps with his mother. It was also an expression of the reawakened impulse toward mastery that was inspired through the analytic relationship. Andrew's first drawing became one in an unfolding series of 32 drawings over the next months.

In the new routine, Andrew would sit down at the table each morning and ask, "What will happen today?" He would take a fresh sheet of 8 × 10 inch paper and start another scene of a road moving through suburbs, cities, and countryside, across flatlands and over mountains. The road would become a superhighway or a dirt path, barely passable by a car. After a day's drawing was completed, it would be taped to the scroll; the scroll became a travelogue of Andrew's experiences and dreams.

Along the road, cars and trucks of varied shape would travel, sometimes in caravans and sometimes alone. Chief among the vehicles in its prominence and as the frequent location of Andrew, the storyteller, was a bright, adventurous, little red car. This car often played the hero in the historical novel being brought to life in front of us. The road passed shopping centers and pastoral scenes with farmyards and crops. It moved through neighborhoods and by stores like those near Andrew's home. Seasons changed; warm sunshine was replaced by winter sledding, and then by summer again. As he finished an episode, Andrew would be surprised. "Who would have guessed I was going to draw that?" he would say, while surveying a marvelously alive circus or the details of a shopping center.

The epic world of the scroll was not without tragedies. Cars crashed and trucks fell off open bridges; doctors and police would rush in emergency vehicles, sometimes arriving too late to be of help. People would drive "away" or "by themselves"; refrigeration would fail in food trucks and their contents would spoil. These crises were part of the natural rhythm of the scroll in which sequences of destruction and turmoil were followed by rural tranquillity and resolution. Increasingly, the drawings become bolder in feeling. There were violent scenes and richly human ones. In one "funny" hour, Andrew laughed at his drawing of a boy stranded on top of a pile of luggage in Andrew's dream paradise, Arizona. He could then recognize how mixed the boy's feelings were while waiting to fly somewhere or to greet someone. It was only years later, after the termination of analysis, that I learned of the origin of Arizona as the repeated destination of dream trips: it was to Arizona that his mother fled during one of her sudden trips, and when she wrote postcards home about the ranches and scenery, Andrew and his sister were envious and enraged at being left behind.

Over the course of its several months of life, the picture scroll provided a deeply felt continuity from hour to hour; it lent its continuity to the disconnected fragments of Andrew's life and fantasies. We were traveling together, simultaneously moving forward and backward. And there was no lack of pride in the visual splendor of the long roll.

As drawings came out of Andrew's crayons, I would sit with quiet watchfulness. An idea would dawn on Andrew and become elaborated. Thoughts would pop into his head or into his hand; sometimes they would be put into words as well. Most often a question from me was answered with a short response, and sometimes with a pictorial denial. When he was working on a circus, I commented on the danger and excitement in watching the man on the tightrope. "You wonder if he'll fall and if the net will catch him." In response, Andrew drew the "funniest" scene with clowns standing one on top of another: a negation of the fear, and, with the same stroke, an expression of the experience of standing on a wobbly foundation. At times, an interpretation hitting its mark set off a new line in the drawing. "The driver in the car is frightened and surprised. He's driven over the bridge before and it seemed so strong. Today, it just crashed open beneath him." This led Andrew to a furious airplane attack on the helpless car falling into the river and then an attempt by helicopters and firetrucks to reach him. Andrew drew, and I interpreted, the experience of being held, of falling, and of being caught or allowed to sink; of unanticipated danger and the danger of trusting; of searching for someone, and of finding and not finding pleasure, fun, security, and calm.

The road one day came up to the shore of the ocean. The cars could proceed no further. Andrew drew a large ocean liner at dock. Over the next days, the ocean liner prepared for voyage by taking on oil from large oil tanks and food from trucks and helicopters. But the steamer never managed to sail. Instead, a man, who became a boy, drifted off to sea on a raft and was threatened by sharks and submarines; eventually, he was saved, or perhaps not. The child was attacked by forces far beyond his power.

During the last days of the scroll's life, Andrew christened the boat, in the most unselfconscious manner, with the name of his mother. It was a name that was suitable for this purpose. Let us call her Mary.

The *Queen Mary* never left port.

The epic scroll led Andrew to the object of his desire. With this realization, Andrew "did not feel" like doing any more drawings on the scroll. He attempted one more scene, but could only manage an enormous truck looming over two small cars; this was a crude drawing by previous standards, and was out of context. It was a mother truck with babies at the breast, I ventured, or a child overwhelmed by a large adult. The next drawing was a blank page with the sun shining and was the end of the scroll.

Weeks after the scroll was put aside, Andrew drew again: sharp-pointed, glorious racing cars, in the most vivid red color. They were capable of beating any other cars in the world. After these, Andrew put away his crayons and colored pens and drew only a rare sketch over the next year.

During the height of his artistic creativity, Andrew's new gift for drawing was recognized by his teachers. When the work on the scroll ended, and with the final drawings of red racing cars, the drawing in school faded as well.

Boats

Andrew returned to his building. With a clear sense of purpose, he set out to construct a seaworthy schooner from scraps of wood and bits and pieces of other materials. The boat was fitted with a colored sail and two life boats; it was finished in time to become the U.S.S. *Xmas*. With its launching, Andrew started to build a battleship that required weeks of planning and construction. A cannon that launched missiles provided adequate protection against enemies; in any case, enemies could be detected before the need for attack by the very sensitive, silver-painted radar tower. An airplane was always ready to fly if the boat was hit by torpedoes, and nuclear-powered shells were stacked in case of need. Construction of an aquaplane followed completion of the building of the boats; the plane was a solid vehicle big enough to carry "a whole family." Following the construction of the fleet of vehicles, Andrew built a dock at which they could tie up. He shared pleasant thoughts of sitting and fishing on the dock on "summer days" with his "mother and father."

Andrew's careful observation of boats at the seaside during summer holidays provided sufficient detail for his realistic models. And his thoughts about voyages to Europe and their dangers provided more than enough material for his always quite short trips into shared fantasy. With this oceanic project, the analysis came to an end. The boat trips, the pleasures and fears in exploration—he as Columbus and I as his navigator watching out for icebergs—served as a metaphor for our relationship. In the future, he would be required to play both roles, a responsibility for which he was perhaps better equipped through the mutative effects of psychoanalysis (Strachey, 1934).

To this point, I have described the various modes Andrew used in his analysis for communication of ideas, fantasies, and feelings about his life and our relationship. I will now review several major, recurrent themes.

Bodily Concerns

During a summer preceding the start of analysis, Andrew visited with his mother and paternal relatives in England. At one point in the summer, a small sum of money was found to be missing from the grandmother's house, and Andrew felt that it had been stolen. The summer ended with the father's departure for the United States while Andrew was to remain for a time with his mother. Soon after his father left, Andrew developed appendicitis and required emergency surgery. His father returned to be with him during the uneventful convalescence. Far more often than the event seemed to justify, Andrew returned to the stolen money. "Remember the time someone broke into my grandmother's house," he would say, and repeat a detail or two of the screen memory. The emergency appendicitis was pushed to the side as "nothing special," as was the abandonment by father and the time with mother.

One autumn, after the start of analysis, Andrew's body reflected his anxiety about returning to school; he complained of "upset stomachs" and "stomachaches" every morning and quietly pleaded to remain at home. Andrew and I wondered together about the stomachaches, and this led almost directly to the retelling of the story of the stolen money. The money, he could gradually see, was so important to him because it reminded him of the bodily integrity he so much feared losing during the time in the hospital when his stomach hurt so badly; the stolen money also reminded him of the loss of his father, who stood as the protection against the fearful closeness with his mother for which he wished so deeply. He, like she, became sick and had to go to the hospital; he, too, felt frightened by his feelings of sadness and the pains in his body; and, like his mother, he wanted someone to take care of him. The pain in his stomach in the morning was a sign from within himself of his worries, a sign that he learned should not be ignored but listened to carefully.

This line of analysis was more tortuous than conveyed by its recounting. As it progressed, Andrew suggested that we work on a cartoon. Since the days of Andrew's drawing were over, he dictated the dialogue for each box and I served as the stick-figure artist. The story was titled "Oscar's Adventures" and had three characters in the following, first episode:

Skimpy (a small boy): Hi people. Hi Oscar.

Oscar (a bigger, red-headed boy): Hi Skimpy. What are you up to?

Skimpy: Getting ready to go to school.

Oscar: Ugh!

Sister (a big girl): You surely look like quite a bunch.

Oscar: What do you mean?

Sister: It's a school day, but you're just standing around.

Skimpy: It ain't a school day for all of us.

Oscar: I'm not going.

Sister: Why not, Oscar?

Oscar (lying down on bed): I'm sick.

Sister: You didn't look sick a second ago. Where are Mommy and Daddy?

Skimpy: That's a good question.

Oscar (standing tall): Don't I look sick?

In the second adventure, the story continued:

Sister: No.

Oscar: Well, I've a terrible pain in my throat . . . and a worse pain in my frungle.

Sister: What's a frungle?

Skimpy: Frungle?

Oscar: I'm not sure but it isn't good. I'm sure of that. . . .

The story unfolded for several more days of talking and cartooning. Father came home and wondered about Oscar, and

Oscar wondered about his "frungle"—a term invented, at the spur of the moment, to convey a sense of bungled confusion and fun in making things inside more understandable. The cartoon dramatized, and provided further access to, Andrew's concerns about the loss of bodily integrity, as shown in his stomachache symptom. The symptom could then be placed in the spectrum of developmental reworkings of this theme: disruptions of narcissistic unity, loss of mother, identification with mother's illnesses, father's caretaking when Andrew was ill and his return when Andrew had appendicitis, and the symbolic significance of the abdominal discomfort in relation to Andrew's feelings of deprivation and fear of oral aggression and incorporation. The symptom disappeared.

Sister

The sister in "Oscar's Adventures" played an obviously maternal role. She prepared supper, organized trips to the bowling alley, and helped the children dress warmly to play outdoors. In one episode of the cartoon, Sister waited with Oscar and Skimpy for the father to return home and later led the children on a search for the father on a snowy day.

In the analysis, Andrew's older sister was sometimes vague and shadowy; when she entered into discussion, she was generally viewed by Andrew as helpful or kind, even if at times she was preoccupied with her own activities. Andrew would jealously describe his sister's greater freedoms, her circle of friends, and the treats she received. However, along with terse comments about muted rivalry and brief reports of occasional fights, Andrew conveyed that he recognized her concern about him. His sister was in the house waiting for him when he went to play or returned from school; she helped prepare snacks or meals; she gently explained a plan or something that occurred in school. He even could use her skepticism about his stomachaches to see his somatic concerns from another perspective. When his sister was sharp or critical—as she was about his table manners—Andrew tended glumly to accept the validity of her complaints.

In spite of the support Andrew received from his sister, he offered relatively little about her as a richly articulated person with importance in his life. The low-keyed, almost bland quality of his descriptions of his relations with adults—the result of his quiet emptiness—extended to his portrayal of his relations with his sister as well. Her stabilizing, nurturant, and substitutive role in his life was, however, apparent; she was a constant presence in the background of his daily life and in the reconstruction of his history. Toward the end of the analysis, her long-standing significance emerged more explicitly. Andrew began to enjoy doing things with her. And he saw how important it was to him that she was with him through the most difficult times, for example, when they moved with their mother to her second husband's house and returned to their father's home together.

Neither of the children spoke openly about their mother, except at rare moments such as those surrounding her notes or visits. Andrew, in particular, could not share openly what he felt inside. In spite of this familial reticence, Andrew knew that his sister was also worried, lonely, and angry. And he was quietly pleased when she occasionally put into words the dissatisfactions and questions that he suffered in silence and they they experienced in common.

Mother's Returns

Andrew could never bring himself to tell friends where his mother was. He would laconically say that she was "not at home." For a long time, he accepted her fantasy about when she would return. "When the new office building for her company is finished in New York, she'll move back." He told this story over and over, but as years went by, he lost his conviction and could no longer reconcile her absence with the many buildings which he saw being constructed around him.

While she was not present, she was also not dead. Andrew's mother sent postcards and letters every few months. She sometimes announced she would be arriving for a visit on a certain date. These dates passed without visits. During the analysis, Andrew saw his mother twice: once during a difficult trip abroad, once during an upsetting visit she paid to his home. On this latter trip, she arrived with luggage and expressed her determination to stay. Only with much confusion did she finally leave for a hotel.

What sense could a child make of all this? Would she come one night to take him back with her? Would she stay away forever? Why did she go so far away? Whom did she love in England? Andrew would recall being in bed with his mother when he was a young child, or being left behind as she dashed off. I would interpret his sense of abandonment, in all the forms in which it was experienced. "You feel you drove her away." "You wonder if she loved some other child more than you." "Did she leave because you wanted too much from her?" "At times, you feel that she left you because you were bad" or "because you failed to make her love you enough." The abandonment was, of course, interpreted from other directions as well: "It hurts so much to think your mother was bad (or unloving, or angry)." "She was so mixed up you could not understand what she was doing or what made her go away . . . you tried and tried and then gave up." Andrew recalled his envy of the small pet dog that his mother carried away with her, and then his wish to be that dog, the pet to whom so much love was shown and who did not suffer the pain of separation (Kramer, 1979; Furman, 1974). I interpreted how he became that dog, in his barking on the floor, and how his wish that she would return to care for him again was disappointed.

Slowly, Andrew shared his daydream of what it would be like when he was older—18 or 20 years old. Then he would be strong enough to build a new house for his mother and father to live in again, like the pioneer house. He would force his parents to get together. And this house would be much better than the new house into which his mother and Andrew moved when she married her second husband, that short, bitter period that preceded her final departure. It would be like the houses he built himself and like the sturdy building we watched grow in front of our eyes. After telling his tale of rebuilding his family, Andrew would become silent and sometimes tearful. The longing was too intense to be contained within the fantasy, and its realization seemed impossible.

Andrew knew that while he lived with his father, legal custody rested with his mother. His father spoke of this with the children and warned them, when the mother visited, of the danger that she might wish to take them away and of the need for caution. After many years, the father was able to change this legal situation and establish rightful custody. This was accomplished with great relief for Andrew's father; his mother could no longer snatch Andrew away. When Andrew spoke about this new arrangement, however, he began, for one of the very few times in the analysis, to cry with sobs and thick tears: "She'll never come back. I know that. Why should she now?"

Romance

In the presence of adults, Andrew kept his peace. He rarely showed enthusiasm for plans, activities, or people. During the analysis, there was one exception to this general restraint.

Over the course of the years of analysis, Andrew's father dated several women. Only one became a truly serious involvement, Lucy, a young, lovely, gentle, and energetic woman, who delighted in the children and wished for her own. At night, Andrew engaged Lucy in a romantic routine. He shut the lights in his bedroom, turned on a lamp, and played music on the radio. When the "atmosphere," as his father called it, was correct, he invited Lucy into the room where she read a story and they talked until he fell asleep. On weekends, Andrew and Lucy went on day trips, and on holidays, the whole family went on longer trips.

A glow came to Andrew's eyes and face as he spoke of Lucy. If his father was a serious rival, Andrew did not appear to notice it. Andrew was intensely possessive. The strength of feeling reflected more than his nonspecific hunger for friendship, since teachers, the housekeeper, and others had failed in arousing such lively engagement. Nor did the child's romance simply mirror the father's, although Lucy's importance derived, in part, from her special value to the man Andrew admired. What appeared to fuel Andrew's passion and loyalty, to a degree that ultimately surpassed his father's, was the fusion of Lucy with the earliest object of a child's desire. Lucy was the returned mother; she evoked the joy of narcissistic unity as well as, at a higher level of registration or organization, the capacity for oedipal triumph (Loewald, 1979b). Unfortunately, the romance did not run its normal course.

Andrew was deeply grieved, and felt wronged again, when Lucy left the house because his father could not solidify the relationship that she needed. Andrew was unable to keep the

woman of his dreams or transmute the relationship along the
lines of normal waning of the oedipal complex. His sadness
about the loss, through no fault of his own, of this love affair
paled the loss of the housekeeper who had been with the family
for many years. Yet, even in discussion about the departure of
Lucy, Andrew answered questions about his feelings with "Okay.
Nothing special." But there was no way for him to conceal the
tears that flowed to his eyes when the loss was tied to that primary
loss of years before and the recognition that, for him, "too few
things have turned out okay." He worried that he did something
wrong, or didn't do something he should have to keep Lucy, and
he could not help blaming himself, his father, Lucy, or someone.
Mourning for Lucy brought about the most intense revival of his
mother and of her loss (Klein, 1948, 1957).

Termination

The termination of analysis was talked about as the "time
when we won't see each other every day" or "so often" but not as
"never again." After the termination of daily sessions, Andrew
wished to return once a month "just to talk." The talk took several forms, including the review of the picture album, kept more
or less current from the start of the analysis, and cataloging the
construction of the building and Andrew's physical and emotional growth; talk about school and friends; and my continuing
comments and interpretations of the major themes in Andrew's
life. It was during this time that Andrew's whimsy flourished in
the form of work on "the thing . . . or whatever you want to call
it."

The "thing" grew from the stockpile of scrap wood and glue in
which Andrew would poke around from time to time. It was a
colossal (2 feet by 3 feet), free-form, wooden sculpture which
grew in various directions: a tall man was built and a funny hat
was plopped on his head and a cigar in his mouth; he was given a
square pet dog, tied to his arm with a string. A series of wooden
blocks became a skyscraper. Interesting shapes were related to
each other with no plan. At one point, a curved piece of wood
became an ocean with a fish sailing on it through the air—
another working through of themes of boats, distances, and
dreamlike travels played out so often before. The sculpture was

painted in a rainbow of colors, in sharp contrast with the more realistic painting of previous models.

"I never thought I'd ever do something like this," Andrew commented as he surveyed "the thing." It was his testimony to a discovered freedom in the special transitional space of the analytic relationship that exists between reality and fantasy. The bold and whimsical thing embodied the possibility of fantasy and hope. The completion of the thing was followed soon after by the more definite termination, punctuated by visits every three to six months during the next years.

Symptoms

At the end of analysis and during the years subsequent to it, Andrew was without the major, overt symptoms with which he had entered treatment. The dog-barking and thumb-sucking were long gone, as was the distaste for new foods and the pervasive sense of loneliness. He was an average student, still plagued by spelling, but no longer the lowest boy in the class on the precipice of being held back. His great dexterity on a 10-speed bicycle and on a team in Little League baseball dispelled any doubts about gross motor incapacities, as did his fine model building during analysis for fine motor coordination. He had best friends and spent pleasurable time away from home involved in sports and cruising his neighborhood.

Yet, in spite of all this, Andrew remained a quiet, sober boy who was, at the core of his personality, alone in a world of grown-ups. Detailed psychological testing several years after termination of analysis documented Andrew's depressive feelings and continuing, mild learning troubles; in his daily life, however, he showed increasing social warmth and good humor, and he spoke more easily and with greater clarity.

DISCUSSION

AFFECTIVE DEVELOPMENT

The child's desire to understand the world of adults—their coming and going, what brings them near and what drives them away, how they respond to his behavior and moods—is the leading edge in his cognitive development (Bell, 1970; Caparulo and

Cohen, 1977; Cohen et al., 1978). Upon the rules or patterns he extracts about how adults behave, a child constructs models of the physical universe and of himself as a person in the world (Piaget, 1937).

As the child increasingly understands the world of adult behavior, he takes into himself, bit by bit, aspects of the caregiving others (Jacobson, 1964). The child evolves representations of his parents; his sense of their goodness is based on such phenomena as the pleasures he experiences with them, the tensions reduced by them, and the mastery he achieves by being able to predict and manipulate their actions. Concurrently, he develops the capacity for feeling good and secure through evocation of the representations of beloved adults. These representations sustain the child during separations and in his response to fear, anxiety, and discomfort.

There are, thus, two simultaneous and intertwined developmental processes which radiate from the child's engagement with his primary caregivers. The first process is the child's construction of the real, felt, external world based upon his understanding of human relations; the second is the emergence of the sense of self and the inner world based on the unique emotional bonding of child and parent and the gradual incorporation of aspects of the caregivers. The child's motivation to understand and to take in the parents derives, in large part, from the experiences of the mutually gratifying relationship of the early parent-child phenomenological matrix (Loewald, 1971, 1978a; Tolpin, 1971). In various ways, the object of understanding and desire—the Other—is also constructive of the agency of inquiry and wish—the Self (Lacan, 1968).

Even in the average expectable environment provided by fortunate, loving parents, an infant or young child experiences not only pleasure but also frustration, psychic pain, and disappointment (Hartmann, 1958). The mother may feel a loss, as well as something gained, at delivery; and both parents may feel tension, unhappiness, and anger in relation to the demanding and, at times, uncompromising infant. Similarly, the child will not remain satisfied, comforted, or calm at all times—or even at those times when one would expect him to have a reason to be.

Analytic theorists have seen these episodes of distress, disharmony, and delay in gratification as important determinants of the tone and forward movement of personality development. Various concepts have been offered in relation to these experiences, including the depressive and paranoid positions, the need for optimal frustration, wish fulfillment through thought and action, and the creation of psychological structures (e.g., defenses) in response to deprivation (E. Kris, 1962). The child's tension, unhappiness, and rage also color representations of the primary caregivers as bad, unintelligible, cruel, and the like; to the degree to which these representations shape the emerging self, they contribute to the child's sense of who he is and what he can expect from others.

Affects, such as anxiety, depression, calm, and joy, are inextricably associated with the representations of self and others; in turn, the capacities to bear the painful affects and appreciate the positive ones emerge from the matrix of early relationships and the crystallization of internalized object relations into psychological structures (Fairbairn, 1952; Zetzel, 1970). The structure of affects can be understood as being built out of the two simultaneously developing psychological processes noted earlier: the origin of the self as the locus of initiative and feelings and the representations and emotional tones originating in relations with others (Jacobson, 1964). The lines of development of self-love and other-love may later diverge, with increasing psychic differentiation (Kohut, 1971); it seems doubtful that they are sharply split early on (Cohen, 1980). Thus, while the dating of the appearance of fantasies about relations between self and object may have been placed too early by some analytic writers, following Melanie Klein (1948, 1957), it seems useful to recognize with her the centrality of the child's representations of others in the formation of his representation and regard for self.

Andrew's disorder can be seen as an empty, hopeless, despairing depression. Its earliest experiential roots may be traced to the first year of life and to what was, most likely, an anaclitic depression of infancy (Spitz, 1946). The dampening of activity, apathy, resignation, and paucity of speech all point to difficulties in the earliest phases of development; they demonstrate how symptoms, arising from deprivation and recurrent loss, become transmuted into character. The affective disorder can be traced stage by developmental stage, in Andrew's incapacity for fun and play, in his distance from peers, in his withdrawal from adults, in his learning problems in school. The dramatic symptoms of age 6 that announced his depression, and called for treatment, such as the identification with his mother's pet dog and passive thumb-sucking, thus represented a breakdown of a compliant false self and an exposure to long-standing pain. To say that Andrew was fixated at the earliest phases of development, however, would oversimplify the phenomena of developmental progression (A. Freud, 1965). Even in a child like Andrew with interferences during the phase of symbiotic or oral closeness, capacities also emerged for more advanced psychological structures, as evidenced in his life and analysis through such phenomena as his romance with Lucy. Yet, each phase of emotional growth carried with it and was suffused by his recurrent losses and what had not been accomplished in early childhood (Winnicott, 1958, 1965). Andrew clearly showed the wounds of self and object representations that were never left alone long enough, in a caregiving world, to be able to heal.

CONSTITUTION AND EXPERIENCE

There is no contradiction, within psychoanalysis, in recognizing the role of early and recurrent experiences and, at the same time, in acknowledging the role of endowment (Cohen, 1974, 1975; Dibble and Cohen, 1980; A. Freud, 1965; Greenacre, 1958; Ritvo et al., 1963; Young and Cohen, 1979). The dual meaning of "genetic" is not accidental. Analysts are aware that in many ways a child's personality is shaped before he emerges into the world; biological genetic endowment as well as early experiences assert their influences throughout the development. Among the major contributions of analytic child observation has been the description of how children alter the behavior of caregivers and how children's perceptions and responses are shaped by the continuous interaction between constitution and environmental provision.

The tendency to fall ill with depression may be among the best studied examples of genetics in both its biological and psychological senses. The biological predisposition to serious depressive disorders seems, at this point, well established (e.g., see Winokur et al., 1971, 1973, 1979). That this predisposition is not expressed in each potentially vulnerable individual, and that there are individuals who develop depressive disorders without familial histories of illness, suggest the importance of the vicissitudes of experience.

Andrew was, thus, a double victim. From the biological perspective, he was vulnerable to the mood difficulties that were so prevalent in both his mother's and father's families. From the perspective of environmental provision, he received little of joyful, pleasurable, soothing, unambivalent, and appropriately timed "good enough" mothering (Winnicott, 1958). Basic preconditions for the normal development of cognitive competence were not fully satisfied through the continuous availability of trustworthy caregivers (Goldstein et al., 1973, 1979). It was difficult for him to understand his parents and feel understood by them, and emerging social comprehension could thus not serve as a solid basis for creating models of a predictable world (Cohen, 1978). He was inhibited in the process of taking in beloved others and using these representations in the formation of his self representation; and the disturbances in earliest object relations and recurrent losses were reflected in impairments in the development of positive affects. He was unable to lay secure foundations for the capacities to bear, recognize, and do something about anxiety and depression. Thus, he became long-suffering and confused.

TECHNIQUE

For Andrew, speech did not come easily. His mother did not speak to him during his infancy; later, his father did not readily communicate his own thoughts and feelings through talk (Katan, 1961). In Andrew's analysis, speech played an even more peripheral role than is usual for children his age. Instead, through the empathic relationship with a listening adult who was there to understand, and who could not in reality be blamed for recurrent losses, Andrew learned that he could communicate as a builder and creator (Kohut, 1959, 1977; Schafer, 1959). He recognized, through his pleasure in creating and sharing, that works of art, when they are authentic, can move between the primary process (from the earliest relationships of child and parents) and the secondary processes, as well as between the one who wishes to give voice to his pain and the one who strains to hear (Winnicott, 1971).

The psychoanalytic task, the problems of technique, can be reviewed from this perspective. The analyst was there to help Andrew see the first photographs in his album about the history of a building as a step toward remembering and then telling his own history, with a past as well as a future (Kennedy, 1979; Neubauer, 1979). The analyst needed to await, accept, and remain surprised by the appearance, from somewhere, of each drawing in the scroll of the highway travels. Finally, the analyst was required to relive with Andrew, and to place in a higher level of psychological organization, the painful wrongs that were inflicted upon him, through no fault of his own, and to alleviate the guilt and shame which he experienced because of his mother's departures (Kennedy, 1971, Kohut, 1959).

The child analyst offers himself as a new, caring friend; also, as an analyst, he is aspects of all the important people the child has ever known (Ritvo, 1974; Schowalter, 1976). For Andrew, the analysis of the negative transference, of his reactions to what the analyst tacitly offered or aroused but could not provide, was only partially interpreted or worked through. The analyst could neither resurrect nor be his mother, nor would he let her ghost lie in peace. Thus, analysis, as life, was also a cause of disappointment. Perhaps the pain of Andrew's predicament prevented the deepest pursuit and unearthing of the grief and unrequited love that are inherent in analysis (Gitelson, 1952). It is possible that this work had to be left undone, to be pursued later when life may provide Andrew with more evidence of its possible satisfactions (A. Freud, 1971). Thus, much remains for a later analysis, during adolescence or adulthood, when new competencies may help Andrew act out the analytic drama on the internal stage of mental representations (Loewald, 1979a; Valenstein, 1962). At this future date, he may be able to give fuller expression to his rage, without fear of driving away the analyst or destroying, in one fell swoop, the analyst, his father, and himself. Whether, given his history, the core mood of a child such as

Andrew can ever be fundamentally altered remains an open question. With some pleasures and stability in his life, and with the fuller understanding of narcissistic disturbances, such transformations of the self remain a possibility for his adulthood (Kohut, 1977).

The phenomenological portrait should not be painted only in dark colors. As described, the early development of affect reflects, in large part, the emergence of object-related structures derived from the complex of the child's relationships; fantasies, instincts, defensive operations, and self and other representations are distillates, not reproductions. Andrew's development reveals, in boldface, the critical role of his father as an early, redemptive object. That Andrew did survive, and was in so many ways an alive child, in spite of painful trauma and good reason for despair, speaks for the importance of his father in the formation of basic emotional competencies. The function of the father is especially rich in families such as Andrew's, when the father must play various roles at once. To a greater degree than can be portrayed here, Andrew's father provided motherly tenderness and fatherly order. That Andrew fell ill with his type of depression is barely in need of explanation; that he could find, within himself and through analysis, the forces for recovery does require explanation. This recovery was, in large part, related to what Andrew could take in over the years from his father and, through the availability of these father-mother representations, from the new mother-father analyst (Tolpin, 1978).

THE ANALYTIC PROCESS

During his three years of analysis, from 7 to 10 years, a latency-aged boy became consciously aware of the meaning of recurrent separations from and loss of his mother in early childhood. He gradually felt understood, and he experienced a self-understanding of the origin of his feelings of emptiness and despair (Kennedy, 1979). He experimented with feeling the anger at being left and of having his hopes for reconciliation dashed over and over. He heard about his loneliness and the right to feel furious, rather than bad, for what he had suffered; and he learned of the potential to express himself, and to try to make his own life in a form he wanted by knowing what he was feeling and what was happening to and inside of himself (Winnicott, 1965).

The synthetic account of a psychoanalytic process in childhood, as described in this essay, draws upon our understanding of the influences on a child's development and of the nature of the therapeutic action of psychoanalysis in allowing development to proceed in areas where it has been restrained or distorted (A. Freud, 1965; Zetzel, 1970). For Andrew, the construction of physical objects and the creation of routines served as the chief modes of communication. His album, drawings, models, and sculpture, as well as his morning coffee-milks and style of sharing thoughts or holding them back, were the materials which allowed Andrew and his analyst to reconstruct the recurrent processes, experiences, feelings, and unfulfilled aspirations of his life. The analytic relationship was, in its own right, a unique construction. For Andrew, as for other children, the analytic relationship existed as a new friendship, a pattern of activities shared in the here and now. This social construction also expressed the potentialities which derived from Andrew's earlier and concurrent relations with his parents. The internal and external constructions of Andrew's analysis were the means of reviving the past and bringing it into consciousness, as well as, to a lesser extent, into speech.

Andrew's development was influenced by the failure of a special type of empathic relationship between himself and his mother, as well as by exposure to various types of traumatic overstimulation and confusion (Kohut, 1971; E. Kris, 1956b). With a disturbance at the level of earliest object relations—characterized as the sphere of self-object relations by Kohut—there may be pervasive and long-lasting impairments in the regulation of self-esteem. In Andrew, these impairments were manifested not by marked sensitivity to rejection but, more ominously, by withdrawal of expectation. He felt that he "didn't care" what happened around and with him; he felt he had little right to care.

Multiple processes lead a child to a trusting, secure attachment to caregivers to whom he can turn in reality and then in fantasy. When development proceeds smoothly, the child can generalize the close, life-sustaining relationships with primary caregivers to others, to whom he can then turn and from whom he can also receive sustenance. This network of internalized objects provides the child with models or standards and with felt competence for recognizing and bearing anxiety, mastering his environment, dealing with defeats, and planning for the future. For Andrew, repeated trauma and failure of environmental provisions during the oral phase of development, when attachments and their vicissitudes are the foremost of the child's developmental tasks, led to persistent disturbances in libidinal organization, in the expression of aggression, and in ego and superego functions. He could not organize his experience into meaningful relations and expectable occurrences, nor could he feel that life had a pleasurable, forward-moving coherence. He feared the expression of his anger and withdrew into passive acceptance or quiet refusal to participate in events or show feelings. His difficulties in motor control and learning reflected, in large part, the failure he experienced in the differentiation and protective isolation of autonomous ego functions; his erection of superego functions on the shaky foundation of disturbed archaic object relations exposed him to feeling out of harmony with his deepest longings. He could not remake his family, bring back his mother, or find pleasure or inner peace in a world of chaos where he was always the loser. For Andrew, the world felt ungiving; he felt bad, as described by Klein, for having made it so.

The therapeutic action of the psychoanalysis lay in the possibility of constructing and reconstructing (Freud, 1937). This possibility was based, in turn, on what Andrew had been able to accomplish during the first years of life. With all his difficulties, Andrew's father could offer himself to Andrew as an exemplar of survival and, in their own ways, both parents could show human warmth. Perhaps the artistic flair that was unearthed during analysis can be traced back to the vitality his mother was able to display when she was well. With less doubt, his father's endurance in the face of hardship and quiet sense of humor became the templates for Andrew's own solidity and capacity for controlled whimsy.

Thus, analysis proceeded through an unfolding series of interrelated processes. It started with the creation of a relationship with an empathic adult; Andrew re-created the routines of early, preseparation feeding and closeness. The construction of external objects then expressed the longing for and, to some extent, the realization of continuity for the ongoing analytic relationship; this construction became a means for reviving and projecting continuities over the course of Andrew's life. The building of actual objects uncovered and externally exercised internal capacities for expressing and sharing feelings and for reflecting on them. The reconstruction of earliest deprivations led to the conscious awareness of sadness, longings, and rage. Finally, the newfound capacities for creativity allowed Andrew to bridge the gap between the archaic, unspeakable past and the conscious awareness of who he was and could be. He learned that he could communicate his pain to someone who wished to hear and bear it with him, to someone who was not overwhelmed by his painful feelings but who could not make them disappear.

Child analysts do not, or at least need not, shy away from seeing the role of the analyst as a new object for the child (A. Freud, 1965; Ritvo, 1978). They can see analysis as building a house, writing a history, dramatizing a family in action, or creating an object of whimsy. What else can child analysis be if it is to be real, lived, and useful? The child analyst, as worker and player, cannot keep his hands clean, or remain unchanged by participation in these activities. Current understanding of the therapeutic action of analysis with adults appreciates the continuities between the child and adult in analysis (Loewald, 1960, 1979a; Stone, 1961, 1967; Winnicott, 1956, 1965). As a developmental psychology, psychoanalysis suggests that a sharp split between the epochs is impoverishing, in the practice of analysis, as well as in life (Loewald, 1978b).

BIBLIOGRAPHY

Bell, S. (1970), The Development of the Concept of the Object As Related to Infant-Mother Attachment. *Child Develpm.*, 41:291–311.

Bornstein, B. (1945), Clinical Notes on Child Analysis. *This Annual*, 1:151–166.

Caparulo, B. K. & Cohen, D. J. (1977), Cognitive Structures, Language, and

Emerging Social Competence in Autistic and Aphasic Children. *J. Amer Acad. Child Psychiat.*, 16:620–645.

Cohen, D. J. (1974), Competence and Biology. In: *The Child in His Family*, ed E. J. Anthony & C. Koupernik. New York: Wiley 3:361–394.

—— (1975), Psychosomatic Models of Development. In: *Explorations in Child Psychiatry*, ed. E. J. Anthony. New York: Plenum Press, pp. 197–212.

—— (1978), The Concept of the "Stimulus Barrier" in Psychoanalyti Theory. In: Colloquim on 'Trauma,' rep. A. E. Geerts & E. Rechardt. *Int. J Psycho-Anal.*, 59:365–375.

—— (1980), The Pathology of the Self in Two Neuropsychiatric Disorders o Childhood. In: *Narcissism and the Psychopathology of the Self in Childhood*, ed. K Robson. Philadelphia: Saunders (in press).

—— Caparulo, B. K., & Shaywitz, B. A. (1978), Neurochemical and Devel opmental Models of Childhood Autism. In: *Cognitive Defects in the Develop ment of Mental Illness*, ed. G. Serban. New York: Brunner/Mazel, pp. 66–100

Dibble, E. D. & Cohen, D. J. (1980), Biological Endowment, Early Experience and Psychosocial Influences on Child Behavior. In: *The Child and His Family* ed. E. J. Anthony & C. Chiland. New York: Wiley-Interscience (in press).

Fairbairn, W. R. D. (1952), *An Object Relations Theory of the Personality.* Nev York: Basic Books.

Freud, A. (1965), Normality and Pathology in Childhood. *W.*, 6.

—— (1971), Problems of Termination in Child Analysis. *W.*, 7:3–21.

Freud, S. (1937), Constructions in Analysis. *S.E.*, 23:257–269.

Furman, E. (1974), *A Child's Parent Dies.* New Haven & London: Yale Univ Press.

Gitelson, M. (1952), The Emotional Position of the Analyst in the Psycho Analytic Situation. *Int. J. Psycho-Anal.*, 33:1–10.

Goldstein, J., Freud, A., & Solnit, A. J. (1973), *Beyond the Best Interests of th Child.* New York: Free Press.

—— —— —— (1979), *Before the Best Interests of the Child.* New York: Free Press.

Greenacre, P. (1958), Early Physical Determinants in the Development of the Sense of Identity. In: *Emotional Growth*, 1:113–127. New York: Int. Univ Press, 1971.

Hartmann, H. (1958), *Ego Psychology and the Problem of Adaptation.* New York Int. Univ. Press.

Jacobson, E. (1964), *The Self and the Object World.* New York: Int. Univ. Press.

Katan, A. (1961), Some Thoughts about the Role of Verbalization in Earl Childhood. *This Annual*, 16:184–188.

Kennedy, H. (1971), Problems in Reconstruction in Child Analysis. *This An nual*, 26:286–402.

—— (1979), The Role of Insight in Child Analysis. *J. Amer. Psychoanal. Assn Suppl.*, 27:9–28.

Klein, M. (1948), *Contributions to Psycho-Analysis, 1921–45.* London: Hogart Press.

—— (1957), *Envy and Gratitude.* London: Tavistock.

KOHUT, H. (1959), Introspection, Empathy, and Psychoanalysis. In: *The Search for the Self,* 1:205–232. New York: Int. Univ. Press, 1978.

—— (1971), *The Analysis of the Self.* New York: Int. Univ. Press.

—— (1977), *The Restoration of the Self.* New York: Int. Univ. Press.

KRAMER, S. (1979), The Technical Significance and Application of Mahler's Separation-Individuation Theory. *J. Amer. Psychoanal. Assn. Suppl.,* 27:241–262.

KRIS, E. (1956a), On Some Vicissitudes of Insight in Psychoanalysis. In: *The Selected Papers of Ernst Kris.* New Haven & London: Yale Univ. Press, 1975, pp. 252–271.

—— (1956b), The Recovery of Childhood Memories in Psychoanalysis. In: *Ibid.,* pp. 301–340.

—— (1962), Decline and Recovery in the Life of a Three-Year-Old. In: *Ibid.,* pp. 172–212.

LACAN, J. (1968), *The Language of the Self.* New York: Dell Publishing Co.

LOEWALD, H. W. (1960), On the Therapeutic Action of Psycho-Analysis. *Int. J. Psycho-Anal.,* 41:16–33.

—— (1971), On Motivation and Instinct Theory. *This Annual,* 26:91–128.

—— (1978a), Instinct Theory, Object Relations, and Psychic-Structure Formation. *Amer. J. Psychoanal. Assn.,* 26:493–506.

—— (1978b), *Psychoanalysis and the History of the Individual.* New Haven & London: Yale Univ. Press.

—— (1979a), Reflections on the Psychoanalytic Process and Its Therapeutic Potential. *This Annual,* 34:155–168.

—— (1979b), The Waning of the Oedipus Complex. *J. Amer. Psychoanal. Assn.,* 27:751–775.

MAHLER, M. S., PINE, F., & BERGMAN, A. (1975), *The Psychological Birth of the Human Infant.* New York: Basic Books.

NEUBAUER, P. B. (1979), The Role of Insight in Psychoanalysis. *J. Amer. Psychoanal. Assn. Suppl.,* 27:29–40.

PIAGET, J. (1937), *The Construction of Reality in the Child.* New York: Basic Books, 1954.

RITVO, S. (1974), The Current Status of the Concept of Infantile Neurosis. *This Annual,* 29:159–181.

—— (1978), The Psychoanalytic Process in Childhood. *This Annual,* 33:295–305.

—— McCALLUM, A. T., OMWAKE, E., PROVENCE, S. A., & SOLNIT, A. J. (1963), Some Relations of Constitution, Environment, and Personality As Observed in a Longitudinal Study of Child Development. In: *Modern Perspectives in Child Development,* ed. A. J. Solnit & S. A. Provence. New York: Int. Univ. Press, pp. 107–143.

SCHAFER, R. (1959), Generative Empathy in the Treatment Situation. *Psychoanal. Quart.,* 28:342–373.

SCHOWALTER, J. E. (1976), Therapeutic Alliance and the Role of Speech in Child Analysis. *This Annual,* 31:415–436.

SOLNIT, A. J. & KRIS, M. (1967), Trauma and Infantile Experiences. In: *Psychic Trauma*, ed. S. S. Furst. New York: Basic Books, pp. 175–220.

SPITZ, R. A. (1946), Anaclitic Depression. *This Annual*, 2:313–342.

STONE, L. (1961), *The Psychoanalytic Situation*. New York: Int. Univ. Press.

—— (1967), The Psychoanalytic Situation and Transference. *J. Amer. Psychoanal. Assn.*, 15:3–58.

STRACHEY, J. (1934), The Nature of the Therapeutic Action of Psycho Analysis. *Int. J. Psycho-Anal.*, 15:127–159.

TOLPIN, M. (1971), On the Beginnings of a Cohesive Self. *This Annual* 26:316–352.

—— (1978), Self-Objects and Oedipal Objects. *This Annual*, 33:167–184.

VALENSTEIN, A. F. (1962), The Psycho-Analytic Situation. *Int. J. Psycho-Anal.*, 43:315–327.

WINNICOTT, D. W. (1956), On Transference. *Int. J. Psycho-Anal.*, 34:386–388.

—— (1958), *Collected Papers*. New York: Basic Books.

—— (1965), *The Maturational Processes and the Facilitating Environment*. New York: Int. Univ. Press.

—— (1971), *Playing and Reality*. London: Tavistock.

WINOKUR, G. (1979), Familial (Genetic) Subtypes of Pure Depressive Disease *Amer. J. Psychiat.*, 136:911–913.

—— CADORET, R. J., DORZAB, J., & BAKER, M. (1971), Depressive Disease *Arch. Gen. Psychiat.*, 24:135–144.

—— MORRISON, J., CLANCY, J., & CROWE, R. (1973), The Iowa 500. *Compr. Psychiat.*, 14:19–106.

YOUNG, J. G. & COHEN, D. J. (1979), The Molecular Biology of Development. In: *Basic Handbook of Child Psychiatry*, ed. J. Noshpitz. New York: Basic Books, 1:22–62.

ZETZEL, E. R. (1970), *The Capacity for Emotional Growth*. New York: Int. Univ Press.

Transference and Externalization in Latency

ERNA FURMAN

THIS PAPER FOCUSES ON THE RELATIONSHIP BETWEEN TRANSFER-ence and externalization. I shall explore how aspects of this relationship are linked to the latency period, how they manifest themselves clinically, and which technical measures they imply. Last, I shall present some tentative thoughts on how counter-transference may interfere with our understanding and clinical handling of the interrelated phenomena of transference and externalization.

DEFINITIONS

In his discussions of transference Freud (1905, 1912, 1915, 1916–17, 1937) stated repeatedly that all people transfer uncon-cious libidinal aspects of their relationships from primal objects to current ones. The neurotic's transference, inside and outside the analytic setting, differs only in quantity due to his or her lack of real gratification and regression—or introversion—from cur-rent realities. Freud noted that some aspects of the transference tacitly and helpfully contribute to the patient-analyst relation-

From the Cleveland Center for Research in Child Development and the Department of Psychiatry, Case Western Reserve University, School of Medicine.

Presented as a contribution to the panel, "Transference and Counter-transference in Latency and Preadolescence," at the joint scientific meeting of the Association for Child Psychoanalysis and the International Psycho-Analytical Association, July 29, 1979, New York City.

ship and further their joint work; others—and he specifically named the negative transference and the erotic nature of the positive transference—manifest themselves as resistances and potential impediments. It is one of the main tasks of an analysis to turn these latter aspects to therapeutic advantage by helping the patient to become aware of them, to explore them, and to understand their infantile origins. The analytic setting and the analyst's interpretative work not only make this utilization of the transference possible but facilitate a special flourishing of the transference, focused on the person of the analyst and unique in its depth, breadth, and intensity. This development constitutes transference in the narrower and specifically analytic sense of the term.

In 1936 Anna Freud brought the earlier concept of transference in line with Freud's later theoretical formulations. She pointed out that the transference of aggressive as well as libidinal impulses in object relations occurs under the influence of the repetition compulsion, and she introduced structural considerations; i.e., in addition to a transfer of instinctual derivatives, transference of ego and superego aspects takes place. Anna Freud underlined the importance of analyzing all aspects. She also discussed the transference of defense and the value of understanding the origins, functions, and vicissitudes of defense mechanisms in the context of the patient's total personality. I wish to stress this because it and her next statements bear directly on the aspects I shall discuss. Returning to the topic of transference in 1965, Anna Freud wrote that with the child, and perhaps to a lesser extent with the adult, some relations established or transferred in analysis are due to externalizations, "i.e., to processes in which the person of the analyst is used to represent one or the other part of the patient's personality structure" (p. 41). She refers to the tendency of children defensively "to externalize their inner conflicts in the form of battles with the environment" (p. 35). Anna Freud terms externalization a "subspecies of transference," adding, "Treated as such in interpretation and kept separate from transference proper, it is a valuable source of insight into the psychic structure" (p. 43).

Sandler et al. (1969) have traced the history of the concept of transference in great detail. Loewenstein (1969), in his concise paper on the developments in the theory of transference, also addresses himself to the wider implications and relates them to the differing views of other analysts and analytic groups. In 1975, Sandler et al. further discussed transference, externalization, and their relationship with special reference to child analytic technique. Under the wider heading of transference, they distinguish (1) transference predominantly of past experiences, where—in the form of transference reactions or transference neurosis—"past experiences, wishes, fantasies, conflicts, and defenses are *revived* during the course of the analysis, as a consequence of the analytic work, and which now relate to the person of the therapist in their manifest or latent (preconscious) content" (p. 423); (2) transference predominantly of current relationships, in which current wishes, conflicts, or reactions are displaced or extended into the analytic situation and/or involved with the person of the therapist. These may be related to current experiences and include "regressive as well as phase-appropriate manifestations" (p. 418); and (3) transference predominantly of habitual modes of relating which are not specific to the therapist but form a part of the child's character. Although they represent "residues of earlier relationships [or defenses against earlier object-directed impulses, they] have now spread to the world as a whole and may be regarded as having attained a degree of autonomy" (p. 414).

According to these authors, the Hampstead Index includes in these different aspects of transference various forms of externalization. Like Novick and Kelly (1970), they define externalization as "any aspect of the person . . . attributed to the external world" (p. 413). In the context of this paper, I shall use the term externalization similarly to this and Anna Freud's above-cited definitions, and I shall utilize Sandler et al.'s (1975) categories of transference.

EXTERNALIZATION AS A PHASE-APPROPRIATE DEFENSE IN EARLY LATENCY

From earliest childhood on various forms of externalization and internalization manifest themselves as developmental phenomena and as defensive maneuvers, but, by their very nature, internalization and externalization of superego attitudes are specifically linked to the onset of latency (E. Furman, 1980).

In observing young children during entry into latency, one is struck with how uneasy they feel with their newly acquired superego, how little it as yet feels like a part of them, and how hard it is for them to understand its signals and to utilize them effectively in their behavior. In the Hanna Perkins Kindergarten (R. A. Furman and A. Katan, 1969) we usually have several children who complain that their mothers constantly "yell" at them, or that their teachers are "mean" to them; and, if they are in treatment, that their analysts say they are "bad." Closer scrutiny shows that these children attribute the harsh voice of conscience to the outside authorities. When it is pointed out that the mother, teacher, or analyst was actually encouraging and soft-spoken and that perhaps something inside the children is very angry at them, they sometimes listen half-bewildered, half-thoughtful, with an inward-looking expression on their faces. As they become more aware of what goes on inside them, they learn to distinguish better the inner from the outer reality, recognize more readily the demands of conscience, and their relationships suffer less interference. Some weeks or months later these children occasionally comment, "My conscience's yelling at me today." Or, "You like my writing, but I think it's terrible." It seems that their attributing the criticism to the outside is initially not a defense but a sign of unfamiliarity with the new inner agency and lack of its integration into the rest of the personality. The adult—parent, teacher, analyst—best helps the child with this developmental process when he or she educationally supports and encourages the child's ego functions of testing inner and outer reality, of weighing and resolving inner conflict, and of adapting accordingly. In analytic terms, this kind of assistance to the child's ego might come under the heading of confrontation and clarification. Were the analyst to interpret the patient's externalizing behavior as a defense, he would create unnecessary anxiety. Should he, however, interpret it as a transference from current or past relationships, he would, I believe, interfere with, and possibly impede, the developmental integrative process.[1]

Since the newly internalized superego is often harsh and un-

1. A. Katan (1979) stresses that all defenses undergo some changes in the course of development. Developmental mechanisms and defenses proper shade into one another, or overlap, in their progression. The definition of a specific defense tends to apply to its "advanced" developmental stage but fails

compromising, many children experience such intense anxiety and painful guilt feelings that they employ a variety of defenses against them. Anna Freud (1936) noted in this connection the defense of identification with the aggressor. Our observations at the Hanna Perkins Kingergarten suggest that the most widely used mechanism in early latency is externalization of superego attitudes to ward off inner conflict. In this form externalization is no longer a sign of developmental unfamiliarity with the superego but a phase-specific transitional defense. It is often combined, in varying degrees, with a need to seek punishment. This combination of mechanisms is similar to that in the adult criminals from a sense of guilt (Freud, 1916). In other respects, it is similar to projection. I am referring here to the relationship between externalization and projection as described by Novick and Kelly (1970) and Sandler et al. (1975). The latter authors define projection as referring to "the attribution to another person of a wish or impulse of one's own toward that person, *and felt by the subject to be directed back against himself*. . . . Projection has, therefore, been regarded as a specific instance of the wider class of externalizations" (p. 413; my italics). In externalization of superego elements to ward off inner conflict, the child relegates the superego function to a potential authority whom he then defies but whom he also "invites" to control or punish the displayed misdeeds. This externalization, like projection, thus has the feature of tying the patient to the person onto whom he externalizes and from whom he expects criticism. However, the externalization not only changes an inner battle into an outer one; it also supplants a very harsh inner threat with a usually milder punishment from the outside. Further, the "crime" is often displaced; e.g., naughty behavior may be shown instead of a guilt-provoking masturbatory activity.

CASE EXAMPLE

The case of Jimmy illustrates the use of this defense and how his parents helped him to become more aware of it and to achieve

---

o fit its initial, more primitive stages. For example, the early stages of externalization, as described in this paper, are characterized by what I termed "unfamiliarity with the new superego."

better mastery of his conflicts. Jimmy had attended the Hanna Perkins Kindergarten where he was treated via his parents, and I was still assisting them with his early latency development when he was in first grade of public school.

Jimmy was a very "good" first-grader, always well behaved in class, somewhat timid and easily hurt by the least unkind remark, but fairly glowing when praised and appreciated. His work was generally very good, but sometimes he hurried through it to be "the first finished" and then felt guilty and crestfallen when he found that his rush had produced a few mistakes. At home Jimmy was less concerned with criticism and perfection, and enjoyed his activities and relationships with the family. Every now and then, however, Jimmy became quite "naughty" with his parents.

His "naughty" times appeared to start with minor disobediences or mishaps, e.g., playing rambunctiously with a peer and not heeding the first call to come into the house, or spilling a dish accidentally. Instead of an apology or effort to put matters right, Jimmy would become inappropriately angry and provocative. He defied his parents' admonitions and requests, loudly proclaimed how little he cared about their expectations, and insisted that he would do just as he pleased. When the parents became very firm, and especially when they sent him to his room or instituted a sanction, Jimmy's outburst eventually subsided; but when they tried to reason with him or kindly disregarded his misbehavior, his naughtiness crescendoed as he yelled abusively, sometimes hit out, or caused minor damage to things. Usually these episodes subsided in a few hours, but they could also continue for several days with intermittent outbursts and provocations. At these times Jimmy also became much more tense and worried about school, fearing that he was "dumb" and that the others would not like him.

Jimmy's parents began to tell him that he tried to give *them* his conscience at these troubled times and wanted *them* to be angry at him and punish him, perhaps because he felt so bad about himself. Would it not be better to be his own boss and let himself know what he felt he had done wrong? They added that then he would be able to get himself in control again, would not have to make others punish him at home or worry about not doing well at school. This helped Jimmy to cut short his "naughty" episodes. Closer observation showed that the incidents which precipitated his outbursts were either displacements from masturbatory concerns or "confessions" of masturbatory indulgence, but this was not discussed with him. In time he was able to cope better with his inner conflict, and his behavioral disturbance subsided.

Whereas Jimmy's defense of externalization interfered primarily with his behavior at home, in other children we have observed it manifested itself mainly at school or in both places. In early latency children in analysis, the externalization of superego aspects usually extends into the analytic setting or even is its focal point because having to go into treatment in the first place and having to face inner conflicts there put special stress on the child's vulnerable spot, the newly internalized superego. Bornstein (1951), Williams (1972), and others have described the child's special touchiness and sensitivity to criticism in this phase.

Instead of making the child aware of his defense and supporting him in dealing with his inner conflict, as Jimmy's parents did, educators are tempted to fall in with the child's defense of externalization.[2] They either fulfill the assigned superego role of harsh disapproval and punishment, or they attempt to counteract it by lowered expectations and increased reassurances of love. Both approaches fail to help the child with his developmental struggle, both tend to perpetuate and intensify the use of the defense mechanism, and both may add further pathological elements, e.g., stimulation of regressive sadomasochistic strivings in the case of harsh punishments, and failure to develop age-appropriate behavioral self-controls and skills in the case of permissiveness. In some instances these forms of environmental mishandling may constitute a developmental interference (Nagera, 1966) and contribute to pathological exaggerations of developmental conflicts or to the establishment of maladaptive character traits. Anna Freud (1936) noted that identification with the aggressor too can lead to a specific characterological

---

2. Kestenberg (1975) discussed related aspects of the latency child's effect on teachers and parents.

pathology if the use of this defense mechanism fails to be supplanted by a more mature internalization of the superego.

The analyst, one hopes, is less likely to become a party to the child's defense by punishing or reassuring him. *His* temptation lies in the area of mistaking the defense for a transference manifestation and to interpret it in these terms in relation to the child's current or past relationships with primal objects. For example, if Jimmy were to provoke and misbehave with his analyst, the latter might link such material to Jimmy's behavior with his mother and perhaps to earlier toddler struggles with her which now serve as oedipal gratifications in a regressed form. I have observed that the mistaken interpretation of transference in place of externalization can lead to an intensification of the defense and deterioration in the child's ability to participate in the analytic work. Most important, however, the transference interpretation can become an interference in the phase-appropriate formation and integration of a new structure within the child's personality. Whereas the child's defense of externalization attempts to live with the superego by diminishing the anxiety it arouses, the analyst's transference interpretation disregards the superego and directs itself to the id sources of its origin.

EXTERNALIZATION AS A PATHOLOGICAL DEFENSE

Externalization of superego attitudes ceases to be a phase-specific, self-limited, early latency defense when its intensity or rigidity precludes progress toward mature and appropriate integration of superego demands. In these pathological forms we find it in all phases of latency as well as in some later characterological disturbances. In contrast to the transitory externalization of superego attitudes, the pathologically exaggerated and characterologically rigid forms of this defense cannot be approached educationally but require therapeutic measures.

Latency children who use externalization of superego attitudes to a pathological extent are easily misdiagnosed as not having entered latency or having regressed from it instinctually and structurally, and their misbehavior is then attributed to inadequate superego development. Actually, cases of complete arrest or structural regression are rare and usually manifest widespread additional pathology. When a latency-aged child exhibits apparently guiltless aggressive or libidinal behavior, it is quite likely that his difficulties are of a defensive nature.

CASE EXAMPLE

Steven was a handsome, almost 6-year-old boy when he entered Hanna Perkins Kingergarten. He had been well prepared for this new venture and had shown by his behavior during the previous year that he was emotionally and intellectually ready for it, with signs of beginning latency development. It was therefore quite disconcerting for everyone when Steven, almost from the first day on, allied himself with the most aggressive and disobedient peer, followed the latter in disruptive behavior, initiated trouble on his own, and seduced others to join him. He was impervious to the teacher's admonitions, indulged in excited play, and would not apply himself to learning tasks. His reply to reminders was, "There are no rules in kindergarten and there are no rules inside me."

At home with his mother, however, Steven was well behaved and enjoyed many activities with her and on his own. Helped by her treatment-via-the-parent interviews, the mother told Steven that she thought he could not really be pleased with himself at school, that his naughtiness there was a trouble, and that she hoped he would work with her on understanding it as they had understood and helped to resolve other troubles during the previous year. She suggested that, at school, he passed on to his teachers all that he knew inside himself about rules and how to keep them, and then fought against that part of himself on the outside because it made him feel so bad and worried to hear it inside himself. As Steven began to face his anxiety, he improved at school but experienced night fears. We now learned that during the summer, several events had served to heighten Steven's anxieties, culminating in a nightmare and a week of severe fears at bedtime just prior to his entry to kindergarten. With the onset of school these worries had disappeared, and his uncontrolled school behavior had started. In the course of our work, his dictum, "no rules for me," could be related to his masturbation and

oedipal fantasies. The fear of punishment was linked to his extremely harsh superego, which, in turn, was based on his experiences with his father's debilitating illness. Steven could be helped
to modify his threatening introject and to improve his outward
adjustment. The incipient nature of his difficulty at a time of
developmental flux and his mother's therapeutic skill made it
feasible to assist him by means of treatment via the parent.

The pathological exaggeration of externalization of superego
attitudes during early latency or its characterological entrench-
ment in subsequent years may result from internal or external
developmental interferences during early latency. It may combine with the conflicts caused by the normal partial libidinal
regression which marks the beginning of latency, and it may be
complicated by fixation points at earlier levels. The consistent
use of externalization also brings about a measure of functional
ego regression (e.g., in reality testing), of drive regression, and of
regression in object relationships (e.g., aggression directed outward against objects rather than inward against the self). Although these regressions are of a secondary nature and differ
from the more serious conditions of arrest at the prelatency level
or from structural regression, they may overdetermine and
obscure from view the crucial unmastered conflict with the
newly formed superego, so specific to latency development.

The initial diagnostic difficulties are not readily clarified during the analysis because it becomes hard to distinguish defensive
externalization from transference proper, and regression in
drive and object relationship secondary to externalization from
similar phenomena caused by arrest or defensive regression.
One may argue that at the point in development where internalization of superego and defensive externalization coincide so
closely, it may not matter much whether the analyst directs his
interpretations at the defense against the inner conflict with the
superego introject or whether he approaches, via the transference, the child-parent relationship which underlies the superego
formation. I have found, however, that transference interpretations do not lead to the patient's awareness of his or her inner
conflict or to an understanding of the factors that make it so
difficult to resolve. The reason lies in the fact that the exter-

nalized superego differs from the internalized superego which, in turn, differs from the primal parental figures. As the process of internalization does not replicate the external reality, so the subsequent externalization does not represent the internalized inner reality. When we interpret the defensive externalization first, however, the patient begins to experience anxiety generated by the structural conflict and the way is paved to understanding the nature of his superego. Only then, and in the course of analyzing the introject, can the original object-directed impulses manifest themselves in the transference. Excerpts from Kevin's analysis illustrate this.

CASE EXAMPLE

Kevin began five-times-weekly analytic treatment at age 9½ years because of his problem of withholding bowel movements and soiling, which had persisted since he was a toddler. Although close scrutiny showed considerable disturbance in all areas of Kevin's personality functioning, this handsome, wiry boy impressed most people as a well-adjusted latency child. He achieved well at school, was popular with peers, and active in sports.

During the initial sessions Kevin revealed his high inner standards, the conflict they caused him, and his defense against them, namely, externalization. He carefully hid from view his painstaking work on a stereotyped paper construction. When I asked if I could help him with it, he replied, "I don't let people see unless it turns out perfect." He wanted my help with only one thing: what to tell others about his coming to treatment, or rather, how to prevent them from finding out, because he was sure they would ostracize him as the only and most inadequate boy if they learned that he saw a psychiatrist. I sympathized with his dilemma and suggested that perhaps he sometimes felt about his troubles as badly as he assumed others would feel if they knew.

Kevin's externalization of conflict soon shifted to another area. Increasingly he behaved like a provocative, dirty, controlling toddler. It was my business to work on his troubles, his business to prove my efforts useless. He contradicted everything

I said, passed gas, hurled streams of anal invective at me or withheld speech for days, expected me to clean up the room after him, tried to boss me around, walked out of the office during sessions, and threatened to quit the analysis. I learned that Kevin maintained a similar relationship with his mother. She was responsible for everything from getting him up in the morning to tying his shoes, washing his soiled pants, remembering to take him to lessons. He also made it her job to endure his rudeness, uncooperativeness, and hurtful withdrawals, to take the blame for his soiling, and to feel unhappy and hopeless about it. His relationship with his father contained the same features, lessened only in degree. As Kevin's behavior in the analysis worsened, he improved at home. It was possible to view this material in different ways: the sympathetic and confidential analytic setting allowed him to displace and isolate his home difficulties and to register, by means of his behavior, his angry protest and hurt over his current disappointments in his parents; e.g., he acted much worse when his parents planned to leave town for a few days. Also, his sadomasochistic relationship pointed to genetically earlier conflicts during his toddler years. Furthermore, his striking avoidance of positive feelings and increased nastiness whenever he would have had occasion to feel a liking for me suggested that his sadomasochistic interplay represented a regression from, and regressive gratification of, phallic-oedipal impulses in the transference. To me, the most pertinent aspect appeared to be Kevin's habitual defense of externalization of superego attitudes which he had extended into the analysis and, in part, transferred from his current love objects. I told him that I knew there was a 10-year-old part of Kevin that wanted to be a regular guy like all his buddies, or even better, and that that part of him must feel badly about his 2-year-old behavior and his misuse of the treatment. I wondered where that 10-year-old Kevin was. Later I suggested that sometimes a person can have such a terrible fight inside himself over wanting to do the right things and never being able to, that it feels safer to have a fight with people outside because one can be mad at them and get away from them, instead of feeling no good all the time.

Kevin responded with more age-appropriate behavior. He assumed responsibility for his body care at home and for his problems in the analysis. He began to share difficulties that caused him great concern, but of which his parents had only the slightest inkling. He suffered from severe insomnia as well as repetitive nightmares and fears when alone in his room. He engaged in excited quasi-delinquent exploits with peers when the parents were out. He was terrified of the very sports he did well. Above all, he felt hopeless and stupid. As he put it, "It's no use trying, nothing can get better." Work on this material led, among other things, to a better understanding of Kevin's superego with its perfectionist demands, prohibition of success, and contempt for inadequacy. Kevin's parents were warm, loving people who had always done their best with and for their children. However, they could not recall much of Kevin's past, and they were unaware of how and when their own difficulties had affected him. As a result, the analytic understanding of Kevin's superego and of the primal relationships and events which had shaped it proceeded almost entirely via the transference.

The origins of Kevin's defense of externalization of superego elements could be traced to his early latency when his inner conflict was so severe that he developed many fears and phobias and when his soiling took a marked turn for the worse. The particular harshness of his superego was to an extent related to events at the time of its formation. Prominent among these was a primal scene which Kevin fully observed at 5½ years of age. The father noticed Kevin only after the coitus and took the boy to his room. The mother made no move. Nobody said a word at the time or afterward. Kevin internalized his sense of the father's awesome phallic perfection, the impossibility of successful competition, the mother's assumed contemptuous rejection of him, as well as the guilt which the parents should have felt. The parents confirmed the facts after they had been reconstructed and recalled in the analysis. Although the primal scene made an overwhelming impact of itself, it also served as a catalyst for ongoing conflicts in the parent-child relationships. The father's pervasive exhibitionistic qualities and his relentless quest for perfection in all he did had deeply impressed Kevin and made him feel very inadequate. Kevin had felt especially hopeless about phallic and oedipal competition for the mother because she seemed always to make herself available for the father. She enjoyed accompanying him hither and yon at a moment's notice and forgot about her boy's needs and feelings at these times.

Kevin's controlling provocative behavior returned in the second year of his analysis. This time it was a true transference phenomenon, focused solely on the analyst. His improvement had brought with it an emergence of positive oedipal feelings from which he regressed following a brief vacation. From the mother transference we learned, for example, that his passing of gas and swearwords represented displaced erections. The father transference included his being blocked with bowel movement and impervious to my words as a protection against being penetrated. Kevin's anal-sadistic difficulties were partly regressive and also related to an earlier primal scene around 20 months of age. This scene, like the one referred to above, was traumatic in itself and was experienced by Kevin in the context of other, then-current stresses. The mother's many sudden absences and emotional withdrawals into sleep had often left Kevin feeling hurt, rejected, and unprotected. It was characteristic of the mother's difficulty that she was quite unaware of the impact of her behavior on the child at these times and that she did not expect Kevin to have a feeling response. His hurt and helplessness were unbearably painful. In addition, he thought that something was wrong with him to have such feelings at all. In time these narcissistic injuries contributed to the formation of harsh superego precursors and to an identification with the mother's "uncaring" attitude. His rude contrariness also served as a defense against the hurt of rejection. In a moving session, after I had sympathized with his deep concern over his recently acquired hamster, Kevin accused me, "How would you know? You don't even care!" I told him that he could not believe I cared as he could not believe his mother had cared, and as indeed he could not allow himself to care, because to care meant to risk getting hurt. In response Kevin allowed himself for the first time to cry. Soon afterward he stopped withholding because his bowel movement represented not only his hidden big penis but also his vulverable feelings.

Latency cases like Kevin, showing widespread and rigid use of externalization of superego attitudes, are not unusual. In some instances the defensive pattern derives not only from the child's developmental conflict but also from an identification with a parent who exhibits the same personality difficulty. I have no analytic experience with adults. I suspect, however, that externalization of superego elements in adults, both in its characterological form and as a transitory transference manifestation, may indicate a conflict during early latency and/or a postoedipal identification with the parent's similar pathology.[3]

After I had completed my own thinking on externalization and transference and began to research the literature, I came across this succinct statement by Anna Freud (1965): "When this defense [externalization of inner conflict] predominates, the child shows total unwillingness to undergo analysis, an attitude which is frequently mistaken for 'negative transference' and (unsuccessfully) interpreted as such" (p. 35f.). Have I merely invented the wheel once again? Perhaps. But I hope I have also clarified some details of its construction and fitted it into the framework of the carriage.

COUNTERTRANSFERENCE

My own experience to date and, as far as I know, that of my male colleagues suggest that the gender of patient or analyst has no significant effect on the areas I have discussed. The fact that the case vignettes in this paper have referred only to boys is accidental. I should, however, like to conclude with some remarks on the relation between countertransference and the defense of externalization of superego attitudes.

First, some thoughts on definition: Freud's (1910, 1915) early comments on countertransference refer to the analyst's inappropriate affective and behavioral responses to the patient's material. Freud did not specifically relate his idea about the universality of transference to the analyst-patient relationship. Hoffer (1956) assesses this as follows, "I should think there is ample justification for differentiating between the analyst's transference, which affects all his object relationships, and the counter-

3. Becker (1974) has discussed the significance of early latency stress on other aspects of adult pathology.

transference which refers to his propensities including his limitations in comprehending the patient's unconscious material; whereas the analyst's transference refers to his human appreciation and responses, to the patient's realistic needs in the various stages of psycho-analytic treatment" (p. 378). Several Kleinian authors (Heimann, 1950; Money-Kyrle, 1956; Racker, 1957, 1968) have explicitly discussed countertransference in this sense of the analytic instrument and have perceptively pointed out its uses and misuses, as well as some of the analyst's attitudes which commonly enter into his work with his patients. Kabcenell (1974), by contrast, reserves the term countertransference for the interfering responses which may be triggered within the analyst by his resonance with the patient's material. "Yet, this very receptivity to external and internal perceptions also makes the analyst vulnerable to many internal conflict-laden distortions. The vehicle for the analytic understanding also is the vehicle for countertransference reactions" (p. 31). I shall adhere to this definition.

Kabcenell, and earlier, Bornstein (1948), Anna Freud (1965), and others, have also addressed themselves to the special stresses the child analyst experiences in terms of his or her transference, countertransference, and use of the comprehending analytic instrument. According to Money-Kyrle (1956), a parental attitude always forms a part of the analyst's view of the patient. Bornstein (1948) in this context discusses the countertransference distortion of a superiority-inferiority attitude toward the child. I wish to focus on another, though related, distortion, namely, the child analyst's propensity to invest the child with his id strivings by way of externalization. In these instances the analyst defensively externalizes some of his id strivings onto the child patient. The latter's behavior, material, or whole personality is then viewed as the analyst's id. Depending on his attitude to the id, the analyst may then tend to indulge the child, for example, encourage instinctual or regressive behavior under the guise of eliciting analytic material, or he may need to control the child, for example, by taking over the analytic work without engaging the patient's participating ego. Most commonly, he may tend to misjudge the structural n aturity of the child's personality and fail to address himself to the internalized conflict. One of Bornstein's special gifts was her ability to empathize with the child as an equal and to comprehend his intrapsychic situation. Brody (1974) reported an anecdote about Bornstein:

> She told me that one day a little boy had asked her what she would do if he stole something from her desk; she replied, "I would think to myself, 'I wonder what has happened to make an honest person act as if he were a thief'" [p. 18].

Anna Freud (1965) comments that children tend to view the analyst as well as all adults as superego representatives. This tendency forms the natural counterpart to the analyst's view of the child as the id, an attitude that is particularly evoked when the child uses externalization of superego elements as a defense. In doing so he may also trigger the countertransference reaction of accepting the assigned role and treating the child as the id. It is my impression that the frequency with which analysts attribute to latency patients a lag in superego development and fail to distinguish externalization from transference can be, in part, attributed to this difficulty.

BIBLIOGRAPHY

BECKER, T. E. (1974), On Latency, *This Annual*, 29:3–12.
BORNSTEIN, B. (1948), Emotional Barriers in the Understanding and Treatment of Young Children. *Amer. J. Orthopsychiat.*, 18:691–697.
———— (1951), On Latency. *This Annual*, 6:279–285.
BRODY, S. (1974), Contributions to Child Analysis. *This Annual*, 29:13–20.
FREUD, A. (1936), The Ego and the Mechanisms of Defense. *W.*, 2.
———— (1965), Normality and Pathology in Childhood. *W.*, 6.
FREUD, S. (1905), Fragment of an Analysis of a Case of Hysteria. *S.E.*, 7:3–122.
———— (1910), The Future Prospects of Psycho-Analytic Therapy. *S.E.*, 11:139–151.
———— (1912), The Dynamics of Transference. *S.E.*, 12:97–108.
———— (1915), Observations on Transference-Love. *S.E.*, 12:157–171.
———— (1916), Some Character-Types Met with in Psycho-Analytic Work. *S.E.*, 14:309–333.
———— (1916–17), Introductory Lectures on Psycho-Analysis. *S.E.*, 15 & 16.
———— (1937), Analysis Terminable and Interminable. *S.E.*, 23:209–253.
FURMAN, E. (1980), Normal and Pathological Aspects of Early Latency. In: *The Course of Life: Psychoanalytic Contributions toward Understanding Personality Development*, ed. G. H. Pollock & S. I. Greenspan. Washington: National Institute of Mental Health (in press).

FURMAN, R. A. & KATAN, A., eds. (1969), *The Therapeutic Nursery School.* New York: Int. Univ. Press.

HEIMANN, P. (1950), On Counter-Transference. *Int. J. Psycho-Anal.,* 31:81–84.

HOFFER, W. (1956), Transference and Transference Neurosis. *Int. J. Psycho-Anal.* 37:377–379.

KABCENELL, R. J. (1974), On Countertransference. *This Annual,* 29:27–33.

KATAN, A. (1979), Personal communication.

KESTENBERG, J. S. (1975), The Effect on Parents of the Child's Transition into and out of Latency. In: *Children and Parents.* New York: Jason Aronson, pp. 267–281.

LOEWENSTEIN, R. M. (1969), Developments in the Theory of Transference in the Last Fifty Years. *Int. J. Psycho-Anal.,* 50: 583–588.

MONEY-KYRLE, R. E. (1956), Normal Counter-Transference and Some of Its Deviations. *Int. J. Psycho-Anal.,* 37:360–366.

NAGERA, H. (1966), *Early Childhood Disturbances, the Infantile Neurosis, and the Adulthood Disturbances.* New York: Int. Univ. Press.

NOVICH, J. & KELLY, K. (1970), Projection and Externalization. *This Annual,* 25:69–95.

RACKER, H. (1957), The Meanings and Uses of Countertransference. *Psychoanal. Quart.,* 26:303–357.

——— (1968), *Transference and Countertransference.* New York: Int. Univ. Press.

SANDLER, J., HOLDER, A., KAWENOKA, M., KENNEDY, H. & NEURATH, L. (1969), Notes on Some Theoretical and Clinical Aspects of Transference. *Int. J. Psycho-Anal.,* 50:633–646.

——— KENNEDY, H., & TYSON, R. L. (1975), Discussions on Transference. *This Annual,* 30:409–441.

WILLIAMS, M. (1972), Problems of Technique During Latency. *This Annual,* 27:598–617.

Countertransference and the Psychoanalytic Process in Children and Adolescents

IRWIN M. MARCUS, M.D.

IF I WERE TO DRAW AN ANALOGY FROM THE FIELD OF BIONOMICS, the term countertransference would be an endangered species in psychoanalytic semasiology. On the other hand, there are those who feel that the term should be restricted to one territory, "when the analyst uses his child patient as a transference object" (Maenchen, 1970, p. 194). At the other end of the spectrum, countertransference becomes vague, blurred, and perhaps even useless when it is seen as everything experienced by the analyst toward his patient or within the analytic situation. Between the two widely spaced extremes, a range of concepts has evolved over the course of more than three quarters of a century of psychoanalytic history. The multiplicity of meanings suggested during this development necessitates a presentation of my current usage of the term. During the course of my career, my views have altered, and even now I offer only a tentative impression which invites contributions to help build a more meaningful structure for this concept.

Countertransference is here defined as a complex phenome-

Clinical Professor of Psychiatry, Louisiana State University Medical School; Adjunct Professor, Tulane University; Chairman of the Child/Adolescent Psychoanalytic Program at the New Orleans Psychoanalytic Institute, New Orleans, Louisiana.

This paper was presented at the meeting of the Association for Child Psychoanalysis, Washington, D.C., March 18, 1978.

non which has origins in the *unconscious* or *preconscious* processes
of the analyst; has *specificity* to the patient, to the transference, or
to other components of the patients' material; and defensively
interrupts or disrupts the analyzing function. The analyst may or
may not act upon the ensuing thoughts and feelings he or she
experiences. The analyst may submit the countertransference
reactions to self-analysis, which leads to new insights into the
patient's mental activity, behavior, or situation, and may then
employ these insights therapeutically to promote the unfolding
of an analysis. Some therapists and supervisors more often associate countertransference with its role as a source of errors. An
injudicious response by the analyst usually produces errors in
technique. Sooner or later these uncorrected responses interfere
with progress in analysis.

As the founder and principal developer of psychoanalysis,
Freud taught us to bring under surveillance the most intimate
details of a patient's behavior and communications, as well as our
own personal experiences, during the analytic process. As heirs
to a unique scientific methodology which views therapy and investigation as inseparably linked, we perceive both the patients
and ourselves as essential elements of the psychoanalytic process. Among the basic issues which have prevailed is the premise
that the analyst should respect the patient's integrity and avoid
imposing personal values and prejudices on the patient.

Freud described countertransference as "a result of the patient's influence on his [the analyst's] unconscious feelings"
(1910, p. 144). Here countertransference may be interpreted to
be an influence that activates a developmental residue and
creates or revives unconscious conflict, anxiety, and defensive-
ness, thus impairing the analyzing activity. The view of countertransference as an unfavorable contamination interfering with
the development or understanding of transference phenomena
led to the requirement that the analyst undergo a personal
analysis. However, the analyst's use of countertransference in a
thoughtful manner to conduct the variety of analytic interventions, including interpretations, was also one of Freud's basic
contributions to technique. At least, this is how I interpret
Freud's statement that "everyone possesses in his own unconscious an instrument with which he can interpret the utterances

of the unconscious in other people" (1913b, p. 320). Thus, early in the history of analysis, the analytic process was characterized as the resonance which takes place between the patient's unconscious and that of the analyst.

In treating young patients, one also encounters problems in restricting the term countertransference to a single mental response, either to the specific unconscious response incited by the patient's transference or to the transference by the analyst to the patient. The child's and adolescent's desire and need to use the analyst as a "new object" for new experiences are both impressive and more active than those of adults. This element in the analysis is not a transference reaction representing the patient's unconscious urge to repeat past experiences, but it nevertheless may stir a countertransference response. The child and adolescent partly do experience the analyst as a "real" person and the analytic situation as a new experience, but the analyst need not abandon the analytic posture and actively assume a parental role or that of a "friend"—the complementary identification (H. Deutsch, 1926; Racker, 1957). When countertransference is aroused, its manifestations are quite variable and overdetermined. Among these are transference factors, projective identification, a revival of omnipotent feelings, and sibling or oedipal rivalry with the patient's parents. Analysts may rationalize some of their activity as being a part of the "new object" aspect, but deliberately presenting oneself as a model for identification is a manifestation of countertransference. Setting forth one's own attitudes, values, and solutions to problem areas in order to manipulate or foster the patient's development forfeits the opportunity for developmental progress based upon the analytic process. Even exercising the "auxiliary ego" function, which may be necessary with very young patients, is usually a temporary activity, but is not to be employed to gratify the patient's libidinal needs.

Another common phenomenon which does not involve a countertransference in response to transference occurs when the patient uses externalization. The analyst becomes the representative of the patient's impulses, ego, or superego, which in a functional sense cannot be considered manifestations of object relations. The unconscious activity triggered in the analyst by

such externalized intersystemic and intrasystemic conflicts leads
to erroneous interpretations if these are forced into the context
of object relations. Externalization does have a relationship to
transference, insofar as all intrapsychic conflicts originate in
early object relationships, but it cannot be viewed as transference
in the usual sense. Because externalization may occur in the
analyst as well as in the patient during the analytic process, I am
reluctant to restrict countertransference either to the therapist's
response to the patient's transference or to his own transference
to a patient.

At the other end of the scale, it is equally untenable to view
countertransference as all of the analyst's emotional responses;
and as a general reaction which includes all unconscious and
conscious attitudes, feelings, and actions. The unlimited concept
is too inclusive and extends too far into such areas as our natural
human and professional feelings experienced as an interest in
the patient and pleasure in our work. The warm, affectionate,
and respectful feelings for our patients (not the overemotional
responses) are nonspecific, and thus are not countertransferences.

The "work ego," as defined by Fliess (1942), refers to the usual
activities of the analyst in conducting an analysis, including empathy. The activities encompassed by the concept of "work ego"
are also too general to be labeled countertransference. The style
of conducting an analysis may include ego-syntonic qualities
which are quite conscious. An aggressive trait which may cause
the analyst to be too active in analyzing defenses or labeling
affects can be a problem for analysis, but it is not a countertransference. The danger of the analyst's real personality coming through too clearly is that the analyst is then less "nonde-
script" a screen for the patient's transferences (Benedek, 1953).
In the course of analysis, identification with the patient is usually
confined to the transitory sampling, a valuable instrument
among several employed to understand the patient. Reich
(1960) referred to these as "trial identifications" and Racker
(1957) suggested the term "concordant identification" to include
the analyst's impulses, attitudes, and defenses which closely
parallel those of the patient. Only the persistent or "sticky" identifications signal a countertransference. When the analyst's re-

sponse is stereotyped and consistently adverse to the analysis of certain types of patients, pathologies, or developmental levels, reflecting an intrinsic aspect in the therapist's character, he is operating in a "gray area." Reich (1951) viewed this as a "permanent type" of countertransference, which necessitates a return to the couch for the analyst. I think this recommendation can be attenuated if the countertransference does not precipitate a serious disruption of the analytic work and the analyst becomes aware of his or her personal problem. By self-analysis and "working through," the analyst may achieve a favorable change. Because these reactions are predictable, evoked by all such patients for that analyst, they lose the quality of specificity that I would prefer for a workable definition.

A young male candidate complained about the aggressive, seductive sexuality of a mid-latency girl who sat with her knees up, exposing her underpants. He felt anger and anxiety, but was not aware of any sexual response of his own. He then mentioned that he had had similar feelings in a room where a young woman had sat on the other side facing him; she had crossed her legs in the usual manner, yet he had been exposed to a view of her thigh. His expressed annoyance with such "castrating females who tease and torture males" and other related comments indicated that he needed more analytic work. His fixed attitude toward females of any age in whom he perceived sexuality had the character of transference and was likely to manifest itself as a generalized or permanent type of countertransference.

Although lack of experience and nondefensive reactions to the patient, which alter perceptions and responses, are common sources of technical errors, they do not constitute countertransference (Tower, 1956); nor does the sudden reaction by the analyst to a real event.

To summarize these approaches to defining countertransference: the analyst synthesizes attention, intuition, self-analysis, and empathy, yet responds flexibly and spontaneously in the analytic situation. Disturbances experienced by the "work ego" of the analyst are noticeable to him. This countertransference signal interferes with the analyst's mobile attention and arouses emtions which alter "analytic neutrality." A shift in his analytic stance, at least temporarily, upsets the intention to function in a nonprejudicial manner toward the various manifestations of transference and other communications by the patient.

COUNTERTRANSFERENCE IN ANALYSIS AT DIFFERENT DEVELOPMENTAL LEVELS

In analysis our goals are basically the same, whether we treat children, adolescents, or adults: "The business of the analysis is to secure the best possible psychological conditions for the function of the ego" (Freud, 1937, p. 250). One need only add, especially in the case of children, that these conditions allow for the resumption of normal development. An alternation of these goals toward a specific therapeutic or educational issue makes one suspect the existence of a countertransference. Child analysts are now less pressed to do things with the child and to use the verbal communications they would use in adult analysis, shifting from clarification to interpretations within the framework of a therapeutic alliance (Marcus, 1977). In order to have a workable relationship, the child analyst must be capable of empathy; and in order to communicate comfortably with a young patient, he must have knowledge of cognitive development.

A disturbance in establishing empathy may or may not be due to countertransference. However, if the child's symptomatology, libidinal regression, impaired ego function, transference reactions, and other factors arouse unconscious issues in the analyst, the variety of countertransferences is considerably large. These responses may be to the child's narcissistic behavior and withdrawal; to symbiotic needs expressed symbolically in play or via insistence upon physical closeness for merging; to demands for need fulfillment; or to the usual elements derived from oral, anal, and phallic-oedipal phases. Countertransferences may be provoked by the demanding, stubborn, or hostile child as well as by the passive, submissive one whose fears of object loss and needs for love remain concealed.

EARLY DEVELOPMENTAL PHASES

Each developmental phase has its own challenges for the analyst. The preoedipal child requires that the analyst understand the strong, though often subtle, mother-child interaction. The therapeutic alliance involves mother and child in combination; thus, if there is unconscious vulnerability on the part of the analyst to a specific mother's personality and her behavior in the analytic situation, countertransference may be expected. In working with a 3½-year-old asthmatic boy, I found myself uncomfortable, mildly anxious, and disliking his mother. She displayed very little affect, maintained a relatively narrow range of facial expressions, showed no warmth that I could detect, and appeared detached from her son. The woman's own mother chided her for her infrequent contacts with and apparent disinterest in their family. I soon discovered that the analysis had been initiated by the father, who had been treated earlier in his life by an analyst. His wife and their allergist were opposed to analytic therapy. The allergist had attempted to desensitize the child with injections and oral medication for the prior year and a half. He was convinced that asthma occurring at such an early age had to be organic in origin. However, there had been no improvement in the course of the illness; thus the father took matters into his own hands and initiated the referral. My response to the mother was neither just an empathetic reaction to her underlying hostility, nor a complementary identification. I did not respond as other rejecting figures had in her past. My reaction was overdetermined by transference and other mechanisms. It was specific, because I am usually comfortable and not hostile toward anxious, insecure mothers; nor am I prone to overidentifying with the child. I thought that the accumulation of experience and self-analysis necessitated in daily work had diminished my vulnerability to the impact of patients' pathology. In general it had, but this woman seemed to have the right combination to revive a long-forgotten early childhood memory, a fear of the darkness, where I usually was sure I could see a large bear. The fear was partly related to separations at bedtime. The asthmatic boy was withdrawn, apathetic, and depressed, and felt frightened and alone. His rapprochement phase was problematic, and he had given up on expecting comfort and approval upon his return from separations. There was not much closeness apparent when I saw this mother and child; he separated easily from her in the analysis. I recommended the "bear" to another analyst, and eventually my contacts with her became more "bearable." Although the mother was initially skeptical regarding child analysis, yet very demanding of it, she gradually became more accepting and cooperative. The little boy became free of asthma during the analysis. Medication had been discontinued at the onset of the therapy. Several years later, the couple separated. However, the patient remained free of asthma and continued in his development.

LATENCY PHASE

A 7-year-old boy, whose analysis I supervised,[1] illustrates the impact on the analyst's oedipus complex and the therapist's defenses against it when oedipal material is vividly enacted by a latency child. The candidate had a variety of countertransference reactions which he successfully analyzed in the course of his own growth as a child analyst.

The child had a compulsion to check faucets at home and elsewhere to make sure they were not leaking, and he had an obsession with numbers, reciting them in specific sequences. His mother was a postgraduate student and a competitive, controlling, aggressive woman. The child's father was a mild, quiet, passive-dependent man. The patient was frequently under the care and influence of the maternal grandmother and a maid, both of whom approved of his effeminate behavior and encouraged his modeling costume jewelry in play. In analysis, he related to the analyst in a passive, dependent, seductive manner, actively seeking physical contact. He flaunted his effeminacy, was exhibitionistic, and spoke in a high-pitched falsetto voice. His teacher complained to the parents that he acted like a nursery school child.

His play displayed libidinal and developmental regression to oral and anal levels, as well as an expressed wish to reestablish a symbiotic union with his mother. He brought bubble gum to his sessions and demanded that the therapist chew the same piece with him. He wanted to have the gum held by their mouths, lip to

1. The personal data from supervised candidates in the examples which follow were offered for this paper, with permission granted, and ordinarily are neither obtained nor desired during usual supervisory work.

lip, and to stretch it as they separated. He raged at the analyst, threatened to quit, ridiculed, mocked, and chanted ditties as he danced around the office in efforts to induce him to participate in these games. The analyst had to hold off the patient who repeatedly tried to jump into his lap.

The unfolding of the analysis is a fascinating issue of its own, but I must return to the countertransference. It became apparent during supervision that the candidate had become so enthralled with the activity of this patient that the analysis was bogged down; efforts gradually to shift the patient from acting out his fantasies and wishes to verbalization by the usual analytic intervention had ceased. The analyst felt blocked in his thinking during his sessions with the patient and in efforts to discuss the case with me. The supervisory learning alliance was good, and the candidate, who was no longer in analysis, revealed with considerable anxiety that he was experiencing sexual excitation during the moments when the patient was attempting physical closeness. Through self-analysis the candidate was able again to work through certain issues in his own childhood, following which he began to analyze the patient's passive-dependent wishes for closeness with his father, as well as the wishes to incorporate his father's penis. The analytic material gradually shifted from a preponderance of oral material to intense anal-sadistic concerns and phallic-castrating wishes toward the father. The analyst became markedly more relaxed in the course of this analysis and subsequently commented that he had been more intensely affected by the sexual material and behavior of this latency child than he was by comparable experiences with adolescents or adults. Certain aspects of this example suggest that the analyst's superego activated massive ego defenses to inhibit his "work ego," in relation to both the patient and the supervisor. Through externalization and projective identification the candidate viewed the patient as an unbridled id engaged in a successful and overwhelming onslaught on the analyst. This onslaught activated a variety of conflicts and defenses, which disturbed his empathy with the patient. The analyst was not just rejecting the patient's transference, nor was he having a transference of his own. The process was highly overdetermined and far more complex.

The material demonstrates the strong regressive forces that can become active in a child analyst, who must be able to sample identifications, but resume to function in accordance with his "work ego." A defensive superego response can produce a nonanalytic, rigid "adult posture" or a paralytic withdrawal from the analytic situation. One of the developmental tasks of latency is to achieve a more benevolent superego. If the analyst's superego is not functioning flexibly, there is no chance for the patient to develop healthier superego and ego attitudes through the analysis.

COUNTERTRANSFERENCE IN THE DIFFERENT PHASES OF ANALYSIS

In addition to being stimulated by specific phases of development, countertransference reactions may occur in response to certain elements in the phases of analysis. Whereas the adult's effort at cooperativeness in the early phase of analysis conceals the early resistance, the child's resistance may be an immediate and obvious problem. Many children exhibit conscious, unconcealed, dramatic opposition (Weiss et al., 1968). The child analyst must rely on the parents' motivation and insight to support both the initial phase and the carrying through of the analysis to a satisfactory termination. The parents must serve as the auxiliary ego for the child, not only initially, but also in maintaining support for a therapeutic alliance, especially when the hostile elements of the transference appear and the child's ego is entangled in resistance. This parental help is the sine qua non for child and adolescent analysis. If parents side with the child's resistance, an abrupt interruption is inevitable. In later stages of the analysis, parental understanding of the changing attitude in the child is necessary to avoid the parents' sabotaging the analysis when the young patient develops a strong positive (affectionate) transference to the analyst. If parents feel competitiveness or respond to the taunting rejection by the child of one or both of them, the analysis may be discontinued. The child or adolescent often acts out a wish for developmental separation and a defensive independence. Parents under this form of attack may aggravate the patient's loyalty conflicts between parents and analyst.

A 10-year-old girl initiated analysis with a candidate in supervision with another analyst. She had nightmares, still sucked her thumb, suffered from bouts of nausea and vomiting unrelated to any organic factors, and had disturbed peer group relationships. Chronic, recurrent urinary infections since age 3 had resulted in frequent urological procedures for urethral dilatation. At age 6, she had bladder surgery, which brought an end to the urethral manipulations. She was quite angry about feeling forced by her parents into analysis. She immediately told the analyst not to ask her questions, because she did not want to lie. Then she expressed her anger at both parents, at her mother for being too bossy and at her father for being "mean." Thereafter, for many sessions she would arrive on time, but fall asleep during the session. The analyst noted that she would sleep in the lithotomy position, thus repeating her earlier traumatic experience with the urologist. Her wish to avoid both the analyst and her conscious and unconscious material was obvious. The analyst's effort to empathize with her anger and anxiety or to note the defense was answered with more sleep. However, if he waited and was accepting of this behavior, she would wake up. If there was a session in which he felt that some rapport had been established, she would follow it by missing the next session, coming very late, or sleeping.

Intense, dramatized manifestations of both conscious and transference resistances early in analysis threatened the analyst's narcissism and engendered anxiety. He wanted to be accepted by the patient, family, and supervisor; and he wanted the analysis to go well because of its implications for his progress in the training program. It was difficult for the analyst to maintain any analytic neutrality; he felt rejected, deprived of both the relationship and the material, and angry. He was unaware of these countertransference feelings and instead persisted in analytic interventions, noting the defensive distancing and attempting clarifications and even interpretations. His analytic activity had the quality of an attack, and the patient both felt criticized and experienced the inducements to talk as seductions. The pa-

tient externalized her own impulses onto the analyst, had transference reactions and even a transient transference neurosis in
her new symptom of sleeping in the treatment sessions. The
analyst, who at that time was under stress in his own life situation,
had a transference to the patient as a depriving figure and became aware of hunger during her sessions. He was also reacting
to her transference and had a complementary identification with
her parents who said she must be analyzed. The analyst, who had
previously denied his hostility and rationalized his technique,
did some self-analysis and changed his approach to the patient.
He had reacted too aggressively with a pseudoanalytic approach
to a resistant child. Upon dealing with the sources of his hostility,
he relaxed and allowed the analytic relationship and alliance to
develop more gradually.

Frantic interpretative work in response to early resistance can
be a disaster at any developmental level. This girl had regressed
to much earlier levels of ego and libido development; thus the
analysis should have begun with a nonintrusive technique.

TERMINATION PHASE

The termination phase is associated with analytic material and
behavior that can evoke countertransferences. The regressive
intensification of the transference, symptom revival, and
mourning of the analyst as a transference object who is being
relinquished may test the therapeutic alliance to the extreme.
The analyst may again question the analytic goals: is the patient
ready for the termination or should the work go on? Will the
analyst's own narcissistic needs and anxieties alter his analytic
neutrality and switch his position toward support and guidance?
Analysts usually are more comfortable with making termination
decisions for young children, but they are less certain in their
assessments of whether older children and adolescents have
achieved structural changes.

A candidate treated a girl who entered analysis at 15 years and
successfully terminated at 19 years of age. Analysis was initiated
because she had become agitated, developed insomnia, and become inappropriate in her affect following the sudden death of
her closest girlfriend's father. Early in analysis she had a transient psychotic episode, threatened to kill her mother, and was

briefly hospitalized. The analysis continued upon her return, and a good therapeutic alliance developed. The major themes included rage about being a woman, feeling castrated, penis envy, and a variety of intense transference reactions ranging from wishes to torture the analyst and defeat the analysis to running away with the analyst. Preoedipal and oedipal material came under the scrutiny of analytic work, as did the reworking of separation-individuation processes (Marcus, 1973).

During the termination phase she taunted the analyst with statements that she had engaged in intercourse without taking precautions (which she later admitted was not true). At one point she expressed a desire to sit up again, as she had early in analysis at the time when she was becoming disorganized and psychotic. Material derived from many developmental levels was flowing in and out of the analysis: oral, demanding dependency feelings as well as anal-sadistic desires to control and attack the analyst. The analyst became aware of his own separation anxiety and thoughts of becoming supportive, but he analyzed the countertransference and did not alter his analytic stance. He continued to analyze the patient's oedipal fantasies and defenses and her anxiety about independence and separation. Her last session was one of complete silence. Six months later she wrote him a note, the "good-bye" that she could finally express, and showed her ability to engage in self-analysis. She also announced her engagement and plans to marry in two years. She was pleased with her independence, but could not share this with the analyst until she had completed her mourning (Marcus, 1974).

CONCLUSION

A working definition of countertransference is suggested. It seems preferable to me to view this phenomenon as complex and as not exclusively dependent upon one mechanism, such as a transference by the analyst or his reaction to the patient's transference. On the other hand, the concept can be limited in scope. It may be viewed in the same way as all unconscious mechanisms: overdetermined in origin, uncontrollable at the source, but useful when the information is integrated by a receptive ego. The thoughtful therapeutic application of self-analysis and patient analysis provides both the analyst and the patient with a pleasurable, exciting, unforgettable, and unique experience. Each of the participants can then continue in progressive development—the goal of analysis.

BIBLIOGRAPHY

BENEDEK, T. (1953), Dynamics of the Countertransference. *Bull. Menninger Clin.,* 17:201–208.

BREUER, J. & FREUD, S. (1893–95), Studies on Hysteria. *S.E.,* 2.

DEUTSCH, H. (1926), Occult Processes Occurring During Psychoanalysis. In: *Psychoanalysis and the Occult,* ed. G. Devereux. New York: Int. Univ. Press, 1953, pp. 133–146.

FLIESS, R. (1942), The Metapsychology of the Analyst. *Psychoanal. Quart.,* 11:211–227.

FREUD, S. (1910), The Future Prospects of Psycho-Analytic Therapy. *S.E.,* 11:139–151.

——— (1912), Recommendations to Physicians Practising Psycho-Analysis. *S.E.,* 12:109–120.

——— (1913a), On Beginning the Treatment. *S.E.,* 12:121–144.

——— (1913b), The Disposition to Obsessional Neurosis. *S.E.,* 12:311–326.

——— (1937), Analysis Terminable and Interminable. *S.E.,* 23:209–253.

——— (1950), *The Origins of Psychoanalysis.* New York: Basic Books, 1954.

GITELSON, M. (1952), The Emotional Position of the Analyst in the Psycho-Analytic Situation. *Int. J. Psycho-Anal.,* 33:1–10.

MAENCHEN, A. (1970), On the Technique of Child Analysis in Relation to Stages of Development. *This Annual,* 25:175–208.

MARCUS, I. M. (1973), Report of Panel: The Experience of Separation-Individuation in Infancy and Its Reverberations Through the Course of Life: 2. Adolescence and Maturity. *J. Amer. Psychoanal. Assn.,* 21:155–167.

——— (1974), Transition in Adolescence: School to Work. In: *American Handbook of Psychiatry,* ed. S. Arieti. New York: Basic Books, 2nd ed., 2:306–315.

——— (1977), The Psychoanalysis of Adolescence, Technique. In: *Int. Encyc. Neurol., Psychiat., Psychoanal. & Psychol.,* 1:260–265. Boston: Van Nostrand Reinhold.

RACKER, H. (1957), The Meanings and Uses of Countertransference. *Psychoanal. Quart.,* 26:303–357.

REICH, A. (1951), On Counter-Transference, *Int. J. Psycho-Anal.,* 32:25–31.

——— (1960), Further Remarks on Counter-Transference. *Int. J. Psycho-Anal.,* 41:389–395.

TOWER, L. E. (1956), Countertransference. *J. Amer. Psychoanal. Assn.,* 6:224–255.

WEISS, S., FINEBERG, H. H., GELMAN, R. L., & KOHRMAN, R. (1968), Technique of Child Analysis. *J. Amer. Acad. Child Psychiat.,* 7:639–662.

WINNICOTT, D. W. (1949), Hate in the Counter-Transference. *Int. J. Psycho-Anal.,* 30:69–74.

Negative Therapeutic Motivation and Negative Therapeutic Alliance

JACK NOVICK, PH.D.

FOR OVER A QUARTER OF A CENTURY SOCIAL SCIENTISTS, INCLUD-
ing many psychoanalysts, have been engaged in large-scale,
costly projects evaluating the results of psychotherapy. The
guiding principle in most of these studies has been to define,
measure, and predict success. The results of this vast expendi-
ture of time and money have been uniformly disappointing. Not
only are the research efforts beset by seemingly insurmountable
methodological difficulties, but, more important, the salient dimension of success has proved almost impossible to define, except in an arbitrary, often superficial way. There is a similar
emphasis on success in psychoanalytic writings, especially those
concerned with the areas of termination, goals of treatment, and
assessment of analyzability. Here too we find authors referring
to "fragmentary and contradictory knowledge" (Namnun, 1968)
and "the lack of well-defined criteria" (Limentani, 1972). In a
study of termination (Novick, 1976) I suggested that the criteria
of success are irrelevant to clinical practice since they often reflect ideals of mental health rather than goals set in the context of
the person's individual pathology. This study revealed the extent to which criteria reflected theoretical, cultural, and personal
predilections rather than clinical perceptions. I would now go
further and say that our training and experience are such that

Clinical Associate Professor of Psychology, Department of Psychiatry, University of Michigan Medical Center, Ann Arbor, Michigan.
Earlier versions of this paper were presented at meetings of the Association
of Child Psychotherapists, London, England, January 1977, and the Michigan
Psychoanalytic Society, October 1977.

we are not especially well equipped to define, measure, or predict success. We are, however, experts in the area of failure. Our patients are products of failure and manifest varying degrees of failure in development and functioning. As Tartakoff (1966) demonstrated, even those privileged to have candidates as patients are dealing with failure. The treatment of failures often ends in a failure of treatment, for, as Freud (1937) said, "Analysis . . . [is] the third of those 'impossible' professions in which one can be sure beforehand of achieving unsatisfying results. The other two, which have been known much longer, are education and government" (p. 248). This emphasis on success may be partly, as Freud suggests, "a child of its time, conceived under the stress of the contrast between the post-war misery of Europe and the 'prosperity' of America, and designed to adapt the tempo of analytic theory to the haste of American life" (p. 216). We should add here the impact of the recent explosion of alternate methods of treatment promising quick results, success with relatively little cost in time, money or psychic pain. The increasing role of third party insurance with its insistence on cost efficiency should not be underestimated as a factor leading to the emphasis on success.

The total immersion in failure has a devastating impact on psychoanalysts, leading many into areas of work, treatment, or theory which promise protection from such an onslaught on their self-esteem. This, of course, is not a recent phenomenon, and I would suggest that many of the early and later psychoanalytic dissidents were not only competing with the father Freud, but were also, if not mainly, dealing with their own experience of failure in their theoretical and clinical work. Freud (1937) saw Ferenczi's therapeutic experiments as a response to the frustration of analytic work rather than as a rebellion. After outlining the many obstacles to treatment, Freud says, "From this point of view we can understand how such a master of analysis as Ferenczi came to devote the last years of his life to therapeutic experiments, which, unhappily, proved to be vain" (p. 230).

I have become increasingly convinced that failure is not only an area of expertise but a most fruitful area of investigation. My own research has turned increasingly to the question of the rela-

ion between failure and omnipotence, the role of failure in
normal and pathological development, and the factors related to
failures of treatment.[1] In 1937, Freud suggested, "In this field
the interest of analysts seems to me to be quite wrongly directed.
Instead of an enquiry into how a cure by analysis comes
about . . . the question should be asked of what are the obstacles
that stand in the way of such a cure" (p. 221). One such obstacle
Freud called the negative therapeutic reaction (1923). As with
many of Freud's concepts, later writers have tended to expand
the meaning and application of the term, a fact noted by many
others (Brenner, 1970; Olinick, 1964; Sandler et al., 1973).
Some use the negative therapeutic reaction as the explanation
for any protracted resistance to or failure of treatment. Freud
used this term to refer to a specific reaction in treatment—a
negative reaction to progress or to words of encouragement.
"When one speaks hopefully to them [the patients] or expresses
satisfaction with the progress of treatment, they show signs of
discontent and their condition invariably becomes worse" (1923,
p. 49). It is thus a specific clinical response occurring during the
course of treatment and following a period of "successful
therapeutic management" (Moore and Fine, 1967). Amending
his original views on the subject, Freud (1918) later said that this
reaction was more than "defiance towards the physician and
. . . fixation to the various forms of gain from illness" (1923, p.
49). It was a moral factor, a sense of guilt. In 1924, he was more
specific and saw the cause of the reaction in a "need for punishment," a clinical manifestation of moral masochism (p. 166).
Freud viewed the negative therapeutic reaction as a powerful
resistance to treatment, but not necessarily the most powerful.
Further, it is but one of many factors leading to failure or protracted treatment.

In this paper I shall explore another factor contributing to
failure in treatment—*negative therapeutic motivation*. Unlike the
negative therapeutic reaction as described by Freud, the negative therapeutic motivation occurs long before the patient sees
the analyst or has any idea what analysis is about. The negative

---

1. A series of interrelated studies of omnipotence and failure are being
conducted at the Youth Service, University of Michigan Medical Center.

therapeutic motivation is the motivation to go into analysis or
therapy in order to make the analyst fail. Before I illustrate the
phenomenon or try to elucidate some of the underlying
mechanisms, it is important to point to a logical error which
occurs most frequently in discussions of obstacles to treatment.
We are accustomed to think of a continuity between normal and
abnormal, between health and illness. The difference is, in
Freud's terms, an economic one or one of degree. However,
when we talk of obstacles to treatment, we often create
"pseudospecies" of patients and call them narcissistic, borderline, or "negative therapeutic reactors" (Olinick, 1970). In my
view, a negative therapeutic motivation, i.e., a wish to enter
treatment in order to make the analyst fail, is part of every
treatment, regardless of degree or type of pathology. The phenomenon is, of course, more visible in certain types of patients,
such as those with severe masochistic disturbances, and at certain
ages, such as adolescence.

NEGATIVE THERAPEUTIC MOTIVATION

I shall present illustrations of how the negative therapeutic
motivation manifests itself in the treatment situation and is related to the defensive need of both patient and parent to maintain an idealized image of a loving, loved, and omnipotent
parent.

CASE 1

A. was a 14-year-old boy, who was referred because he was severely depressed, tearful, failing at school, and feeling increasingly socially isolated. He said he felt that his whole world was
shattering. The referring psychiatrist believed that he was highly
motivated for treatment. When I saw A., it was evident that he
was indeed experiencing a great deal of psychic pain and that he
very much wanted to be helped. It was not evident, however, that
at the same time there coexisted a need to turn me into a failure.
His parents were in the throes of a separation battle and the air
was filled with accusations and blame. After the third session A.
stopped talking to me and did not say a word during the next
nine months of treatment. Although this resistance was multi-
determined, it became apparent that a major impetus stemmed

from A.'s conscious and unconscious wish to make me fail in my therapeutic efforts. My interventions became effective only after I recognized my feelings of failure as a counterreaction to his need to make me fail. Slow, but gradual change occurred after a lengthy period during which I maintained a steady level of therapeutic composure, accepted and shared with A. my limited power in the face of his resistance, made very few but often accurate interpretations of his nonverbal expressions, and interpreted his silence as an attempt to make me fail and thus externalize and displace hated aspects of his self and object representations onto me. Further confirmation that this long period of silence was a manifestation of negative therapeutic motivation occurred years later when he referred to that silent period as 'the greatest year of my life." It had been. I had become the failure. His parents, especially his mother, had been restored to something approximating his view of their former perfection. Whatever her failings, they were not as great or as evident as mine. In later years, when I had become a transference object and could interpret the sadomasochistic battle with me, he recalled that even before he had met me he had decided that he would not talk to me.

CASE 2

J., a 16-year-old girl, was referred to a colleague because of uncontrolled bouts of crying, severe depression, and pervasive feelings of inadequacy. In her initial session she presented a bright, cheerful façade and claimed that others said she did not need treatment. The slightest critical comment on her part about her mother was immediately followed by a statement that she respected her mother and that her mother was nice. After her second session she left feeling convinced that the therapist had rejected her and that evening she made a medically serious suicide attempt.

On the basis of such little information one could posit other determinants of the treatment failure more salient than a negative therapeutic motivation, including a lack of skill or sensitivity in the therapist. However, we do have much more information on this girl, because following her suicide attempt she was included in a psychoanalytic study of attempted suicide in adolescents (Friedman et al., 1972). She was seen five times a week for five years. The material from her analysis was part of the information obtained from eight such cases, four boys and four girls (Hurry et al., 1976). One major finding of this study is germane to the topic of negative therapeutic motivation. The suicide attempt in each of the cases was not a sudden act but the end point in a pathological regression. Suicidal thoughts had been present for a considerable period prior to the attempt. Although there were important differences in these patients, and especially between boys and girls, they all showed a similar pattern in the regressive sequence. The regression started with the experience of failure in the move toward independence from mother. The cause of failure was externalized and attributed to the mother (Novick and Kelly, 1970), who was experienced both as a failure and as someone who rejected them and withheld the magical solution. The blame and the experience of rejection and failure were then shifted once more to themselves and then most decisively to an external object. In each case the immediate precipitant to the suicide attempt was the experience of rejection consequent upon the failure of an external object to meet his or her needs. One girl had told her friend at school of her wish to kill herself and she was told to go to a psychiatrist. A boy had pinned all his hope on being accepted at a particular university; when he was rejected, he felt that there was nothing for him but to kill himself; and J. construed her analyst's words as a rejection and left the session saying to herself, "What's the use, she doesn't care either" (Hurry, 1977). It was only well into the analytic process that the unconscious need to make the object fail could be elucidated. For example, the young man who was rejected by the university of his choice often came late or came extremely early to a session and then blamed me for failing to see him immediately or for his full time. Once he canceled a session, but appeared anyway. Since I make it a practice to be available even during cancellations, his attempt to make me fail did not succeed and we could begin to look at his own need to make people fail him. He then recalled that he had applied to the university of his choice after the deadline.

Once these patients succeeded in placing the blame and failure onto some person or thing other than their mothers, they could, without the inhibiting factor of guilt, put their suicidal wishes into action. These adolescents illustrated a phenomenon I have now seen in many types of children, adolescents, and adults—the need to make objects fail as related to a need to defend the mother from their own aggression and maintain an idealized image of a loving, omnipotent mother. Struggling with lifelong intense feelings of failure in major areas of functioning, these patients oscillate between externalizing and internalizing the blame for this failure. Either solution is painful and terrifying, and they soon obtain relief by finding some object other than mother to blame, to hate, and then to reject by turning that person into a failure. The failed object represents the "significant other," people such as fathers, siblings, teachers, friends, who could draw the child out of the maternal orbit. With each failure of a significant other, the child becomes ever more intensely and pathologically tied to the mother. The analyst becomes yet another in the series of objects who fail, and the negative therapeutic motivation is the manifestation in analysis of the primitive mechanisms of externalization and displacement of negatively cathected parts of self and object onto the analyst.

Work with children and adolescents highlights an important feature of the negative therapeutic motivation—the fact that the need to make objects fail is a motivation shared by mother and patient. Both mother and child seek help from others in order to make those others fail. The fact that parents often interfere with and sabotage treatment is well known, and the causes and types of parental resistance have increasingly become a topic of research (Rinsley and Hall, 1962). To the descriptions of the many kinds of parental resistances I would like to add the hitherto neglected, yet potent factor of the negative therapeutic motivation. It has been my experience with child and adolescent workers that once the concept is presented and defined, many cases spring to mind illustrating the phenomenon.

CASE 3

The following material is taken from a case I supervised. At the insistence of their doctor the parents referred their 16-year-old boy, B., for treatment because of severe psychogenic chest pains and his fear that he would die. During the lengthy and detailed evaluation the parents were seen as being forthcoming and cooperative, as was B. in his interviews. It was felt that his motivation for treatment was high, and that the parents would be supportive. It was an intact middle-class family, without any obvious signs of severe parental pathology. In addition to his anxiety, B. was also doing very poorly at school, was becoming increasingly abusive and physically aggressive toward others, especially girls, and was engaged in numerous delinquent acts.

He came to his first session with his shirt unbuttoned down to the waist, lolling over his chair, seemingly expecting a sexual response from his female therapist. He saw no difficulties with the times or frequency of sessions and spoke as if he had expected that he would be staying all day, every day. By the end of the first session he said that he was bored, and by the second session he said that everything had changed and he was feeling much better. During the third session he presented what we later learned was his mother's assessment of his difficulties and her solution. He said that his difficulties were entirely due to his boredom with school and the failure of his principal and teachers to meet his educational needs. The mother then convinced the school that he needed a special educational program and she also arranged for her sister to provide additional tutoring. The mother had the matter in hand, she had made all the arrangements, and now everyone felt better. He did not come for his fourth session, and the mother telephoned, saying that he refused to attend the sessions, and then added, "You must be so disappointed." The therapist did feel disappointed and that she had failed.

At my suggestion the therapist had weekly meetings with the parents which continued for a period of four months. During these meetings the mother spoke of herself as the only one who could and did respond to the boy's needs. She said he had been a difficult and unmanageable child from birth, but she could always handle him. However, the time before the referral was a period during which she felt she could not cope with him, could not meet his needs, nor manage his increasing anger. Although she made no conscious connection with her feelings of failure,

she added that this was also a period during which he had begun
to make his sexual needs more apparent in the home in a manner
similar to his behavior during the first session.

In analytic work with adolescents I have seen a number of
cases where patients insisted that their parents had a claim on
their sexual wishes, that their sexual aims, usually passive ones,
should be gratified by their mothers. I have also seen parents of
adolescents who feel that as perfect parents they should be
gratifying their child's sexual needs. Unable to do so, and unwilling to allow anyone else the possibility, they encourage regression to pregenital modes of functioning which they can gratify.
Although we lack analytic data to confirm our speculations about
this boy and his mother, it seems that the mother felt that, just as
she had been the only one capable of meeting his other needs, so
she should be the only one to gratify his sexual wishes. In that
period before the referral the mother had had a serious
gynecological infection which required surgical intervention.
According to her, she had neglected the infection and had almost died. She was incapable of intercourse many months prior
to the operation, and she was too frightened to have sex afterward. Her own motivation for continuing the weekly sessions
was her concern about her sexual inhibitions and her feelings of
sexual failure. The material from her sessions revealed that she
felt that she had failed her child. She was no longer the perfect
parent and B. would blame her and be disappointed. He did
blame her, and his fear of dying represented a defense against
his rage at his mother and his conviction that he could destroy
her. She felt that to be accused of failure was a destruction, a
death to be defended against by abandoning the object. The
mother walked out in the middle of her last session with her
therapist and then telephoned to say, "I know what you were
going to say, you were going to say that I am a failure." She
expressed her fury at the therapist, blamed her, and accused her
of failing to deal adequately with the situation. She never returned to treatment.

Thus, B.'s accusing his mother of failure would destroy her
and would lead to abandonment. To protect her and to stay part
of her he took on the perceived failure, the mother's imminent
death, and he became the one who was helpless and about to die.

The internalization of blame and failure was equally terrifying
In a manner which must have represented a lifelong pattern,
mother and child found relief and restored the idealized omnipotent unit by locating the failure, disappointment, and blame
in the therapist, someone external to the closed world of their
now purified omnipotent dyad.

There is a group of children and adolescents in whom the
degree of disturbance is such that the parental role in the negative therapeutic motivation remains hidden. These are patients
who can loosely be labeled borderline. Common on referral are
problems of overwhelming anxiety, with panic attacks and tan-
trums occurring frequently. Severe disturbances in drive and
ego development are evident, and the extensive use of externalization and a tendency to confuse and fuse self and object representations are prominent. They often rule the house with tan-
trums and rages, making the parents feel helpless and terrified.
The referral usually is made because of a fear that the child will
kill or seriously hurt a younger sibling. In cases of this type, the
initial period of treatment was marked by the immediate discharge of wishes into action, which presented severe management problems. The preadolescents would rage, shout, break
things, and throw objects out of the window. One boy came in
with a BB gun, shouting that he would kill me and firing the
pellets at me. Adolescents sometimes also present management
problems in treatment, but usually the analyst has to contend
with their unrelenting, abusive attack in which he becomes the
recipient of all the negatively cathected aspects of self and object
representations. With both children and adolescents of this type,
the analyst not only is accused of being a failure but also is turned
into a failure as this relentless attack on his or her competence,
skill, and experience is carried on for years. Even more devastating is the attack on the analyst's identity as a separate person, for
during this lengthy period he exists only within the narrow limits
of their externalizations and everything else is denied. Then,
possibly because he has survived this unceasing attack, these
patients begin to perceive the analyst as someone other than the
hated parts of themselves and their mothers. As they gradually
perceive the analyst as a separate and valued object, they can

begin to have a transference relationship to that object. It becomes evident then that the negative therapeutic motivation reflects, in part, a defense against the positive transference. At this point, when the analyst is acknowledged as a separate and valued object, an object of positive transference, the maternal negative therapeutic motivation becomes visible and operative. It is at this point that parents remove the child from treatment, often going to such lengths as changing jobs or professions and moving to another city. Or one or both parents may become depressed and show other signs of severe disturbances resulting from the disruption of the pathological family pattern (Brodey, 1965; Novick and Kelly, 1970).

CASE 4

This case illustrates another reaction that once more underlines the relationship between failure, externalization, and the negative therapeutic motivation. When I saw C., a 16-year-old boy, he had been in analysis for four years, since the age of 11. Originally he had been referred for treatment because of his uncontrolled rages and his attacks on his younger brother. He and his parents saw the first period of treatment as a total failure. He had spent each session reading comics, slowly sipping from a container of soda pop, and talking to his mother by calling her on the telephone. When I first saw C., he looked more like an 11-year-old than an adolescent about to turn 16. Every area of functioning was a total failure. He had gone through a progressive school without learning anything, and it was evident that he could never pass a final high school examination. He had no friends, was bullied and teased by everyone, and showed severe disturbances in most facets of drive and ego development. In the sessions he shouted and raged at me, saying that analysis was a jail, that all his problems were due to analysis, and that everything would have been fine if he had not been sent to therapy. He said that he wanted his mother to be his therapist, and after each session he would use the pay phone to call her and tell her what we had discussed.

He knew that he had made the previous analysis fail, and he was conscious of his wish to do the same to me. During this time the parents were very supportive and encouraged him to go to treatment. They would keep me informed of the "terrible things" he said to them about me, and they offered sympathy for his contemptuous treatment of me and for my failure to change him. Gradually, however, C. began to develop a positive trans-ference and a treatment alliance. Through our work together he began to change, but as each change became apparent or about to be translated into action, the mother would do something to obliterate my role and his, so that the credit for the positive change would become hers alone. For example, as we worked on his need to remain a little boy, not only mentally but also physi-cally, he began to grow and mature. As soon as these changes began to appear, she took him to a "growth clinic" where he was given a course of hormone injections. He became physically ma-ture and of average height, but he did not attribute these changes to something internal or to something possibly linked with the analytic work. He viewed the physical changes as some-thing due entirely to his mother's intervention. Each further progressive step was taken over in a similar fashion by his mother. His desire to leave school and start work, his moving from his home and living in a youth hostel, his changing to a better job, and even his first sexual experience were matters arranged by his mother. Thus, each success became a source of failure—my failure and his—and he remained tied to an image of his omnipotent mother who could magically grant all his wishes.

I represented the significant other, the father and teacher, the carriers of the reality principle curtailing his omnipotent fan-tasies and demanding active and sustained effort for the fulfill-ment of realistic wishes. Painful and difficult as this may have been, he probably could have made the shift had he not been simultaneously overwhelmed by the terror that his relation to me would destroy his mother and leave him totally abandoned by her. She offered him safety from the terror of abandonment. By carrying her failure and by being the devalued, helpless, dam-aged parts of her, he became extremely important to her and she would not—in fact, could not—abandon him. By inducing him to be a passive failure and making others, like his analyst, fail him, she could then become the omnipotent source of everything good. To the end he retained the fantasy that he would become a famous writer, even though he could barely read, or a famous pop star, even though he could not play any instrument or sing. By being the passive, damaged infant, he felt he controlled the omnipotent mother and together they lived out the mythological fantasy of the golden age, the Garden of Eden, a purified pleasure dyad.

My contributions to his development were repeatedly denied by both C. and his mother. There was a collusion between them to nullify and obliterate my significance in his life. This manifestation of the negative therapeutic motivation is a repetition of an established pattern where mother and child obliterate the significance of any object other than mother. The most important significant other is the father, and in most such cases the phenomenon of "the bypassed father" (Asch, 1976) is evident. In the cases I have seen, the fathers were physically or emotionally absent. They were often passive, ineffectual men who were viewed by their wives and children as another damaged child rather than a father. In work with adults in whom the negative therapeutic motivation is often more subtle and difficult to perceive, the material relating to a bypassed father is often a warning concerning the operation of negative therapeutic motivation.

NEGATIVE THERAPEUTIC MOTIVATION AND THE REFERRAL PROCESS

Case material from a postgraduate seminar I led for child psychoanalysts revealed how often referrals from other professionals were made, not at a point of crisis or treatment readiness in the patient, but at a point of actual, imminent, or feared failure on the part of the referring person. The referral was then made in a highly ambivalent manner containing both magical, omnipotent expectations and actions designed to make treatment fail. Analogous to the parental negative therapeutic motivation, professionals may also, at times, unconsciously wish for a failure in order to externalize their own feelings of failure and remain an idealized, omnipotent figure for the patient. Like the parent, the referring professional may be unconsciously conveying the message that if he cannot succeed with the patient then no one can.

For example, a 16-year-old obese girl was referred after a suicide attempt. She had been known to the hospital since birth and had been to every department except psychiatry. When her obesity became life-threatening, she was referred to the obesity clinic, where she managed to lose considerable weight. She then attempted suicide and was referred to psychiatry. In terms of her own readiness for treatment, this was the least propitious moment for referral, but it was the moment of maximum failure for the referring physician because the medical department now worried that the girl would succeed in killing herself and they would be blamed. Psychiatric treatment was viewed and presented to the girl as a panacea, the magical cure for all her problems. At the same time the referral to the child analyst read as follows: "Once weekly treatment for a trial period of six weeks with the play lady."

The unconscious negative therapeutic motivation of the referring professional reinforces the patient's negative therapeutic motivation, and many premature terminations, especially during the early phases of treatment, can be traced to the unconscious intensification of a negative therapeutic motivation by the referring professional. This can occur even when the referral is from a psychoanalyst, as illustrated with one of my cases.

CASE 5

At the time when I was planning to leave England, I referred a young woman for continuation of analysis to a colleague. The patient and I had agreed that she required further treatment, and she asked me to suggest someone she could see. For a variety of reasons we decided she should meet the new analyst while she was still in treatment with me. After seeing him she decided that she could not work with him, and the attempt to arrange further treatment failed. She blamed herself and felt that she had failed me after all my efforts to find a suitable person. My colleague also felt that he had failed and, at first, her description of the interview made me think that indeed he had. Of course, it was all too comfortable, and my own tinge of pleasure at being considered the only one and the best one alerted me to the collusion. The patient and I had created a purified pleasure dyad. I was loved for finding such a good substitute for me and doubly loved because he was not as good as I was. All this was to avoid the woman's intense rage at me for failing her both as an omnipotent, idealized object and as an analyst, since I was in reality stopping her treatment before she was ready. Termination involves the relinquishment of a transference relationship stemming from all levels of development and having both positive and negative qualities. A forced termination, one in which a premature termination is initiated by the analyst, adds further reality-based complications to the transference relationship, particularly the real failure of the analyst to meet the legitimate needs of the patient.

The defensive need of the mother and patient to externalize the failure and retain the illusion of an idealized, purified pleasure dyad has its counterpart in the situation of a forced termination. In addition to the usual working through necessary, in the case of a forced termination both patient and analyst have to come to terms affectively with the real failure of the analyst. This is extremely difficult and painful for both and the above case illustrates how a referral at the point of termination can, in addition to other determinants, have a negative therapeutic motivation in which patient and analyst unconsciously create an external failure to maintain an idealized patient-analyst relationship. In the particular case referred to and in others undergoing a forced termination, I have found it best to avoid making a referral and to leave the responsibility for this decision to the patient. Thus the question of further analysis and the means for attaining further help becomes analytic material similar to other major decisions such as career or marital choice.

In the case of the failed referral the patient and I realized the defensive collusion, the mutual unconscious wish to have the other analyst fail, and through this we could both acknowledge and feel my real failure, the real broken promise. The intense rage, disappointment, and hurt had to be experienced, survived, and integrated. At the end she decided, and I concurred, that although there was much work still to be done, she needed a period without analysis, to mourn and integrate what she had achieved. She wrote to me about a year later and it was evident that this had been a good decision as she not only maintained the analytic achievements but also continued to grow in many areas. She told me that certain areas remained unchanged and worry-ing and that she was seriously considering further analysis but did not ask me for a referral. About a year after this I received a New Year's card from her with a note that she had reentered analysis and after an initial difficult period was settling in and making progress.

THE NEGATIVE THERAPEUTIC ALLIANCE

I have described the negative therapeutic motivation as one among many motives within the patient, as something shared with the mother, and indicated how this motivation to have treatment fail can be shared and reinforced by the professional person making the referral. Similarly, one can speak of a *negative therapeutic alliance,* an unconscious collusion between the therapist, the patient, and others to produce a failure. This is not due to the analyst's deficiencies of skill or training or to the countertransference reactions produced by particular patients. As in the patients I have described, the analyst carries the seed of failure with him into the treatment situation; his need to make the therapeutic enterprise fail relates, as in the patients, to issues of omnipotence, magical expectation, failure, and externaliza-tion of blame.

The negative therapeutic alliance often becomes manifest in an overvaluation or a devaluation of the analyst's own skill, his importance as an object, and his therapeutic effectiveness. I shall highlight just a few of the effects of these attitudes.

Overvaluation is often part of an omnipotent quest based on the fantasy that there is a perfect mother with a perfect tech-nique who can kiss away all the pain, create what Balint termed "a new beginning" (1968), and Kohut (1977) refers to as "the restoration of the self." Anna Freud (1969) has said that the view that the analytic setting fosters a regression to the original mother-child dyad, and the possibility of undoing the primary "basic fault," is one which does not warrant much belief. This approach, however, often involves a direct clash with the patient's external or internalized omnipotent mother, one in which the mother-child duo is more powerful. The result will often be failure of treatment.

Another effect of the omnipotent quest for success is the overvaluation of technique. Omnipotence is a human fantasy, but it is not a human attribute. Only nonhuman objects such as machines can begin to approach omnipotent perfection. The quest for therapeutic omnipotence often leads to an overemphasis on technique, as a result of which the analyst may become an inhuman interpretive machine. As noted earlier, the negative therapeutic motivation functions as a defense against the positive transference by denying any human attributes of the analyst. The analyst's technical fervor may thus reinforce the defensive aspect of the negative therapeutic motivation and obscure the possibility of the emergence of a transference relationship.

Finally, I would like to emphasize the analyst's failure to detect the quality of sham and deceit in the negative therapeutic motivation of certain cases. These patients survive by becoming what others want them to become, by confirming the mother's externalization. They have become experts at counterfeit; they have become what one adult patient described as "an empty canvas waiting for you to paint a picture." Another adult patient described herself as a hologram produced by the intersecting projections from both her parents. She may look real, she may seem three-dimensional, but, like the hologram, she is nothing more than the intersection of two projecting beams. These are the patients who can do anything we would like them to do. They confirm our omnipotence, they can become a success for us, they can validate our theories. They are very quick to pick up our expectations, and in this way they can control us, retain us, and ultimately destroy us. Abraham (1919) and Joan Riviere (1936) described this type of complaint, cooperative, pleasant patient as one who can speak of the resolution of the transference before the transference itself has ever been broached.

To summarize: by overvaluing our importance, our technique, and our therapeutic effectiveness, we can enter into an open clash with the omnipotent mother, collude with the patient's need to avoid the human contact by becoming an omnipotent interpreting machine, and fail to see the sham and deceit behind the seeming cooperation and progressive development of certain patients.

The relation between the negative therapeutic alliance and a devaluation of one's skills, importance, and technical effectiveness is more apparent as the patient's need to make the analyst fail meets with a readiness on the part of the analyst to fail. The feature I would like to highlight is the extent to which we allow others to dictate the conditions of our work and the hesitancy we have in giving treatment the priority it deserves. This is apparent in child and adolescent work where we often see therapists giving afterschool activities and even television programs priority over treatment. It is not unusual for parents urgently to seek help and then argue with the therapist about the frequency or time of the sessions because it would interfere with the child's swimming or music lessons. I have had psychologically sophisticated parents express their gratitude for the help I was giving them and their child, and in the same breath say they were going to cancel a session for a visit to grandmother or because it was the last day before a vacation, there was so much to do and it didn't matter anyway. Some of these requests seem very reasonable, but, in my experience, to accede to them is to strengthen the negative therapeutic alliance.

Patients often set a time limit for treatment, and this is usually a manifestation of the negative therapeutic motivation. I have referred to this as the "unilateral termination plan," which exists before the start of treatment, is the condition for entering treatment and the means by which treatment is avoided (Novick, 1976). Describing the analysis of a 17-year-old where the unilateral termination plan was a way of avoiding the transference and becoming even more tied to the omnipotent mother, I suggested that "at some point in the treatment, the patient must be confronted with the seriousness of his disturbance and the necessity of giving himself up to the analytic process by relinquishing the plan for unilateral termination. Analysis cannot become terminable until it is experienced by the patient as interminable" (p. 411). I would now add that what I called the unilateral termination plan is a manifestation of a negative therapeutic motivation. It is a need to make the analyst fail and a defense against a transference relationship with the analyst. As such it becomes a part of the analytic process to be dealt with in the appropriate technical manner. However, to accept the patient's rationalization as reasonable, to agree, for example, that university is more important than treatment, is often a collusion with the patient's negative therapeutic motivation, the formation of a negative therapeutic alliance, and the production of a misbegotten child—the therapeutic failure.

THE VALUE OF FAILURE

Beyond the clinical phenomena of the negative therapeutic motivation and alliance is a larger, more general issue of the role of failure and omnipotence in normal and pathological development. To many patients the alternative to omnipotence is abject failure and total inadequacy. In their striving for omnipotence and their total intolerance of failure, the mothers I have referred to become inhuman objects producing inhuman children. As analysts we can provide these patients with the experience of a human acceptance of limitations and failure. Patients can see that we are not destroyed by failure and that failure often leads to positive growth and development. The "good enough mother" knows this and she slowly becomes less available to the child; she gradually increases the degree to which she fails the child, and this helps the child move beyond her body to the larger world of other objects.

The history of psychoanalysis provides us with a model for the adaptive response to failure. Each change in psychoanalytic theory and technique was a response to failure. It was the failure of patients to respond to hypnosis that led to the changes in technique which culminated in free association and the psychoanalytic method of inquiry. It was the failure of Freud's seduction theory which led to the discovery of the oedipus complex, instincts and their vicissitudes, and in general the intrapsychic world of instinctual drive derivatives and fantasies. Finally, it was the failure of patients to respond in an expected way to encouragement and praise that led Freud to describe the negative therapeutic reaction, relate this clinical phenomenon to the operation of the superego, and from this make the major theoretical change from a topographic to a structural point of view. So it is with Freud's comment on his own failure that I would like to end this paper. In a letter of September 21, 1887 to Fliess, Freud said,

> I no longer believe in my *neurotica*. [He detailed the reasons for rejecting his seduction theory and then wrote,] I might be feeling very unhappy. The hope of eternal fame was so beautiful, and so was that of certain wealth, complete independence, travel, and removing the children from the sphere of the worries which spoiled my own youth. All that depended on whether hysteria succeeded or not. Now I can be quiet and modest again and go on worrying and saving, and one of the stories from my collection occurs to me: "Rebecca, you can take off your wedding-gown, you're not a bride any longer!" [1950, pp. 215–218].

SUMMARY

Freud described the negative therapeutic reaction as one of many factors leading to failure or protracted treatment. In this paper another factor contributing to failure in treatment is identified as the negative therapeutic motivation, which exists long before the patient sees the analyst or has any idea what analysis is about. The negative therapeutic motivation is an unconscious wish to go into analysis or therapy in order to make the analyst fail. This motivation is part of every treatment, regardless of degree or type of pathology. The phenomenon is, however, more visible in certain types of patients, such as those with severe masochistic disturbances, and at certain ages, such as adolescence. Material from several cases, especially suicidal adolescent cases, is used to illustrate the patient's need to make the analyst fail in order to maintain an idealized image of a loving, loved, and omnipotent mother. This is maintained by the externalization and displacement of negatively cathected parts of self and object onto the analyst. The negative therapeutic motivation is shared by mother and patient. Both seek help in order to make others fail. The negative therapeutic motivation is a repetition of an established pattern where mother and child obliterate the significance of any object other than mother. In most of the cases presented the negative therapeutic motivation relates to the phenomenon of the "bypassed father." The defensive need to maintain the illusion of a purified pleasure dyad and the inability of both patient and mother to move beyond the stage of dyadic omnipotence underlie the negative therapeutic motivation. The therapist too must learn to modify and adapt omnipotent fantasies; issues of therapeutic omnipotence or impotence can interact with the patient's need to make the therapist fail, to produce a negative therapeutic alliance. It is suggested that analysis can provide the patients with the experience that failure does not lead to destruction and, as with the "good enough mother," failure can lead to positive growth and development.

BIBLIOGRAPHY

ABRAHAM, K. (1919), A Particular Form of Neurotic Resistance Against the Psycho-Analytic Method. In: *Selected Papers on Psycho-Analysis*. London: Hogarth Press, 1927, pp. 303–311.

ASCH, S. S. (1976), Varieties of Negative Therapeutic Reaction and Problems of Technique. *J. Amer. Psychoanal. Assn.*, 24:383–407.

BALINT, M. (1968), *The Basic Fault*. London: Tavistock Publications.

BRENNER, C. (1970), Origins of the Negative Therapeutic Reaction. In: Olinick (1970), pp. 662–663.

BRODEY, W. M. (1965), On the Dynamics of Narcissism. *This Annual*, 20:165–193.

FREUD, A. (1969), *Difficulties in the Path of Psychoanalysis*. New York: Int. Univ. Press.

FREUD, S. (1918), From the History of an Infantile Neurosis. *S.E.*, 17:3–123.

——— (1923), The Ego and the Id. *S.E.*, 19:3–66.

——— (1924), The Economic Problem of Masochism. *S.E.*, 19:157–170.

——— (1937), Analysis Terminable and Interminable. *S.E.*, 23:209–253.

——— (1950), *The Origins of Psychoanalysis*. New York: Basic Books, 1954.

FRIEDMAN, M., GLASSER, M., LAUFER, E., LAUFER, M., & WOHL, M. (1972), Attempted Suicide and Self-Mutilation in Adolescence. *Int. J. Psycho-Anal.*, 53:179–183.

HURRY, A. (1977), My Ambition Is to Be Dead. *J. Child Psychother.*, 4:66–83.

——— LAUFER, E., NOVICK, J., LAUFER, M., FRIEDMAN, M., GLASSER, M., & WOHL, M. (1976), Attempted Suicide in Adolescents. Center for the Study of Adolescence, Report to Grant Foundation, New York.

KOHUT, H. (1977), *The Restoration of the Self*. New York: Int. Univ. Press.

LIMENTANI, A. (1972), The Assessment of Analysability. *Int. J. Psycho-Anal.*, 53:351–361.

MOORE, B. E. & FINE, B. D. (1967), *A Glossary of Psychoanalytic Terms and Concepts*. New York: American Psychoanalytic Association.

NAMNUN, A. (1968), The Problems of Analyzability and the Autonomous Ego. *This Annual, Int. J. Psycho-Anal.,* 49:271–275.

NOVICK, J. (1976), Termination of Treatment in Adolescence. *This Annual,* 31:389–414.

—— & KELLY, K. (1970), Projection and Externalization. *This Annual,* 25:69–95.

OLINICK, S. L. (1964), The Negative Therapeutic Reaction. *Int. J. Psycho-Anal.,* 45:540–548.

—— (1970), Report of Panel: Negative Therapeutic Reaction. *J. Amer. Psychoanal. Assn.,* 18:655–672.

RINSLEY, D. B. & HALL, D. D. (1962), Psychiatric Hospital Treatment of Adolescents. *Arch. Gen. Psychiat.,* 7:78–86.

RIVIERE, J. (1936), A Contribution to the Analysis of the Negative Therapeutic Reaction. *Int. J. Psycho-Anal.,* 17:304–320.

SANDLER, J., HOLDER, A., & DARE, C. (1973), *The Patient and the Analyst.* London: Allen & Unwin.

TARTAKOFF, H. H. (1966), The Normal Personality in Our Culture and the Nobel Prize Complex. In: *Psychoanalysis—A General Psychology;* ed. R. M. Loewenstein, L. M. Newman, M. Schur, & A. J. Solnit. New York: Int. Univ. Press, pp. 222–252.

The Gender of the Analyst

In Relation to Transference and Countertransference Manifestations in Prelatency Children

PHYLLIS TYSON, Ph.D.

IN THE ANALYSIS OF YOUNG CHILDREN THERE IS A RANGE OF CIR-
cumstances in which the gender of the analyst becomes an important factor for consideration. First, the analyst's gender may
influence the content of nontransference configurations such as
the use of the analyst as a figure for displacement or as a real
object to accomplish a developmental step. Second, the gender
of the analyst may contribute to an evolution of transference and
countertransference manifestations, and this influence may be
felt more at some phases of the analysis than at others. Third, the
gender of the analyst may assume more importance for the child
at certain developmental stages than it does at others, which may
then be reflected in the transference. It remains my impression,
however, that the primary motivating force behind the content
and evolution of transference manifestations stems from the
pressure of the child's intrapsychic world.

Ferenczi (1909) quoted Freud as having remarked that patients treat themselves with transference: "we may treat a neuro-

Graduate of the Hampstead Child-Therapy Clinic, London; and Research
Candidate at the San Diego Psychoanalytic Institute.

Presented to the Association of Child Psychoanalysis, Charleston, S.C.,
March 17, 1979, as part of a panel on the "Vicissitudes of Transference and
Countertransference Related to the Gender of the Analyst and of the Child."

tic any way we like, he always treats himself psychotherapeutically, that is to say, with transferences" (p. 55; italics omitted). Freud's writings on transference seem to imply that a patient will evolve a series of transferences of particular form and content, which will be determined by a number of forces reflecting the individual's unique historical experience and development. Factors having an important influence on the evolution of transference manifestations, regardless of the patient's age, include the developmental level of underlying conflicts and their associated defenses; the intensity of the patient's relevant needs and wishes; the degree of psychic structuralization achieved, and its relative autonomy and availability to the patient for this new or regressively reactivated relationship. An additional factor which may influence the evolving transference is the way in which the patient perceives particular "real" qualities of the analyst, assigns meaning to these qualities, and then utilizes them in the transference. It is as part of this factor that the gender of the analyst finds its place, not exclusively as part of the so-called real relationship, but as a consequence of the meaning it has for the patient.

There has been a long debate about the validity of various transference manifestations in children because of questions of immature structuralization, incomplete ego autonomy and superego maturation, availability of and dependence on primary objects, ongoing development, the need for a real object, the tendency to externalization and enactment, and the impact of the analytic situation on the child's world. In an effort to clarify our understanding of transference manifestations as they appear in analytic work with children, Sandler et al. (1975) proposed a useful, though somewhat arbitrary, set of four categories of patient relationship to the analyst. The first, transference predominantly of habitual modes of relating, is clearly not transference in a strict sense; it is not specific to the analyst but represents a residue of earlier and ongoing relationships which have attained a degree of autonomy. The second category, transference of current relationships, refers to the extension or displacement of current conflicts with primary objects into the analytic setting. This frequently occurs for defensive reasons and raises the question how much of the current conflict has relevance to the past. The third category refers to transference predominantly of past experiences that are revived as a result of the analysis; these conflicts can still be related to primary objects but displaced onto the analyst. The last category is transference neurosis, referring to a new edition of repressed infantile conflicts, concentrated on, yet inappropriate to the person of the analyst or to the situation, together with a diminution of symptoms expressed elsewhere.

These definitions provide a framework for the technical handling of the treatment situation in child analysis. There are well-known difficulties in teasing out children's transference manifestations clearly, for the child's relationship to the analyst becomes a complicated mixture of elements of a real relationship, an extension into the analysis of current relationships, and a repetition or revival of the past. Developments in the relationship with the analyst may be the expression of a new developmental step, or the child may have cast the analyst in a particular role in order to express neurotic conflicts from the past. The effectiveness and precision of our interpretations are guided by the way in which we understand the content of the child's material, as well as by our understanding of the patient's transference needs, developmental needs, reality needs, and our own countertransference. Certainly, it is timely that we examine the role of gender in these aspects of the child analytic situation.

Freud (1917) considered the transference to be the key to analysis, "by whose help the most secret compartments of mental life can be opened" (p. 444). He discovered transference through the tendency of his women patients (beginning with Dora, 1905) to develop intense feelings of affection which were justified neither by his behavior nor by the situation that had developed during the treatment (p. 441). He thereafter made occasional references to the gender of the analyst and its effect on the treatment. In 1917, he stated that with his male patients there was a greater propensity to a hostile or negative transference; in 1920, he felt that the resistance to the transference he encountered in the analysis of a female homosexual was attributable to his gender; and in 1931, he noted that women analysts with female patients were able to perceive factors of preoedipal sexuality more easily and clearly because they were helped by the transference to a suitable mother substitute. Thus,

Freud appeared to see the gender of the analyst influencing the treatment by: (1) providing a focus for resistance to the transference; (2) exaggerating a negative transference used as resistance to positive transference; and (3) transference enhancement.

THE GENDER OF THE ANALYST IN CHILD ANALYSIS

In applying these ideas to work with children we come to recognize that the gender of the analyst becomes important when the reality of the analyst's gender has a particular meaning to the child. The child in any case will attempt to use the analyst for the expression and gratification of his transference as well as developmental and real needs, but at some stage of the analyst the actual gender of the analyst *may* become a critical issue in the expression of one or more of these needs. One immediately thinks of the analyst's gender helping to fulfill a developmental need which has been inadequately fulfilled elsewhere, a need which may be more important to the child at some developmental stages than at others. An example of this would be those cases where issues regarding gender identity, gender role, or gender of the chosen love object are of particular concern to the child. In some children these needs may have to be satisfied before any transference development of analytic work is possible. Yet the very satisfaction of these needs may serve to enhance the revival of past conflicts, which may then find expression in the transference.

We can therefore add to Freud's list and say that in child analysis not only can the gender of the analyst enhance the transference, provide a focus for resistance to the transference, or highlight the use of transference as a resistance (Harley, 1967), but it can also serve a developmental need which may then enhance the transference.

The circumstances under which the gender of the analyst influences the child's analytic material now become an important consideration. There are, first of all, nontransference ways in which the analyst's gender as well as other real factors (such as age, or physical features) may very well determine the child's initial reaction, and where the child's character may be highlighted in his habitual modes of relating. However, the situation becomes increasingly complicated when the analyst is dealing with the displacement of current conflicts, the revival of past experiences, and the transference neurosis, if one develops. In these instances the gender of the analyst will become important in certain phases of the analysis, but with the increasing revival of the past and the increasing use of the analyst to rework past conflicts, the importance of the gender of the analyst tends to recede into the background, and conflicts from all prior levels of development and modes of relating to both parents will eventually find expression in the transference. In order to illustrate the range of circumstances in which the gender of the analyst needs consideration, a series of clinical vignettes will be presented, the first group relating primarily to the expression of preoedipal conflicts, the latter to oedipal configurations.

PREOEDIPAL CONFLICTS

Hester, a 5-year-old girl, was referred because of constipation and asthma and was treated by a male colleague. Hester showed the preoedipal ambivalent nature of her relationship with her mother by fighting with her analyst for control. She controlled all the games by making up her own rules, for example, "Today it's a Hester game." She was stubborn and extremely bossy, and her sadomasochistic character traits were readily extended into the analysis. Hester's father was terminally ill and had been largely unresponsive to any oedipal gestures made by the child toward him. However, in the treatment situation, the male analyst's responsiveness enabled her to gain more confidence in her femininity, and emerging positive oedipal wishes counterbalanced the battles for control. Although the transference continued to contain elements of sadomasochistic struggles, these gradually gave way to the expression of a new developmental step. After the attenuation of the preoedipal transference, the treatment relationship served a developmental need, which then enhanced the analysis of disappointments in the father; eventually this led back to the analysis of preoedipal disappointment in the mother and the child's narcissistic vulnerabilities; finally, the roots of the sadomasochistic struggle could be analyzed. This brought symptomatic relief, and conflicts with the mother gradually abated. Here we can conclude that in the earliest phase of analysis, when habitual modes of relating were extended into the analysis, the analyst's gender did not appear to be of central importance. However, the analyst's gender later served to fulfill a real need, enabling the girl to take a previously delayed developmental step, which then enhanced the transference and subsequently made it possible to analyze the preoedipal elements.

Lisa, a 4½-year-old girl, came to analysis with the presenting symptom of encopresis, which developed subsequent to a bilateral hernia operation when she was 2½. Lisa maintained the fantasy that prior to the operation she had been a boy, and she was convinced that another penis would eventually grow. The relationship with her female analyst contained the sadomasochistic traits described in the case of Hester, but underlying this was an extreme narcissistic vulnerability. The disappointment and anger with her mother for not protecting her from the operation and for not giving her a penis were transferred to the analyst. She became extremely bossy, was envious of other patients, constantly demanded new toys, and stubbornly refused to leave sessions, demanding to take something home. Analysis of her disappointment in her mother and of the underlying fantasy that her mother would have preferred a boy enabled her to take on more feminine identifications; the fecal mass began to represent more often fantasies of babies rather than of growing a penis, and she began tentatively to move toward positive oedipal fantasies. However, the pervasive nature of her sadomasochistic character provided a focus for resistance to the transference, and the persistent hostile transference was then used to defend against her underlying passive dependent longings, which aroused such anxiety (Greenson, 1967). Unfortunately, once the sadomasochistic conflicts became focused on the analyst and somewhat contained in the treatment situation, giving some symptomatic relief, Lisa's mother broke off treatment.

When girls with preoedipal ambivalent struggles with the mother, like those demonstrated by Hester and Lisa, are treated by female analysts, it is my impression that there is a greater proclivity to repeat the earlier and ongoing conflicts in their original intensity in the treatment situation. In such cases the analyst's gender serves to heighten resistance to the development of a positive transference, and the analysis often becomes characterized by sadomasochistic struggles, which provide such secondary gain that the child is reluctant to give them up and little progress is made. In contrast, with an analyst of the opposite sex, the concurrent expression of positive oedipal strivings, which may represent a new developmental step, seems to be facilitated by the reality of the analyst's gender. In this case, these strivings enhance the development of a positive transference, which can then be used to facilitate the analysis of the regressive conflicts. However, the analyst's gender has somewhat of an attenuating effect in that the regressive sadomasochistic struggles appear not to become the central focus of the analysis because of the concomitant positive oedipal configurations.

There are two more ways in which the analyst's gender seems to me to be of importance in the analysis of children who are arrested at or have regressed to the anal-sadistic conflict levels and modes of relating to objects, that is, in regard to the countertransference and in reference to the mother's transference to the child's analyst.

Freud (1905) commented that the analysis of the transference was one of the hardest parts of analysis. Bird (1972) suggests that one of the reasons for this difficulty is the strain it puts on the analyst due to his own transference. From discussions with colleagues over the years, and from my own experience, I have the impression that one of the most difficult clinical situations is the treatment of a little girl arrested at or regressed to the anal-sadistic level of conflict and of object relating when the analyst is a woman. The preoedipal ambivalent struggles with the mother can be one of the most difficult developmental conflicts for a young girl. Blos (1979) discusses how fervently the adolescent girl struggles against the revival of these conflicts. Hence, if these conflicts are revived in the countertransference, as they often are in the treatment of such girls by female analysts, they may be expressed in action before the analyst is aware of the countertransference, and the relationship may become a revival of the past for both patient and analyst. Sandler (1976) suggests that this situation can usefully be understood as a compromise between the analyst's own countertransference tendencies and the patient's transference attempts to impose a special interaction or "role relationship" with the analyst as a means of reexperiencing a gratification.

Because of the analyst's "free-floating responsiveness" in addition to his free-floating attention, Sandler feels that rather than regarding particular responses to the patient as irrational reactions of the analyst, which his professional conscience leads him to see entirely as a blind spot of his own, these responses may sometimes be usefully regarded as a "compromise-formation between his own tendencies and *his reflexive acceptance of the role* which the patient is forcing on him" (p. 46).

Sandler notes that some analysts may be more susceptible to certain roles than others. It may be in this area that gender is an important factor, and that women analysts are more liable to accept the role these little girls are forcing upon them. Once this compromise is made, the secondary gains make it a difficult relationship to analyze.

The mother's transference to the child's analyst may also be affected by the analyst's gender. Rosenfeld (1968) discusses the nature of the mother's involvement in the child's pathology in cases of retention and soiling. She pointed out that the mother's inconsistent, controlling, and ambivalent behavior to her child is a frequent factor in the child's choice of symptom. The mother's need for control is often reflected in the relationship she establishes with the child's analyst. She may find it difficult to share her child with another woman. The female analyst is often seen by her as an idealized mother. Once the child establishes a positive relationship with the analyst and symptoms are alleviated, the mother's unresolved conflicts with her own mother are aroused. The mother feels in competition with the analyst for her child's loyalty and in competition with her child for the analyst's time. Feelings of inadequacy and jealousy emerge; the mother finds it progressively more difficult to share her child with the female analyst; and the treatment is broken off. I have come to feel that such cases would benefit from simultaneous analysis, with a view to helping the mother separate her feelings about the child from her feelings about her own mother and feelings about the child's analyst. Otherwise, the ambivalent nature of her tie to the child and her ambivalent reactions to the child's analyst may significantly interfere with the child's analysis.

So far, I have given examples of the range of situations in which the analyst's gender is an important consideration in the treatment of children presenting with preoedipal, ambivalent struggles with the primary object. Next, I will illustrate another type of preoedipal disturbance, one in which the child suffers chiefly from narcissistic difficulties, and the analyst's gender appears to play an insignificant part.

At the age of 4½, Susie's developmental arrest was such that her object relationships had not yet achieved a triadic form. She was referred by the nursery school for impulsive behavior, having alienated all the children by pinching, pulling hair, or biting. Whenever she was frustrated or reprimanded, she would tearfully hide and sob, claiming that no one liked her. She longed for, yet feared, any kind of intimacy in relationships, suffering an excessive dependence on others for maintenance of her self-esteem. I concluded that Susie had only tenuously established libidinal object constancy. Her mother was an equally disturbed and narcissistically fragile soul who, because of her poorly modulated anxiety, would respond with abrupt, unempathic, and excessively intense and frightening expressions of anger and assertions of control over Susie's behavior. The mother verbally and sometimes physically abused Susie, comparing her unfavorably to her 2-year-younger sister and to all the other children in the neighborhood, until Susie was completely demoralized and heartbroken. The father, who was actively involved in all aspects of Susie's care because of the mother's vulnerability, attempted to modify the mother's influence, yet found himself responding in equally negative fashion to Susie's behavior.

In Susie's ongoing analysis a major transference wish that we be twins emerged. In making drawings, Susie felt that if mine were better, hers would seem no good at all. If hers appeared superior, she feared I would get angry, which would leave her feeling devastated; so it would be better if we were the same, i.e., twins. Therefore, we spent a long time making "twin drawings," and I had to do exactly as she did. In this way, Susie re-created in the transference not only the regressive wish for symbiotic attachment, but also her search for the acceptance and approval she sought in both her mother and her father—factors that are so crucial to the development of the child's self-esteem. In the transference she used me as an object for the extension and displacement of past as well as current conflicts. I was encouraged by a recent remark she made: "You're the only one who likes me; everyone else just says 'dumb Susie.'"

I felt this was an illustration of Ritvo's point (1974): "When an arrest or deviation in the child's development is due to an incompatibility between the parents' personality characteristics and the child's needs at a particular period, the therapist can function as a new object who may be more available to the child for the satisfaction of inner needs and enable the child to reach a higher developmental level" (p. 164). Susie's trust in my regard for her represented her use of me as a new object and was a hopeful, beginning step in the development of new inner structure that would allow her to internalize a positively invested representation of me which could eventually be incorporated into her self representation. Morgenthaler (1969) has suggested that some patients can maintain their narcissistic equilibrium only so long as the analyst is experienced as sexually undifferentiated, and this is my understanding of Susie's position—at this point in her development the narcissistic vulnerability expressed in her wish that we be twins is not yet related to sexual issues in which the gender of the analyst might assume importance.

OEDIPAL CONFLICTS

In my review of the range of circumstances in which the gender of the analyst becomes important, I have thus far considered preoedipal situations where the gender of the analyst can function as a focus for resistance to the transference (Lisa), as an enhancement or attenuation of the transference (Hester), and in the service of developmental needs, including those of narcissistic equilibrium (Susie). The child in the oedipal situation commonly displaces conflicts into the treatment situation from the parent of the same gender as the analyst, especially at the beginning of treatment.

Thus, the order in which the conflicts of the infantile neurosis are expressed in the treatment can be affected by the analyst's gender. To illustrate this point, I will describe an early portion of the analysis of Norman, a 5-year-old boy of divorced parents.

Norman was referred for analysis because of difficulties in social adjustment, daytime enuresis, a deteriorating relationship with his mother, and apparent problems in gender identity in that he expressed a wish to be a girl. At the age of 1½ Norman had been put in daycare, and subsequently at 2½ was abandoned by his mother when she separated from his father. Although he later had intermittent contact with her, he did not again live with his mother until he was 3½. Dual custody was then arranged; this meant that he and his sister would live six months first with one parent and then with the other. At the age of 5, after having lived with his mother for the second six-month period, Norman requested to live permanently with his father, and he was eventually allowed to do so. Prior to this move, Norman would fight about returning to the mother's home after weekend visits with the father. After the move to his father's home, Norman refused to talk with his mother in person or on the telephone.

The early months of the analysis reflected Norman's negative oedipal longings for his father and his hostility to his mother. He reacted to me as the castrating, rejecting mother whom he envied and feared; he also fought against revealing any dependency needs or weaknesses. He expressed envy and jealousy of women, saw no advantage in having a penis because his sister's friends always teased him about being a boy. He longed to play with them and become an accepted member of their group. The analysis of the early separation revealed that Norman felt his mother had left him not only for his anal messiness but also because he was a boy. (The mother had openly stated that she felt she could deal with his sister, but not with Norman.) He experienced the separation as an enormous narcissistic wound and saw nothing valuable in being a boy or in assuming a male role,[1] for

---

1. In this context it is useful to distinguish between gender identity, gender role, and sexual partner orientation because the developmental line is different for boys and girls in this regard (Tyson, 1979). *Gender identity* in its broadest sense includes all those characteristics which comprise each individual's combination of masculinity and femininity, determined not only by biological sex but also by psychological factors such as object relation's, identifications, intra-

men were denigrated and devalued. When Norman's fear of loving me became a significant part of the transference, his wish for his father as a source of affection, love, comfort, and protection emerged in an expression of a negative oedipal configuration. The analysis of his fear of the phallic, castrating mother revealed that his daily wetting served as a reassurance that his penis was still intact; fantasies of urinating on the whole world with his powerful phallus then emerged.

As these conflicts were increasingly verbalized in the analysis, Norman began to establish a better relationship with his mother; but the conflict then appeared with me, to the extent that his father commented that I seemed to have replaced Norman's mother in his struggles. During this phase Norman would go happily to visit his mother, but he put up the familiar resistant struggle every day before the treatment sessions. As the analytic work continued, Norman's behavior in the sessions took on the regressed character of an angry, messy, and sulky toddler. His wetting became confined to sessions, while his behavior outside continued to improve in all areas. There was progressively less emphasis on the reality of my gender as conflicts from the past were revived in the transference. I was then used for the expression of conflicts with both parents. Later in the analysis, the reality of my gender again took on notable significance, however. After Norman had been able to rework earlier conflicts, forward movement began to take place. Although there remained a fear of expressing positive feelings to me, for fear of being abandoned, he increasingly identified with a male gender role, became less of a messy toddler, and began to look forward to sessions. He started to behave more like an oedipal child, oscillating between a negative and a positive oedipal position.

In this example we can see that the reality of the analyst's gender was an important element in the early part of treatment

psychic and bisexual conflicts as well as cultural and social influences (Stoller, 1976). *Gender role* refers to one's behavior in relationship to other people, i.e., the subtle, complicated, conscious, and unconscious exchanges of messages, and conscious and unconscious experience of interactions (Sandler and Sandler, 1978) between self and objects vis-à-vis one's gender identity. *Sexual partner orientation* (Green, 1975) refers to the sex of the chosen love object, and is a separate yet related process.

and provided a focus for resistance to the transference. Later, as past conflicts with both parents were revived, gender influences receded into the background, but again emerged as an important factor in enhancing a new developmental step.

In introducing this example, I said that the analyst's gender may influence the order in which the conflicts of the infantile neurosis are presented. However, there is an unknown variable, in this or any case, in the extent to which the intensity of neurotic conflicts and the urgency of the inner pressures felt by the child right from the very beginning dictate which conflicts appear first, without regard to the analyst's gender. As an illustration of this latter situation, I present the first of several excerpts from the treatment of Colin, a 4-year-old boy.[2] Colin's early analytic work centered around fears of abandonment and loss of love. He had suffered a series of traumatic separations from both parents in his first 3 years, and he was emotionally abandoned by his mother, because of her depression, before the rapprochement crisis could be adequately resolved. Although libidinal object constancy was established through the help of a loyal and loving father, Colin's self-esteem was tenuous and still very dependent on outside sources. I became aware of a new development in the transference when, after several months of treatment, I had to cancel a session. The following day Colin panicked on seeing his father drive away. The canceled session had revived conflicts around his early separations from his mother, which then came to be vividly expressed in the transference. Following this, preoedipal conflicts over instinctual wishes, sibling rivalry, and feared loss of love were revived. The transference manifestations of these concerns did not appear to be gender related, because Colin expressed fears of being abandoned by his father as much as by his mother.

When, as a consequence of our work together, Colin's trust in me and his libidinal attachment had grown, my being a real woman came to be of great importance to him at this particular stage in his development and at this phase of the analysis. At the time he began treatment, Colin had not established oedipal phase dominance, partly because he had not found in his mother a suitable object for oedipal elaboration, and he appeared "ob-

2. A fuller version of this case can be found in Tyson (1978).

ject hungry." Apparently he first had to work through the more pressing preoedipal issues before positive oedipal fantasies could flourish with me as the central and real object. Thereafter he was able to move forward in his development.

Now we have two examples in which the gender of the analyst appears to be important in regard to oedipal manifestations. With Norman, it may well have influenced the order in which his oedipal conflicts were presented in treatment, encouraging the negative oedipal side to appear first, because of a preoedipal fear of and anger toward his mother. But there remains room for doubt on two points: first, the child's inner pressures may have acted to determine the order of appearance of the clinical material; and second, it is possible to understand Norman's earlier use of me as being in the service of a defensive displacement of his negative feelings from the mother, and thus not to be transference at all, in the strict sense of the term. With Colin it was clear that my gender was not important in the preoedipal material which appeared in the first part of treatment, but that it did matter when he became able to utilize me as a real object. As is often the case with deprived children, Colin's use of me as a real object enabled him to elaborate the next developmental step, which temporarily served some resistance to transference. As treatment progressed, however, it became clear that the fulfillment of the developmental need ultimately enhanced the transference and led to the expression of old conflicts with both parents. I will give a second example from his treatment in which my gender was irrelevant because I represented the father.

Colin's envy of his father began to emerge. He believed his father had a very powerful penis, a belief that was reinforced by the appearance of baby after baby at home, and his father's increasing professional success. I became father in the transference and Colin became envious of all my possessions—my jewelry, my money, my power. He thought if he could be rich like me, then he would be powerful and have everything he wanted. The offer of some play money provoked a violent temper tantrum, whereupon he attacked me screaming, "This is worthless! How could you give me anything absolutely worthless!" He claimed it was I who gave him worries anyway; he never felt like this anywhere else!

A third example shows the analyst's gender having an attenuating effect on particular transference manifestations, reminiscent of a similar situation in the case of Hester. While there had been hints of the topic, it was in the third year of treatment that Colin gave clear evidence of negative oedipal feelings toward me as representative of the father. Colin wished he could be a girl and make babies for me like his mother did for his father. He bemoaned his belief that the woman has everything—in intercourse she gets the penis *and* the baby. Colin's negative oedipal longings for love and affection from his father-analyst could not be fully worked out, I believe, partly because of the castration anxiety this engendered, partly because his father was the only real object in his life at home who could be counted on, partly because of his concomitant positive oedipal wishes toward me which were emphasized because I was a woman, and partly because he had begun his oedipal development with me as a real positive oedipal object. Thus, the reality of my gender served to have an attenuating effect on the analysis of the negative oedipal configuration.

I nevertheless have the impression that Colin's use of me as a transference figure enabled him to rework and reorder old conflicts to the point that he was eventually able to transfer the positive relationship with me back to his mother and to reestablish a long-forgotten positive relationship with her, as well as to become less clinging and more secure in his relationship with his father.

DISCUSSION

This paper focuses on the role of the analyst's gender in the treatment of children who manifest primarily either preoedipal or oedipal conflicts. Although in the past there has been a tendency in the analytic literature to underplay any essential differences in the transference developed toward male and female analysts (Fenichel, 1945), in recent years increasingly more attention has been paid to the real factors which might influence the developing transference. Blum (1971) emphasizes that not only transference distortion, but realistic perceptions of the analyst, the therapeutic alliance, and the analyst as a new object and developmental reorganizer are overlapping dimensions of the analytic relationship. He notes that real attributes of the therapist may color the developing transference; and that the transference is probably influenced by variables in the therapist such as age, style, sex, and character traits. He says, "With a female analyst a maternal transference will usually appear first" (p. 50), implying that the analyst's gender influences the order in which particular transference manifestations appear.

In the analysis of children, their perception of "real" qualities of the analyst seems to be of special importance, particularly as they continue to have an ongoing relationship with their primary objects. It must be continually emphasized, however, that the gender of the analyst assumes importance not exclusively as a part of the "real" relationship, but as a consequence of the meaning it has for the patient.

In the examples that were presented it became clear that the analyst's gender may have importance in nontransference ways such as determining the child's initial reaction, but that very soon the child's habitual modes of relating were reflected in the relationship, regardless of the analyst's gender. (Both Lisa and Hester brought sadomasochistic character traits early in treatment, although they had different-sexed analysts.) The analyst's gender appears to be of some importance when the child uses the analyst in the defensive displacement of negative feelings to primary objects, as in the case of Norman, but this too should not be considered transference in the strict sense of the term. The child's use of the analyst as a real object may very well take advantage of the analyst's gender, enabling previously untraversed developmental steps to be made, as in the oedipal configurations described in the cases of Hester, Norman, and Colin. However, in the case of Susie, it appeared that the analyst's empathic understanding was the primary factor in her use of the analyst as a real object to achieve a new developmental step. The analyst's gender appeared to be of little importance.

With regard to more specifically transference-related phenomena, the role of the analyst's gender seemed first to operate as an influence on the order in which conflicts were expressed, some preference perhaps being given to those conflicts with the parent of the same gender as the analyst. However, inner pressures and defensive needs must be taken into consideration as well. As the transference develops, it becomes increasingly obvious that the primary motivating force behind the content and evolution of transference manifestations stems from the pressure of the child's intrapsychic world. These manifestations are not necessarily influenced by the analyst's gender, but when this becomes a factor, this influence may result either in an attentuation of some aspect of the transference, or in an enhancement of it.

SUMMARY

I have tried to illustrate through selected case material that there is a range of circumstances in which the gender of the analyst becomes important in a young child's evolving relationship with the analyst. Significant among these are nontransference configurations, such as the defensive use of the analyst as a figure for displacement of conflicts from primary objects, or in the use of the analyst in achieving a new previously untraversed developmental step. I have also briefly discussed instances in which the gender of the child appears to have some influence on the developing countertransference, especially in relation to preoedipal manifestations in young girls and women. With regard to evolving transference manifestations, I have indicated that the use of gender is representative of particular qualities of the analyst which are given meaning by the patient and subsequently utilized in the transference. I have also tried to demonstrate that the ways in which the gender of the analyst becomes important in transference or transference-related areas reflect particular conflicts and developmental phases with which the child is involved. Finally, I have indicated that the gender of the analyst can provide possible foci for resistance to transference development, serve to exaggerate a transference resistance, and work for the enhancement or attenuation of particular aspects of transference manifestations.

BIBLIOGRAPHY

BIRD, B. (1972), Notes on Transference, *J. Amer. Psychoanal. Assn.*, 20:267–301.
BLOS, P. (1979), Modifications in the Classical Psychoanalytic Model of Adolescence. In: *The Adolescent Passage.* New York: Int. Univ. Press, pp. 473–497.

BLUM, H. P. (1971), On the Conception and Development of the Transference Neurosis. *J. Amer. Psychoanal. Assn.*, 19:41–53.

FENICHEL, O. (1945), *The Psychoanalytic Theory of Neurosis.* New York: Norton.

FERENCZI, S. (1909), Introjection and Transference. In: *Sex in Psychoanalysis.* New York: Basic Books, 1950, pp. 35–93.

FREUD, S. (1905), Fragment of an analysis of a case of hysteria. *S.E.*, 7:31–122.

—— (1917), Transference. *S.E.*, 16:431–447.

—— (1920), The Psychogenesis of a Case of Homosexuality in a Woman. *S.E.*, 18:145–172.

—— (1931), Female Sexuality. *S.E.*, 21:223–243.

GREEN, R. (1975), Sexual Identity. *Arch. Sex. Behav.*, 4:337–352.

GREENSON, R. R. (1967), *The Technique and Practice of Psychoanalysis.* New York: Int. Univ. Press.

HARLEY, M. (1967), Transference Developments in a Five-Year-Old Child. In: *The Child Analyst at Work,* ed. E. R. Geleerd. New York: Int. Univ. Press, pp. 115–141.

MORGENTHALER, F. (1969), Disturbances of Male and Female Identity As Met with in Psychoanalytic Practice. *Int. J. Psycho-Anal.*, 50:109–112.

RITVO, S. (1974), Current Status of the Concept of Infantile Neurosis. *This Annual,* 29:159–181.

ROSENFELD, S. (1968), Notes on a Case of Retention. *J. Child Psychother.*, 2:38–49.

SANDLER, J. (1976), Countertransference and Role-Responsiveness. *Int. Rev. Psycho-Anal.*, 3:43–48.

—— KENNEDY, H., & TYSON, R. L. (1975), Discussions on Transference. *This Annual,* 30:409–442.

—— & SANDLER, A.-M. (1978), On the Development of Object Relationships and Affects. *Int. J. Psycho-Anal.*, 59:285–296.

STOLLER, R. (1976), Primary Femininity. *J. Amer. Psychoanal. Assn. Suppl.*, 24:59–78.

TYSON, P. (1978), Transference and Developmental Issues in the Analysis of a Prelatency Child. *This Annual,* 33:213–236.

—— (1979), A Developmental Line of Gender Identity, Gender Role, and Choice of Love Object. Unpublished manuscript.

APPLICATIONS OF
PSYCHOANALYSIS

The Cornerstone Treatment of a Preschool Boy from an Extremely Impoverished Environment

THOMAS LOPEZ, Ph.D. AND GILBERT W. KLIMAN, M.D.

MONROE WAS THE KIND OF CHILD FROM WHOM USUALLY LITTLE IS expected therapeutically. A member of a disadvantaged ethnic minority, he lived in the poverty of a big-city slum ghetto; as do so many children from such circumstances, he had as presenting problems marked intellectual retardation, a nearly psychotic degree of withdrawal, impoverished affect, and episodic difficulties with impulse control (Meers, 1970, 1973). The fact that his treatment ran dramatically counter to the usual pessimistic expectations makes the fascinating adventure it turned out to be especially worth reporting. It also is worth reporting because it serves as an example of the therapy of several dozen similar children treated by the Cornerstone method, all of whom have been helped.

The Cornerstone Method (Kliman, 1968, 1969, 1970, 1975, 1978) is an attempt, in the context of a community clinic, to integrate psychoanalytic therapy with the therapeutic nursery

Dr. Lopez is on the staff of The Center for Preventive Psychiatry, White Plains, N.Y., and on the child analysis faculty of the New York Freudian Society. Dr. Kliman is Principal Investigator, The Center for Preventive Psychiatry's NIMH-sponsored Project to Assess Preventive Interventions with Foster Children, founder and formerly Medical Director of The Center.

A shortened version of this paper was presented at a scientific meeting of the American Psychoanalytic Association on December 14, 1979.

education of preschool children in order more fully to exploit the properties of each. A child psychoanalyst or psychotherapist works in the classroom alongside two teachers for about two of the daily three hours of class time, four to five days each week, with seven or eight children. The psychoanalyst or therapist treats the children individually right in the classroom, in sessions of 20 to 25 minutes; each child receiving three or more such sessions weekly.

The teachers simultaneously conduct a therapeutic nursery program. By means of affection, example, limit setting, guidance, and stimulation, they work to promote the children's interest, skills, and talents; aim at taming their "drive" behavior in order to divert it into play, learning, and work; and encourage their gaining independence from primary objects by helping them to establish other relationships (Edgcumbe, 1975). The teachers also provide guidance for the children's parents. Where possible, each child's parents are seen once weekly by a teacher, except for once every fourth week, when the therapist sees them.

The teachers and therapist also become involved in complex interactions with one another and with the children (Kliman, 1968, 1975), aspects of which can only be touched on in this paper. It is important to bear in mind, however, that a consistent effort is made to maintain the roles of therapist and therapeutic teacher separate: the former adhering as closely as possible to the interpretive stance of the psychoanalyst; the latter, to the stance of the therapeutic educator of the preschool child.

CASE PRESENTATION

Monroe was the second of three sons born to an impoverished black couple. When he was 2½ years old, his mother suffered a psychosis following the birth of her third child, who was born with a defect requiring a chronic tracheotomy. The mother's psychosis—about which no more than the most fragmentary information was ever gained—included delusionary fears a man would enter her window and attack her. She was hospitalized for nine months and then treated by drugs, the dosage level of which induced her face to take on a masklike appearance and caused her to become grossly obese and slow in her movements. While she was in the hospital, Monroe and his brother, older by 2 years, were cared for by their father and paternal grandmother. The baby was placed in permanent foster care. When Monroe's mother returned home, his father moved out for good, and remained out of contact with the family, except for occasional visits. Throughout Monroe's treatment, neither his mother nor anyone associated with the case knew where his father lived, nor were they able to meet with him. The combination of father's absence and mother's condition made it impossible to gain information about Monroe's early development.

Monroe was referred by a daycare center as a result of his obvious profound developmental lags and grossly atypical behavior: he had little ability to relate to peers and adults; very sparse use of language (limited to occasional phrases such as, "I don't know" or "Thomas hit me"); grossly deficient capacity to learn; a withdrawn, detached appearance, interrupted only by occasional outbursts of obstreperousness; overall, a joyless lack of vitality. On intake, he was described in terms of wandering gaze, lax facial musculature, paucity of expressive interchange, impoverished affect, and scored an IQ (WISC) of 53. However, the examining psychiatrist (G.W.K.) noted some positive features. Monroe's receptive comprehension of verbal communication was at a higher level than his active linguistic expression: he readily brought a toy elephant and a yellow truck when asked to, finding them in the middle of a cluttered floor. On request he built an excellent tower of blocks with some 25 pieces. And he seemed very pleased at the examiner's admiration and encouragement.

Monroe began what were to be two years of Cornerstone method treatment at age 4. Prior to it, he had been seen individually by Mrs. H. Baskerville of The Center for Preventive Psychiatry in educational psychotherapy (Stein and Ronald, 1974)—an approach similar to that discussed by Weil (1973)—for some ten months, three sessions weekly. Educational psychotherapy, though it may have enhanced Monroe's response to treatment in the nursery, brought about no appreciable improvement in his functioning.

A "homemaker," a woman employed by the county, spent

eight hours of each weekday with the family to help care for it. A "therapeutic companion," a female graduate student, was provided by the Center to spend time with the family, one day of each weekend.

THE FIRST YEAR OF TREATMENT

When Monroe arrived at Cornerstone, accompanied by his seemingly barely ambulatory mother and the homemaker, he fully fitted the description of him at intake. His eyes appeared glazed; his visage, like that of many institutionalized patients, blank; his affect flat.

However, in the very first session, when, in an attempt to make emotional contact with him, I[1] cautiously rolled a toy truck to him, a somewhat livelier facial expression immediately developed. More important, Monroe rolled the truck back! I suggested we were getting to know each other. Monroe managed to smile through his sad vacant look and actually seemed delighted. Then he smiled broadly and rolled the truck to other people in the room: to the teachers, to his mother, and to other mothers, present because it was the first day of school. He responded to my remarking on his discovering other people eager to play with him with an almost uncanny show of ecstasy: he squirmed about the floor, seemingly trying to rub as much as he could of his body on it. A thing as good as this, I commented, ought be made contact with by as much of one's being as possible.

Monroe quickly became more active. In the second session, he jumped off a table into my arms, declaring he was a baby and I his mother, and assigning to me the task of his caretaker. By the end of the first week, when another child was in possession of something or someone he coveted, or when the day's class session had come to an end, Monroe shrieked in a deeply pained, almost unearthly manner, though without tears. At the end of one session, he attempted to destroy the watch on a teacher's wrist, seemingly in an effort to halt the passing of time. Within two months, Monroe cried and wept continuously during the

---

1. T.L. was the analyst, supervised by G.W.K., the method's originator.

greater part of three sessions immediately following the three-day interruption of school.

Within a month of entering Cornerstone, Monroe became very difficult to cope with. He would kick, bite, spit, punch, scratch, and make a shambles of the classroom, create chaos and drive the teachers to near despair. He would ingest great quantities of food, storming the cupboard where it was kept or attempting to appropriate all of what had been set out for the entire class. When he was stopped and scolded, his frenetic activity might well dissolve in a flood of tears, as he would fervently hug and kiss his scolder, ask to sit on her lap and be cuddled by her. As infuriating as Monroe might be one moment, as lovable he became the next. In one session, he bit a very attractive female psychologist who had come to administer tests. Then he stuffed himself with pretzels and potato chips. My verbalizing that the recipient of his bite was a "yum-yum" brought forth ecstatic nods of agreement from Monroe. He then declared a wish to go camping with her in a nearby forest.

Despite the turmoil there was a general feeling that Monroe's condition was improving. Following his morning session in Cornerstone, he continued to attend the daycare center, where he was functioning better: he was following his teachers' instructions and getting on better with the other children. It appeared that the attention, tolerance, and affection—and, of course, the food—Monroe was receiving from the nursery were enabling him to feel more nourished and intact outside of it (Kohut, 1971, 1977). Confirmation came from a most unexpected source and for reasons that were astonishing: Monroe's mother, her pitiable appearance unchanged, volunteered that her son was improved because he seemed more lively and troublesome at home! While it was difficult to know to what extent she was suffering from mental illness, and to what extent from her drug treatment, it was clear that she was no longer actively psychotic. We failed in our efforts to prevent continuing overmedication to which she was subjected by a nearby aftercare clinic, but we were able to engage her in nearly weekly parent guidance.

Within three months, Monroe was affectionately feeding a dog outside the school; playing at being a fireman at the local fire station which we often visited at his request; proudly presenting

Ms. Balter, one of his teachers, with splendid phallic structures made of blocks; affectionately hugging her while wearing a mask he had cut out of paper to disguise himself as a grown man; and once playfully urinating on her hand when she helped him with his trousers in the toilet. He emerged as the most competent among the children at cutting designs from paper, and radiated a charisma which made him very popular among his peers.

Nevertheless, Monroe's ego limitations were glaring. His thinking was so stimulus- or context-bound (Goldstein, 1939; Werner, 1940, 1957), he was unable to engage in conversation because he could not, at will, call up relevant ideas within himself. For example, to deal with the fact that waiting for him to produce material relevant to therapy invariably resulted in little more than his ignoring me, I would at times begin work with Monroe either by throwing him in the air and catching him, or by holding him by his feet upside-down—activities which delighted Monroe. When asked which he preferred, however, Monroe was unable to verbalize his choice, simply saying "yes" when I did so.

His affects had an unmodulated, all-or-none quality (Fenichel, 1941; Rapaport, 1953). Rage, anxiety, despair, affection, happiness would emerge, dominate his entire being, and then recede only after they had seemingly exhausted themselves or in response to a dramatic change in the environment, such as a scolding, a cuddling, a frustration, or, at times, an interpretation.

By the middle of the fourth month of treatment, Monroe's entire demeanor—the sound of his crying; the clinging torturing manner by which he related; his preference for drinking from a baby bottle; his occasionally becoming incontinent with regard to urine; the manner in which he sought adults' laps for "refueling"—increasingly took on the qualities of a toddler, frequently of a desperately grieved toddler. Time and again, on little or no pretext, or on one he had largely manufactured himself, he spent long periods crying pitiably on a teacher's lap. Gradually I had changed my approach and stopped the game of throwing him in the air and catching him so that we might work on "ideas." In response, Monroe clawed and hit at my watch. When I verbalized how terrible it was that good things, like our playing, come to an end, Monroe became desperate, pleaded to be given a baby bottle, and calmed only after he had received it.

But when I verbalized the hurt "baby feelings" that had been stirred in him, Monroe again broke down into desperate crying and continued uninterruptedly for some 20 minutes. During this time Monroe repeatedly called for his mother and cuddled close to me while sitting on my lap. Presently, he picked up a plastic shell shaped like an egg split in half (a container for pantyhose), placed it on my chest, and mouthed and sucked it as a baby would a breast. At that time I attempted an interpretation that related his behavior to his mother's current psychically impoverished condition and past breakdown. I reconstructed: long ago, his mother became sick, and had to leave him to go to a hospital. He could not be with her, sit on her lap, or get "good feeling" from her. She still was very sad, slow, and difficult to feel close to. Now, when he is unable to get something he wants, the terrible pain of being unable to feel close to his mother comes up.

For the next four months this was the main line of interpretation. The results were dramatic. A way had become available for making sense of Monroe's internal chaos and desperation. Although the reconstruction may have been valid only in a "hazy way" (Valenstein, 1975, p. 63), and though they surely made use of much that Monroe had since pieced together from discussions with his mother and perhaps from other sources, dialogue became possible where previously only comforting and restraint could be resorted to. Material became accessible for understanding and mastery which otherwise almost surely would have remained out of reach.[2] In one session, after having become furious at me for working with other children before working with him, Monroe ostentatiously ignored me when his own turn came. I verbalized Monroe's rejecting me as a retaliation, and said how difficult it was to wait for someone one wanted to be close to and how often Monroe must have felt and still feel rejected at home by his mother. He continued to ignore me. I then became more concrete. I first enacted Monroe's feeling rejected when I worked with other children, playing both Monroe's and my own role, and verbalizing his pain and anger. Then I enacted Monroe's trying to gain his mother's attention, imitating Monroe's and his mother's mannerisms and vocal qualities.

2. Settlage and Spielman (1975, p. 46) offer a similar formulation.

Monroe abandoned his withdrawal. He alternated between furiously attacking me with spit, bites, kicks, and punches, on the one hand, and desperate crying, on the other. Finally, with great venom, he loudly accused me of being crazy. I pointed out that Monroe's mother had been crazy when he lost her, and might still seem crazy to him. Moreover, her withdrawn state might often make Monroe feel crazy. He sobered, went to a doll representing a woman, undressed it and caressed it. Then he twisted its movable limbs so that they became hopelessly tangled. I interjected that Monroe's mother had become all mixed up. Monroe dressed the doll and again caressed it. "How you love your mother and want to care for her," I commented. Again Monroe began to cry, but this time, instead of hitting out, he hugged and kissed me.

In many of the ensuing sessions Monroe continued to hug and claw me while crying desperately. I in turn attempted to facilitate Monroe's expressing his emotions. I verbally elaborated on the persistence in Monroe of "bottled up" feelings, which originally had been evoked by his mother's disappearance, and were still aroused by her withdrawn state. I imitated Monroe's and his mother's manner of speaking to dramatize their mode of interacting: Monroe seeking; mother unable to respond; Monroe becoming frantic. After a period of intense crying, Monroe usually became calm and sat quietly for a time, often continuing his sobbing with a teacher. During this period other material emerged:

1. Monroe ran out of the classroom, as if to escape. However, he quickly ran back in, said he was scared, and sought refuge in the arms of one of the teachers. In response to my comments on how frightening it must be to live with his unresponsive mother—how often he must want to run away, and then how terrifying the prospect of being totally alone must become—Monroe volunteered a considerable amount of information about the baby whose birth had apparently precipitated his mother's breakdown. He said his mother had told him about, and had shown him pictures of, the baby. He described the hole in the baby's throat and told of his currently living with another family. In this interchange the concretistic quality of Monroe's thinking was not as evident. Invariably when he described matters which deeply engaged him, his thinking was less concretistic.

2. Monroe walked about aimlessly, seemed terribly sad, and said he was scared. He turned to me and pleadingly asked, "Who took my Mommy away?" To my question who he thought had done so, Monroe answered that he himself had. Then, extremely sad, he fetched a teacher's sweater and her apron. He went to a corner of the room, curled up on the floor, held them to his face, and sobbed. Relying on dramatization, I elaborated the idea that in his mother's absence, a child may try to hold onto things that belong to her, like her clothes. Perhaps Monroe had done so when his mother was away, and, to help tolerate her emotional absence, still did so. Monroe's crying became almost unbearably desperate. At times he literally clawed the walls. Several times he came to hug me, only to push me away as if I were not the person he was looking for. I commented that there are other people, but they do not easily replace the mother we love. Finally, tired from crying, Monroe hugged the teacher whose garments he had gathered. "It's so good to have a woman to hold and love," I said.

3. I took up Monroe's rejecting another child's efforts to befriend him in terms of his identification with his mother in her past and present rejection of him. He responded by asking who took care of him in her absence. I gave a completely factual answer to his question, feeling that such an answer would be the most helpful to Monroe's efforts to organize his experience (Buxbaum, 1954).

4. I related Monroe's crying at not gaining the attention of a teacher occupied with another child to the pain he felt when a person he loved was unavailable to him. He responded by crawling under my chair and declaring he wished to eat my feces. I then elaborated on the terrible drop in self-esteem and immense hunger Monroe felt when the person whose attention he was seeking was unavailable; on how lonely and hungry for his withdrawn mother Monroe must often feel. Next I used Monroe's wish to eat my feces to reconstruct that such a wish would have been a natural reaction on his part to the loss of his mother at the age of 2. Monroe emerged from beneath the chair and sobbed quietly while sitting on my lap.

5. I took up Monroe's ignoring me in terms of retaliation for my ignoring him while I was working with other children. Monroe fetched a set of keys from the teacher's desk and attempted to unlock the door to a closet. He claimed he was trying

to release his mother from the hospital. In response to my saying how much Monroe had missed her, he sat on my lap, sucking and biting my chest. Then smiling, he tenderly combed my hair. Understanding Monroe's actions in terms of displacement, I acknowledged Monroe's love for his mother and his wish to care for her. I also underscored that although she no longer was in the hospital, she still seemed very much locked up—not in an institution, as she had been, but within herself. How often Monroe must want to unlock the barrier that separates them and sink his teeth into her.

6. Monroe kicked me in the stomach while vehemently calling me a "fucker," in response to my having interpreted his obstreperousness as a defense against painful affect. I linked his outburst to rage at his mother for having left him to "fuck"—to have intercourse—and have the baby whose birth precipitated her breakdown. He furiously grabbed at my throat, thus enabling me to take up Monroe's rage toward the throat-damaged baby. Monroe sobered and became calm.

7. Seemingly in response to my having missed a week due to illness, Monroe again hit me in the stomach and called me "fucker." He also howled "Mommy" time and again while crying desperately. Again I acknowledged that Monroe understood that his mother's breakdown had been precipitated by the birth of his brother. I also pointed out that my own absence had aroused in Monroe feelings similar to those he had experienced when his mother was absent.

8. Monroe stared out of a window for a time, in an effort, he said, to find ambulances among cars he saw in the street. He then set himself to draw a face which he called "the Easter bunny monster." For the eyes, mouth, and nose, he drew holes. Asked to tell me about the drawing, he said the picture reminded him of his little brother and the hole in the latter's throat. He elaborated the similarity further with one of the teachers, after his time with me had ended.

Monroe's fixedness to a prephallic position was loosened considerably by this line of work. The four months during which it had been central were followed by nearly a month during which remarkably conflict-free phallic material and behavior were dominant. Monroe's despair and his obstreperous, provocative, sadomasochistic ways receded. They were replaced by his strutting about wearing a fireman's hat or an Indian headdress; demonstrating expertise in riding a tricycle; building handsome towers of blocks which he delighted in presenting to his teachers; proudly waving a flag at the end of a sizable stick; and lifting cardboard boxes by inserting the same stick into their handles. He often assumed a very "manly," responsible role in the nursery: he eagerly volunteered to do chores, such as serving food during snacktime, or cleaning up. Frequently, he assisted smaller or less able children. Once he stopped a fight involving two other children.

A clear yearning for a paternal figure he might love and admire—in whose strength he might participate—began to emerge. He frequently requested that we take walks and on these occasions displayed great skill in attracting the notice of the neighborhood "father figures." At the fire station, firemen patiently demonstrated their fire-fighting equipment to him. Construction workers similarly displayed their shovel-wielding techniques. A guard at a nearby museum we occasionally visited allowed himself to be placed under arrest by Monroe, who had dressed himself to look like Batman. Often, following an interaction in which his self-esteem had been raised by participation in the manly strength with which he had endowed me, Monroe made romantic overtures to one of the teachers. In addition to employing his impressive displays of phallic prowess to woo them, on one occasion he shyly presented a teacher with a necklace he had patiently constructed from beads and thread.

Then a shift in the material occurred. What had been an ebullient seeking of association with men to gain a feeling of strength became rigid, compelling, and clearly defensive in character. It became a means of escaping from closeness to women—in the nursery, from closeness to the teachers. When I became aware of this shift, I began to frustrate Monroe's desire to go into the neighborhood to seek men and focused on his need to take flight. Monroe's reaction was dramatic. Outbursts of chaotic ambivalence returned full force: hitting, throwing, spitting, and biting on the one hand, desperate clinging and crying on the other. He fell frequently, on occasion hurting himself. Once he threatened to jump from a balcony in the school's stairwell, and was convincing enough to cause the teacher accompanying him to become quite frightened.

The turn of events was, at first, puzzling. My focusing on Monroe's longing for a father to rescue him, and on guilt causing him to turn aggression against himself, as manifested by his suicidal gesture, was probably at least partially valid, but it seemed not truly to hit the mark. Finally, information conveyed by Monroe's therapeutic companion shed light on what was happening. His mother's condition had deteriorated. She had become even more inert and less involved with her children. This information was now made use of in working with Monroe, and care was taken that his home was visited weekly. (The therapeutic companion had missed a week, leading to the delay in my gaining this information.) A closer tie with the homemaker was established.

For the next two months, the further deterioration of his mother's condition was the main focus of my work with Monroe. His experience and expression of pain became more intense, but our work appeared to be effective in helping him to cope. I shall describe in detail three sessions from this period. They illustrate that despite the dreadful grimness of the situation, Monroe's grip on it actually improved.

1. Following a day when I had been absent, Monroe frenetically insisted that we leave the classroom and visit the fire station. Ms. Schnall, the head teacher, nonjudgmentally reported that prior to my arrival that morning, Monroe had been demanding all manner of food he knew he was not permitted and creating chaos when refused. As Ms. Schnall spoke, he became even more insistent that we go out. When I linked the behavior his teacher reported to his yearning for the emotional nourishment his mother's involvement might provide him, and which she now was even less able to give, Monroe became truly beside himself. He hit, bit, spit, and attempted to turn the classroom upside down. I caught him and placed him atop a closet where I could maintain him relatively immobile without actually sitting on him. Ms. Schnall now added that on the previous day Monroe had cried frequently and had asked for his mother. I commented that Monroe must also have missed me, whereupon Monroe broke down in a flood of tears. I verbalized how painful it was for

Monroe to live with a mother as unresponsive as his, and to be a whole day without a person, like myself, with whom Monroe was able to have good feelings. I also commented that if only his father were with the family, Monroe might gain some relief from his mother's emotional absence. For a time Monroe's crying did not decrease; then, perhaps as a result of fatigue and discharge, it abated, and he asked for a baby bottle. He spent the next half hour sucking on it, while cuddled on Ms. Schnall's lap.

2. This session, from the middle of this period, illustrates Monroe's increasing symbolic elaboration. He again began by requesting that we visit the fire station, but he was no longer frantic. I reiterated the importance of our staying in the classroom to work on issues we might otherwise avoid. Seemingly appreciating my position, Monroe began to play with a baby doll. He declared he was its mother, and alternated between affectionately bathing and caressing it and blandly throwing it about the room; carefully applying talcum powder to it, and bizarrely burying it in the powder. I wondered whether Monroe could trust his mother to care for him; not to hurt him; even not to kill him? Monroe, very serious, looked up and said, "Don't take my Mommy away." I focused on Monroe's fear that if he told me what his mother was like, this might well cause her to be taken away. I then linked these fears to Monroe's angry wishes to be rid of her, which his mother's withdrawn, frightening state aroused in him. Monroe walked about aimlessly for awhile. Then he wandered to where clothes used by the children as costumes were kept. He dressed in women's garments—a hat, high-heeled shoes, a shawl—but in such a way as to make himself look ridiculous, accentuating this appearance by the manner in which he carried himself. I interpreted that Monroe was conveying how mixed up his mother seemed to him. Again, Monroe dissolved into tears, and this time pleaded that I be his mother. While holding him, I elaborated on the pain of his situation.

3. The next session is taken from the latter part of this period. In what had by then become almost a ritual, Monroe began by requesting that we visit the fire station. My usual refusal, for the usual reasons, brought on demands for cookies and, when these were refused, another of Monroe's colossal storms of obstreperousness. Again, I contained him by placing him atop the closet.

While crying desperately, Monroe positioned himself on my shoulder, much as a baby being burped by his mother. As Monroe cried, he dribbled saliva down my back. I said he seemed like a baby, and asked him why he was crying. Through sobs Monroe answered, "I'm crying for my Mommy." He gradually calmed down as I focused on the baby feelings stimulated in him by his mother's worsened condition, then asked to get off the closet, and returned to ground level with the other children. Behaving more maturely, Monroe appeared to create a family of his own. He protected a smaller boy, whom he called his brother, from attack by a larger boy. Then he rested his head on a teacher's shoulder, and "jokingly" called her "Mommy." I verbalized his enactment and enumerated the terrible things that had happened to his own family. As I spoke, Monroe once again was unable to maintain his composure. He broke into tears and ran to raid the food cupboard. When he was prevented by a teacher, he furiously hurled everything he could lay his hands on at her. His fury, however, soon gave way to fear and then to a desperate affection, as he hugged and kissed her when she succeeded in holding him. He then hugged and kissed the other teacher, several of the children, and me. I reflected on how painfully empty within it makes a little boy feel to love his mother so, and have her to unable to return his love.

Presently new stresses burdened Monroe's beleaguered ego. The Cornerstone Therapeutic Nursery remains in operation 12 months a year. When summer came there were vacations and substitutions of the nursery's teaching staff. Ms. Balter announced she would be leaving permanently in early July. Despite these losses and changes, Monroe did not substantially deteriorate, though his dramatic storms recurred. Previous work clearly had provided him with an enhanced capacity to cope. Monroe had learned to use the nursery as a family which was fluctuant but generally reliable and enduring. He clearly came to understand that in it he could safely express and experience the agony within. As his affects remained accessible to his ego, mastery of his inner life continued.

A few days prior to my own one-month summer holiday, and about one month following Ms. Balter's departure, Monroe began a session by telling me explicitly that his mother had seemed very sad that day. He then played with a toy ambulance, aimlessly rolling it about. I verbalized both Monroe's sadness and his recurrent fear that his mother would again be hospitalized. Monroe responded by placing a toy sheep in a small rectangular wooden box, the lid of which he shut. The resemblance of the box to a coffin led me to take up Monroe's fear for both his own and his mother's life. Monroe began to cry softly, but he did not fall to pieces. He hugged and kissed two teachers; then sat quietly sucking a baby bottle and listening to a story. I commented only that Monroe was bearing his terrible situation better all the time.

In another session, just after the children had been informed of the nursery team's summer vacation schedule, I began working with Monroe while sitting on a wooden ladder laid horizontally between and bridging two climbing frames. Monroe ran under me, shouting, "Move your big butt!" I did not, instead suggesting to Monroe that we examine the ideas that emerged. Monroe responded by poking his head up into my buttocks. He said that he wished to pull down my trousers so that he could go into my "butt" and get my "doo." I stopped Monroe from undressing me, and with great formality indicated to Monroe that children of his age were able to use words in place of actions. I then drew a pair of large buttocks on the blackboard and offered him a board eraser in place of feces. Monroe refused it, insisting it stank.

To elicit more material, I went along with Monroe's maneuver. I cried pitiably at his refusal of my fecal gift, and loudly protested that Monroe did not care for me at all. Monroe, sensing victory, now refused my gift even more strenuously, declaring for all to hear that its stench was horrible. As my crying achieved "uncontrollable" intensity, Monroe ran behind Ms. Herzog, the teacher who had taken Ms. Balter's place, hugged her around the hips, and stuck his tongue out at me.

I commented that Monroe seemed to be saying he did not need my buttocks. Ms. Herzog's were softer, warmer, bigger, and in every way superior—more like his mother's. Ms. Herzog gently stroked Monroe's head and showed absolutely no sign of discomfort. I elaborated my understanding of what Monroe was communicating: Monroe was experiencing the coming vacation of the nursery's team, on the one hand, as an anal rejection of him, as if he were feces, causing him to try to "reenter" my anus, and, on the other, as a rejection at the anal level of his own gifts of love, of his fecal products. Moreover, he was defensively turning passive into active by becoming the rejector. I also linked this material to its roots in the anal phase of Monroe's development and to his mother's illness, which had occurred during that phase. Monroe listened quietly, his receptiveness greatly enhanced, I felt convinced, by his identification with his teacher's comfort with what was being said.

THE SECOND YEAR

When I returned from vacation, Monroe at first withdrew emotionally, but by the second day became angry, tearful, obstreperous, and difficult to manage. Several times he lost control of his urine in class, something he had not done for some time. However, within a week and a half, his behavior indicated that he had in fact not deteriorated in my absence, but rather was reacting to my return. The following session marked a turning point: Monroe was supplied with a fresh pair of trousers after he had urinated in his own. Embarrassed, he sat sullenly, staring straight ahead. When I sat next to him, he looked up and called me "stinky." I accepted Monroe's externalization, pretended to cry, and wailed that Monroe did not like me. No longer withdrawn, Monroe railed at me, insisting that he did not like my smelly feces, and inducing other children to join him. My pretending to be further driven to despair made Monroe wild with power. As was his wont, he proceeded to wreak havoc in the classroom, knocking furniture and toys about. I caught him and held on to him. I interpreted his having felt discarded like feces by me during my absence, and again related these feelings to similar ones he had when his mother was withdrawn and therefore absent. As I spoke—and dramatized to improve my communicativeness—Monroe broke into tears and cried terribly for some ten minutes. Seemingly spent, he became quiet. Then he fetched a stick and furiously tried to hit first me and then a child with it. When I again contained him and urged him to express himself verbally, Monroe asked to be taken to the toilet.

On the way he stumbled and had a painful fall down the stairs. I comforted him, and interpreted his rage at having been left, his guilt over his own aggression, and his turning this aggression against himself by hurting himself. Monroe hugged me and again cried pitiably, to which I responded by once more emphasizing how much Monroe had missed me.

After the toilet, at Monroe's request, we went outside and came upon a group of physically impressive workmen digging a large hole. Monroe looked longingly at them for some time. At intervals, he whispered to me that he wanted to handle one of their shovels. Finally, a workman noticed him, and Monroe had his wish fulfilled. As we walked back to the classroom, Monroe asked me to carry him, and again cried, this time softly and sadly. I verbalized Monroe's desperate longing for a man to help him feel strong and good about himself, and I related this longing to his having missed me.

Once Monroe's relationship with me had been reestablished, this session turned out to be the beginning of a period of progress, sustained throughout the year. Monroe achieved a level of functioning far superior to what had been possible for him previously. Soon after this session, it became commonplace for Monroe to strut about the classroom waving a flag; wearing masks he had cut out of paper, representing children's current superheroes; and imitating the shovel-wielding men at whom he had so movingly stared. It became especially commonplace for him to eat great quantities of food in an effort, he said, to make himself big; and insatiably to ask me to throw him in the air and catch him.

Monroe turned to women for support of his emerging phallic self. On one occasion when Ms. Solomon, the teacher who had permanently replaced Ms. Balter, failed to attend him, he impulsively kicked her in the face. Shocked and hurt, she responded first with anger, then with withdrawal. Monroe was shaken and frightened, until my verbalizing of what had happened helped his teacher regain her composure and again relate to her charge. Greatly relieved, Monroe hugged her and apologized. Then after sucking from the barrel of a toy gun, he delivered a dramatized rendition of Superman to his now attentive teacher. On other occasions, when women observers were present, Monroe cavorted exhibitionistically before them in ways that ranged from demonstrations of athletic prowess to ogling at them like a grossly undersized King Kong.

Sexual wishes manifested themselves in other ways: Monroe invented a way of making bow and arrows from plastic drinking straws, and affectionately shot these at the teachers and children. He delighted in my drawing a Valentine heart with an arrow through it, as an aid in interpreting the loving connotation of his activity, and also in my underscoring Monroe's getting people to "fall for him," as they often playfully did when hit by one of his arrows.

Monroe created family groups and situations, assigning roles of mother, father, and son to himself and to the adults and children whose participation he enlisted. For example, Monroe had been playing family with two other boys, assigning himself the role of "baby," to one of the boys the role of father, and to the other boy that of mother. When his turn came to work with me, he asked to visit the fire station, but stipulated that he and I be accompanied by Ms. Solomon. Monroe walked between us, holding hands with each, contentment on his face—an obvious continuation of his play with the boys. He proudly told us that his father was planning to buy him a tricycle. This was the first hint we had of his father's reappearance.

After a very successful visit to the fire station, Monroe set about digging for a "brown snake," which he said lived in the ground outside the classroom. He declared he wished to bite the snake, and also to keep and hide it. When it did not materialize, he angrily beat the ground with his spade. I suggested that he was searching for his father, the man with the brown penis, who was so hard to find. Monroe was serious for a time, then said he wished Ms. Solomon would come to live at his home. I interpreted that Monroe's thought might be: if Ms. Solomon lived at his home, his father might be persuaded to live there too. He must feel it was his mother's illness that had caused his father to leave. Monroe nodded sadly.

After some quiet contemplation, Monroe noted that Ms. Solomon, now with another boy, lacked a spade with which to dig. He lent her his. Then, almost manly in his demeanor, he demonstrated his prowess at running up and down a nearby hill. If

Monroe could not have his father, I interpreted, he could act in fatherly ways toward others.

At about midyear, Monroe scored 73 on an IQ test (WISC)— 20 points higher than on intake. As the year progressed, his intelligence appeared steadily to improve; he probably would have scored even higher by the end of the year, had it been possible to retest him. He displayed leadership qualities as he organized other children for dramatic play, or to hunt for insects and worms which after capturing he placed in paper cups. He exuded an air of competence and became so helpful with less able children and teachers, that he earned the title, "Dr. Monroe Macher." The classroom took on the quality of home for him. He even set himself the responsibility of keeping the grounds immediately outside of it free of debris. Late in the year, he conveyed a clear recognition of his parents' intellectual retardation. Wearing a mask he had cut from paper, Monroe enacted robbing a bank. He planned to use the money, he said, to buy food with which to fill his refrigerator. However, he planned to hide whatever money remained from his parents. He feared his mother would either burn it or wash it down the sink, and his father might leave it on the street where it could be stolen. I underscored Monroe's belief that he was the cleverest person in his family. He responded by hugging me affectionately, in clear appreciation of having been understood.

In the latter part of November, unexpectedly, Monroe's father emphatically entered the scene. By way of the therapeutic companion, we learned that he had come unannounced, without a word had taken Monroe and his brother with him, and had kept them at his home for the four-day Thanksgiving weekend.

The stay with his father truly moved Monroe. He described it with delight in the immediately following sessions, conveying affection for the woman who was living with his father and telling of outings the four of them had had together. Guilt over his pleasure soon intruded, however: Monroe began calling himself a "bad boy"; enacted a thief attempting to evade the police; took prohibited food from the cupboard, clearly in order to be caught at it; and once hurled himself headlong into a large garbage can. In the course of several sessions, I took up Monroe's guilt in terms of his feeling disloyal toward his mother for wanting to leave her and live with his father. Monroe met my attempts at first with protest and avoidance, but then with a kind of resigned, sad acceptance.[3]

A new spurt in the direction of positive development followed. During the next three weeks, Monroe showed a greater seriousness about his schoolwork and again made use of me (e.g., rides on my shoulders) as a fueling base for his phallic forays.

Then, as unexpectedly and unannounced as the first time, Monroe and his brother were once more taken by their father to spend time with him—this time for ten days, including Christmas. On this occasion, however, it was possible to elaborate his experience considerably, because material relating to it remained central for two months: Monroe talked of what had occurred at greater length than he had after his first visit. He described the appearance of his father's apartment and of the room he and his brother had slept in. He told of how kind the woman living with his father had been: she read bedtime stories, gave them medicine when he and his brother's tummies hurt, and cooked tasty meals for them. He told of the four of them having gone fishing. In class he rendered elaborate and sustained dramatizations of family groups and situations, enlisting both adults and children for the purpose—clearly efforts to re-create the familylike situation he had enjoyed with his father.

However, as had been true after his first stay with his father, Monroe's good feeling frequently gave way to painful affect and outbursts of crying. He often hurt himself by falling and mishandling toys. Repeatedly he would be overcome by a depressive mood. At the core of his pain was the conflict over his wish to leave his mother and be with his father. In one session he called me, in another, one of his teachers, "Mom." On each occasion, as if to escape, he then ran to the telephone and frantically but randomly dialed it, in an effort, he said, to reach his father. Each time, when there was no answer, Monroe lapsed into helpless crying, allowing me to put my understanding of what he was saying into words. I was also painfully moved by Monroe's enacting the part of my son, after he had disguised himself as Caucasian with the help of a mask he had cut out from paper.

Monroe's efforts to separate psychologically from his mother

---

3. Mannoni (1972) and Berger and Kennedy (1975) present similar material.

manifested themselves in another striking way. The final nine months of his treatment were marked by good progress interspersed with episodes in which he would call desperately for her—at times insisting that her hospitalization or even her death was imminent. Vomiting, complaints of stomachaches and head pains, painful minor accidents, and another threat to jump from the balcony on the stairwell outside the classroom accompanied his tears. However, no relationship between these episodes and his mother's actual condition could be discerned from home visits and interviews with her.

It dawned on the nursery team that the key to understanding these episodes lay in Monroe's concretistic mode of thinking, causing intensely experienced ideas to become confused with reality. Thenceforth I related these episodes interpretatively, not to Monroe's mother's imminent departure, but rather to Monroe's own efforts to detach himself psychologically from her both by functioning independently and by going beyond her inadequate mentation. In each instance my efforts were rewarded: Monroe regained his composure rather quickly and resumed his progressive development. For example, Monroe was carrying on in his all-too-familiar provacative, obstreperous, sadomasochistic manner in a session which followed one in which he had responded to an attractive female observer by being stimulated to ecstatic heights of phallic exhibitionism. When I focused on this shift in his material, Monroe sobered, turned to me, and said, "My brother killed my Mommy and sent her to the hospital." I verbalized Monroe's wish to be rid of his mother, especially after having been exposed to the visitor of the previous day, his guilt over this wish, and his displacing responsibility for it onto his brother. Monroe stopped and nodded sadly. He then engaged in a variety of activities, including instructing a boy with a tested IQ of more than 130 on how to make bow and arrows out of drinking straws; hugging a teacher and two children affectionately; and playing at being an Indian warrior battling imaginary adversaries on the nearby hill.

In early May, Ms. Solomon announced that she would be leaving the nursery within a month. Monroe's coping with her departure conveys something of the progress he had made. He acknowledged the fact and pain of it, and at the same time demonstrated a readiness to seek and accept substitutes. Initially, he responded by stuffing himself with food and by angrily shouting obscenities. Soon, however, a more complex response emerged. In one session, I attributed Monroe's being especially difficult with Ms. Solomon to her leaving. Monroe responded by hugging and kissing her and then by proposing that I marry her. I interpreted: "Since I was not leaving, if Ms. Solomon and I were married to one another, she would not be leaving either." Monroe developed a surprising variation on this theme in the following week. When his turn came to work with me, he hurled obscenities first at Ms. Schnall and then at me, but he ostentatiously ignored Ms. Solomon. When I became the target of Monroe's abuse, I gradually moved closer to Ms. Solomon in an attempt to undo the displacement. The strategy worked as Ms. Solomon soon became the unequivocal focus of Monroe's rage. Monroe loudly declared he hated her for leaving him. But when I interpreted the pain underlying Monroe's anger, he melted, cried, hugged his beloved teacher—and more! He proposed another solution. He would marry Ms. Solomon, and I would be his and his bride's child. Accepting this role, I focused on the dilemma small boys find themselves in. Because they are not able to marry, they repeatedly lose the women they love so dearly. Monroe sadly agreed, but that did not stop him from further elaborating his solution. He enacted being caring and affectionate to the family he had created and set up a home for it. He took me, as his son, for a walk, gave me money, and bought gifts for me. Finally, he built a handsome phallic structure of blocks for Ms. Solomon, his wife.

In a later session, Monroe submitted yet another solution. He had been withdrawn and in a melancholy mood, but intermittently he launched into angry verbal tirades against his teacher for leaving him. When I verbalized his grief and anger, Monroe stuffed rags under his shirt in the region of his chest and announced elatedly that he had breasts just as Ms. Solomon did. I focused on Monroe's identification with his soon-to-be-lost love object, and took the opportunity further to explicate Monroe's depleted state prior to treatment by stressing his earlier identification with his barely available, depleted, intellectually retarded mother.

On Ms. Solomon's last day, Monroe loudly proclaimed he

wanted nothing to do with her because she was leaving. Then the teacher who was to replace her entered the classroom for a visit. Monroe already knew her from several occasions on which she had substituted for a temporarily absent teacher. Ascertaining that Ms. Solomon was aware of him, he flamboyantly presented the new teacher with a plant he had taken from the windowsill. When I verbalized that though he was losing a person he loved, he was looking forward to a new relationship, Monroe became very sad. He placed a chair in front of a window, sat on it and stared into the distance. I focused on Monroe's not wanting to look into the room where Ms. Solomon would no longer be, and on his staring far away where she would shortly go. Monroe turned to Ms. Solomon, tried to smile, but, finding the effort beyond him, ran and enclosed himself in a large metal box. I did no more than put into words the pain of it all.

In the session that followed, Monroe openly and soberly verbalized how much he missed Ms. Solomon. Then in appreciation of love objects still present, he went around the room kissing each of the children, the teachers, and me. Smiling, he announced that he had "other friends."

Monroe's treatment ended shortly thereafter. In August, without warning, his mother moved with him and his brother to a rural area in the South to be with her own mother. A letter sent them by registered mail was received, but there was no reply. A half year later, however, another letter was sent, and this time there was a reply! Monroe's grandmother wrote, stating simply that the family was doing well. Perhaps more important, Monroe wrote back! In his letter he demonstrated that he could spell his first and last names and write the numbers from 1 to 20. Three and one half years later, just prior to publication, we reached Monroe's mother by phone and, through her, his school and teacher. Though she did not have a recent IQ score available, the latter said: "If you treated him, you must have cured him. He's a most wonderful, outgoing little boy. He talks like a cricket, and is most enthused about learning. Though he was placed in a learning disabilities class, and left back one grade, we're going to move him up to grade level. He's too smart to be left back. If he keeps up his enthusiasm, he should easily keep up." His mother, in a very lively voice, said that she and the children were "happier than ever" and doing well. She added that she had wanted to visit Cornerstone for some time, but had not had the money. Our hope that his grandmother and rural life—perhaps less stressful than the urban ghetto he left—would be good for Monroe and his mother, it seemed, was being fulfilled. The team also suspected that the move was a successful escape on the mother's part from her debilitating chemotherapy.

DISCUSSION

Contrary to what might all too easily have been assumed, Monroe's treatment established that he was not a child who had been catastrophically deprived and unalterably damaged by life with a mother whose personality had been profoundly impoverished throughout. Rather it showed him to be a child, living in the dismal conditions of a big-city slum (Meers, 1970, 1973, 1975), who in addition was impinged upon by three monumental interferences with his early development (Nagera, 1966): (1) at the age of 2, he lost his mother for nearly a year due to her psychosis; (2) then he was forced to live with the barely recognizable shell of her former self who returned to him; (3) on her return he lost his father and his paternal grandmother, leaving his heavily sedated, pitifully inert mother as sole caretaker.

The detachment, passivity, and flat affect he manifested on intake became clarified as states into which he had to withdraw in order to survive in the grimly unsupportive circumstances in which he lived (Kliman, 1977). Joffe and Sandler (1965), discussing detachment, the third of three phases described by Bowlby (1960) as children's reactions to prolonged separation from love objects (protest, despair, and detachment), aptly state:

> Whereas in the phase of despair we can discern a general inhibition of both id and ego functions, in the phase of detachment we can postulate a partial lifting of the generalized inhibition which is characteristic of the depressive response. This is made possible by a form of ego restriction, in particular a restriction of attention and a flattening of feelings. It shows itself in a devaluation of the unique affective importance of the mother or indeed of any object. The child settles, so to speak, for its actual state of the self. It is a type of resignation which can be

seen as an attempt to do away with the awareness of the discrepancy between actual self and ideal self, and in this sense it is a
form of adaptation which stands in contrast to the process of
mourning. . . . [It] is not an inherent response to a separation
experience but rather one fostered by deficiencies in the supporting environment . . . "detachment" may occur even in
situations where there is no actual separation, but rather
chronically inadequate mothering [p. 409f.].

The gross interferences which impinged on Monroe's development, in combination with his environment's failure to
compensate for them, caused the basic integrity of his very
young personality to be profoundly undermined. His ego became inundated and overwhelmed by diffuse anxiety, the pain
of narcissistic collapse, and unintegrated, unneutralized libidinal and aggressive strivings. It could do little more than capitu-
late and retreat into the dedifferentiated state into which it
did—one in which substantial detachment from his mother and
from the object world were central. The alternative surely would
have been even greater psychic disintegration and damage (A.
Freud, 1967; Kohut, 1971, 1977). For, stultifying of his capacity
for life though it was, Monroe's detached state also performed a
protective function. It acted to diminish, to dull, the amount of
stress his environment could inflict upon him.

In Cornerstone, Monroe's pathology began to reverse itself.
Efforts on the part of teachers and analyst to gain access to the
"person within" Monroe resulted in his forming increasingly
strong attachments to them. Nurtured, sustained, and enhanced
by interpretive work and by analytically informed acceptance,
these new ties began to provide him with the empathic, caring
objects of which his life was so starkly devoid. Detachment
began to lift. Aided by the presence of a supportive environment (Aichhorn, 1925), he began to reexperience his despair
and thereby to diminish it. As hopelessness lessened, for the first
time in more than one year, Monroe became able to protest, and
protest he did! Potentials for interacting with the world about
him (Erikson, 1950) were stirred from dormancy. Since he had
been so little exposed to the taming effects of participation in
social life for so long, their awakening was accompanied by repeated storms of intense affect (Fenichel, 1941; Rapaport, 1953).

Time and again Monroe ran rampant, made a shambles of the classroom, and became generally very difficult to control. But he had come to life! The beauty of his rebirth helped the nursery team to endure.

With Monroe's self revitalized, the social world (Erikson, 1950)—the world of love objects beyond that of his depleted mother—also became revitalized (A. Freud, 1951). Incentives to "improve his relationship" to it (Hartmann, 1939), to resume development (Aichhorn, 1925; A. Freud and Burlingham, 1943; A. Freud, 1960), were activated. For only by so doing could he hope to reside in this more vital world he was becoming increasingly aware of, and increasingly able to love.

Neurotic conflict, the pain of narcissistic injury—indeed, Monroe's whole inner world, largely inactive behind the wall of detachment—now became vividly reactivated (Meers, 1970, 1973). Kept consistently in contact with this revived inner world by therapy, Monroe's ego was stimulated to efforts to master its chaotic state. Thereby his ego also was stimulated to greater differentiation and development (A. Freud, 1936).

The treatment which Monroe underwent in Cornerstone can be thought of as having two distinct, though highly related foci: one, its basically nonanalytic, "upbringing," educational aspect; the other, its more specifically psychoanalytic aspect.

With regard to the nonanalytic aspect, it became commonplace for Monroe to use teachers, analyst, and children to create familylike situations and relationships, in an effort to compensate, however partially, for the terrible deficiencies of his home environment. Spurred and sustained by the teachers' and analyst's pride in him (Mannoni, 1972; Berger and Kennedy, 1975), Monroe strove to become more adept in the realms of language, cognition, and social interaction. He became, in a sense, "addicted" to his new love objects, nourished more and more preferentially through them, and increasingly reactive to them as objects for identification and as auxiliaries to his own ego functions.

This manner of using objects was substantially enhanced, we believe, by the concerned, nonjudgmental way in which teachers and analyst routinely discuss each child, right in the child's presence, immediately before and after the child works therapeutically with the analyst. These interchanges give the child, often for the first time in his or her life, an experience of being thought and cared about by two collaborating adults. Further, they promote verbalization and self-observation in the child by contributing to a group-supported atmosphere in which talking about one's feelings and about what motivates one's behavior is the accepted norm. The discussions, at the same time, give the analyst the advantage of broad knowledge about recent events or behavior and often about themes the child has been developing with one of the teachers immediately after or before working with the analyst. Never, in our experience, has a child objected to these discussions.

There are many values in the "teamness" of the therapy, not only for the children, but also for the analyst and teachers. The team members support and provide narcissistic supplies for one another. This helps counter the development of "burnout," emotional fatigue, and depletion, which are otherwise likely to occur when therapists deal for years with large numbers of depleted patients.

Finally, we would like to underscore a special feature of the Cornerstone method, one amply illustrated by this case. The analyst's interpretations, as they do in individual treatment, appear to release in the patient considerable quantities of libido and aggression. But instead of becoming available only for further analytic work, as these energies are in individual treatment, in Cornerstone they are provided with a therapeutically novel opportunity. They can immediately become employed in intense relating to the teachers and other children. These relationships, in turn, provide the child with myriad opportunities for sublimation and structure building, both in the social and in the cognitive realms (Rapaport, 1960; Lustman, 1970). The value of these opportunities for Monroe is strongly implied in the way in which he explored the environment in and around Cornerstone; took pride in and tended to its upkeep; charmingly and skillfully courted his teachers; constructed headdress, bow and arrows, and necklaces; and in the end vigorously asserted himself as rational, social, and dignified, rather than remaining the depleted, dull, unsocialized, almost "feral" child he started out as.

We are convinced, however, that the nonanalytic aspects of the

Cornerstone method could not by themselves have accounted for Monroe's coming to life in the way he did. Otherwise, the educational therapy offered him during the previous year, together with the provision of daycare, homemaker, and therapeutic companion, should have had more evident value than it did. In our opinion, the crucial difference lay in the analytic approach. Indeed, we believe it was the analytic work which permitted the nonanalytic aspects of the treatment to be effective at all.

Our reasoning is as follows. By the time Monroe began treatment the stress and deprivation to which he had been subjected had rendered his capacities to make use of empathic understanding and narcissistic supplies defensively inoperative. We mean by this that under ordinary, i.e., nonanalytic circumstances, Monroe could no longer "open up" to people. He could no longer benefit from people's affection, support, or generosity, however well intentioned. Analytic work was required to lift Monroe's pathogenic defenses so that his needs and capacities could again become operative and available to him. Once these were operative and available, analytic work was required to maintain them against persisting resistances, to permit working through.

Consistent with this view is the experience one of us gained in supervising Monroe's very dedicated educational therapist during the year prior to his entering Cornerstone. Two factors seemed central in the minimal impact educational therapy made on Monroe's pathology. One was the therapist's inability—unequipped as she was with the tools of analytic understanding—to deal, without herself withdrawing emotionally, with Monroe's primitive chaotic material. The other was educational therapy's inability as a method to cultivate and work through a transference illness.

A transference illness was, however, in our opinion, activated and cultivated in Monroe. His analytic treatment evoked in him a condition in which all of the basic elements of his previous pathogenic experiences and pathology were repeated, though in a form which was entirely new. From at least the age of 2, Monroe was chronically subjected to object loss and deprivation as a result of his caretaker's emotional withdrawals and absences.

These losses and deprivations were, in the treatment situation, replicated both in reality—though, of course, in highly muted forms—and, most importantly, in Monroe's imagination. In Cornerstone, however—in all likelihood for the first time in his life—on experiencing his desolate aloneness, Monroe was responded to in a consistently empathic way. This, in our view, made it possible for him to develop a transference illness in the only form he could—in the form of affect storms and intense, persistent crying, or at times in the form of violent, destructive, and near-suicidal behavior. The illness, in turn, was responded to neither with emotional withdrawal nor with efforts to tone it down. Rather, teachers and analyst worked to help Monroe tolerate, understand, and conquer it. They made themselves affectively and physically available to provide Monroe with a holding environment (Winnicott, 1965) that would enable him to express and experience his illness. Further, his transference illness was analytically interpreted to him, in order to help him gain insights into its topographic, economic, dynamic, genetic, and adaptive aspects.

As far as we know, Monroe's stormy behavior in Cornerstone was unprecedented in his life prior to treatment. We believe it had the quality of what Blos (1972) referred to as a latent infantile disorder, which for the neurotic patient is an infantile neurosis. According to Blos, this infantile disorder or illness is activated only by analysis, is a product of analysis, and is not to be equated with an actual preceding childhood illness. It is an iatrogenic illness, but one which seemed essential to accept and cultivate in order to help Monroe.

The view that his crying, storms of affect, and his pain placed a therapeutically unfruitful strain on his already all-too-fragile ego has been put forth by some who know our work with Monroe. In our view, however, the center of Monroe's pathology was not a precarious balance between ego and id which could easily be overthrown by a large influx of affect. Rather, we saw as central to it a psychic apparatus massively depleted of libidinal and aggressive energies. Amelioration was possible only through Monroe's suffering the pangs of love and hate aroused by the transference and "real object" ties fostered and maintained by the Cornerstone personnel and treatment situation. It is well to remember that Monroe's tearless shrieking of the early sessions turned into tearful crying only after he had become emotionally attached to the Cornerstone personnel. Thus, it was his ability to experience himself and others as more fully human that made the communicative, discharge, and self-soothing functions of tears relevant and active (Greenacre, 1965; Löfgren, 1966; Kliman, 1978). A related view has been put forth, that Monroe's affect storms and intense crying were little more than ways on his part to protest against the agonies being stirred in him by the analytic work. We regarded them, however, as indicative of re- vivals in the transference of past agonies, which earlier in his life had led to despair and detachment. They were consistently in- terpreted accordingly. Monroe's response to these interpreta- tions with steady improvement in his condition seems to lend support to our view.

We believe that the affective intensity which accompanied Monroe's crying actually had an enlivening effect on his psyche, and that its pain was more than compensated for by the positive experience it gave him in causing him to feel more alive. This is attested to by the fact that throughout Monroe made no pro- longed effort to avoid analytic work. He was generally enthusias- tic about his sessions with the analyst, usually clamoring loudly for his turn to come. He also produced ever more elaborate material in the course of his episodes of crying, which in turn permitted consistently more elaborate interpretations. A period of intense crying during a session with the analyst was usually followed by a period of calm, during which Monroe often cud- dled with one of the teachers, and his appearance took on a more "normal," affectively richer quality.

In this regard, it also was striking that we received no com- plaints from his mother, homemaker, or therapeutic companion about Monroe having become especially difficult to manage at home, as might be expected from his opening up in Cor- nerstone. On the contrary, his mother expressed being pleased by his greater liveliness. It is possible that Monroe's long experi- ence of living with a withdrawn mother had taught him to expect and demand very little from her. It is also possible that once his condition had improved, he knew better than to put extra pres- sure on her, and he turned to others or even to himself for comforting and gratification. We feel, however, that our understanding of the situation is too limited to permit us to make a confident formulation.

Interpretation as a therapeutic tool played a key role in Monroe's treatment throughout. At the beginning it was instrumental in setting therapy in motion by helping to overcome his resistances to relating and by helping to overcome his defensive flight taking. Dynamic, genetic, economic, as well as transference elements entered the interpretive work. Genetic reconstruction, especially of his mother's breakdown, was of great importance in helping Monroe to achieve increased mastery over the archaic affective chaos, narcissistic injury, and conflicts rooted in his chronic deprivation. It was of great importance in making explicit and thereby promoting his efforts to compensate for the gross deficiencies of his early environment, at the same time making more understandable the gross deficiencies of his current environment.

Nonverbal indicators—changes in affect and symbolic play—had to be relied on to a greater extent than is usually the case, to determine whether or not interpretations were reaching Monroe, given his initially limited intellectual and verbal capacities. During the first period in which the analyst heavily relied upon reconstructive interpretation, the extremely dramatic, affective discharge responses were considered the main indicator of its effectiveness. Monroe almost immediately changed from acting obstreperously in the service of maintaining emotional distance from objects or driving them into states of helplessness. Instead he became a boy experiencing profound pain, pain which motivated the very opposite kind of behavior. Instead of trying to keep distance from human objects, Monroe began turning to them in desperation, to gain comfort, affection, and support. At times the analyst could now infer the correctness of interpretations on the basis of Monroe's responses in symbolic play. For example, Monroe twisted a female doll's arms in every which way, in a "crazy" manner, in response to the analyst's interpretively linking his chaotic behavior in the classroom to his mother's formerly psychotic, currently withdrawn, "crazy" states. At other times the analyst inferred that Monroe understood his interpretation on the basis of affective responses. For example, following an interpretation Monroe might calm down and take on a sober appearance; or the opposite, he might become aroused or agitated as a result of affect released by the interpretation.

Modifications in the basic technique of child analysis were required by Monroe's pronounced tendency to defensive flight from intimacy, and by his stimulus-bound mode of thinking (Werner, 1940, 1957). The analyst's persistent, highly active, indeed stubbornly intrusive refusal to be "shut out" by Monroe (Radford, 1972); the analyst's relying heavily on dramatization to bring Monroe's material concretely to life; and the analyst's allowing, indeed encouraging Monroe to hug and claw at him as the inner chaos emerged—these were, in our opinion, of greatest importance as parameters.

The analyst's intense activity—which the context of the nursery classroom made less threatening than it might have been had he and Monroe been meeting in individual therapy (perhaps to them both)—was necessary in countering Monroe's overriding tendency to detachment. Without it, we believe, it would have been impossible to gain his attention and to involve him in a significant relationship. Monroe's detachment, like that of so many other pseudoretarded ghetto children, constituted a "Maginot line" of resistance which had to be circumvented, in part even overwhelmed, before he could utilize interpretations. The analyst's use of parameters such as initiation of play, employing dramatization, and accepting, at times even encouraging, physical contact are not unlike those used by many child analysts to reach psychotic or withdrawn children.

The high degree of dramatization employed by the analyst also helped to compensate for Monroe's concretistic thinking. It acted to provide a cognitive framework in which Monroe's emerging material could "fit," much as Goldstein's (1939) brain-damaged patients could conceive of a phenomenon such as rain only if it actually was raining. The dramatization also enhanced dialogue and gave boosts to Monroe's self-esteem. On the one hand, it provided him with relief, albeit at first only temporary, from his stultifying inability to communicate with other people—relief to which he reacted early with grateful elation (Freud, 1905) and increased responsivity. On the other hand, it provided him with the privilege of seeing his thoughts and ideas spur other people, adults and often children, into lively, fascinating enactments. In these, the existence and value of his inner life were graphically mirrored.

Finally, the analyst's physical availability in the classroom ten hours each week concretely diminished Monroe's sense of being alone and overwhelmed by inner chaos. It provided his over-taxed ego with the auxiliary it needed in the palpable way he needed it. Without it, we believe, mastery by means of repetition, interpretation, and working through could not have occurred. Though, at the end of two years, Monroe was clearly far from being a "normal" child, during no appreciable period in the time he was in Cornerstone did his functioning fail to show continual improvement.

In our approach we were fortified by our previous experience with detached and seemingly retarded blind children who appeared to be unlikely candidates for any form of psychoanalysis (Lopez, 1974) and by previous successful Cornerstone work with pseudoretarded ghetto children (Kliman, 1969, 1970) who ordinarily would not be treated analytically. We hope that this report will in turn fortify others who work with the far too many children in circumstances similar to Monroe's. We also hope it suggests the value of the Cornerstone method as an application of child analytic techniques integrated synergistically with therapeutic education.

BIBLIOGRAPHY

AICHHORN, A. (1925). *Wayward Youth.* New York: Viking Press, 1935.
BERGER, M. & KENNEDY, H. (1975), Pseudobackwardness in Children. *This Annual,* 30:279–306.
BLOS, P. (1972), The Epigenesis of the Adult Neurosis. *This Annual,* 27:106–135.
BOWLBY, J. (1960), Separation Anxiety. *Int. J. Psycho-Anal.,* 41:89–113.
BUXBAUM, E. (1954), Technique of Child Therapy. *This Annual,* 9:297–333.
EDGCUMBE, R. (1975), The Border Between Therapy and Education. In: *Studies in Child Psychoanalysis.* New Haven & London: Yale Univ. Press, pp. 133–148.
ERIKSON, E. H. (1950), *Childhood and Society.* New York: Norton.
FENICHEL, O. (1941), The Ego and the Affects. *Psychoanal. Rev.,* 28:47–60.

FREUD, A. (1936), The Ego and the Mechanisms of Defense. *W.*, 2.
———— (1951), An Experiment in Group Upbringing. *This Annual,* 6:127–168.
———— (1960), Discussion of Dr. John Bowlby's Paper. *This Annual,* 15:53–62.
———— (1967), Comments on Psychic Trauma. *W.*, 5:221–241.
———— & BURLINGHAM, D. (1943), *Infants Without Families. W.,* 3:543–681.
FREUD, S. (1905), Jokes and Their Relation to the Unconscious. *S.E.,* 8.
FURMAN, E. (1971), Some Thoughts on Reconstruction in Child Analysis. *This Annual,* 26:372–385.
GOLDSTEIN, K. (1939), *The Organism.* New York: American Book Company.
GREENACRE, P. (1965), On the Development and Function of Tears. In: *Emotional Growth,* 1:249–259. New York: Int. Univ. Press, 1971.
HARTMANN, H. (1939), *Ego Psychology and the Problem of Adaptation.* New York: Int. Univ. Press, 1958.
JOFFE, W. G. & SANDLER, J. (1965), Notes on Pain, Depression, and Individuation. *This Annual,* 20:394–424.
KENNEDY, H. (1971), Problems in Reconstruction in Child Analysis. *This Annual,* 26:386–402.
KLIMAN, G. W. (1968), *Psychological Emergencies of Childhood.* New York: Grune & Stratton.
———— (1969), The Cornerstone Method. Read at New York Society of Child Psychiatry.
———— (1970), Treatment of a Ghetto Preschooler with Drug-Addicted Parents. Read at Vulnerable Child Workshop, American Psychoanalytic Association, New York.
———— (1975), Analyst in the Nursery. *This Annual,* 30:477–510.
———— (1977), Psychoanalysis and Preventive Psychiatry. Read at Westchester Psychoanalytic Society, White Plains, N.Y.
———— (1978), Treatment of Vulnerable Preschoolers. Read at Vulnerable Child Workshop, American Psychoanalytic Association, New York.
KOHUT, H. (1971), *The Analysis of the Self.* New York: Int. Univ. Press.
———— (1977), *The Restoration of the Self.* New York: Int. Univ. Press.
KRIS, E. (1956), The Recovery of Childhood Memories in Psychoanalysis. *This Annual,* 11:54–88.
LÖFGREN, L. B. (1966), On Weeping. *Int. J. Psycho-Anal.,* 47:375–381.
LOPEZ, T. (1974), Psychotherapeutic Assistance to a Blind Boy with Limited Intelligence. *This Annual,* 29:277–300.
LUSTMAN, S. L. (1970), Cultural Deprivation. *This Annual,* 25:483–502.
MANNONI, M. (1972), *The Backward Child and His Mother.* New York: Pantheon Books.
MEERS, D. R. (1970), Contributions of a Ghetto Culture to Symptom Formation. *This Annual,* 25:209–230.
———— (1973), Psychoanalytic Research and Intellectual Functioning of Ghetto-Reared Black Children. *This Annual,* 28:395–418.
———— (1975), Precocious Heterosexuality and Masturbation. In: *Masturbation from Infancy to Senescence,* ed. I. M. Marcus & J. J. Francis. New York: Int. Univ. Press, pp. 411–438.

NAGERA, H. (1966), *Early Childhood Disturbances, the Infantile Neurosis, and the Adulthood Disturbances.* New York: Int. Univ. Press.

RAPAPORT, D. (1953), On the Psychoanalytic Theory of Affects. *Int. J. Psycho-Anal.,* 34:177–198.

——— (1960), On the Psychoanalytic Theory of Motivation. In: *Nebraska Symposium on Motivation,* ed. M. Jones. Lincoln: Univ. Nebraska Press, pp. 173–247.

RADFORD, P. (1972), Personal communication.

SETTLAGE, C. F. & SPIELMAN, P. M. (1975), On the Psychogenesis and Psychoanalytic Treatment of Primary Faulty Structural Development. *Association for Child Psychoanalysis: Summaries of Scientific Papers and Workshops,* 2:32-63.

STEIN, M. & RONALD, D. (1974), Educational Psychotherapy of Preschoolers. *J. Amer. Acad. Child Psychiat.,* 13:618–634.

VALENSTEIN, A. (1975), Comments in Scientific Meeting: The Analysis of (Nonpsychotic) Children with Structural Deviations. *Association for Child Psychoanalysis: Summaries of Scientific Papers and Workshops,* 2:32-63.

WEIL, A. P. (1973), Ego Strengthening Prior to Analysis. *This Annual,* 28:287-304.

WERNER, H. (1940), *Comparative Psychology of Mental Development.* New York: Int. Univ. Press, 1957.

——— (1957), The Concept of Development from a Comparative and Organismic Point of View. In: *The Concept of Development,* ed. D. B. Harris. Minneapolis: Univ. Minnesota Press, pp. 125–148.

WINNICOTT, D. W. (1965), *The Maturational Processes and the Facilitating Environment.* New York: Int. Univ. Press.

Adolescent Love and Self-Analysis as Contributors to Flaubert's Creativity

FRANCIS D. BAUDRY, M.D.

GENERALLY, THE EARLY WRITINGS OF A GREAT AUTHOR ARE APT TO reveal the intrusion of autobiographical aspects of his life much more clearly than the later, more polished works.

Flaubert's decision to become a writer and give up any attempt to compete in the real world may have been related in some way to a very moving, platonic love affair that had occurred at age 14. He first describes the details in thinly disguised form in a brief novelette, "Memoires d'un fou," written at age 17, some three years after the event (Flaubert, 1900). By that time Flaubert had already been introduced to sex. In studying his adolescent works prior to his first great novel, *L'Education sentimentale*, I was struck by the repeated occurrences of some aspect of his first love. Its unsuccessful resolution probably had much to do with Flaubert's turning away from a lasting real relationship with a woman. It is of interest to trace the vicissitudes of this experience—the ways in which it seemed to resonate with previously unresolved conflicts and contributed to Flaubert's choice of a literary career.

I plan to study the manifest content of Flaubert's adolescent writings in the hope of identifying and tracing various transformations and echoes of the platonic affair. This may permit the reconstruction of a hypothetical process of attempted working through of a conflict situation, interwoven with the development

Lecturer, New York Psychoanalytic Institute.

I am indebted to Dr. William Grossman for his many thoughtful suggestions.

of creativity. These writings span the period of 1835 to 1842, that is, the time when Flaubert was 14 to 21 years old.

My efforts will be directed, not at a literary analysis, but instead toward the examination of the many uses that an author may make of his artistic talents. It appears that Flaubert used his creativity as an aid to introspection, at least in adolescence. The converse is also true—that is, his attempts at introspection fed his creativity. This possibility was first suggested to me by the description of the method Flaubert attributes to the narrator in the "Memoires": "I will put down on paper everything that comes to mind—my ideas, my memories, my impression, dreams, fantasies—everything that goes on in my head and soul" (p. 230). These memoirs, consistent with the romantic theme of confession and self-revelation, include a moving document of the torments of an adolescent soul on the threshold of the discovery of love.

There is a difficulty in reconstructing the actual events inasmuch as the sources are mostly Flaubert's own writings. Other contemporaries allude in passing to one or another aspect. Most biographers, including the most scholarly, have taken Flaubert's description of the actual events I am about to detail at face value. In psychoanalytic terms, one might say that these events had psychic reality for the author. We can be reasonably sure about the broad outlines, as they are well described by his friends, such as Maxime du Camp (1892) in his *Souvenirs Litteraires* written in 1882.

Let us go back in fantasy to the lovely Trouville, a seaside town in the rich province of Normandy with its immense, flat, unencumbered beach and a rough-hewn fishing village cozily nestled against a hill surrounded by apple orchards and pastures. In the summer of 1836, at 14½, Flaubert chances upon a red coat while walking on the beautiful beach. He rescues it just in time from the rising tide. Later that day, at the pension where his family has been staying, a young woman thanks him profusely for having picked up her coat. He blushes in embarrassment, notices her beautiful, burning eyes, "looking at me like a sun"; without speaking to her, Flaubert is fascinated by her charm and falls under her spell. He notices her Greek nose, her fiery skin, and her magnificent shoulder-length hair.

The young woman's real name was Elisa Schlesinger. I shall

not be concerned with her real life beyond indicating that she was, or appeared to be, the wife of Maurice Schlesinger, a Prussian music publisher with a somewhat unsavory reputation. At the time Flaubert met her, she had an infant named Marie Adele, approximately 6 months old. Flaubert's virginal passion is stirred to greater heights as he sees the young mother fondle her infant and breast-feed her.

As the summer wears on, Flaubert becomes friendly with the couple, enjoys horseback rides with the husband, a warm and jovial man, who goes out of his way to bring back tempting melons from a neighboring village for the three to enjoy.

Another day, the trio goes rowing together across the Touques estuary, the river flowing into the Manche, and they briefly get caught in the strong tide. Like a true romantic, the adolescent boy spends hours daydreaming about the lovely Elisa—watching her bathing or walking on the lonely beach that still bears her footprints, and fantasizing that he is the clothing that encircles her lovely, full-breasted figure. He engages the husband in conversation, does errands for him, and strolls with the couple at night, taking leave of them at their lodgings. As the fall approaches, Flaubert bids adieu to Elisa and her husband; he is driven by his passion to have his first sexual experience. He loses his virginity as quickly as possible in the attic of his father's hospital with one of his mother's maids.

The French scholar Jean Bruneau, who wrote the definitive literary study of Flaubert's adolescent works (1962), believes that at the time of the incident Flaubert was not consciously aware of his love for Elisa. He bases this assertion in part on the assumption that there is no trace in Flaubert's writings of his love for Elisa until the "Memoires." I hope to demonstrate that fragments of the incident, its development, and its consequences do in fact appear, somewhat disguised, in the adolescent writings over the next two years. Most scholars agree that aspects of the adolescent passion are to be found in all of Flaubert's novels, whether in its erotic, passionate aspect as in *L'Education sentimentale*, or in its tender, ideal form as in the first part of *Madame Bovary* (Leon's platonic love for Emma or Justin's silent adoration), or in its guilt-arousing propensities as in *La Tentation de St. Antoine*.

It is safe to assume that if the incident with Elisa could convincingly be shown to have such a lasting presence in Flaubert's writings, the encounter must have lent itself to the expression of his own particular basic infantile conflicts and attachments, including a love for an idealized, unavailable maternal figure. The manifest story of the Elisa episode may well have served as a convenient screen for the expression of complicated unconscious fantasies.

In Flaubert's personal life, there is a marked break after the end of his adolescent period. Following a number of epileptic attacks in 1844, failures in his studies, and his continuing shyness with women, he made the conscious decision to withdraw from the world; he would no longer attempt to satisfy himself in "reality" but rather would seek a solution in the career of a writer.

Separation from the world, in part determined by his various failures, became the source of a literary technique. He writes to his mistress, Louise Colet,[1] in 1846:

> The one who is alive now and is me does nothing but contemplate the other who is dead. I have had two distinct lives; external events symbolized the end of the first and the beginning of the second. . . . My active, passionate, emotional life, full of contradictory movements and multiple feelings, ended at age 22. . . . Then, for my purposes, I divided the world and myself into two: on the one hand, things external, which should be colorful, diverse, harmonious, superb, and which I accept only as a spectacle to enjoy; on the other hand, things internal, which I compress to make as dense as possible [1:214].

His poetic persona was made up of equal parts of boredom and disdain, a studied indifference. "I have come to look upon the world as a show and to laugh at it" (September 1838). Finally he expresses a wish to defile and trample the sacred values, including women. He writes to his friend, Ernest, in December 1838, "Since you are no longer with me, you and Alfred, I analyze myself and others more. I dissect ceaselessly; I enjoy this

1. Since I was unable to procure English versions of the early works and the correspondence, the rather literal translations are mine. All letters are quoted from *Flaubert Correspondence*. Flaubert did have a stormy and extended liaison with a secondary romantic poetess, Louise Colet, for about a year (1846–47), and then again during most of the period of composition of *Madame Bovary* (1851–56).

especially when I come upon an element of corruption in something I generally considered pure and when I discover gangrene in 'nice' places, I raise my head and laugh. Well, I am convinced that vanity is the sole moving force and conscience is little more than internal vanity." As a concrete illustration of the above, he had written a year earlier (June 1837): "The most beautiful woman is hardly beautiful on the dissecting table of an amphitheater, with guts hanging in her nose, a leg cut open, and an unlit cigar resting on her feet. How sad analysis becomes . . . to understand the world only to find misfortunes" (1:25).

This use of "analysis" is of special interest to psychoanalysts, since its purpose seems to be to confirm a particular view of the world rather than to arrive at self-knowledge.

All of Flaubert's output will deal in some way with adolescence and his attempts to come to terms with his disillusionment. All the basic literary themes of Flaubert may be found in his adolescent writings. According to Bruneau, Flaubert has scantily utilized any events or memories beyond those of 1843–44. At that point, he had stopped living his own life to nourish his creations by his past life. All his characters are transpositions of the passionate and anxious youth prior to his becoming an artist. As Bruneau indicates, Flaubert "died" around 1844. The whole of his work brought him back to life.

THE YOUNG FLAUBERT

A few words about Flaubert's early history and psychological situation at age 14 are necessary as background material. He was the second son of a highly successful surgeon in Rouen, the capital of the province of Normandy. His mother was a constricted, controlling woman, yet self-effacing and absolutely devoted to her children and husband. She had several miscarriages and could not stand separation from Gustave. We are lucky in possessing some brief descriptions of Madame Flaubert by Gertrude Collier, a young English girl who met Flaubert the summer before the involvement with Elisa. She writes in her memoirs, "She was dark as a gypsy with melancholy black eyes and glossy hair and a face perfectly colorless, grand and solemn, she looked as if she had never smiled. She seemed to have had some great sorrow in her past and to be expecting some great sorrow to overtake her in the future" (quoted by Spencer, 1954, p. 103). Her firstborn son, Achille, became a surgeon. The future author was born 9 years later in December 1821, following the death of two children some time in their second year. A miscarriage preceded the birth of Caroline, 3 years younger than Gustave. She was the first love of his youth; she idealized him, and he was the overseer of her intellectual development.

Their correspondence, which lasted until her tragic death from puerperal fever a year after her marriage in 1845, is full of tender reminiscences and loving allusions to a shared past. He refers to her as his *raton* (little rat). Caroline, in a letter dated June 1845, writes from Paris shortly after her wedding, "Do you think in the morning of your Medor who came and jumped on your bed when you awakened and whom you condescended to consider a learned dog from 11:00 to 12:00 A.M. to explain Shakespeare to? . . . It [the dog] feels more and more like scratching on your door and playing on your bed, poor old fellow; how I long to see you again and how much I love to reflect on all the times we spent together all alone, away from everybody" (1:243). Flaubert answers with a long, chatty letter in which he says, "[Now that you are gone] I have no one I can strangle with both my hands, saying 'old rat,' old rat! . . . When you will be here again, if you like, we can start a play together. You will once again romp on my bed like the dog, and for my part, I will play the part of the nigger—'yessuh, I love missy, me love missy.' At times I feel a need to kiss your good ruddy cheeks—firm as seashells. The saying of a classical seventeenth-century author really applies to you, 'a sight lovely to behold—a pleasure for the eyes'" (1:142).

The flavor of such a letter hints at a lifelong intimacy of shared memories, including a physical closeness lasting well into Caroline's twentieth year. In 1842, around the time of Flaubert's withdrawal, he wrote her: "Oh rat, my good old rat, please be sure to have enough ruddy cheeks left for me because I am hungrily wanting to kiss them. . . . Assuredly, when I think of it, I won't be able to stop myself from hurting you a bit. Do you remember when my hearty *baisers de nourrice* [literally, kisses of a wet nurse] were so noisy that mother said, 'Leave her alone, this

poor child'; and you yourself, a bit overwhelmed and pushing me away with both hands, were saying, 'Oh, my good fellow!?'"
(1:140).

Flaubert's early years were spent in the gloomy surroundings of the hospital at Rouen. A number of early memories refer to frightening and exciting visual scenes of Gustave and Caroline watching their father through cracks in the hospital fence as he performed autopsies; they were fascinated by the vision of disemboweled women, with cigars between their toes and carrion flies buzzing around the table and landing on the children. Flaubert's intellectual development seemed to lag far behind; a late talker and a late reader, he would spend hours daydreaming and was rather shy, awkward, and very naïve: when he was 5, a servant could send him on an errand to the family kitchen asking the cook if the servant were to be found in the kitchen!

From age 10 to 18, he attended boarding school, for somewhat unclear reasons. Flaubert often felt alone, isolated, and withdrawn, adopting a cynical, superior stance toward his contemporaries, who teased him without mercy (see the first scene of *Madame Bovary*, which involves such an event). He developed very close friendships with three young men, who played a leading role in his career. It is not always clear whether his isolation and withdrawal were genuine or were part of a romantic image he was creating.

Unfortunately, we have little information about Flaubert's relation to his father; the traditional view has it that the two men were far apart and that Dr. Flaubert never appreciated his son. There is a contrast between the few mentions of his father in Flaubert's correspondence and the constant references to his sister. There is an even more puzzling paucity of comments about his death, in contrast to the clearly expressed reactions of grief following his beloved sister's death. One anecdote hints at why Flaubert may have quickly abandoned any attempt to share his writings with his father. Dr. Flaubert had fallen asleep shortly after his expectant son had started to read passages to him from one of his early novels, *La Tentation de Saint Antoine*. The father awoke and left the room without making any comments. On the other hand, Gustave occasionally accompanied his father on his rounds in the countryside in his calèche, as the famed surgeon visited farms and hamlets to minister to his ailing patients, receiving payment more often in vegetables and local produce than in money. Both Bruneau and Francis Steegmuller, who translated Flaubert's diary (to which I shall refer later), feel that the traditional view of father-son estrangement does violence to the real feelings Flaubert had for his father, as expressed in the portrait of Dr. Larivière in *Madame Bovary* and in some letters he wrote around the time of the father's death. The problem remains unresolved, as I see it.

Very quickly, Flaubert attempted to overcome disappointments by a retreat into his inner world, followed either by writing stories or by putting on playlets of his own invention. At times the plays were so graphic that the family had to put a stop to them—as on one occasion when they were very upset at the mimicry of a poor dilapidated hobo.

Flaubert's awakening sexuality found a frequent outlet in masturbation, described openly in his correspondence, and fantasies of an increasingly perverse, sadomasochistic character infiltrated his daydreams. The struggle against temptation of all sorts was to occupy many pages of and give the title to *La Tentation de Saint Antoine*. His correspondence during his fourteenth year, particularly that addressed to Alfred le Poittevin, is replete with various obscenities and allusions to all aspects of sexuality, particularly the theme of degradation of women.

It was around this time that the summer incident described in the early part of the paper took place.

THE LOVE TRANSFORMED: REALITY VERSUS FANTASY

In Flaubert's work, several related themes suggest that the writer attempted to integrate his adolescent passions. A comparison of some of the devices and underlying mechanisms in the several youthful stories permits us to discern a process of working through. Different types of short stories allow consideration of different aspects of the event and related fantasies. I shall treat the manifest content of the stories as thinly disguised elaborations or fantasies related to the summer incident. The justification for doing this lies in the formal aspects of these stories. Their style is typically adolescent; their tone is very personal, awkward, with rapid alternation between outbursts of lyricism, passionate confessions, and attempted philosophical discourse; the affect shifts between irony, cynicism, candor, and superficial bombastic pessimism. Obvious conflict is in evidence right on the surface.

I realize some of the theoretical pitfalls of such an approach—for example, the danger that inappropriate significance could be attributed to a feature whose presence might not reflect a psychological dynamic as much as the intrusion or contribution of a genre. I hope to show that the question has not an "either/or" answer but an "and" possibility; data derived from some understanding of the author's life and character traits will serve as additional guideposts along my interpretive path; I draw as few inferences as possible without giving some of the evidence to buttress my conclusions; since I primarily describe variations in manifest content, there will be no room for disagreement about the data. It is more difficult, however, to demonstrate the connections between one story and another in a dynamic sense. To do this in detail would require a delving into many additional factors about Flaubert's adolescent period in a depth that is not feasible in this paper, even if the data for such reconstruction were available. Nevertheless, I hope that the limitations of my method still leave room for some additional understanding of the literary process and its relation to the author's psychic reality.

I

At age 14, as early as 1835, that is, only one year prior to the incident at Trouville, Flaubert was already preoccupied with love, incest, and adultery, and certain repetitive themes recur in his various projects and notes. Although Bruneau takes considerable pains to trace the relationship of these projects to the readings, newspaper stories, and various genres with which young Flaubert was acquainted, the analyst is tempted to single out certain repetitive patterns and outcomes as having personal significance for the psychology of Flaubert, the other aspects studied by Bruneau acting very much in the fashion of a day residue for a dream.

A project written in 1835, entitled, "Two Loves and Two Coffins, Drama in Five Acts," illustrates the concerns of young Gustave. Only the bare outline exists. A young countess married to an older nobleman loves him much more than he loves her. She had rebuffed several potential lovers. One of them takes pity on her, loves her out of compassion, then really falls in love. She becomes aware of it and asks him to leave, but consents to keep him "as a friend." Another woman comes on the scene; jealous of the wife, she steals from her "everything she possesses," eventually putting arsenic in her milk. The countess dies. The "friend" kills the husband, who had denounced him as the poisoner, saying in so doing, "You are the culprit and I am the executioner."

Another fantastic tale dating from the end of 1835, entitled "The Bridge and the Tomb," also deals with the themes of unhappy love, revenge and mutilation of bodies, and temptation by the devil. Can we see in these repetitive themes of young women submitting to older men, loving their husbands more than they are loved, and secretly harboring a lover or friend who cannot possess them some personal preoccupation of Flaubert's? Some of the crudity in these barely sketched plots, not intended for publication, suggests that these early drafts represent a transformation of some barely disguised daydreams or masturbatory fantasies. (I shall return to this theme in my discussion of disturbances of creativity).

II

I now turn to the stories that followed the summer incident of 1836 and examine the basic motifs.

The first is a novelette in 10 chapters called "Un Rêve d'enfer" ("Dream from Inferno"), written in March 1837, some six months after the summer encounter. In the Prologue, a voice indicates that other men have complained about being weak and overcome by passion, but "this one will be strong and without passion." Duke Arthur of Almaroes is an alchemist, or appears to be one, even though he spends many hours in his laboratory with his fires out and the pages of his open books unturned. He is a cold man, unsmiling, an automaton, thinking without feeling. People are awed by this man whose parched lips seemed to open only upon the sight of blood, who exhales through his white teeth an odor of human flesh—a ghastly vampire. He is afflicted with a boredom that gnaws like a cancer and ends up by driving a man to suicide. He leaves humanity behind, feeling alone among his fellow creatures. He hopes that on his own he can have a life that mirrors his daydreams and fulfills his ideal vision of himself.

Satan then enters the scene, offering to help him. The two go for a walk on the empty beach, watching the stormy sea. Satan says threateningly that he will force him to love, to be happy. As Arthur complains that because he does not want anything he is bored, Satan replies, "Doesn't your body provide you with the pleasures available to men?" Arthur answers, "Human pleasures, I hold them in contempt." Satan: "But a woman?" Arthur: "Ah, I would strangle her in my arms, I would crush her with my kisses. I would kill her with my breath. Oh, I have nothing, you are right, I want nothing, I love nothing. And you, Satan, you would want my body—right?"Satan, having only a soul, desperately wants Arthur's body and asks him whether he would like a soul like that of other men—a fall from illusions to reality, madness, idiocy. A wager is then made between the two that Satan can make Arthur fall in love with a woman.

The scene now shifts to the lovely shepherdess Juliette, age 16 (Flaubert's age at the time he wrote the story). She is sad, dreamy, oppressed, wanting something uncertain, lost in the past, imagining that some devil's face might be grimacing behind her.

The Devil then appears to her and forces her to sit down with him on the flank of a white cow. Juliette is unable to struggle out of the Devil's grasp, overcome by a strange paralysis as the animal moans and groans, moving its head on the ground as if it were dying with pain. Satan tempts Juliette by describing Arthur as having exactly the same wishes and longings, "You love the sea, the shells, the moon, and your dream at night." As Juliette returns home and her frightened father comforts her, she goes to get a pail of milk, which turns out to be blood! The father attempts to kill Satan but fails. Juliette does not sleep that night but spends the whole time listening to the plaintive moan of her white cow, described as being locked in her stable, suffering and perhaps writhing in agony on her bedding, wet with sweat. In the morning the cow bears the mark of a fang on her neck.

As Juliette walks in a field, she suddenly becomes aware that in fantasy she has fallen in love with a stranger, "the devil incarnate, a lofty and poetic creature." She imagines love scenes with him. Eventually she meets him, looking at him with love, envy, and jealousy. She calls him by name, "begs him to listen." She runs after him, falls on her knees, and then lies on her back as if to die. She wants to tear her hair out, then moans softly with forced laughter. Her knees are scorched and bleeding, because she loves with a bursting, possessing, satanic love. This love is devouring her. It is mad, bounding, and exalted. She threatens to kill herself unless he returns the next day, but elicits only a contemptuous "I'll see you tomorrow."

Weeping, Juliette waits for the duke night and day, for four years. Her hair becomes white because "misfortune ages." She is pale and thin. Finally, she desperately attempts to infuse life into Arthur's loveless body. Frenzied, she tries one last effort—she jumps over the cliff. Satan admits defeat as Arthur's reaction to the sight of the cadaver washed up by the waves is "So what."

This story seems to be the first to develop in any length the theme of love—Juliette's longing is suspiciously similar to Flaubert's own longings of the past summer. In fact, it is possible to discern elements of Flaubert's internal conflicts in each of the characters as the youth struggles with the emerging passion. Does it seem farfetched to attribute his own desires for the woman to Satan's voice, struggling against ascetic narcissistic tendencies as represented by the duke? Finally, there is the desperate wish to love and be loved, expressed by Juliette. The fascination with the ideal love and the impossibility of attaining it, a typically Flaubertian theme, is fleshed out in less disguised fashion. The sadomasochistic, murderous fantasies of the primal scene and the devouring, cancerous, feared aspect of the woman and of himself are right on the surface and represented via the personage of Satan.

This story, then, could be seen from the point of view of an internal dialogue with himself, already suggesting a resolution of the conflict away from a real relationship, yet retaining a struggle with varying alternatives. Satan forcing himself on Juliette is a mirror of Arthur fearing he would strangle a girl with his kisses and very reminiscent of Flaubert's use of the same words in the correspondence with his sister. The comparison of

Arthur and Juliette in their search for an ideal, their suicidal tendencies, and their attempts to find a mate—a recurrent theme—suggests the basic bisexuality of Flaubert. Juliette's listening at night to her cow in the stable moaning and suffering, ending up with a fang mark, certainly suggests the primal scene theme—a recurrent motif in Flaubert.

The basic pessimism of the characters, particularly Arthur's, and his impermeability to human emotions, especially love, does not bode well for the author.

I have left out of this summary hints of earlier conflicts that are present in the novelette. Arthur also embodies many aspects of Flaubert's father's personality—cold, aloof, distant—and if we add the biographical fact that as a younger child Flaubert desperately wanted to be loved and admired by him, then Juliette in the story might also represent the feminine aspect of his relationship to his father.

If we accept Bruneau's thesis that Flaubert's initial reaction to Elisa was not sensual, then this story suggests that the summer incident gave impetus to the emerging sensuality, which had to be repressed partly because of its intensity, partly because of its frightening, sadomasochistic character. A note of caution is necessary before the conscious statements of a sadomasochistic nature in any story can be equated with similar elements in the author. It is conceivable that a story could contain such elements for other dynamic purposes—for example, the author may wish to shock the audience or to write something preposterous or to ward off some more threatening motif. Finally, the genre could be dictated by some current fad. Monsters and Satan were certainly frequent personages of Romantic literature, influenced by Goethe's *Faust.* However, in the case of Flaubert, the sadomasochistic tendencies are found in all of his works as a leitmotif and also are in evidence in his correspondence, which clearly was not written for publication. Hence, I feel I am on reasonably safe ground in attributing certain sadomasochistic fantasies of the narrator to the author as well.

That playing with some of these fantasies served a function of mastery is suggested in a letter to Louise Colet, July 7 and 8, 1853. After a passage in which he recalls the influence of the morgue, he writes: "Madness and debauchery are two things whose depths I have plumbed. . . . I shall never be (I hope) either a sadist or a madman. . . . I have toyed with madness and the fantastic as Mithridates with poison. Considerable pride gave me courage and I vanquished the foe by my persistent grappling and wrestling with it head-on" (3:266).

III

At around the same time (spring 1837), Flaubert was planning a brief historical drama, "Madame d'Ecouy." The outline of its plot was described by Bruneau (1962, p. 98f.). A baron is in love with Madame d'Ecouy, whose husband had died four years previously. Her son Arthur is in love with his mother's maid, Maria, who had been bought by his father. Arthur is waiting in the garden for a rendezvous with Maria at 10, not realizing that his mother has a rendezvous with her own lover at 9. In the ensuing confusion, Arthur mistakes his mother for Maria. A man suddenly appears. Arthur attacks him and asks what he wants; when he hears that the baron is his mother's lover, he kills him on the spot. When Maria appears a few minutes later, dressed in white, Arthur realizes his deed and says, "Oh, my God, I am damned."

The themes of adultery and mother-son incest were to preoccupy Flaubert his entire life. The date of "Madame d'Ecouy" would place it in contiguity with Flaubert's first sexual experience with the maid. This raises several questions. Was Flaubert living out some aspects of an unconscious fantasy—his life being the externalization of a story? Or was he attempting to express his unconscious fantasies, conflicts, and real experiences in his stories? It is also possible that there was no special relationship between the affair and his writing. It is possible for an author to model a story or several writings on some meaningful experience of his own for motives not connected directly with the incident in question, or connected only tangentially? This seems unlikely if the incident was sufficiently emotionally charged.

The connection between Elisa and the theme of maternal love will come up many times in the ensuing stories. Here I mention only that the name "Maria" chosen for the maid is the same as that chosen for the Maria of the "Memoires" and is also the name of Elisa's daughter. Moreover, Flaubert first chose this name for the heroine of *Madame Bovary* before settling on Emma.

In fairy tales a servant often represents an alter ego of a master. The sibling position of Maria also suggests the brother-sister incest which preoccupied Flaubert. The name Maria was connected with the Virgin Mary, who played an important role in Flaubert's life and novels. In a note on Flaubert's intimate notebooks, Steegmuller describes Flaubert's religious upbringing—a combination of freethinking and traditional French Catholicism. Gustave and Caroline were baptized, but whereas Caroline made her First Communion, there is no record of his having done so. Flaubert's early novels, *Madame Bovary* and of course *La Tentation de Saint Antoine*, are full of religious mysticism and pantheistic ecstasy (Steegmuller, p. 54).

IV

The next story to be considered, "Quidquid Volueris [Whatever You Wish]: Psychological Studies," was written in October 1837. The story, a 12-chapter novelette, is presented as a quasi daydream or fantasy of an insomniac, as the references to the author's nightmares in the opening sentence indicate, "Come to me, memories of my insomnia, dream of a poor deranged mind. [Flaubert's capacity to fantasize and be frightened of the results is well known and frequently commented on by him in his correspondence.] Come, all little devils, you who at night jump on my feet, run on my window panes, walk on the ceiling . . . and with your breath and green lips make the flame tremble and pale." Such is the author's introduction to the tale.

The story itself takes place in a chateau owned by the aunt of a desiccated scientist, Mr. Paul. It opens two weeks before the wedding of Mr. Paul to his cousin Adele, a beautiful, ethereal, romantic young woman. Paul is asked to tell of his trip to the tropics. Adele is described as loving (in this order) her swans, her monkeys, her birds, her squirrel, the flowers in the park, her beautiful books gilded on the edge, and Paul, her cousin and childhood friend. Flaubert presents Paul as a selfish bourgeois, embodying all the hated attributes of that class—calculating, shrewd, and materialistic, "taking advantage of a woman's love" as with a suit one wears for a while and discards along with worn-out feelings no longer in fashion. He has no use for literature. Before the story unfolds further, we are introduced to a half-human creature Paul had brought from the tropics, Djalioh, who glimpses on the sleeping Adele: "He wanted to say a word, but he said it so low, so fearfully, that it sounded more like a sigh." Djalioh has never spoken, and much is made of his silence: some thought him in a daydream, others saw him as melancholic. Flaubert has this to say about him: his physical appearance is half human, half bestial; his hands are strong, with nails bent crooked; his lips are big and reveal two rows of long white teeth similar to those of monkeys and blacks; his general demeanor is that of a young man seemingly born to die, "as these young trees which are broken and without leaves." "His heart is vast and immense like the sea—empty and alone—at times he would fall into a lethargic state, then his soul would shine through his body like the beautiful eyes of a woman behind a black veil. . . . He had loved no one because he felt such inner chaos of strange feelings and sensations. Poetry had taken the place of science."

We then see the wedding scene through the eyes of Djalioh, who is in the audience. Inflamed and angry, he is assailed by a memory of a funeral ceremony and is seized by a horrible thought as he glances at Adele's milky white bosom. He muses that one day a physician might discover that two inches below her décolleté, she had a hidden cancer and would die. Djalioh also wonders why the happiness he sees at the wedding has been refused him. As the procession goes by Djalioh, he digs his nails in Adele's gloved hand and blood drips.

Paul is then prevailed upon to regale the gathering with Djalioh's story. While Paul was in Brazil, a friend's slave had refused him her favors, so he had bought her. Bored one day, Paul had also bought a beautiful orangutan. Out of a wish for revenge, Paul had mated the two, and Djalioh had resulted from the ensuing pregnancy. The slave had died a few hours after giving birth. Paul had brought up the child, loving him as a father would his own son. Djalioh is then described as an idiot, afraid of sex, unable to read.

There follows a monologue in which Djalioh laments his fate. Why do women flee him when he smiles? Why is he so bored, and why does he hate himself so? He expresses a fantasy of abduction, ripping the clothes off the woman as he takes her far away to an exotic country.

Later that night as he struggles to get to sleep, he lingers on the joys of daydreaming, "and then in the shadows a friendly head appears—a mother, a friend, and all the ghosts sliding along the blackened wall." He alternates between his thoughts of Adele and her bare breasts. A savage laughter echoes in him, followed by images of Paul's smile and the kisses of his wife. He imagines their lovemaking as he wanders alone in the park through the night. He sees some swans and wishes to be one of them.

The next day Paul, Adele, and Djalioh go rowing together. Adele feeds some swans and each time she bends to drop bread, her hair and cheek barely touch Djalioh.

In the next section the author reflects, "I do not like monkeys and yet I am wrong, they seem an exact imitation of human nature. When I see such an animal, I believe I see myself in a deforming mirror—same feelings, same brutal appetites, a bit less pride—that's all." Adele had some monkeys and fed them nuts, and Flaubert adds that young women sometimes like monkeys, probably as symbols of their husbands.

In the final chapters, the couple and Djalioh have moved to Paris. It is two years later. A child 1 year old is sleeping in a carriage in the garden. Djalioh comes upon the sleeping child and suddenly seizes him, throws him with all his might on the grass, spattering his brain some 10 feet. He laughs in a cold and frightening way. He then goes inside the house, locks all doors, throwing the keys out the window. He approaches Adele, casting a devouring glance. He kisses her on the neck, pinching her as in a snakebite. Then he feels hopelessly rejected as the terrified Adele says she will call her husband, who will kill him. Somehow Adele senses that something may have happened to her child. Djalioh seizes her, kisses her, rapes her, and kills her without meaning to. He then runs head first against the chimney in a fit of passionate rage, falling motionless and bleeding on Adele's dead body. Mother and child are buried together.

If we take Flaubert's lead and consider the story as a disguised daydream, the plot is so transparent that one is puzzled by the lack of distortion of the oedipal fantasy and sibling rivalry, acted out in all their gory, sadistic aspects. The primal scene, the oral, cannibalistic impulses, and the guilt for them—leading to inhibition, low self-esteem, and passivity—are apparent. The responsibility resulting from the acting out of the sadistic impulses is subtly displaced onto Paul. After all, since he initiated the bizarre mating, he alone should shoulder the blame for the result, a bit like Victor Frankenstein in Mary Shelley's story. This is all on the surface. The formal elements, the devices by which the fantasies are transformed into a story, can also be described. The displacement to the monkeylike human being, with concomitant identification, and some of the more subtle symbolism of various elements of the oedipal theme are clear—with rowing and playing on the violin representing sexual activity. The identification also extends to the feeding of the swans, with the oral regression emphasized as a means of representation of the later fantasy. The theme of revenge and rejection by a woman predominates, as does the inability of man and woman to be happy, each pursuing a different dream.

The overt identification of the narrator with the monkey suggests that we might gain considerable insight into his psychological situation if we examine with care his description of the feeling state of the half-human being. First of all, Djalioh is half man, half beast, and his behavior expresses the constant irreducible contradiction between humanity and bestiality (the base instincts). An experiment in nature, he is born to experience suffering that will inevitably impel him to crime and suicide. His most characteristic quality is the impossibility of surviving. The child produced of a rape is driven to repeat the experience. Paul, the scientist, cold and aloof, is momentarily transformed into an orangutan, who, blind with rage, rapes the slave who rebuffed him. The woman is the helpless victim of man's lust.

The description of Djalioh's character is practically identical with that of the adolescent Flaubert. Particularly relevant are his inability to express his feelings in words and his tendency to daydream; his bisexuality ("his soul would shine ... like the beautiful eyes of a woman behind a black veil"); his never having loved a woman in spite of the violence of his passions; and, finally, his almost total isolation from those around him, who misunderstand and misjudge him. Also stressed is his belief that he is forbidden to taste and have women because of some fantasized unjust crime he is accused of, so that he can only witness the happiness of others and envy what he cannot share. The retreat into idiocy and stupidity is both a protection against the outbreak of sadistic strivings, an expression of inferiority in competition with real men, and finally a narcissistic retreat.

A note is necessary to account for the statement that Djalioh had "never . . . loved a woman, in spite of the violence of his passions," in the light of Flaubert's experience with Elisa. Does this mean that Flaubert, like Djalioh, had never loved a woman—that is, experienced tender feelings without the emergence of sadistic fantasies? Or perhaps that he had never been loved by a woman? Or that the experience of loving a woman was totally alien to Flaubert's profound narcissistic tendencies? The last point would confirm Bruneau's hypothesis that by this time—one year after the Elisa incident—Flaubert had not yet "discovered" his love.

If we compare the Djalioh story with "Un Rêve d'enfer" in terms of the characters Juliette-Adele, Arthur-Paul, and Satan-Djalioh, we can describe an evolution. It is as if Flaubert tried out another ending. What if the marriage had occurred, what then? But the contemplated marriage is, on the surface, not his own but rather that of the parental figures, who clearly make a mess of things. Happiness is for others. Djalioh-Flaubert can only love what he cannot have and destroy the very object of his passion; the theme of guilt is also introduced openly for the first time.

If we assume that Paul also represents an aspect of Flaubert, as indeed he might, the story becomes richer. Flaubert then tries out what marriage might be like. We know that Flaubert was deeply convinced that he could not make any woman happy, that he was far too selfish and unable to give of himself.

The theme of deception and of being the outsider was emphasized by another real event in the life of young Flaubert, occurring a few months before the composition of "Quidquid." During the winter of 1836–37, he visited the Chateau de Héron to attend a ball, which is described by Bruneau:

> As the dancing began, Flaubert, who never learned to dance, listened to the noise of the shoes as they slid over the waxed floor. . . . At three in the morning, there was a cotillion and then the older ladies went to their rooms. Eventually, miserable and angry, the boy took a candle and went to bed, the music

ringing in his ears and desire for one of the ladies coursing
through his body; he got up and looked out of the window;
eventually he dressed again and went for a walk in the park, his
shoes rustling amongst the leaves. Reaching the lake, he sat
down in a boat, paddled idly about looking at the swans, and at
last returned [p. 494].

After the encounter with Elisa, the episode seems to have exposed Flaubert to the luxury of nobility and beautiful women, a
world he idealized and from which he felt unjustly excluded.
The same ball scene will, of course, recur in the well-known
passage in *Madame Bovary*.

There are so many points of similarity between the Djalioh
story and the encounter with Elisa that I believe I am not over-
stepping the limits of credibility in seeing the story as a further
attempt to express the impact of the summer's events: (1) the
resemblance between Paul, Mr. Schlesinger, and Flaubert's
father; (2) the similarity between Adele and Elisa; (3) the theme
of refusal of favors (slave refuses Paul, Adele refuses Djalioh,
and in fantasy Elisa refuses Flaubert); (4) the most obvious
theme of revenge and envy; (5) some factual similarities in details of story—for example, rowing together.

According to Bruneau, at the time Flaubert wrote "Quidquid"
he was not yet consciously aware of his passion. If this is truly the
case, the underlying storm suggests that the passionate feelings
were not far beneath the surface and were finding an expression
in his creativity. It would not be the first time that Flaubert
discovered his own true feelings indirectly—that is, he needed to
write as a way of mirroring and giving reality to his inner world,
as a substitute for an external world that was experienced as alien
and threatening. It does not seem unreasonable to suggest that
this story gives shape to the connection between the love for Elisa
and its oedipal antecedents and defenses against them. The
Djalioh story also suggests the existence of intense rivalry with
the child born of the parental union, founded particularly on an
envious projective identification which will recur many times in
the theme of the adoration of the Virgin Mary suckling a child.
In clinical work, analysts know that surviving children often har-
bor the unconscious fantasy of having murdered the siblings
who died. Could this story give expression to such a theme?

Bruneau feels that until the "Memoires," written in 1838, there is no trace of Flaubert's passion to be found in his writings (p. 222). I believe he is able to make this claim because the evidence that he is looking for is probably too close to the manifest content of the episode, and he does not consider as clues the type of derivatives in the Djalioh story which are acceptable in the eyes of an analyst.

Of course, we lack sufficient data to be certain about the specific meanings which the story had for its author. I can only raise some of the questions that could be used as cautionary arguments against my assumptions. What is the emotional state in which Flaubert wrote the story? Some elements of the content—beasts, jungle—are, of course, part of the Romantic paraphernalia, but more evidence is needed to infer the sadomasochistic personal meaning. If Flaubert was not aware of his love for Elisa at the time he wrote the story, what could be the motive impelling him to write? It could not be the preconscious working out of the love. The creative person will, of course, borrow material from his unconscious fantasies (what else does one have to borrow from, if not from himself). This is not to say, however, that he does so for the purpose of discharge or working through; the latter implies an attempt to deal with unfinished business. Other motives might include a certain grandiose posturing or some narcissistic aim or self-aggrandizement or the wish to assume a cynical, sarcastic stance, or some competitive feelings toward another author.

The crudeness of the story may perhaps be related to derivatives of certain adolescent masturbation fantasies. This seems especially important in light of difficulties Flaubert experienced in writing. Writing was at times for him an agonizing process— torture. He refers to writing as the ejaculation of the soul. To the degree that creativity for him was sexualized, a relationship could exist between disturbances of his creativity, the vicissitudes of his sexuality, and his attempts to come to terms with it throughout his adolescence.

The uses Flaubert made of his creativity are often well spelled out in his correspondence. He attempted to analyze himself in order to master and control a situation he had endured passively, and to immortalize or recapture—through a reliving and identification with his creation—an event or emotion which was very dear to him. In an adolescent work composed at 15 "Un Parfum a sentir," Flaubert writes (section 12), "You perhaps do not know what pleasure it is to compose, to write; to write is to encompass the world, to take hold of its prejudices and sum them up in a book. It is also the process of feeling one's thought being born, growing up, living and raising itself up on its pedestal and remaining there always!" Thus, writing may serve an organizing function very much related to the formation of screen memories, allowing for processes of discharge, defense, and synthesis.

V

The next story, "Passion and Virtue," is a philosophical tale written some time in December 1837, two months after "Quidquid Volueris." It is headed by a quote from Shakespeare's *Romeo and Juliet*, "Thou canst not speak of that thou dost not feel" (act III, scene 3), spoken by Romeo to Friar Laurence, who is attempting to convince him that banishment is, after all, not a bad punishment when death is the only alternative. Could Flaubert have been applying the theme of banishment to himself in relation to Elisa? We recall that Juliette was the name of the heroine of the story "Un Rêve d'enfer." The possibility of a self-reproach may not be excluded as an alternate meaning.

The tale, inspired by an article published in the *Gazette des tribuneaux,* narrates the saga of an adulterous woman who commits suicide. The heroine, Mazza, a married woman, falls prey to the advances of Ernest, a Rodolphe-like individual. He decides to leave her forever after "one day in a transport of rage and delirium Mazza bit him in the breast and dug her nails in his throat." Seeing their passion result in flowing blood, Ernest understands that Mazza's passion is ferocious and terrible and that around her reigns a poisoned atmosphere that might eventually strangle and kill him. Her love is an active volcano that could crush him in its convulsions. The choice is between leaving forever or joining her in this "turmoil that drags you like a vertigo in this endless road of passion, which starts with a smile and ends only in a tomb."

One can hardly blame the poor fellow! In any case, Mazza, succumbing to her passion, eventually kills her husband and two children, finally poisoning herself when Ernest fails to return; she removes her clothes so as to be discovered naked by the police. The author's sympathy is clearly on her side, as his comments show.

The only indirect allusions to the summer's events are the description of Mazza's black eyes and Ernest's attempts early in the story to ingratiate himself with the husband, children, and domestics, going to visit his mistress every day. However, the story does give us a good basis for understanding why Flaubert could never allow himself to achieve any long-lasting intimacy with a woman.

Continuing the comparisons of the manifest content, we see that in this story the roles are reversed. The devouring sadistic monster is no longer Djalioh, or Satan as in "Un Rêve d'enfer," but the woman. The unacceptable parts of the author-narrator are then projected outward and reacted to phobically: I am not the one who is dangerous and destructive—she is; and I will attain safety by running away from her. The bisexuality inherent in Flaubert, evident from his frequent conscious statement of wanting to have the experience of being a woman, suggests that this particular mechanism of projection is also coupled with identification with the aggressor, for the murderous actions are taken by the woman rather than the man. Finally, the abandonment of the woman might also express the theme of revenge.

VI

Before I consider the next story, the major autobiographical work "Memoires d'un fou [madman]," it is necessary to call attention to another event in the life of the young Flaubert—his passionate friendship for Alfred le Poittevin, who introduced him to Rabelais and Sade. According to another biographer, Maurice Bardèche, Flaubert loved him with a passion that dwarfed his earlier love for Elisa. Alfred de Poittevin (5 years older than Gustave) and his sister Laure were childhood friends of the Flaubert family. For the first time, Gustave felt understood by an older male friend, who very likely replaced the father and older brother who were emotionally so removed.

The depth of Flaubert's attachment can be fathomed from two passages from his correspondence. In 1863, several years after Alfred's death, he wrote to Laure about Alfred: "How I loved him! I even believe that I never loved anyone, man or woman, as I loved him. I even experienced, when he married, a deep jealous sorrow, it was like a rupture, a tearing apart. For me he died twice" (5:72).

The other passage was written while Flaubert was accompanying his beloved sister and her husband (Emile Hamard, for whom he had the utmost contempt) on their honeymoon trip. "This afternoon while walking along the river, I recited to myself a piece starting with the line 'suddenly bounding with insane joy.'[2] I again was thinking about you in the arenas of Nîmes and under the arcades of the Pont du Gard; that is to say, in those places I longed for you with a strange lust: because when we are separated, there is something in us wandering, vague, incomplete" (1:165).

The relevance of this attachment is manifested in the personal dedication of the "Memoires," which details his adolescent love for his friend Poittevin. The great interest of the "Memoires," from our point of view, lies in the break in their composition, during which Flaubert took a fateful second trip to Trouville, which allowed him to crystallize or recapture the memory of his first love. Although the timetable of the composition of the "Memoires" is a bit confusing, most scholars agree that Flaubert met Elisa in 1836. He began composing the early part of the "Memoires" in 1838. He interrupted the writing for a period of three weeks, going back to Trouville, drawn to the locations of the events of the incident with Elisa.

The revisit was responsible for the bursting forth of his passion described in the "Memoires"; this section was written after the trip. Flaubert introduces the narrator's most personal reminiscences in a very moving and direct way, warning the reader that he will approach them with a feeling of religious veneration:

2. In the *Correspondence*, Bruneau supplies the complete stanza, which deals with girls passionately kissing the lips of their lovers amidst orgies.

"They are alive in my memory. . . . They created an eternal wound in my heart, but just upon embarking on this venture my heart quickens as though I were about to unearth loved ruins."

The work presents us with the most direct narrative version of the summer of 1836. It is divided into 23 short chapters, of which the tenth is entirely devoted to the adventure with Elisa, here given the name of "Maria." Very quickly the tenderness and veneration of the memory are soiled by the intrusion of a mocking, sarcastic, vivid description of savage, bestial intercourse between Maria and her husband. The narrator mocks the two lovers, "thinking perhaps that happiness is a crime and lust a shameful thing," in contrast to platonic love, which is sublime but just a dream, as is everything beautiful in the world! The narrator then apologizes for sullying and tarnishing these reminiscences, adding, "I thought a woman was an angel. Oh, how Molière was right to compare her to a soup!" A scene of breast-feeding follows. The narrator writes, "One day I witnessed her baring her bosom and offering the child the breast. Never had I seen a woman in the nude. Oh, the ecstasy that the sight of this breast plunged me into; I devoured it with my eyes. I would have so much wanted to touch it. It seemed to me that if I so much as touched it with my lips, my teeth would have bitten it with rage; and my heart melted in swoons as I thought of the sensuality of the kiss."

It is not clear, of course, how much of this scene actually took place and how much was imagined, and whether the fantasies were later editions retrospectively projected. The name Maria also reminds us of Elisa's daughter, whom Flaubert envied. The love of the two is then fused, reminiscent of the situation with his sister Caroline. The rowing scene which had caused him so much happiness is elaborated and followed by a dramatic break-through of sadistic fantasies. He writes of that evening: "She was there, close to me, I felt the contour of her shoulders and the touch of her dress." The adolescent's happiness is of short duration as he walks the couple back to their lodging. He leaves them, sees the light go out in their room:

> "She is sleeping," I told myself, and suddenly I was assailed by thoughts or rage and jealousy—"Oh, no, she isn't sleeping." I began to think of her husband, this common and jovial man,

and the most hideous visual images forced themselves on me. I was like those caged people condemned to starvation surrounded by banquets.[3] . . . This man only had to open his arms and she came to him effortlessly—without waiting she came to him. They made love and kissed. To him belonged all the joys and pleasures. To him, everything. To me, nothing. I began to laugh because jealousy inspired me with obscene and grotesque thoughts; then I would soil them both. I heaped on them the uttermost of scorn and ridicule and all these images that made me cry with envy; I tried to laugh and pity them.

The self-contempt and resulting abasement lead to the typical Madonna–prostitute split, and the narrator then recounts his first sexual experience, mirroring Flaubert's own, a purely carnal affair which leaves him empty and hateful. "I had guilty feelings, as though Maria's love were a religion which I had desecrated."

The narrator longs to regain his spiritual virginity: "Who will give me back all the things I lost?—my virginity, my dreams, my illusions—all these things wilted—poor flowers killed prematurely by the frost before their bloom." As he takes leave of Maria forever, he vows she will always have a place in his heart and recalls bitter fantasies of his own death. The narrator's bitterness and disapointment lead him to espouse a more pessimistic philosophy:

> You think you are free! From your birth on you are a victim of your father's shortcomings. You receive, along with life, the seeds of all your vices. . . . They will bring you up warning you against loving in a carnal way your mother and sister, even though you and all other men are the fruits of an incest, since the first man and the first woman were as their children, brother and sister. But first of all why were you born? Had you asked for it? Did they consult you? You were, therefore, born out of a fatality because your father came back one day from an orgy, his mind heated by wine and debauchery and your mother took advantage of this to arouse him. . . . No matter how great you are, you were first something as dirty as saliva and more fetid than wine.

---

3. At the wedding, Djalioh wonders why he is denied such happiness.

It is not surprising that throughout his life one of Flaubert's greatest dreads was of becoming a father.

The last three chapters of the "Memoires" describe the narrator's return to the site of his first love two years later. In a confessional mood, the narrator admits to having lied to the reader, as he is unable to recapture his past love. "How could she have seen I loved her since I did not love her then? In everything I told you up to now I lied. It was now that I loved her, that I wanted her, that alone on the banks, the woods, or the fields I created her—there, walking next to me, talking to me, looking at me. . . . I reconstructed in my heart all the scenes she played a part in. These memories became a passion." The narrator's capacity to re-create his love reaches hallucinatory intensity. One day while walking in a field, he falls into an altered state of consciousness. "The regular motion lulled me to sleep, so to speak. I thought I heard Maria walk near me. She held my arm and turned her head to look at me. . . . I knew very well this was a self-created hallucination, but I could not help smiling at it and I felt happy." It may well be that what Flaubert fell in love with was more the fantasized version of Elisa than the real person.

This capacity to utilize a real event, to project himself into it at a later time and give it an intensity that it did not originally have, is quite characteristic of Flaubert and forms a major component of his method of artistic creation. One gains the impression that in order to regain or even attain spiritual love, Flaubert had to divest himself of the sensual love for the real person whom he could not possess and substitute instead someone unreal—his own creation.

At the end of "Memoires," the narrator appears reconciled to establishing a quasi cult and special communication between himself and the idealized Maria. A last yearning to possess her in reality is quickly dispelled.

From a psychological point of view, we are left uncertain as to whether the "Memoires" should be taken at face value or whether the belated discovery of the narrator's love is not connected with a woman at all. It is possible that Maria-Elisa and love are united because of the plausibility and acceptability of such linkage, but that the real dynamic element is the budding love and passion for Alfred de Poittevin. The love for Elisa may have been resurrected as a screen for the more troublesome feelings. Much of the "Memoires" has the flavor of a wish to recapture youthful innocence long gone. The emergence of the love via a story also suggests a wish-fulfilling function. The return to Trouville and the discovery of the love could also serve in part to undo the youth's loneliness, and the story might then be a model for the resolution of Flaubert's conflict through writing rather than through a real relationship with a woman like Elisa.

One is somewhat uncertain about the insertion of the sadistic fantasies into the platonic love. Were they a later addition to justify the self-degradation and masochistic tendencies, or, as is likely, had they existed before the summer incident? Was it necessary for them to be indirectly expressed in the Djalioh story before the entire incident, somewhat divested of certain of its more unacceptable attributes, could find its way into Flaubert's creative output? Or, to put it another way, did the Djalioh story perform a cathartic function, an abreaction allowing the emergence of the past summer's incident?

One concrete aspect of the screening function might be illustrated via the scene of breast-feeding, which the narrator claims was the first time he was ever exposed consciously to a naked breast. We know from the correspondence that Flaubert was a witness to his father's autopsies and that he wrote earlier about the traumatic effect such a scene had on him, particularly when a naked woman was being dissected. In fact, Flaubert suffered from nightmares in which he was attacked by a group of men holding bleeding knives in their mouths. It is more than likely, then, that the view of naked women was very early connected with primitive sadomasochistic fantasies requiring considerable defensive walling off. It would be of interest to know whether Flaubert's sister Caroline was breast-fed and, if so, whether Flaubert ever witnessed such feeding. Bruneau suggested that Caroline was probably sent to a wet nurse, as was the custom in those days.

VII

"Smarh," a mystery play composed in 1839, again takes up the theme of temptation. The main characters are Satan, the hermit

Smarh, Yuk, and a woman. This is a hybrid work combing metaphysical questions about the meaning of life and very personal confessions of the yearning for love and the disillusionment in reality. Combining several forms, including dialogue, reflections, and a play within a play, it includes Flaubert's earliest attempt to work out his philosophy and his adolescent self-reflections, musings, and yearnings. It presages *Madame Bovary* and presents us with several voices, each representing a different aspect of the author's inner life.

The work is relatively long, over 100 pages. I present briefly the sections that are relevant to my theme—the evolution of his attitude toward love and women as it relates to the reworking of the Elisa theme.

Smarh, the narrator, is visited by Satan and an additional character, Yuk, who serves as a reflector, an expressor of Satan's views, and a somewhat grotesque figure in his own right. The character of a woman is presented as an almost faithful copy of Elisa and is dissected by Yuk, who describes her as "married to a good man, a bit on the stupid side, and the night of your honeymoon you had to teach him a few things that women know too well but pretend to ignore. . . . But you, in spite of having married, remained wise as the virgin . . . you have children resembling their mother."

Yuk, the grotesque god, serves as the tempter and goads her further: "You have had to compromise, you are disappointed in love, you have private fantasies of lascivious orgies, and every day you began to wonder when will it happen." He continues in the same vein to excite her: "Well, the first of these men you will see, perhaps a youth of about 16, blond and pink, who will blush under your gaze; take this child, bring him to your room, and there in the night you will see how he loves you and how much pleasure you will derive from this love. This will be the personification of your dreams and visions of angels." The woman answers, beside herself, "Let him come, let him come. Then how happy I will be. I was foolish to age without love. The voluptuousness of the most passionate nights will be mine." Yuk laughs as the woman runs off, and sarcastically he adds that here is a woman who before morning will have given herself to all the lads in town and all the farm varlets.

This passage might represent a wish-fulfilling fantasy of what could have happened, a rather typical, barely disguised, adolescent erotic daydream, working over the Djalioh theme of the sacrificed wife yearning for true love.

The poet-narrator contrasts the wild recesses of his orgiastic imagination with his inability to portray in his "castrated" language (his words) the bounding flights of his mind. He boasts that one day he will compose a page so lascivious and erotic that if it were pasted on walls, the walls would be in heat and men and women would have intercourse on the street like dogs and pigs.

In the final passage, Smarh, on the brink of spiritual death, sees an angel woman and believes he will be rescued by the power of eternal love. He is just about to reach out and touch her when Satan appears in a blinding flash and says, "Stop, Smarh, she is mine." Yuk—eternity—triumphs, and Smarh tumbles into nothingness.

This melodramatic plot, with its imaginary characters, illustrates the relentless course of the narrator away from a real relationship. The underlying fantasies and fears are clearly expressed behind the romantic excesses and traditional symbols; the failure of reality to measure up to the expectations of the poet is reaffirmed. The option of giving up the unattainable rather than exposing himself to further disillusionment and destruction is the only one remaining. The similarity between the narrator and the woman confirms the role of the latter as a narcissistic object; the ambivalent attitude toward the woman mirrors the narrator's intrapsychic split between a grandiose, idealized self and a degraded, dirty, castrated self.

There also are some hints as to the nature of the conflicts involving creativity—a fear of being drawn into an orgiastic abyss through the cult of daydreaming and writing. The sexualization of the process is complicated by loss of sense of self. In fact, the same dangers that embodied the adolescent passion are present here—fear of loss of control of his impulses and loss of boundary with the loved one. Spinning out some of the derivatives of this conflict will then constitute an important part of Flaubert's creativity. Writing, like women, fails to satisfy the author.

In using the term *narrator* to indicate the protagonist of the story, I have purposely left some ambiguity in not defining clearly the relationship with the author. Literary critics use the term *persona* to convey the image that the author uses to portray himself in a given work. The narrator is clearly related to the author, but in complex ways. The manifest content is a fantasy, just as the concept of self is a fantasy that needs to be analyzed. Thus, the narrator may represent the self, the ideal self, the observing self, or the repudiated self. Only a careful comparison of the narrator with what can reasonably be inferred about the author at the time he composed the story will furnish clues. In the case of Flaubert, multiple identifications prevail, and Smarh certainly represents directly an aspect of his psychological identity. The intellectual discussions about lofty metaphysical problems are very reminiscent of the intellectualization processes described by Anna Freud (1936) as typical of the adolescent's defensive organization.

VIII

Between July 1839 and June 1840, for almost a year, Flaubert wrote next to nothing. He describes in his correspondence his fears of losing himself in daydreams and the way in which he busied himself by making outlines. Did the dangers of unbridled imagination frighten him away, as is suggested above? The struggle between a lyricism that threatened to get out of control and a psychological realism keenly rooted in observation of the outside world persisted throughout Flaubert's life. The danger of losing control of himself and regressing into an autistic state was highlighted by an unusual perceptual sensitivity reaching hallucinatory proportions, and was reinforced in 1844 by the frightening onset of epileptic seizures—probably temporal lobe epilepsy—with visual aura.

Before considering this last youthful work, I will intersperse a few quotations from Flaubert's diary, a private memoir not meant for publication. Entitled *Souvenirs, notes et pensées intimes*, it was first published in 1965 and translated by Steegmuller in 1967 under the title *Intimate Notebooks, 1840–1841*.

The value of this work lies in its frank expression of some of the themes previously exposed by some of the characters in

Flaubert's works, thus allowing us to see more clearly the author's personal views and their transformations. First, a note on sensual pleasure: "Sensual pleasure is pleased with itself; it relishes itself like melancholy, both of them solitary enjoyments, all the more intense because in each case their subject is the same and their object themselves. Love, on the contrary, demands sharing. Sensual pleasure is selfish and deliberate and serious; such pleasures carried to the extreme are like orgasms of self-abuse; their self-contemplation and self-enjoyment are a kind of onanism of the heart" (p. 24). What the notebooks reveal particularly is the narcissistic aspect of Flaubert, his inability to love, and his search for the woman who by the strength of her love could liberate him and almost create him anew: "My heart is full of sonorous chords, melodies sweeter than those of heaven: A woman's finger would make them sing, vibrate—to melt together in a kiss, in a look—am I never to know anything of all that?" (p. 26). This narcissistic aspect is even more clearly revealed here: "Why is it that when we do not share the feelings of people we are talking with, we feel clumsy and embarrassed? I recently saw a man who told me that his brother was dying; he pressed my hand affectionately and I simply let him press it and as I left him, he gave a stupid laugh. . . . I was annoyed at once; that man humiliated me. He was full of a certain feeling and I was devoid of it. . . . I remember how I hated myself and found myself detestable at that moment" (p. 22). Flaubert's admiration of Sade is also clearly expressed, "You cannot resist the hypothesis of limitless mastery and magnificent power that he makes us dream of" (p. 27).

A last statement conveys the purpose and failure of art: "There is a rather stupid axiom which says that the word renders the thought—it would be more truthful to say that it distorts it; . . . I could tell you all my reveries and you will know nothing about them because there are no words to express them. Art is nothing but this strange translation of thought by form" (p. 50).

Flaubert's pessimistic philosophy finds its last statement in "Novembre," written in 1841, which marks the dividing line between the adolescent writings and the commitment to a literary career. "Novembre" holds many clues about the crucial choices made by the young Flaubert. Bruneau sees "Novembre" as symbolizing the failure of sensuality, just as the "Memoires" presented the failure of love. The work ends in the death of its protagonist, who has also failed to achieve success as a writer. It is an epitaph to a way of life. Psychologically, the story tries out one final solution to the problem of love. The story is told by a fictional narrator, who has found a manuscript, written in the first person, describing the life of the hero.

The work starts in the typical Romantic fashion, heralding somber times, "I love autumn—this sad season befits well the search for memories. When the trees are leafless . . . it is soothing to watch everything that once thrived in us gradually become extinguished." The hero imagines viewing his life as a "stroller through the catacombs." He then describes the development of his enthrallment with women; even in early adolescence, he was frightened and charmed by the glance of a woman.

The hero's fantasies are most stirred by the word "mistress"—stressing the power these women have over kings and emperors and artists. What the hero envies is the narcissistic state of power and being loved. Stirred by the illusion provided by actresses on stage, he is driven to search for a woman to love, who will serve as the object of his longings and fantasies. He is aware of the self-deception involved, a bit like a rebel in search of a cause. He fondly reminisces about his early awakening to love. "The puberty of the heart precedes that of the body; then I needed more love, sensuality. I can hardly imagine this love of first adolescence in which the senses are absent and infinity dominates; occurring between childhood and youth it signifies its transition and occurs so quickly it is forgotten."

The woman he imagines is more or less his double—love appears to be a self-love, enveloping, powerful, and destructive of the self, ending in a fusion with the other. Flaubert describes well the course of the hero's sensuality—from total disgust of women to the longing for pain and sadness, self-pity, and martyrdom including stigmata. A passage describing the hero's wish to be a woman admiring herself—naked, with hair streaming down to the ankles—heightens the sense of love as a narcissistic state. The search for the person to fulfill the ever-growing fantasies reminds one of Emma Bovary—states of longing are followed by moods of rage as the narrator feels unfulfilled. Only a great love can rescue him, unless death can give him a way out. The only relief from this pent-up state comes as the hero experiences ecstasies in nature, followed by reminiscences of his singing hymns at the foot of a Madonna and loving the Virgin Mary, as reflected in the image of her showing herself to sailors in a corner of the sky, holding the Christ Child in her arms. But the hero is pursued by the demon of the flesh and fascinated by a single word, "adultery": "a gentleness surrounds it, a magic aura, all the gestures one makes, sing it and comment on it, especially for the heart of the youth, he drinks of it to satiety."

The central episode concerns the encounter of the virginal hero with the prostitute Marie, a female counterpart to Don Juan. The story is modeled in part on a real event in Marseilles involving Eulalie Foucault, a French woman just back from Peru. As Bruneau remarks (p. 335), there are similarities in the first encounters with Marie and Maria. As in the "Memoires," the woman has a white, short-sleeved dress; both protagonists avert their glances, and then the description of the face follows, with the major difference being that Maria's ("Memoires") hair falls in tresses, whereas Marie's ("Novembre") hair is smooth and adheres to the temples. The sensual scene that follows ends somewhat like a section of "Un Rêve d'enfer." Marie asks the hero if he will return. He replies with a noncommittal "Perhaps." His reaction to this encounter is unsettling, a mixture of indefinable sadness, disgust, and satiety. The hero misses the virginal longing—"It was only that." He implies that all his beautiful reveries, daydreams, and boiling desires somehow should not have been "wasted" on such an experience.

As the story unfolds, the figure of Marie takes on heroic virginal proportions. She reminisces about her own adolescence, presaging Emma's youthful ecstasies in front of the statue of Christ. She confesses fantasies similar to those of the young Flaubert, a searching curiosity about the sexual life of men. "I watched my parents kissing each other and at night listened to the noises emanating from their chambers."

Again, an eagerness to find a man led to an attempt by Marie to seduce a young peasant, who became frightened and ran away. Finally, after her father's death, she and her mother moved and she was approached by an old woman who promised her wealth if she was willing to be the lover of an unknown person.

The intensity of Marie's longing, daydream, and frenzied excitement was equaled only by the depth of her despair as she met her master in a castle: he was elderly, toothless, arthritic, crotchety, and limping. Disgust overcame Marie's desperate attempt to love. She felt like a "castrated tiger." Eventually she was led to a life of debauchery, frenetically searching like the sailors in distress who drink seawater to attempt to quench their burning thirst. (During this period, the books she read included *Paul et Virginie,* one of Flaubert's favorites.)

Prostitution became another degradation, and Marie confesses that she feels like running away, back to her nurse in the village where she was born: "when I was small, I went to her and she gave me milk . . . oh, she would love me, I would lull the little children to sleep, how I would be happy!"

The hero recognizes the parallel course in both of their lives: "Without knowing each other—she in her prostitution and myself in my chastity—we followed the same road ending in the same impasse; while I was looking for a mistress, she was searching for a lover. She in the world and myself in my heart. Both eluded us." Marie then suggests the obvious—that the two disappointed youths join forces. After a brief passionate embrace, she becomes startled, "Oh, my God, what if I become pregnant?" Then, "Oh, yes, how that would be. . . . You are leaving, aren't you?" As he flees, the hero asks himself, "Did I love her already? We did not say good-bye. I never saw her again."

The hero's failure leads him to reminisce again and to do what amounts to rather penetrating psychological analysis. "The type of women all men seek is perhaps nothing more than the memory of a love conceived in heaven or during the first few days of life." Flaubert follows this passage with a personal reminiscence. "I once knew a youth who at 15 loved a young mother he had seen feeding her child—long afterward he only liked plump women—the beauty of thin women being abhorrent to him." As he searches deeper in himself, he recognizes his fear that he only loves a conception or fantasy, and that he loves in the woman only the capacity to evoke in himself the fantasy of love. Only several months after having left her did he begin to love her.

The wish to travel, to flee anywhere, follows naturally from these thoughts. At this point, the "manuscript" ends, and the pseudoauthor, who claims to have discovered the manuscript and who tells the story, brings the tale to a close. He writes in an ironical vein: "What a shame the manuscript stops before the hero enters the world; he could have taught us a lot, but instead he retreated into an austere unproductive loneliness. He stopped writing about himself, and I found nothing that revealed his true feelings beyond the time he stopped writing his confession." He turns from all solutions. "To want a married woman and for that purpose to befriend the husband, shake his hand, laugh at his jokes . . . is too humiliating."

He neither wants a prostitute nor wishes to seduce a young girl. He would have felt less guilty raping someone than making her dependent on him. "He thought seriously that there is less crime in killing a man than in making a child . . . because you are responsible for all his tears from cradle to tomb. . . . This is why he never married, had no mistresses; there remained widows. He did not think about that." (This passage is of interest because Flaubert spent all of his adulthood with his mother, widowed since 1845, the year of Flaubert's father's death.) The main protagonist is then described as sinking into drug addiction, a state between apathy and nightmares. Finally, as December comes about, he dies, but slowly, through the mere intensity of his thought, without any diseased organ.

The narrator is aware of the irrevocable split between the spiritual love and the sensual current. He has lost the former and is unsatisfied by the latter. The only remaining path is a regressive one—longing to be reunited with a nursing mother. The narrator has also come to the realization that what he loves in a woman is her capacity to evoke. She has no value in her own right as an independent person. Dependency on a woman is also to be shunned.

More than the failure of a relationship to a woman, "Novembre" presents a dissolution of a whole romantic belief in the search for absolute love. It took some additional external crises in the life of the author to resolve this apparently insoluble dilemma. However, the very attempt at describing the narrator's fear of failure as a person and a writer became the first really creative act, hence the solution to the conflict—that is, the description and sharing of the process of struggling.

Most of Flaubert's contemporaries to whom he showed this piece, including the Goncourt brothers, were visibly impressed. Here was the beginning of a truly great writer.

We have come a long way from the early stories, such as "Un Rêve d'enfer," to the penetrating psychological analysis of "Novembre," in which the narrator finally turns toward and reflects in a sobering mood on his failure to fulfill himself with a woman. There seems to be a thin line separating him from the author. Flaubert once wrote to his mistress, Louise Colet, that if she were to read "Novembre" carefully, she would surmise many things about him that were his intimate secrets. Could there be a connection between the development of creativity and the increased capacity for genuine self-observation?

Discussion

I shall briefly reconstruct the evolution of the themes I have described in the stories, sketching out a process of working through and some of its relation to the development of creativity.

The earliest stories, presented as bare outline or plots, show us the raw fantasies with minimal disguise. Themes of incest, adultery, and the inability of lovers to be united abound.

Following the encounter, the stories become richer. "Un Rêve d'enfer" openly describes in various voices aspects of an internal conflict—a cold, unsmiling, aloof, unfeeling man, torn between insatiable longings and daydreams and an empty reality. Love is equated with destruction and represented by Satan. Juliette, the innocent child victim, deeply in love, is driven to suicide by the duke's haughtiness and cruelty.

The next story amplifies the nature of the inhibition; the danger is not only that of unbridled destructive passion or that of an unresponsive partner but also of incest—a son mistakes his mother for his mistress in darkness. The themes of incest and rage are clearly acted out in "Quidquid Volueris." This story, then, describes the outcome of the expression of pent-up passion—death, infanticide, and suicide. The emergence of a sense of guilt fleshes out the understanding of the impossibility of attaining happiness. The barrier against the possibility of fulfilling one's dreams is strengthened. Multiple identifications enrich the themes. Not only is happiness impossible for internal reasons, but also the woman herself, presented as a mirror of the narrator, will never be satisfied in the marriage. The projection of the destructive rages onto the woman continues in "Passion and Virtue": Mazza is now the erupting volcano. Homosexuality can afford a refuge, and perhaps love of man for woman is an unrealizable fantasy. The split between real love and sensuality cannot be bridged; each follows a separate route. At this point creativity emerges. Since reality is so disappointing, perhaps dwelling on the memories of love will afford a safer solution. The multiple meanings of writing as a compensation emerge: a comfort, a justification, a sharing, a way of controlling, and finally of re-creating a reality more in line with certain wishes. As the writing and the accompanying recognition gradually increase, it becomes possible to diminish the involvement with the troublesome outside world. The unfulfilled fantasies, both sensual and tender, can find substitute outlets, in acceptable form.

"Smarh" seems to express more clearly the theme of revenge on the frustrating woman and the turning away from reality to writing and affecting an audience, but in ways that suggest the return of sexuality ("to compose a page so lascivious and erotic that if it were pasted on walls, the walls would be in heat and men and woman would have intercourse on the street like dogs and pigs").

The last two works, *Souvenirs* and "Novembre," reveal a deepening of the capacity for self-observation and an acceptance of the essentially narcissistic nature of love. Since love is so narcissistic, the external object recedes in importance and the author can search in himself. "Novembre" restates the failure of sensuality and reinforces the regressive pull (Marie the prostitute confesses that she wishes to run back to her nurse in the village she was born in). The psychological analysis of the author relegates the external world to an evocative role. The end of the "real life" seems to be the precondition for the emergence of the writer—a transformation.

Creativity, then, feeds on the author's willingness to share his disappointments and expose his failures. One cannot help but smile at the author's irony in despairing at the end of the "manuscript" prior to the hero's entrance into the world, when he stopped writing about himself.

CONCLUSION

I have attempted to sketch out the evolution of the impact of a platonic love affair as it is reflected in the manifest content of Flaubert's adolescent writings. I have tried to show a relationship between such evolution and an increasing self-awareness in Flaubert as to the meaning of the event for him and its ramifications in the past and in the present, which contributed to his decision to shun real relationships. Along the path I have followed, we have seen:

1. An early preoccupation with incest, murder, and sadomasochistic fantasies prior to the encounter.

2. The encounter itself.

3. The stirring up in puberty of an unresolved conflict between sensuality and loss of control (including loss of self) leading to alternation of orgiastic fantasies of rapes, incest, and suicide.

4. The increasing emergence in Flaubert, as epitomized in the narrators in the stories, of concern with his own narcissistic, grandiose self, and recognition of profound inferiority.

5. Various attempted solutions—idealization, prostitution, adultery—and their abandonment as elements in his life. (Tenderness and love did not emerge until more than two years after the incident and could be tolerated for only a very brief span of time.)

6. The erection and justification of a philosophy leading to withdrawal into an inner world, which became the source of future creativity.

Finally, much as in a therapeutic situation, Flaubert found his solution in the description of the process—in this instance, accepting his inner turmoil and writing about his understanding of it. His creativity and his introspection had converged.

BIBLIOGRAPHY

BARDÈCHE, M. (1974), *L'Oeuvre de Flaubert*. Evreux: les Sept Couleurs.
BRUNEAU, J. (1962), *Les Debuts litteraires de Gustave Flaubert*. Paris: Armand Colin.

CAMP, M. DU (1892), *Souvenirs litteraires.* Paris: Hachette.

FLAUBERT, G. (1900), Memoires d'un fou. In: *Oeuvres completes.* Paris: Edition du Seuil, 1964, pp. 229-247.

—————— (1910-24), Oeuvres de jeunesse, inedites. In: *Oeuvres completes,* 3 vols. Paris: Louis Conrad.

—————— (1926), *Flaubert Correspondence.* Pleiade Edition, ed. J. Bruneau. Paris: Louis Conard.

—————— (1965), *Intimate Notebooks, 1840-1841,* ed. & tr. F. Steegmuller. New York: Doubleday, 1967.

FREUD, A. (1936), The Ego and the Mechanisms of Defense. *W.,* 2.

SPENCER, P. (1954), New Light on Flaubert's Youth. *French Studies,* 8:62-64.

SPECIAL ARTICLE

Psychoanalysis and Academic Psychiatry—Bridges

ROBERT S. WALLERSTEIN, M.D.

PSYCHOANALYSIS AND PSYCHIATRY (ESPECIALLY ACADEMIC PSY-chiatry) have developed over the years an alliance that has been intimate but always problematic and uncertain, and periodically grossly troubled and strained. To call up just one statement (and any number of others would be equally possible and equally cogent) of the kinds of dilemmas that beset this relationship: on the one hand, psychiatry has been the source of the greatest part (and in America, of the overwhelming part) of the manpower recruited to psychoanalytic training and activity, as well as the locus of the greatest application of psychoanalytic knowledge both as basic psychological *theory* infusing and informing the conceptual framework of academic psychiatry under the banner of psychodynamics, and as central psychotherapeutic *technique* under the rubric of psychoanalytic or psychoanalytically oriented psychotherapy. On the other hand, psychoanalysis has always, most ambivalently, asserted itself ideologically and con-

Professor and Chairman, Department of Psychiatry, University of California at San Francisco, School of Medicine, and Director, Langley Porter Psychiatric Institute; Training and Supervising Analyst, San Francisco Psychoanalytic Institute.

Earlier versions of this paper have been presented, initially at the Southern California Psychiatric Society Symposium honoring Leo Rangell at San Diego, September 24, 1978; as the Richard B. Lower Memorial Lecture of the University of Pennsylvania Department of Psychiatry and the Philadelphia Psychoanalytic Society, Philadelphia, October 13, 1978; at the Seattle Psychoanalytic Society, October 12, 1979; and at the American Psychoanalytic Association, New York City, December 14, 1979.

ceptually as a discipline completely distinct from psychiatry (and having many nonpsychiatrists sharing fully in its work and its achievements), but also at the same time pragmatically and opportunistically as a heightened specialization of psychiatric education, entitled, via this organic linkage to psychiatry and thus to the central body of medicine as a discipline, to the many symbolic and tangible advantages of physicianhood.

My own long-time concerns with the nature of this relationship between psychoanalysis and (academic) psychiatry have of course been much more than academic. Like many psychoanalysts and psychiatrists of my generation who occupy (or have occupied) positions of influence in the psychoanalytic and the psychiatric worlds, my own career—and the justification of my career commitments—has been built precisely on this relationship, or this bridge, between psychoanalysis and academic psychiatry. It is this bridge which is, in fact, the intersect of my own professional preoccupations over a lifetime, as a psychoanalyst, as a psychotherapy researcher—an investigator into the process, the how and what, of change in psychotherapy—as a chief of a psychoanalytically grounded department of psychiatry in a community general hospital, and now as an academic psychiatrist, responsible for helping chart the destiny in the sense of the future, the very uncertain future, of psychiatry, of academic psychiatry, as a discipline in itself and as an enterprise within a separate hospital and psychiatric institute, a medical school, and a university. I say uncertain future because academic psychiatry is today in great flux and in a very self-conscious state of searching reappraisal of what it is about and what its proper place in the scheme of things should be.[1] It is central to the theme I will be developing that the currently unsettled relationship between psychoanalysis and academic psychiatry is a major representation of the uncertainty of destiny of academic psychiatry today, and that the reflective elaboration of a conceptually sound bridge or interface between psychoanalysis and academic psychiatry can exert a powerfully

1. Marked, for example, by the currently ongoing activity of a special Josiah Macy Jr. Foundation Commission on the Present Condition and the Future of Academic Psychiatry of which I am privileged to be a member.

clarifying and corrective pressure toward the resolution of the current flux of multiple indecisions within and about academic psychiatry.

To begin to develop my theme, I will have to interweave two main strands, the one something of the nature and the relevant history of American academic psychiatry and the other something of the nature and the relevant history of psychoanalysis as its focal power and scientific leadership was transplanted from its European origin and base to its new American homeland—and by relevant, in this context, I mean, of course, that which bears upon the shifting vicissitudes of the relationship between the two, psychoanalysis and academic psychiatry.

As is usual in psychoanalytic discourse, I begin with Freud, who actually wrote very little on issues of education and the educational enterprise per se. From the small number of his statements in this area, I will quote only his best-known, which touches, at least by implication, some of the roots of the array of issues that are my concern here. In *The Question of Lay Analysis,* Freud states his prescription, as of that time (1926), for the ideal curriculum for the new profession of psychoanalysis that he had single-handedly created:

> If—which may sound fantastic to-day—one had to found a *college of psycho-analysis,* much would have to be taught in it which is also taught by the medical faculty: alongside of depth-psychology, which would always remain the principal subject, there would be an introduction to biology, as much as possible of the science of sexual life, and familiarity with the symptomatology of psychiatry. On the other hand, analytic instruction would include branches of knowledge which are remote from medicine and which the doctor does not come across in his practice: the history of civilization, mythology, the psychology of religion and the science of literature. Unless he is well at home in these subjects, an analyst can make nothing of a large amount of his material. By way of compensation, the great mass of what is taught in medical schools is of no use to him for his purposes [that is, for the purposes of the clinical practice of psychoanalysis] [p. 246; my italics].
>
> [A few pages further on, Freud restated his prescriptive advice even more tersely,] A scheme of training for analysts has still to be created. It must include elements from the mental

sciences, from psychology, the history of civilization and
sociology, as well as from anatomy, biology and the study of
evolution [p. 252].

In these prescriptions of Freud's, more than a half century
ago, for what he considered the requisite or the best possible
training in the theory and practice of the new profession of
psychoanalysis we can discern implicitly, perhaps even explicitly,
Freud's views on the proper context for psychoanalysis, its
proper relationship to academic psychiatry and the medical
school, and even, though less clearly, its proper relationships to
the wider academic university world for which Freud always
yearned, in Walter Lippman's words, the university "that ancient
and universal company of scholars" (1966).

But this idealistic prescription for education and training in
psychoanalysis is a description neither of how psychoanalysis
started nor of what it could ever become, at least till now, in its
European homelands. Its origins and history in Europe are indeed broadly known, and it is something that I have written
about in considerably more detail (Wallerstein, 1974). Here I
only want to state the salient aspects of that historic unfolding in
grossly telescoped form in order to set the historical context for
the subsequent American developments. The elements that I
single out are: (1) the gradual spread of the psychoanalytic idea
through the educated and intellectual strata of European society
with at the same time bitter and often scornful opposition to that
idea both within the general medical practitioner community
and also within the academic university medical community with
its attached teaching hospitals and clinics; (2) the clinical growth
of psychoanalysis in the first instance from the outpatient con-
sulting room practices of neurologists (like Freud and his hand-
ful of early medical followers), dealing with the mass of neurotic
patients, prototypically the hysterical (Freud's first psychological
clinical work was *Studies on Hysteria*)—hysterical patients who at
that time were the special province originally of the neurologist
concerned with differential diagnostic distinctions between organically and psychogenically based disorders of the motor and
sensory apparatuses; (3) the very secondary and far more limited
inroads of psychoanalysis into the understanding of the psychotic and organic patients who were in turn then the special

province of the psychiatrists, caught up in the organically and descriptively centered tradition led by Freud's great contemporary, Kraepelin;[2] (4) the development out of all this of psychoanalysis as an essentially private practice and self-sufficient clinical enterprise that never had the academic entrée and entitlement into either the medical school, as a branch of the healing arts, or, through it, to the university more broadly, as a system of thought, an entrée to which Freud lifelong aspired and in which he was lifelong disappointed; and (5) the need for psychoanalysis to create its own scientific and academic structure, the concept which thus arose of the independent psychoanalytic institute, the original vehicle for psychoanalytic scholarship and training, which can be viewed, both in Europe and in America where likewise it took root and flourished, both from the standpoint of its accomplishments—in the rich propagation of the psychoanalytic idea and in the thorough training of its bearers in which the independent institute has been so successful even under adverse circumstances—and, at the same time, in the limitations and constraints of those adverse circumstances, the pursuit of a major intellectual-educational enterprise as a night school carried on the tired energies of part-time men and women after daytimes of full-time practice.

Such are the highlights of the historical development of psychoanalysis in its European homelands where it had no place, and for several generations actually never won a place, never really penetrated into the medical schools or into academic psychiatry, which remained firmly planted in the organicist and nosologically descriptive world of Kraepelin and his followers. In effect, in Europe, bridges between psychoanalysis, as a quintessentially psychological understanding of the mind and the behavior of man, and academic psychiatry, as an organically conceived effort to understand the functioning (and malfunctioning) of the brain (and the behaviors and misbehaviors linked thereto) via biological mechanisms exactly analogous to those that were beginning to achieve such stunning success in the

2. This inroad into the sphere of the psychotic patient came in the first instance with the adhesion of Bleuler and Jung and their colleagues at the Burghölzli Sanitarium in Switzerland to psychoanalysis.

understanding of the functioning and malfunctioning of the body—bridges between these two enterprises did not for a long time exist, and could not in that historic-social context to which I have been referring be built. And in fact, despite the several generations' headstart of psychoanalysis in Europe over its development in America, it is only in the most recent years—quite a while after it was a commonplace in America—that, in Europe, avowed psychoanalysts could become professors in medical schools and directors in psychiatric clinical centers.

In overall summary, and this is my main point, for various reasons of historical and social context, and with whatever degree of credit or blame we wish to attribute to the defensive responses of Freud and his followers or to the hostile reactions of an unreceptive academic and intellectual milieu, fearful of the Freudian idea, however we wish to parcel out the responsibility for the developing state of affairs, the fact is that psychoanalysis in Europe essentially grew up outside of psychiatry, of medicine, and of academia.

By contrast, the relationship between psychoanalysis and psychiatry (including academic psychiatry) has almost from the beginning been sharply different in America than in Europe and this has played, I think, its major role in the differing initial conceptualization in America of the overall nature of the (academic) psychiatric enterprise, a conceptualization which now, in reverse flow, is developing and picking up momentum in Europe and around the world as well. I should insert the caveat that I am not completely sure of all my historical grounds, especially of whether it was the role of psychoanalysis itself in its transplantation to America and in its penetration into American psychiatry which importantly influenced or even to a major extent determined the way in which the clinical and the academic psychiatric enterprise have been delineated in America, or whether, conversely, it was the nature of the conceptualization of psychiatry in America that made it such a receptive soil for the implantation of the psychoanalytic viewpoint in its very midst— in such marked contrast to the European development. Such questions usually are not susceptible to either-or explanations, but rather are resolved into studies of propitious interactions between powerful ideas, receptive (because prepared) soils, and fortuitous timing, with idea and soil and timing each conjoining in some measure from both sides of the interaction.

What, then, is this conception of the nature of the academic psychiatric enterprise in its peculiarly American stamp that makes for such productive bridge building with psychoanalysis? Psychiatry, like all the branches of the healing arts, is of course a *clinical* discipline dedicated to the amelioration of human disease and distress, in this instance, that caused by mental and emotional conflict and illness. And like all clinical healing disciplines, psychiatry as a branch of scientific medicine rests on and is the clinical application of a base of knowledge in the preclinical or so-called basic science realms, the clinical application of this basic science knowledge in relation to the ills and distresses of the variety of patients within its purview. This preclinical knowledge base for psychiatry is clearly in *three* realms, biological science, psychological science, and social science, since man is a biological animal individually thinking and functioning within a socially organized and constrained setting, and it is the task of clinical psychiatry, of the psychiatric clinician, to integrate the data and the organizing concepts from each of these three knowledge realms into the total understanding of the functioning and malfunctioning of the individual patient in distress and then to translate that comprehensive understanding into ameliorative effort directed toward remediation and change within any or each of these realms as appropriate. This psychiatry, at its best, encompasses the understanding of the mental and emotional conflicts and illnesses of human beings over their entire unfolding life-span, from infancy through old age.

Perhaps I should digress for a moment to state the truism that in theory this characterization of psychiatry as an applied clinical science resting on integrated data and conceptualizations from the *three* coordinate basic science realms is *in principle* not different from that of any of the other medical disciplines (each with their different arenas of clinical application), and the present renewed and intensified concern with the teaching to medical students of the psychosocial aspects of health and disease, especially to those headed for the various primary care or generalist areas covering the span of children, adolescents, and adults, and the families in which they grow up (to which I shall come back in more detail) is but one current expression (among others to which I shall also come back) of that conception. The difference is that in the medical and surgical specialty areas, the data and conceptualizations from the biological basic science realm for the most part have fundamental primacy (with modification, of course, with the so-called psychosomatic diseases) and for the most part the psychosocial data and conceptualizations, though useful and even necessary, can be only secondarily or less immediately vital. To give a trivial example, the first urgent order of business with the victim of lobar pneumonia and complicating pneumococcal meningitis is the institution of proper life-restoring antibiotic therapy and life-supporting physiological reequilibration, and it becomes then a secondary concern, but one that of course need also be addressed when the life-threatening acute illness is conquered, that the pneumococcal infection, pneumonia, and meningitis developed in the setting of chronic deteriorating alcoholism, inclement weather and despairing exposure.

To come back to my main point about what distinguishes psychiatry among the various disciplines in medicine: the data and conceptualizations from the three knowledge base realms are more *coequal* in importance, in psychiatry, a tripod with three more equal legs, though these vary of course in emphasis with each specific clinical instance. Corollary to all of this is the statement that more than any other clinical discipline or branch of the healing arts, psychiatry is a boundary discipline living on the understanding and the integration of its three interfaces, into the biological, the psychological, and the social science realms with an overall concern across all of these for the processes of human development. In this sense psychoanalysis has as its *main bridge* to the world of psychiatry and to the teaching of it and the accrual of new knowledge in it that we call academic psychiatry, not its position as a specific therapeutic modality with its implications for all the psychoanalytically related psychodynamic therapies that are taught to psychiatrists (as well as to other, allied mental health professionals), but rather its position as a psychology, that is, as part of the underpinning basic science base of the psychiatric enterprise.

Opinions of course will differ at this point, not just outside but also within psychoanalysis, as to the proper reach or limitation of psychoanalysis as a psychology and the extent to which it can try to lay claim to being the totality of the psychological theory of psychiatry. In its first generations of expansion, psychoanalysis, born out of the study of conflict in the behaviorally and emotionally disordered, i.e., born out of psychopathology, progressively extended its reach into the study of normal behavior and emotion, and normal development, that is, toward the universalisms of a general psychology—all built on Freud's fundamental insight into the continua between the normal and the abnormal, the abnormal as the inappropriately exaggerated normal. Anyway this was Freud's dream, of psychoanalysis as a comprehensive psychology, a dream carried to its logical furthermost in the endeavors of our great systematizers and architects of modern-day ego psychology, most especially Hartmann (1964) and Rapaport (1967).

This claim of psychoanalysis to be ultimately a completely encompassing and explanatory general and developmental psychology, to be reached finally (at least in Rapaport's view) when it had achieved a satisfactory psychoanalytically integrated learning theory was, however, one never accepted outside its ranks in academic psychology, not even by those academic psychologists benignly disposed to the psychoanalytic contribution. Put simply, even those most friendly to psychoanalysis in academic psychology ranks have seen it primarily, or only, as a psychology of conflict and of motivation, relevant and illuminating in those realms of psychological issues, but only partially relevant and illuminating in the realms of nonconflict-born, nonmotivation-determined psychic phenomena. To Ernst Kris's well-known aphoristic definition of psychoanalysis as *nothing but* human behavior considered from the viewpoint of conflict, they have added the counterview that it is also *nothing more*.

Even within psychoanalysis, however, there is, as one (and not necessarily as the most central) aspect of the great metapsychology debate raging in our theoretical literature (see especially the current writings of Gill, 1976; Holt, 1976; and Schafer, 1976), the falling back from the claim that psychoanalysis can be a completely comprehensive general and developmental psychology and especially from any pretension that it can be the kind of general and developmental psychology expounded in terms akin to those that operate in the natural science or biological science realms. What is important at this point of major theoretical flux within psychoanalysis during which our prevailing ego psychology paradigm is being subjected to such searching criticism and such efforts at fundamental revision (Rosenblatt and Thickstun, 1977; Rubinstein, 1976) or even total replacement, as, for example, by the action language model (Schafer, 1976), or oppositely by a feedback-regulating, information-processing model (Peterfreund, 1971), there is no agreement, not even within psychoanalysis, as to its scope and reach, the validity or not of its claim, or pretension, to generality and universality, and therefore no consensus possible with those outside, as well, on this issue. We will at this point perhaps have to rest more modestly on our well-established positions within the scope of the view of analysis propounded by Kris and then claim for psychoanalysis its place as a psychology in itself, a central developmental psychology and psychological base for psychiatry, interacting (one hopes productively) with the psychological understandings from the other realms of academic psychology. And parenthetically, we see already some such productive interactions with the cognitive developmental psychology of Piaget (Wolff, 1960). This then leaves open, however, properly open for the present, I think, the extent to which all these perspectives and paradigms from the realms of psychological phenomena can and ultimately will be subsumed within a larger, more encompassing (and shall I say ultimately comprehensively psychoanalytic?) psychological framework.

A last point should be added to this part of my statement of the bridges between psychoanalysis and academic psychiatry, or rather of the placement of psychoanalysis as *a* major psychological basic science undergirding clinical psychiatry—and that has to do with the issue already alluded to of psychoanalysis as a therapy, both a specific therapy and a model therapy. This of course brings us back to Freud's well-known threefold categorization of psychoanalysis, first, as a fundamental theory of the mind, as a psychology, that is, and this is the sense in which I have been considering it to this point; second, as a method, an investigative tool, a way of research and of unraveling the reaches of the mind, especially of course its not conscious or its unconscious depths; and third, as a specific therapy originally derived from studies with the neurotic patients, who are still those most amenable to it, but by now varyingly extended to those with wider and deeper ego disorders, the narcissistic (Kohut, 1971), the borderline (Kernberg, 1975), and by some (e.g., Searles 1965) even to the openly psychotic, depending really on one's position in relation to the issue of the properness, the validity of, and the readiness for "widening scope," as against, let us call it, narrowing or focused concentration (Anna Freud, 1954; Stone, 1954).

Considered from this standpoint, as a specific therapy, psychoanalysis is a specific clinical application of psychoanalysis as a basic science, as a psychology, applied to a specifically indicated patient population, and requiring of course rigorous specific training—as carried out in our various institutes. Other specific clinical applications of psychoanalysis as theory, as basic science, are the whole range of psychoanalytically based or psychoanalytically oriented or psychodynamic psychotherapies, however one calls them, ranging from the expressive insight-aiming through to the supportive ego-strengthening that are derived from the theory of psychoanalytic psychology, which have their specific range of indications to their defined appropriate patient populations, partially overlapping with each other and with psychoanalysis per se as well, and a chief subject of teaching in our psychiatric academic university centers and our psychiatric teaching hospitals and clinics—in fact, for many of our students in psychiatry, what they most want to learn in our field.

But now let me return to the thread of my main argument, the nature of the conceptualization of psychiatry in America as a clinical discipline resting on a tripartite basic science base, the biological, the psychological (to which psychoanalysis could so readily become central), and the social: it is clear from this conception that psychoanalysis in the transplantation of its focal power from Europe to America borne on the tide of Hitler refugees found a very different set of contextual circumstances and therefore a very different opportunity available to it in America than had ever theretofore been dreamed possible in Europe.

Alongside then the psychoanalytic beginnings in America

which actually go back even to before World War I and which
took firm root in the interregnum between the two World Wars,
which led to the establishment and evolution in America of the
first training centers and institutes in the established European
institutional form of the independent institutes in New York, in
Boston, in Chicago, in Baltimore-Washington—alongside these
another even more compelling current was gathering, and intensifying, less in defensive, more I think in adaptive response to
the accession to psychoanalytic ranks in America of the large
numbers and the established psychoanalytic prestige of the
psychoanalyst European refugees. Whether self-consciously
thought out and planned in terms of the full array of consequences that subsequently eventuated or, as is more likely, more
the result of only partial and partisan perspectives imposed
upon events, leading through the clash of contention and compromise to outcomes in part unforeseen and for the rest only
dimly thought out, and to that little extent entitled to be called
planned, however this was, certainly in retrospect it is as if a
major strategy was deliberately evolved and pursued. And this
was that psychoanalysis follow a different path in America than
the proud and at the same time lonely isolation that marked it in
Europe, to penetrate into the receptive soil of American
psychiatry—characterized and self-aware within the framework
I have delineated—to capture, in a sense, academic psychiatry
and its formal training centers and to become its prevailing
psychological theory under the banner of dynamic psychiatry
or psychodynamics, and thus to be firmly planted in the midst
of medicine, the medical school, and, at least via this route,
the university as well. Here I speak not specifically of the
university-based psychoanalytic institute, which was a subsequent development in time, but of the more basic effort to
transform the departments of psychiatry in the various medical
schools and teaching hospitals of our nation into bulwarks of
psychodynamic thinking and of dynamic psychiatric practice.

This story too, the success of this effort, in the sense of the
radical transformation of American psychiatry which reached its
high watermark through the decade of the 1950s in which in one
after another of the major departments of psychiatry in the
country, the retiring chairman, characteristically an Adolf

Meyer-trained psychobiological psychiatrist, was replaced by a psychoanalytically committed and psychoanalytically trained psychiatrist (see Wallerstein, 1974) is in its broad outlines well enough known. And I will not digress more than briefly to refer to some of the concomitants of that effort, the decision arrived at after such bitter and divisive debate within the American Psychoanalytic Association to effect what was called the 1938 rule, the barring henceforward of training of nonmedical candidates under the auspices of the American and barring membership in it to nonmedical analysts unless trained before that date. It was as if to strengthen its claim to psychological hegemony within psychiatry that psychoanalysis felt it had to divest itself of its nonmedical cohorts, no matter how glorious the contributions from these rich and diverse nonmedical sources had been. Whether it was a sacrifice that was necessary to the waging of what turned out to be so successful a campaign— because in the sense in which I mean it, psychoanalysis did essentially succeed in establishing itself centrally within the main intellectual strongholds of American academic psychiatry—and whether the campaign would have been more difficult or less successful if this sacrifice had not been made it is hard to know so categorically in hindsight. But certainly it was a heavy sacrifice and one that so many of us have felt to be unwise. The story of our long and slow and painful efforts and by now partial success in the undoing of this total restrictiveness against the training of nonmedical people in psychoanalysis is one with which personally I have been long identified in the affairs of the American Psychoanalytic Association and have written about (Wallerstein, 1974), but the telling of it would be tangential to the main thrust of my exposition here.

The main point is that of the intimate penetration of American psychoanalysis, strengthened enormously by the infusion of numbers and of intellectual leadership of the European refugee pre-World War II transplants to America, its victorious penetration in the decade or so after that war into the central fabric of American academic psychiatry, both as psychological theory, becoming *the* prevailing psychological science underpinning academic psychiatric understanding and teaching, and as derived psychotherapy, psychoanalytically informed and oriented psychotherapy, which in turn became *the* prevailing psychotherapeutic approach taught and learned within most psychiatric training centers. Many departments of psychiatry with psychoanalyst chairmen and heavily psychoanalyst faculty became avowedly psychoanalytic in orientation; almost all, with only a few conspicuous exceptions, explicitly acknowledged their resting on what they called, a little more euphemistically, a *psychodynamic* base. This was officially recognized as early in the post-World War II era as 1952 in the very influential NIMH-supported American Psychiatric Association Conference on Psychiatric Education held at Cornell University in the summer of that year. In the book of proceedings of that conference the chapter on "The Role of Psychoanalysis in Residency Training" states in the very first paragraph that "it is now almost universally agreed that a necessary part of the preparation of a competent psychiatrist is the development of and understanding of principles of psychodynamics" and that "it seems obvious that an understanding of psychodynamics presupposes—indeed, necessitates—... knowledge of Freudian concepts and of psychoanalytic theory and practice" (Whitehorn et al., 1953, p. 91).

Such is what I have called the high watermark during the decade of the 1950s, of the capture, if you will, of the main bastions of American psychiatry by the psychoanalytic idea and its praxis, and of the intimate intermingling and in some locales even efforts at actual fusion of the two, psychoanalysis and psychiatry. But history did not stop here and my accounting rather than drawing to its close at this point must now turn to both the bewildering complexity of the changes and the growths in academic psychiatry which have transpired since the fateful turning point year that I will place, in ways I shall indicate, as far back as 1954, and the consequences of these changes in psychiatry for what has become a necessarily much more complex as well as much more problematic (in the sense of needing to be continuously readdressed and redefined) relationship between academic psychiatry and psychoanalysis.

Since I spoke of high watermark it is natural to think of the receding of the tide, and in many places people have characterized the relationship between academic psychiatry and psychoanalysis during the two decades since the 1950s in just such terms, that the tide has indeed receded, that the era of psychodynamic dominance in American psychiatry is over. As a reflection of this conceptual as well as programmatic shifting of emphasis, in the decade of the 1960s it was no longer the commonplace assumption that open chairmanships in the major influential departments would be automatically offered only to individuals with psychoanalytic credentials; in fact, contrariwise, new breeds of chairmen arose, for example, those identified with the stunning successes in expanding, clinically and research-wise, the whole area of biological psychiatry which they came incidentally to identify in many eyes with scientific psychiatry and research psychiatry—but that is a point to which I shall return.

At this point I would like to sketch out, in somewhat tabular form, the several major dimensions of change and of growth in academic psychiatry over these past two decades that have made for what I have called the increasingly complex and problematic relationship between academic psychiatry and psychoanalysis. These dimensions of change and of growth seem to fit quite well into the tripartite division I have advanced of the basic science realms, basic to the undergirding of the psychiatric clinical enterprise, and I will therefore categorize and briefly discuss them in that order.

First, of course, is the literal explosion of biological knowledge, of brain-behavior interrelations within the field of psychiatry, in the domain of mental and emotional disorder. There are the advances in neurophysiology and in neurochemistry, in knowledge of neurotransmitter mechanisms and of catecholamine metabolism, in psychophysiology and in psychopharmacology. Such discrete areas are involved—both in fundamental investigation and in direct or at least potential clinical application—as studies of average evoked potentials and the conditions of electrical activity in the brain, of split-brain preparations (both experimental and clinical) and the derived studies of cerebral lateralization phenomena, of biofeedback and the control of involuntary autonomic mechanisms, of REM states and sleep-dream research. Biological psychiatry has rapidly become a most significant and most respectable scientific arena and is now the clinical and research focus of many academic psychiatric careers and major psychiatric space and money resources.

The second and related major development, also in the biological realm, is the modern era of psychoactive drugs as a central therapeutic modality in the management and treatment of the psychiatrically ill, especially the sicker, psychotic patients whom we psychodynamically trained psychiatrists have tended to avoid and who have been historically such a heavy, collective, undischarged social responsibility of our profession—historically warehoused in large public mental hospitals, often neglected at best, and badly abused at worst. Here is where the date 1954 represents so sharp a turning point. Prior to that, and in the time when many of us chose psychiatry as our specialty within medicine, our drug armamentarium was limited essentially to sedatives and hypnotics with all the potentials for barbiturate abuse and addiction and for bromide poisoning. It was 1954 that brought Largactil, a drug developed in Switzerland, via Canada, to the United States, where Smith, Kline and French marketed it as Thorazine and inaugurated the era of the modern antipsychotic, major tranquilizer drugs. I do not need to recount the great proliferation of psychoactive drugs and of classes of such drugs in the years since—the major tranquilizers or antipsychotics, the minor tranquilizers, or so-called antianxiety drugs, the several classes of antidepressants, including the tricyclics and the monoamine oxidase inhibitors, or the very special drug lithium with its so poorly understood effects in relation to manic and to depressive disorder. Suffice it to say that the existence of all these drugs has vitally changed the practice characteristics of psychiatrists (not to speak of the ministrations to emotionally and behaviorally troubled individuals by nonpsychiatric physicians) and has forced accommodations in the psychotherapeutic arena where adjuvant or concomitant use of psychoactive drugs has become a commonplace, again especially with the less well-integrated patients, for the most part those outside the normal-neurotic range, and where understanding of drug-behavior interactions and of the psychological meanings of such chemically induced mood and behavior changes has become part of what we must know and teach in our psychotherapeutic endeavors—very much even in our psychoanalytically guided psychotherapeutic endeavors.

The third major dimension of change in the field of psychiatry is in the psychological arena. Here I need only point out that psychoanalysis is no longer the unquestioned prevailing psychological theory guiding and illuminating our understanding of the human mind and its aberrations. It has now been challenged by the astonishing (astonishing to us, anyway) growth of two fundamentally different and competing psychological paradigms, the one the learning-theory and stimulus-response conditioning model (partly classical, partly operant) with the behavior modification technology derived from it; and the other, attacking *both* psychoanalysis and behavior modification as being mechanical and stripped of essential subjectivism and humanism, the so-called third force, the existentialist-phenomenological tradition of European philosophy and letters brought to America as humanistic psychology and leading to the whole encounter and human growth and potential movement both within our profession and, with a larger force even, without. The point at issue here is that these are competing and, despite the efforts at reconciliation or at least at finding common ground (Wachtel, 1977), antithetical paradigms that make it much more difficult now when most departments of psychiatry, no matter how psychodynamic, also have their behaviorists and their humanists, so readily to link psychoanalysis and its theoretical understandings as *the* psychological basic science of the derived psychiatric clinical enterprise.

The fourth major dimension of change is in the social science (and social policy) arena. Here I want to mention another influence, as potent as the psychoactive drug industry in transforming the character of modern American psychiatric and mental health practice, and that is the community mental health center movement and ideology inaugurated by the Kennedy legislation of 1963. This community mental health center movement is clearly the new center of gravity in political power and in access to funding mechanisms in the whole field of mental health and illness, but it is also a succession of linked conceptualizations and ideologies, not necessarily all politically inspired, and many of them developed both before and outside the official community mental health movement. I refer to the concepts of the open hospital and the therapeutic community pioneered by Maxwell Jones in England, and of milieu therapy as designed by D. Ewen Cameron in Canada and further developed with psychoanalytic sophistication by Will Menninger and his colleagues at the Menninger Clinic in Topeka, Kansas, as well as to the very current and very fashionable concept of deinstitutionalization that has already carried us from the era when most of our sicker patients were kept, or rather, incarcerated, in our large public mental hospitals for very long periods of time, even for their whole lifetimes, to the current times when hospitalization is by and large very short and mainly for acute and unmanageable life crises and psychological decompensations and when most of even the very sick, chronically psychotic patients are managing (or not managing) in outpatient lives in the outside world—and when we now see the new untoward consequences of the deinstitutionalized life, the patients once neglected and abused in the state hospitals, now often neglected and abused in board and care homes and cheap inner-city hotels, and the impact of chronically psychotic patients, as parents living at home, upon the children they are trying to raise—anyway, a host of major problems and issues that stamp the whole face of current mental health practice and are necessarily a major concern of academic psychiatry in preparing its students for their professional life ahead!

Fifth, and last in this cataloguing of major dimensions of impact upon psychiatry in these past two decades, are the correlated developments of theory that relate to the changes in emphasis from the therapeutic to the preventive ameliorative models and from the idiosyncratically individual to the socially controlled family and group and social system concerns that characterize the philosophic thrust of the community mental health movement. Some of this theory was developed within psychoanalysis, such as crisis theory as innovated originally by Lindemann (1944); most of it has been developed outside psychoanalysis, in academic sociology and social psychology, such as role theory, theories of deviance, theories of small group behavior, and social systems theory. Again, the main point is that there are other bodies of knowledge, social science knowledge, which are being brought to bear as explanatory frameworks upon many of the phenomena that are within the purview of psychiatry and of psychiatrists, and which in terms of the issues surfaced by the emphases of the community mental health center movement, are putatively better, in the sense of more broadly encompassing or more directly relevant, or perhaps are just more easily understandable or commonsensical explanatory frameworks. There have of course been efforts to link these theoretical understandings from the side of social science to the more centrally traditional psychoanalytic psychological understandings of the phenomena of mental illness, pioneered first by Talcott Parsons (1964) and continued into a current very lively ferment within our field (Wallerstein and Smelser, 1969; Weinstein and Platt, 1973), but such endeavors are at present, and with all due respect, but a programmatic promise, and not an accomplished fulfillment.

So much for a tabulation of some of the major trends of development within and around psychiatry in but the last two fast-moving decades. Where does that leave us today, and what are the implications of all this for the relationship between psychoanalysis and the academic psychiatric enterprise? Basically it is a statement of the diversification of psychiatry as now a *variety* of fields of interrelated endeavors, all more or less closely interdigitated in their various partial, and varyingly overlapping comprehension of and ameliorative influence upon the central phenomena of the field, the range of mental and emotional disorder. In contrast with the time in the immediate wake of World War II, and before all the developments that I have called the major dimensions of change and of growth in the past two decades, the time, that is, when I and most all my contemporaries came to psychiatric training in order to go on and become psychoanalysts because that was where we perceived the field to be, in both theory and in practice, and in essential oneness between dynamic psychiatry and psychoanalysis—in contrast with that time and that climate, today there are multiple equally honorable, equally honored, and at least equally appealing career paths open to the student in psychiatry, and it is no longer a foregone conclusion that the most or the best will be drawn to psychoanalysis. It is not that this multiplicity of options and the internal glamour and external support that some of them seem to enjoy in higher measure than does psychoanalysis has in any sense pressured psychoanalysis into a diminished posture and status. It is just that psychoanalysis is now only one among several, or one among many, and only in some eyes, primus inter pares, the first among equals, and it has both to compete for its share of the allegiances of the students to psychiatry and to justify itself in new terms, including its capacity to relate meaningfully to the conceptualizations and the data that derive from the other basic science realms and then in turn relate meaningfully (and comprehensively) to the phenomena in the patients that must be comprehended in terms of the synthesized understanding that derives from the perspectives brought to bear upon those clinical phenomena from each of the three major basic science realms. This is one way of stating what I feel to be the present-day challenge—and opportunity—in the continually evolving relationship between psychoanalysis and academic psychiatry and is also the arena in which I think the future of that relationship rests.

To spell this terse and bald conclusion out somewhat more, I turn to a variety of the very contemporary, very current, concerns of academic psychiatry and will delineate briefly the particular problems as well as opportunities that they pose for the relationship of psychiatry to psychoanalysis. I will discuss these current concerns under four headings: (1) the remedicalization of psychiatry, a now popular catchword in the field; (2) the evolving relationship of academic psychiatry to the behavioral sciences; (3) the dilemma of what makes basic research basic in our field; and (4) of such central interest to those of us in psychoanalysis, who after all stand first of all for a clinical enterprise, the new questions of the proper relationship of psychiatry to psychotherapy.

1. The theme of remedicalization indeed has several interrelated aspects, adding up in cumulative impact to perhaps the most powerful thrust on the present-day psychiatric scene. Included here are all the developments in biological psychiatry in the most recent decades, the advances in all the facets of neurobiology that I have already enumerated as well as in genetics and the influence of inborn genetic loading upon subsequent behavioral disorder (most notable with manic-depressive illness but also seriously implicated with schizophrenia). And,

corollary of course, also included here is the renewed growth of somatic therapy in psychiatry, the varieties of psychoactive (mood- and behavior-influencing) drugs that are so large a part of the learning experience and of the employed therapeutic armamentarium of today's psychiatrist—and also incidentally of today's nonpsychiatric physicians who in their daily medical generalist practices over the entire developmental life course see so many emotionally and behaviorally troubled individuals. Linked to the new growth in the realm of the biological aspects and interests of psychiatry is the great revival of interest in the psychosomatic-consultation-liaison function and activities, an arena given much of its original impetus in the first decade after World War II under psychoanalytic auspices (see Alexander and French [1948] and many others), now being importantly renewed after the relative decline into which it subsequently seemed to recede, as a complexly integrated biobehavioral research investigative enterprise and a humanistic biopsychosocial clinical science enterprise in hospital ward and clinic.

Concomitant with the surge of knowledge growth in these more "medical" areas and interfaces is the current heightened teaching attention of departments of psychiatry to medical students and to undergraduate medical education, that is, to the total medical student population, only a fraction of whom (and currently it is a rapidly declining fraction) will seek specifically psychiatric careers, and with special emphasis in this teaching to the training of future primary care physicians (the new majority among today's medical students) in the psychosocial dimensions of health and disease: all this, by the way, in contrast to the scene but a few short years ago when departments of psychiatry tended to concentrate their primary efforts not upon medical students or nonpsychiatric physicians, but rather on their own residents, those who had opted for careers in psychiatry, and alongside the psychiatric residents, students from the other clinical mental health disciplines, like clinical psychology and psychiatric social work.

In all of this, I am speaking here under the heading of remedicalization only of the clinical and educational and research aspects of present-day psychiatry. I have not mentioned the obviously linked, more practical, and political considerations; such as (a) that the main extramural funding mechanisms for the academic psychiatry enterprise are flowing the same way, with overall available NIMH monies actually declining, but within that, sharply increased gradients of support to psychosomatic-consultation-liaison programs and to undergraduate medical student education programs; and (b) that the economics and politics of health care with some form of national health insurance on the reasonably near horizon and with massive third-party payment and reimbursement formulas already the ongoing reality of practice—that these livelihood considerations are driving so much of psychiatry and so many psychiatrists back into an intensified "medical" identity and medical allegiance.

What are the implications of this massive and many-pronged, conceptual as well as practical, remedicalization of psychiatry, what are its implications for our concern here, with the bridge or interface between academic psychiatry and psychoanalysis? Clearly, all this has made the biological science knowledge base of psychiatry and the biobehavioral interface with medicine immensely more important within psychiatry than it had been just a decade or so earlier. The risk for us of course is that of the swing of the pendulum. Need we attend to the voices of gloom that assert that the dominant psychodynamic era of psychiatry that so characterized the field during the 1950s and the 1960s is now decisively over, or can we still hold on to the central importance of the psychosocial dimensions of the phenomena in our field, alongside of and in interacting accommodation with the biobehavioral and the biomedical? Can there be here, in these interactions, an even more vital continuing role for the psychological and specifically for the psychoanalytic, for the undiminished importance of its perspective upon human behavior no matter what the growth in cognate realms?

2. Seemingly at the opposite end of the spectrum, we have witnessed the intensifying patterns of relationship between modern-day psychiatry and the array of the so-called behavioral sciences. The issue here is usually posed as that of the proper place of the behavioral sciences, mostly anthropology, sociology, social psychology, and personality and experimental psychology, all now growingly recognized as part of the proper basic science preclinical knowledge base for the physician in training

alongside of the heretofore wholly biomedical or molecular biological basic science knowledge base—what is the proper place of these behavioral sciences within the medical school setting? Should it be as a separate department of behavioral science, a preclinical basic science department, charged to teach for the entire medical student body the behavioral science base for all of medicine, for clinical medicine *and* for clinical psychiatry? Or should the behavioral sciences (*basic* sciences to the phenomena of health and disease though they be) be incorporated as part of the *clinical* department of psychiatry charged to teach its clinical phenomena, psychopathology, psychiatric diagnosis, and psychiatric treatment, but also its own behavioral basic science base, for its own phenomena *and* for medicine in general?

Viewed purely pragmatically, one can say that where separate medical school departments of behavioral science have been established, they have characteristically not fared well; and where some degree of success in behavioral science teaching has been achieved, it has characteristically been from within the umbrella of the department of psychiatry, with this marriage, where most successful, often marked by an actual change in name to Department of Psychiatry and Behavioral Science. Whatever the location, the point is the dialectical one that side by side with the remedicalization or the medical-biological turning of present-day academic psychiatry is the other growing imbrication of psychiatry with the other sciences of behavior. Psychoanalysts will certainly see the parallels to these trends in the issues I have already alluded to surrounding the efforts to link the theoretical understandings from the side of (psychoanalytically informed and sympathetic) social science to the more centrally traditional psychoanalytic psychological understanding of the mind and in the counterpart organizational or structural concerns that linkage to the department of psychiatry of the medical school not be the exclusive avenue of access of the psychoanalytic idea to the academic university world. Here many will recognize the oft-repeated call of David Shakow for another model of psychoanalytic inclusion in the university, that of the separate psychoanalytic institute, linked to the department of psychiatry of the medical school, to be sure, but also to all the various other graduate departments in the social sciences and the humanities that can profitably share mutual discourse. Given the structure and funding base of the American university system, Shakow's dream seems a utopian vision, but perhaps the opportunity to realize it will come after all in a new, more relevant version via the very departments of psychiatry, to which Shakow has been fearful to accord such a monopoly, as more of those departments of psychiatry become in practice as well as in name departments of psychiatry *and* behavioral science. Situated in that setting psychoanalysis can then perhaps find its fullest opportunity at realization of its academic-intellectual ambitions and of its linkages to related academic-intellectual realms of knowledge of the mind. At least with rare exceptions such as in the English department at Columbia University in the days of Lionel Trilling and Mark Van Doren or in Social Relations at Harvard under the leadership of Talcott Parsons (1964) or more currently again in English at the State University of New York in Buffalo with the Group for Applied Psychoanalysis led by Norman N. Holland (1968), aside the happenstances of such exceptions, psychoanalysis to this point has not secured a substantial place in organized academia—*except* within departments of psychiatry.

3. The confusing arguments over what constitutes "basic" research in our field or whether the investigation of the psychological or the psychosocial dimension can be basic continue. This is not merely a semantic or definitional quibble but rather is, to my mind, a fundamental conceptual stance concerning the nature of our field. Here there are two major positions. The one, which I mean nonpejoratively to call the reductionistic, is the prevailing model in much of the medical science and natural science enterprise, that the psychosocial is a complexly higher but also epiphenomenally organized level of understanding which is (as an article of faith) ultimately explanatorily (and therefore causally) reducible to the biological level of understanding. In accord with this conception, basic research in psychiatry, as in every other clinical branch of medicine, is ultimately biological, and the research quest then is to search out what genetic complexity (including behavioral aberration) can ultimately be "explained" by an altered placement of a hydroxyl group on a vital organic molecule. Within psychiatry this has been specifically expressed in the oft-quoted statement, "Behind every twisted thought there is a twisted molecule."

It should be abundantly clear from the body of this whole presentation that my own position is exactly the opposite one. If we take seriously the conceptualization that psychiatry is a clinical discipline in medicine, a branch of the healing arts, and that it rests equally on three basic science knowledge bases in the biological, the psychological, and the social science realms, then it follows that it is a field in which one need be able to do both applied research—at the level of clinical application to the phenomena of mental health and illness—and basic research, and equally basic research in each of the three basic science knowledge realms. Put this way, basic does not mean *just* biological, and is *not* counterposed to the psychosocial since psychosocial investigation can be and should be equally basic, if by basic we mean concern with fundamental mechanisms within the level of discourse, be it biological or psychosocial.

This I would like to assume would be a congenial and an uncontroversial statement at least within the ranks of psychoanalysts with their own appreciation of the fundamental *psychological* contributions of Sigmund Freud to our knowledge of how the mind of man functions. Yet as part of what I have earlier called "the great metapsychology debate" raging in psychoanalysis today, one of the most thoughtful and provocative participants in that debate, Peterfreund (1971), has called for the total abandonment not only of the structure of current metapsychology but of all ego-psychological or psychological-level thinking as an explanatory, causal theory of the functioning of the mind. He calls a purely psychological theory of the mind an "anachronistic vitalistic position" (p. 41) and further elaborates:

> I am abandoning any attempt to theorize about psychological phenomena from a psychological standpoint, as is the rule in current psychoanalytic theory. And I am abandoning the idea implicit in much of current psychoanalytic theory that the mind is an entity with an independent existence, capable of interacting with the body. No simple or direct equation can be made between current psychoanalytic theory and the information-systems frame of reference which I am attempting to present. The focus for theory shifts *away from* psychological experience or behavior to the larger world of information

processes and their links to neurophysiology. The world of man's mind will be viewed from the *larger world* of biology and evolutionary time [p. 148; my italics].

I have quoted at this length from a contemporary psychoanalytic theorist merely to underline the importance of this issue as a fundamental focus of current debate within both academic psychiatry more broadly and psychoanalysis more narrowly. The clarification of this issue is of fundamental importance to both disciplines since it is so critical to the conceptualization of the research enterprise in both arenas, within psychiatry and within psychoanalysis, and thereby to the impact of the research findings on the theory and practice in each of the fields. Here I think academic psychiatry and psychoanalysis stand on common ground; they have a shared and common problem, and conceptual clarification in the one realm will be directly reflected in the other.

4. The last of the major themes preoccupying current academic psychiatry which I will be discussing is the central one of the relationship of *psychotherapy* as an activity to academic psychiatry. At one time, some 10 to 20 years ago, this was not an issue. Psychotherapy was universally and unquestioningly regarded as a central, and mostly *the* central, clinical and therapeutic activity of the psychiatric practitioner and therefore the central pedagogic activity of the academic psychiatric teacher and clinical supervisor. Not an officially or legally recognized discipline in itself, psychotherapy was rather looked at as the central skill that marked the mental health practitioner and therefore central to psychiatry but also to the allied mental health disciplines, clinical psychology and psychiatric social work.

Today all of that is under question in a confusing babel of ideological, social, and political cross-currents. Partly the attack by political opponents on the shibboleth of the "medical model," which they declare to be the outmoded symbol of psychiatry's anachronistic bondage or allegiance to (antihumanistic or even antihuman) medicine, and partly the rise of alternative therapeutic paradigms (behavioristic or existential-humanistic) and their derived alternative therapies (behavior modification, Gestalt, and transactional therapies, etc.); and partly even, to a further extreme, the human potential and encounter movement dealing with issues of growth and of actualization, not of health and illness—all of these together have served both to meld various interpersonal helping processes into more amorphous and a less technically differentiated mix of human helping services and at the same time to push these now less professional helping processes out of the orbit of psychiatry as a clinical helping *profession*, and one suspiciously linked to medical hegemony via its so-called medical model. This feat of attempting to thrust the center of gravity of psychotherapy out of psychiatry can indeed be accomplished fairly readily if most of mental and emotional illness except for the organic syndromes and perhaps the major psychoses is transformed into merely "problems in living," and this one can also recognize as a trend abetted in part from within the center of psychiatry itself (see Szasz, *The Myth of Mental Illness* [1961]).

Put somewhat differently, the question can readily become one of why any therapist would need or want to be a psychiatrist these days; and whether psychiatry, for its part, with its tremendous new surge of biological knowledge and pharmacological therapeutics in the realms especially of severe mental disorder, which everyone acknowledges to be an exclusive province of psychiatry, should not attend more exclusively to those very severely ill for whose care it has an unchallenged prerogative—and a social argument for this can be made out in terms of society's greatest need of psychiatry—and leave psychotherapy or the psychotherapies to all the various practitioners of various theoretical and school persuasions, and all the instant intimacy and self-help movements, to deal with all the many individuals with acknowledged "problems in living."

Stated this way, it is an extreme and a fringe argument and few of us in psychiatry or in the main professional centers of the other traditional mental health professions would subscribe to it; most of us are more than a little aware of not just the antipsychiatric but also the antiprofessional and ultimately the antiintellectual tenor of the whole movement. Certainly psychiatry, and just as certainly academic psychiatry, is in no serious risk of turning its back on psychotherapy, though there are a few psychiatrists who, as I have indicated, are ideologically committed to getting psychotherapy (or rather interpersonal helping) out from under psychiatry, and there are of course more psychiatrists who in their personal commitments within the field are working primarily in the biological arena and eschew psychotherapy as a professional activity that they themselves carry out.

The real danger within psychiatry is rather a subtler one, that the current melange of helping movements, of therapies, of schools, of encounters, and of self-actualizations can in their total impact tarnish the coin, can undermine dynamic psychotherapy—read psychoanalytic psychotherapy—as a principled scientific activity and thus weaken the fabric of something which is central (theoretically and practically) to both psychiatry and psychoanalysis and is a main common ground between the two. Here again, then, psychiatry as an academic and a professional enterprise and psychoanalysis as a discipline indeed have common cause in the continuing assertion of a scientific psychotherapy built on a scientific theory of the mind as the essential centerpiece in the continuing psychiatric enterprise even as its biological science and behavioral science components grow in their importance.

On this overview of the many dimensions of relationship (and many issues of relationship) between academic psychiatry and psychoanalysis, I have followed the historical route that is psychoanalytically so congenial, starting with Freud, as is our wont, but concentrating on the period since World War II and the changing vicissitudes of that relationship over that period as I have been witness to those changes and participated in them. I am sure that my own particular historical perspectives and the emphases that I have accorded to particular issues will not be equally agreed to by all. But I do hope that I have at least persuaded any who have been wavering, or who have been openly skeptical, to my own conviction that academic psychiatry and psychoanalysis are indeed linked together in multiple ways in shared conceptual and clinical endeavor and that the future of each will only be the brighter the more it is shared on broadly traveled bridges with the other.

BIBLIOGRAPHY

ALEXANDER, F. & FRENCH, T. M. (1948), *Studies in Psychosomatic Medicine*. New York: Ronald Press.
FREUD, A. (1954), The Widening Scope of Indications for Psychoanalysis. *J. Amer. Psychoanal. Assn.*, 2:607–620.
FREUD, S. (1926), The Question of Lay Analysis. *S.E.*, 20:177–258.
GILL, M. M. (1976), Metapsychology Is Not Psychology. In: *Psychology versus Metapsychology*, ed. M. M. Gill & P. S. Holzman [*Psychol. Issues*, 36:71–105]. New York: Int. Univ. Press.
HARTMANN, H. (1964), *Essays on Ego Psychology*. New York: Int. Univ. Press.
HOLLAND, N. N. (1968), *The Dynamics of Literary Response*. New York: Oxford Univ. Press.
HOLT, R. R. (1976), Drive or Wish. In: *Psychology versus Metapsychology*, ed. M. M. Gill & P. S. Holzman [*Psychol. Issues*, 36:158–197]. New York: Int. Univ. Press.
KERNBERG, O. F. (1975), *Borderline Conditions and Pathological Narcissism*. New York: Jason Aronson.
KOHUT, H. (1971), *The Analysis of the Self*. New York: Int. Univ Press.
LINDEMANN, E. (1944), Symptomatology and Management of Acute Grief. *Amer. J. Psychiat.*, 101:141–148.
LIPPMAN, W. (1966), The University. *New Republic*, 28 May.
PARSONS, T. (1964), *Social Structure and Personality*. Glencoe, Ill.: Free Press.
PETERFREUND, E. (1971), *Information, Systems, and Psychoanalysis* [*Psychol. Issues*, 25/26]. New York: Int. Univ. Press.
RAPAPORT, D. (1967), *Collected Papers*, ed. M. M. Gill. New York & London: Basic Books.
ROSENBLATT, A. D. & THICKSTUN, J. T. (1977), *Modern Psychoanalytic Concepts in a General Psychology* [*Psychol. Issues*, 42/43]. New York: Int. Univ. Press.
RUBINSTEIN, B. B. (1976), On the Possibility of a Strictly Clinical Psychoanalytic Theory. In: *Psychology versus Metapsychology*, ed. M. M. Gill & P. S. Holzman [*Psychol. Issues*, 36:229–264]. New York: Int. Univ. Press.
SCHAFER, R. (1976), *A New Language for Psychoanalysis*. New Haven & London: Yale Univ. Press.
SEARLES, H. F. (1965), *Collected Papers on Schizophrenia and Related Subjects*. New York: Int. Univ. Press.
STONE, L. (1954), The Widening Scope of Indications for Psychoanalysis. *J. Amer. Psychoanal. Assn.*, 2:567–594.
SZASZ, T. S. (1961), *The Myth of Mental Illness*. New York: Hoeber.
WACHTEL, P. L. (1977), *Psychoanalysis and Behavior Therapy*. New York: Basic Books.
WALLERSTEIN, R. S. (1974), Herbert S. Gaskill and the History of American Psychoanalysis in American Psychiatry. The Denver Psychoanalytic Society *Newsletter*, 1:1–9.

———— & SMELSER, N. J. (1969), Psychoanalysis and Sociology. *Int. J. Psycho-Anal.*, 50:693–710.

WEINSTEIN, F. & PLATT, G. M. (1973), *Psychoanalytic Sociology*. Baltimore & London: Johns Hopkins Univ. Press.

WHITEHORN, J. C. (Chairman of the Editorial Board) (1953), *The Psychiatrist, His Training and Development*. Washington, D.C.: Amer. Psychiat. Assn.

WOLFF, P. H. (1960), *The Developmental Psychologies of Jean Piaget and Psychoanalysis* [*Psychol. Issues*, 5]. New York: Int. Univ. Press.

Bibliographical Note

S.E.   *The Standard Edition of the Complete Psychological Works of Sigmund Freud,* 24 Volumes, translated and edited by James Strachey. London: Hogarth Press and the Institute of Psycho-Analysis, 1953–1974.

W.   *The Writings of Anna Freud,* 7 Volumes. New York: International Universities Press, 1968–1974.

Index

Edgcumbe, R., 342, 373
Education
  psychoanalytic, *see* Psychoanalytic training
  psychiatric, 419–46
  and therapy, 341–71
Educational therapy, 343, 368
Edwards, A., 197, 200, 214, 222, 231
Effectance pleasure, 97
Ego, 270, 369
  in adolescence, 158–60
  autonomous function, 262
  auxiliary, 287, 294, 366
  and cognitive controls, 48–65
  differentiation, 366
  disorders, 429
  and dream, 184–89, 192, 195, 197, 199–200, 205, 207, 211, 230
  incomplete autonomy, 322
  limitations, 346
  modalities, 54–62
  overwhelmed, 365, 369
  precocious, 230
  and psychoanalytic treatment, 287, 290
Ego ideal, 11, 57, 74–75
  see also Ideals
Ego psychology, 6, 42, 428
Ehrhardt, A., 228, 233
Eiduson, B. N., 108, 125, 131
Elation, 80
Elkind, D., 66
Embarrassment, 68, 80
Empathy, 8, 20, 92, 102, 240, 261, 283, 369
  disturbed, 290, 293, 329
Encopresis, 326
Endowment, 257–58
  see also Constitution
English, C. A. and H. B., 43, 65
Enuresis, 119, 201, 331
Environment, 6, 11–15
  average expectable, 13, 255
  holding, 369
  impoverished, 341–73
Envy, 8, 145, 152, 251, 326, 331, 334
Erect posture, 73–81
Erickson, M. H., 181, 214
Erikson, E. H., xi, 13, 33, 76, 81–82, 88–89, 104, 365–66, 373
Erlkönig syndrome, 219–31
Escalona, S. K., 109, 131
Exhibitionism, 68, 77–81, 279, 292, 361
Externalization, 114–17, 303–05, 308, 322, 356, 390
  of blame, 314–15

and countertransference, 287–88, 293
and negative therapeutic motivation, 308–11, 313
and transference, in latency, 12, 267–83, 296

Failures, 300–18
Fairbairn, W. R. D., 256, 264
Family
  of anorectics, 157
  breakup, 241; *see also* Divorce
  depression in, 238, 258
  disruption of pathological patterns, 309
  loosening of ties to, 173–74; *see also* Independence
  myth, 11, 32
  pathology, 16–17, 23, 31
  pressures, 162–63, 172
  psychoanalytic concepts of, 3–10
  single-parent, 123–24, 231, 260; *see also* Father, absent; Mother, absent
Family complex, 8–33
Family romance, 9–10, 22, 25–26, 32, 35
  in adopted children, 112, 128
Fanshel, D., 129, 131
Fantasy, 247, 256, 293
  and adoption, 116–28
  aggressive, 208
  of being (having) twin, 11, 136, 140, 153
  and cognition, 45–62
  and dream, 190, 197, 199–200, 206
  as ego mode, 54–63
  of flying, 77
  homosexual, 149–50
  in mother and child, 15–16
  oedipal, 276, 297, 326, 393–94
  of perfect mother, 314
  power through fasting, 164–67
  of powerful phallus, 332
  reversal of generations, 11
  sadomasochistic, 384–415
  about sibling, 361, 396
Father
  absent: 220–31, 247, 343–60; sudden reappearance, 358–60
  bypassed, 311, 319
  longing for, 223–32, 351–60
  providing main care, 240, 260
  relation to, 209–11, 279–80, 331–32, 383–84, 389
Father hunger, 219–30
Fear
  of abandonment (rejection), 115–19, 333